More Praise
for *When All Hell Breaks Loose: Stuff You Need to Survive When Disaster Strikes*

"*Hell* is, in equal parts: a screed against materialist society, a how-to for post-apocalypse survival, a short ride through crazytown. But what a ride!"
Slate

"This is the urban/suburban thinking person's guide to survival. Focusing on self-reliance, Cody Lundin leads you playfully through a variety of domestic survival scenarios with pep-talks, practicality and plenty of pizzazz."
—*National Geographic Adventure* magazine

"Lundin explains how to treat wounds, dispose of dead bodies, and—of course — how to cook mice and rats over a campfire."
—NPR radio "All Things Considered"

"...in the event that the economy crumbles, and civilization with it, I would appoint Cody Lundin my financial adviser. He is my favorite survivalist ..."
—*The Atlantic* magazine

"Lundin's advice is intensely practical. From detailed information about nutrition and nuts-and-bolts daily functions to spiritual guide pep talks to keep up morale, *When All Hell Breaks Loose* is a comprehensive guide to staying alive when disaster strikes."
—*Suite 101* magazine

"Cody Lundin's *When All Hell Breaks Loose* instructs readers how to get rid of bodies and feast on rats in the event of disaster."
—*Financial Times*, London, UK

"*When All Hell Breaks Loose* is exactly what I envisioned the perfect book on survival to be. The book is unlike any other survival training book that I have ever read. No dogma, just what works. Every single page is loaded with information. Once the first page is read, the reader wants to keep on reading right through to the epilogue, and then wants to get out and practice the skills learned in the book. It is twenty-three chapters of information that we all need to know if we would ever get put into a survival situation of any kind."
—United States Concealed Carry Association (USCCA)

"...you won't need to eat the dog if you're prepared, which is the point of Cody Lundin's hilarious book *When All Hell Breaks Loose*."
—Grist magazine

"*When All Hell Breaks Loose* is aimed at empowering an urban and suburban audience to deal with survival situations BEFORE they happen."
—*SuperConsciousness* magazine

"[The] book's key message—that advance preparation and personal responsibility are crucial in mitigating the effects of a disaster—is an important one."
—Elizabeth Gary
Acting Executive Secretary, National Protection and Programs Directorate, U.S. Department Of Homeland Security

"*When All Hell Breaks Loose* is the essential survival guide for the twenty-first century. It might not be judgment day, but a bridge collapse, a hurricane, flu pandemic, tornado, or terrorist attack can make life pretty unlivable for a dangerous period of time. Every American should have two copies [of this book], one for pre-crisis enlightenment, amusement, and good reading and a second for the Go Bag. This book will make you laugh and might very well save your life."
—Jim Mulvaney
Founder and president of Tactical Intelligence Services, Inc., Pulitzer Prize-winning journalist and member of the Nassau County, New York, emergency planning counsel

"Cody Lundin's knowledge-based material about everything from skewering mice to sanitizing water found in the oddest of places is handy to have in mind. Readers will come away from *When All Hell Breaks Loose* with a variety of passages starred and circled. Lundin's suggestions and encouragements are clear and kind, offering readers a new-found confidence regarding survival *before* crises occur."
—*Tucson Weekly*

"Cody Lundin's *When All Hell Breaks Loose* is not your grandpa's survival manual. Nothing is too gross for his contemplation. So, from preparing alternative protein sources (grasshopper, rat) to digging a potty trench to treating festering wounds and diarrhea, he covers the realities. Practical, feasible preparation—and improvisation—rule. Keep this book by your bedside. Laugh a lot, learn it by heart—this book is just damn entertaining."
—*Read It Here* magazine

"*When All Hell Breaks Loose* breaks survival preparedness down into a common-sense approach, although Cody's style is still 'in your face.'"
—*Wilderness Way* magazine

WHEN ALL HELL BREAKS LOOSE

STUFF You Need to SURVIVE When DISASTER STRIKES

CODY LUNDIN

ILLUSTRATIONS BY RUSSELL MILLER
PHOTOGRAPHS BY CHRISTOPHER MARCHETTI

Gibbs Smith, Publisher

TO ENRICH AND INSPIRE HUMANKIND

Salt Lake City | Charleston | Santa Fe | Santa Barbara

First Edition

16 15 14 13   25 24 23 22

Text © 2007 Cody Lundin

Illustrations © 2007 Russell Miller

Photographs © 2007 Christopher Marchetti

Published by

Gibbs Smith, Publisher

P.O. Box 667

Layton, Utah 84041

Toll-free number to buy more copies for everyone you know:
1.800.835.4993
www.gibbs-smith.com

Edits and general harassment by Leslie Cutler Stitt
Designed by Black Eye Design, blackeye.com
Printed and bound in Hong Kong . . . still land of small, cheap rubber toys.

Library of Congress Cataloging-in-Publication Data

Lundin, Cody.
 When all hell breaks loose : stuff you need to survive when disaster strikes / Cody Lundin ; illustrations by Russell L. Miller ; photographs by Christopher Marchetti. — 1st ed.
    p. cm.
 ISBN-13: 978-1-4236-0105-0
 ISBN-10: 1-4236-0105-X
 1. Emergency management—United States. 2. Natural disasters—United States. 3. Survival skills. 4. Disasters—Psychological aspects. I. Title.
 HV551.3.L86 2007
 613.6'9—dc22

2007018636

This book was written with solar power to the ear-bleeding, head-banging tunes of Vivaldi, Iron Maiden, Led Zeppelin, Bach, The Grateful Dead, Judas Priest, Mozart, Metallica, Handel, Lamb of God, Bob Marley, Rush, and many others.

This book is gratefully dedicated to the Great Ones, and to every thought, feeling, and action, no matter how small, of encouraging harmony, freedom, courage, integrity, and truth for all Life. May the Earth's Light again shine as Freedom's Star and complete the Music of the Spheres.

REALITY CHECK

"Any society that would give up a little liberty to gain a little security will deserve neither and lose both."
—Benjamin Franklin

"I would RATHER be EXPOSED to the INCONVENIENCES ATTENDING too much LIBERTY than those attending TOO SMALL a DEGREE of it."
—Thomas Jefferson

CONTENTS

ACKNOWLEDGMENTS

I wish to thank my grandparents Agnes, Gene, Mona, and Adolph for unwittingly turning me on to what self-reliance is all about. I'll never forget cleaning fish, weeding the vegetable gardens, watching chickens run around with their heads cut off, smelling the freshly cut grass for compost, pruning fruit trees, canning garden produce, bailing hay, seeking refuge in the root cellar from tornadoes and shelter in the house from blizzards, making kolaches and date pinwheels from scratch, and the overall uncanny ability of doing more with less with a smile. Their integrity, honesty, and courage were astounding and they treated others as they wished to be treated. No matter how little they had, their doors were always open for a friend or a stranger in need. Thank you, my grandparents, for the memories and values that continue to shape my life.

Once again, hats off to Russ Miller for the crazy-cool illustrations and to Christopher Marchetti for the beautiful color photography. You two have believed in the madness virtually from its inception and I am most grateful for the company—blessings to you both. A big thanks to Mark Bryans for his invaluable contribution to the self-defense chapter. You *are* the chapter, Mark. Thanks also to Dave's parents, Bob and Debbie, for lending us their house for the photo shoot.

Thanks again to the crew at Gibbs Smith, Publisher, for putting up with my eccentric mannerisms, tantrums, cursing, and control-freak behavior. You have the balls to do something different and I salute you for your courage.

To my Freja Jane (and her extreme patience), and to my sweet family, by blood or by bond, to those who believed in me and my process or at least got out of the way, and to my Brothers and Sisters the world over, this book is for you. I wish freedom for us all.

Finally, I give my greatest loving gratitude and heartfelt thanks to all of the Ascended Masters and Cosmic Beings, the Archangels, angels, Elohim and elementals. Time and time again, They have freely given Their life's energies to me (and all of us), sustaining me in times of self-perpetuated darkness. It will not be forgotten.

> Don't skip this part of the book, dear ones!

INTRODUCTION
MY INTENTION FOR THIS BOOK

This book is written to remind people of their right to self-reliance within a world community and to offer them no-nonsense, home-tested tools and techniques toward the goal of obtaining greater peace, harmony, and independence during troubled times. It's based upon popular lectures and hands-on skills about self-reliance that I've taught to thousands of students around the nation. Using common sense and the hierarchal necessities of human psychology and physiology, *When All Hell Breaks Loose* concisely and humorously outlines the often simple steps needed for preparing a self-reliant home to survive urban and rural emergencies from Los Angeles to Paris and everything in between. My intention is to offer these "survival tools" in the most practical, affordable, simple, efficient, and realistic way as possible.

Don't assume to whip out this book while three feet of floodwater lingers in your living room and expect to be a happy camper. *The information in this manual should be studied and used BEFORE the next emergency.* It's too late to read the book on how to swim when the boat's going down. Proper advanced preparation can mean the difference between your living or dying. There is an old survival saying that's prudent to understand and follow: *Proper Prior Planning Prevents Piss Poor Performance.*

God

This is not a book based upon religious prophecy, dogma, or "end times." Regardless of your faith or lack of it, I'm betting that you reside within a human body that lives upon a physical planet. If this is true, you and your loved ones will benefit from the contents in this book whether Armageddon happens or not. That said, embracing and strengthening a personal and family spiritual path will deepen your connection with the Source, the only truly permanent supply on Earth.

Goosebumps

This is not a book based in fearmongering and paranoia. It doesn't matter what preparedness gear you have stored in your garage or buried in your backyard if you are too much of a mental and emotional basket case to use it. You will learn later in this book about the power of your attention. Whatever your attention focuses upon, you draw that quality into your life to act. Perhaps nothing is needed more in today's world than inner harmony consciously held by the individual. To be able to maintain and hold a harmonious attitude in the face of all things chaotic is true mastery. It is your biggest and best survival skill. Have faith and keep trying. This book is dedicated to your Divine right to think and act for you and your family's welfare—and those serious about advancing on the path will remember that we are all "family" on this planet. Self-understanding and self-reliance minimize fear and manipulation, increase positive attitudes, and allow you to become one of the stronger links in the chain of humanity during times of turmoil.

Goats

This is not a book on homesteading skills. I don't write about growing gardens, planting fruit trees, or milking goats—all of which would be wonderful resources and skills to have during a prolonged crisis. There are books available that deal with small- and large-scale homesteading and I encourage you to learn all that you can about self-reliant strategies. If you have the initiative and the space to raise some or all of your family's food, you have my praise and a hearty slap on the back.

Guns

Unlike some survival manuals that offer handy tips for cooking the family pet, stockpiling ammo and only ammo, improvising explosives, and properly fitting the family with gas masks, this book sticks to the basics of being prepared in a populated environment when shopping at the discount or grocery store is not an option. That said, I'm not discounting the potential weirdness that could threaten our towns and cities in current world affairs. However, planning to survive the *effect* of a catastrophe is very different from planning to survive its *cause*. The former is dictated by a mind-set of fear and hysteria; the latter, a mind-set of common sense and practical wisdom. If you think there's no difference between the two, please rethink your intentions and strategies for your family's preparedness plan.

Gold

I'm not a financial planner and I don't want to be. Through this book, I hope to educate the public on what is truly needed to live during a compromising scenario in which you are "on your own." A friend of mine once told me the sobering story of how his German grandparents, during World War II, witnessed urban dwellers making their way into rural farming areas to trade. He said, "They went to farmhouses with suitcases full of silver dinnerware, gold, and jewelry, and left with suitcases full of very expensive vegetables." The supposed value of an item is dependent upon that which society decrees upon it at the time. Don't repeat history by forgetting your priorities.

Goofs

This is not a survival book that caters to what most "hardcore survivalists" would consider a good read: there is no instruction on booby traps, camouflage, fearmongering, or homemade explosives. No doubt I'll read online "reviews" mocking the book scribbled by underinformed, well-armed, aging, overweight, henpecked wannabe survival gurus sitting in comfortable yet dependent on-the-grid homes with vulnerable water, sanitation, heating, cooling, lighting, and communication systems. While this book is obviously my opinion about survival skills, it is an opinion based on years of self-reliant living and experimentation. I live what I teach by informed choice: I consciously chose to design and build a home that heats, cools, and ventilates itself; I gather power from the sun, catch rainwater for drinking and gardening, compost fecal matter, and grow food. This book is geared toward helping the masses of people on the planet, readers who may or may not have a passion for becoming more self-reliant, not supporting the macho, dogmatic delusions of those who choose to put themselves into a self-limiting box of what urban and suburban survival skills should or should not have.

Gear

Although there is physical gear that you should have on hand during any emergency, I am not a "gear head" and do not wish to entice you into buying items that you don't need. This is not a book about cool survival gear and where to get it, thereby distancing yourself from crucial aspects of personal responsibility. True self-reliance—and the emotional, mental, and spiritual mind-set it perpetuates—allows form to follow function. Don't become mesmerized by people or organizations trying to pitch the sales of survival gear in your direction. Many people that manufacture, test, "improve," and/or market survival gear have little experience in the field. The vast majority don't live what they teach, as this requires a lifestyle commitment on all levels. Unless individuals and organizations offer education aimed at your ultimate freedom and self-reliance (in general, and from their products), they have an agenda, one of which is to make money by selling you their stuff. Even if they are correct that their product seems to be the best, *the maker will always be biased about what they make.*

Keep purchased gear simple and don't forget the core reason why you are buying what you are buying. Complicated specialty gear can be a real drag to service, return, and buy spare parts for, so keep your intention and what you buy as simple as possible. I have my students strive to broaden their motive and identify the *intention* behind the physical act of what their survival gear is supposed to perform. In other words, although there is a difference in quality between many flashlights, *sustained lighting* is the key concept or intention to keep in the forefront of your mind, and there are several ways to accomplish this intention.

Grace

This book will devote a good chunk of time delving into the "cause" and "effect" relationship of energy; *your* energy and the ones whom you love. Ultimately, we are all the cause of the distress in our lives, whether we care to acknowledge the fact or not. Unless this Law of Life is explained, understood, and put into practice, we will all continue to play the victim game in our lives, endlessly blaming persons, places, or things for the seeming failures that pop up in our experience. If we as a people on this planet understood and lived this law, there would be no need to write this book. *Truly understanding that we are masters of our own world by where we put our attention, thought, and feeling, is the essence of personal responsibility.* Personal responsibility is the essence of developing and maintaining a sound family preparedness plan. Work on getting your "inner house" in order with as much or more dedication as you will your outer house.

Most of the topics covered in this book are simple, yet forgotten, common-sense issues that will directly affect your family's life during a short or long-term survival scenario. Other topics are extremely involved, and required much research on my part. Similar to my first book, *98.6 Degrees: The Art of Keeping Your Ass Alive!*, I will reiterate critical points throughout this text, as science and psychology have proven for decades that folks do not remember things unless they are repeated several times. Also, I will strive to give you the necessary background information into why I am writing what I am writing, in the hopes that you and your family will take a proactive role in determining the fate of your preparedness plan.

Furthermore, like my first book, the style in which this book is written, and the accompanying illustrations, are not by accident. If you only read fine literature and drink Earl Grey tea with your pinkie extended, choose another book. I won't conform to so-called world literary standards at the expense of losing the imagery and feeling regarding the information being presented.

I am a survival instructor by profession, and I teach all types of people in order to make my living. I am passionate about what I teach, and I have learned what presentation style keeps a student engaged and awake. Many books on self-reliance are a drag to read. If they bore me to tears, God only knows how your aunt Florence will react to them.

While my presentation style may be unorthodox, I will gratefully risk unsettling a family member in order to give them valid information *in a style that will cause them to remember survival strategies while under great stress and fear.* After all, it's difficult to offend the dead. When you're stressed out or scared, your ability to take in and assimilate information is severely impaired. When your heart rate increases from anxiety or fear, your ability to accomplish fine and complex motor skills suffers. Learn how to swim before the boat begins to sink. Fear not, for the very fact that you are reading this book is proof that you're a swimmer.

The characters living within these pages, Vinny the (Uptown) Cockroach, Robbie Rubbish, Trevor, Holy Cow, and others, are reminding metaphors for essential psychological qualities inherent within all survivors, as well as core needs and intentions for survival, and important items to acquire to prepare for the widest variety of disasters. They are meant to keep your spirits and attitude uplifted, happy, and positive—all significant survivor qualities. Enjoy!

Read this book, and others, and then make up your own mind about what your family requires. Resist the temptation to take this or any other book or opinion on the street as gospel about what you should do about your situation. Unless your preparedness plan is customized to some extent by paying attention to your particular needs, frankly, it's someone else's survival plan.

Special circumstances or limitations involving your family that are above and beyond the scope of this manual are your responsibility to research and deal with, and every family will have their fair share. Face it, combining the unknowns of a chaotic urban or suburban landscape with the personalities of your stressed-out family will be challenging, regardless of how much you have prepared. Once again, like every decent survival manual ought to do, I'll focus as much as I can on dealing with the cause of the calamity, instead of reeling in the aftermath of its effect.

My hope for you and those you love is that the material contained within these pages offers you a positive yet realistic plan for living a safer, happier, more fulfilling life. After all, if your preparedness plan breeds mistrust, paranoia, and fear, you're missing the point.

URBANELY Yours,
—Cody Lundin
September 2007

PART 1

HEAD CANDY

How to USE this BOOK

Head Candy

Many of the chapters in this book are fairly short in length, allowing you to peruse for just the information you require. The chapter subjects are based upon what will most effectively help keep your family alive during a disaster. When the topic changes within a chapter, the heading above the new paragraph will tell you what it's about. Obviously, your training will be most effective if you read the entire book in the order that it's presented.

Surviving a life-threatening scenario is largely psychological on the part of the survivor(s). Get this fact into your head now that living through a survival scenario is 90 percent psychology, and 10 percent methodology and gear. Because of this, the "head candy," or psychological pep talk designed to inspire confidence and a "can-do" attitude is presented first. It will assist you in honestly evaluating, and then improving upon, what your family's *presence* will be under stress and fear and when doing without normal creature comforts. Countless survival stories from around the world and even science itself support the fact that a positive attitude and mind-set are paramount to your living through a survival situation.

Your cheerleader, "Mr. Head Candy," appears throughout the book, delivering encouraging, thought-provoking, humorous, and at times uplifting quotes of wisdom and wonder from various people and cultures around the world. His role is to reinforce the writings in which he appears, and to remind you that you are not alone in your process of preparation and to never give up.

Mr. head candy

Don't blow off the head-candy part of this book as it will give you the common-sense foundation upon which to base your survival plan. Survival supplies don't mean diddly if you're too scared stupid to use them.

Hand Candy

The "hand candy" or material goods that I recommend to keep your physical body alive are presented in the second half of the book. Specific chapters on emergency sanitation, water, transportation, food, communications, and others are presented in the most practical detail as possible. Entire books have been devoted to each of the above subjects, so please don't expect this book to cover every possible aspect of these skills. If, after contemplation, you feel your particular living situation requires advanced emergency communications training, for example, then locate the more specific information you and your loved ones require. This proactive mind-set is the hallmark of healthy self-reliance, so don't lean on this or any other book or instructional source as your one-stop shopping guide to surviving everything.

Within each chapter category are several options that more or less all perform the same intention. For example, under the lighting chapter, several options are given to illuminate the night including flashlights, chemical light sticks, candles, lanterns, oil lamps, and even solar photovoltaics. After reading and digesting the many options, choose which lighting option(s) best fits your family's needs and budget. Resist the temptation to go on autopilot and buy stuff suggested in this book because I recommended or implied that you should. THINK about your family's situation and needs and YOU decide what is necessary to have on hand and what is not.

Super Simple Summary

At the end of each "hand candy" chapter is a super simple summary illustration flagging a section highlighting the critical points of the chapter. This condensed version is ideal for those who are short on time, those who want to refresh their memory on key points, or lazy family members with limited attention spans who feel that you're a paranoid doomsday freak.

Helpful Hardcore Hints

The Helpful Hardcore Hint sections present advanced survival information related to the chapter in which they are found, but beyond the basic needs of most families. Enjoy the options they may provide for you and your loved ones.

A Brief Introduction To Da' Gang

Vinny the (Uptown) Cockroach

Without a doubt, cockroaches are one of nature's ultimate self-reliant creatures and convey innate and uncanny guidance in teaching others the art of survival. Their adaptability and talent for enduring hardships, in both town and country, is legendary.

There are nearly 4,000 known species of cockroaches whose existence dates back more than 400 million years. Of these species, only a dozen or so are considered pests to people.

Cockroaches can live for a week without a head, dying only of dehydration because they lack a mouth to drink, as their brain is scattered throughout the body. They can hold their breath for forty-five minutes, eat literally anything (they have a separate set of teeth inside their digestive system in case they need to eat on the run), run up to three miles an hour, and withstand an amount of radiation equivalent to that of a thermonuclear explosion—between 90,000 and 105,000 rems for a German Cockroach! (A lethal dose of radiation for a human is 800 rems or more.)

Cockroaches have one big nerve connecting their heads to their tails, similar to a motion detector, thus alerting them to danger from behind. The claws on their feet enable them to climb walls, while their eyes, made from over 4,000 individual lenses, allow them to see in all directions at once. When getting out of harm's way, their highly sensitive and specialized antennae, containing between 150 and 170 individually jointed sections, allow them to make up to twenty-five body turns per

second—the highest known rate in the animal kingdom—and they do it all in pitch darkness. They sense minute changes in air currents around their bodies—like a foot about to squish them—with the assistance of tiny hairs on two appendages that feed into a network of fourteen vital nerve cells that process the information.

The cockroach heart is a simple valved tube that pumps blood backward or forward within the body. The roach can slow down or even stop its heart altogether without causing harm. If it loses a leg while out on the prowl, unlike some insects which gradually regenerate a leg over several molting cycles, the cockroach will delay its next molt in order to regenerate its leg first, thereby assuring maximum get-out-of-dodge speed and agility. The roach also excels at the ability to turn valuable nutrients into an energy source that helps it neutralize or lessen life-threatening chemicals.

Always wise to conserving calories, cockroaches spend 75 percent of their day lounging around. Current research has shown that they possess certain complex behavior methods such as group-based decision-making when it comes to divvying up food resources. Most cockroach species give birth to live young—an anomaly in the insect world—to prevent other critters from eating their eggs and if food gets tough to scrounge, the cockroach kids can live by eating their parents' poop.

A dapper survival guide, Vinny's humorous, can-do positive attitude and confidence reflect generations of wisdom and leadership gained from harvesting the trash cans and kitchens of some of the world's better known personalities. His vast, real-time field experience allows him to radiate a natural affinity, awareness, and intuitive knowledge for surviving, and thriving, during and after catastrophic disasters. He's gifted with being able to read situations and the motives of people before disaster strikes, thereby allowing him to devise strategies for successful survival based upon the cause of an issue, rather than its effect. He has a love for authentic Brie cheese.

> **Special Bonus (Irrelevant) Cockroach Trivia Tidbit!**
> The current world record for eating the most live cockroaches in the shortest amount of time goes to Ken Edwards of Derbyshire, England. In 2001, Ken ate thirty-six hissing Madagascar roaches in one minute flat. Way to go, Ken!

Robbie Rubbish

Robbie Rubbish was birthed in a county landfill south of Arivaca, Arizona. We summoned Robbie for his help with this project due to his active persistence in doing more with less. He's known and admired as somewhat of a legend in the landfill and dump crowds for his inventive creativeness and willingness to wing-it on a budget. His intimate knowledge of back-alley resources in urban and suburban surroundings and their wealth of garbage, coupled with his skill at improvisation, make him invaluable when needing to make cheap, multiuse survival gear. Robbie is dedicated to the facts (he abhors survival fads and gimmicks) and is able to convey complex terminology and detail-oriented skills in a practical, no-nonsense fashion. His motto is, "If it ain't broke, don't fix it. And if it is broke, fix it yerself!"

Trevor

Trevor is a constant reminder to strive for simplicity in all things. If there is an easier way to accomplish a task, Trevor will find the natural way, in a calm and collected manner. His open heart, unselfish motive, and eager willingness to learn allow him to continuously improve upon his skills for the benefit of all. This fresh outlook provides needed flexibility in anticipating changing needs of the moment, minimizing static, knee-jerk "stay the course" training methodologies and responses. Although some may attempt to prey upon his good nature, childlike innocence and a lack of ego and bias are his natural protectors, along with a genuine desire to know and follow the truth.

Holy Cow

Although Holy Cow has at times been labelled a busy body, her true intentions have simply been misunderstood by our pass-the-buck society. Her penchant for personal responsibility, creative cooperation, thoroughness, and organization are udderly divine. She takes the bull by the horns with great determination and perseverance, and acts as the great recorder and doer of all that needs to be done. Holy Cow is our patron saint of decisive decision-making and fearlessness. Strong and focused, she balances her fiery courage with great gentleness, love, and respect for all who need encouragement and hope. She embodies the ability to hope for the best and prepare for the worst.

2

FLASHBACK:
Grooving to that Feeling
of IMPENDING DOOM

"Liberty means responsibility. That is why most men dread it."
—George Bernard Shaw

I remember watching the countdown on TV. It was East Coast time so we westerners figured the ensuing calamity would give us a few more precious hours to prepare for the inevitable—Y2K, the mother of all endings. Five, four, three, two, ONE! Happy New Year!!! And by God it was.

For months leading up to the supposed megadisaster, I attended town meetings filled with fearful people barraging a hastily assembled panel of "experts" with their questions, comments, and accusations.

"Whudder yew gonna do when my power turns off!" cackled an old lady.

The panel did their best to smooth things over, saying that everything possible was being done to protect our little hamlet from the impending threat of power outages, stock market collapses, and delayed e-mail. Some from the panel of experts had obtained their wisdom fairly recently, like the stock market broker who lectured the town on how to safely "purify" their water supply from a hastily downloaded Web page.

I watched the audience with awe. Never before had I seen such a display of fear all in one place, of people willing to put their personal responsibility into the laps of others, in fact, to demand that they be taken care of, or else! While I was proud of my town for holding the forums to educate the public, it was a psychological soap opera that was unequaled in my experience.

Survival experts sprung up overnight, eager to join the feeding frenzy of fear by selling an incredible array of freeze-dried foods, solar panels, attack dogs, and nutritional supplements. Generators were on back order at all of the hardware stores. All claimed salvation, hope, and mercy through the purchase of consumer goods by the almighty dollar. The classified

"There has been in recent years **EXCESSIVE EMPHASIS** on a citizen's rights and inadequate stress put upon his **DUTIES** and **RESPONSIBILITIES**."
—Paxton Blair

section of the paper advertised homemade survival kits, assault weapons (pre-ban, of course), and several other items that one might find useful for the coming end of the world. People would buy damn near anything to avoid taking responsibility for their lives. I was personally befriended by several people who haven't talked to me since . . . just in case, I guess.

In the days, weeks, and months that followed an apocalypse gone soft, the world was showered with a plethora of new to barely used survival gear, all at bargain basement prices. After all, the crisis was over. We were all safe now, right? So we might as well unload all of this preparedness stuff to repay back the loans we took out to buy it in the first place. The people that had preached so hard about the end of the world were openly mocked and laughed at. "Urbania," throughout the world, slowly let its guard down, shuffling down the street of complacency and the fact that it wasn't going to happen to us after all . . . right?

At first glance, we seem to be up a creek without a paddle. Even a casual peek at the news can cause one's pulse to quicken. A simple Google search for "fear in America" generates more than 13 million results, and the market is growing. The media on all fronts has and continues to crank up the fear factor and pummel America and the world about impending doom and scandalous "what if?" scenarios. Unfortunately, in recent days there has been much to report.

More than 170,000 people died in a few minutes from a tsunami in Asia, a product of the strongest earthquake ever recorded since the documenting of seismic activity began in 1899. The United States' southern coast reeled from the aftermath of Hurricane Katrina, possibly the largest natural disaster ever recorded on American soil. Despite promises to the contrary preached by politicians, most of New Orleans still lies in ruins, more than two years after the disaster. Two jetliners intentionally crashed into the World Trade Center in New York City, killing more than 2,700 people and bringing pause to the wealthiest nation on Earth, hearkening a new type of warfare based on terror. The so-called "war on terror" is fought in earnest all over the world, oftentimes reaching out to strike a shadow that quickly disappears only to resurface elsewhere. Fear of what has happened, or what could happen, played an integral role in the most important presidential election on Earth.

New and continuing proof of global warming threatens to change the very fabric of our ecosystem. In the eastern United States, record snowfall and ice routinely knock out power, communication, and transportation options for thousands. Two years ago, Florida had one of the most extreme hurricane seasons in recent memory. Multiple storms ripped up homes and brought urban life to a standstill, causing more than $30 billion in property damage and killing 130 people.

In the past few years, America and the world have entered a new era of change and the unknown. Perhaps like no other time in history, our dependence on outside technology as an urban society has become painfully real. Whatever the cause, when the power grid fails, urbanites the world over feel the pinch of their personal, city, state, and/or country's lack of prior preparation. Bogus, fear-based advice for dealing with urban calamities from "experts" (remember the rush on plastic sheeting and duct tape?) further fuels the fires of chaos and powerlessness.

Every day, people become compromised from a breakdown in the greater system that could have been prevented or minimized with advanced preparation and knowledge. From neighborhoods to nations, we believe it can't happen to us, until, to our shock and disbelief, it does.

What is **URBAN** and **SUBURBAN** **SURVIVAL?**

"Dear Mr. Lundin: Thank you for your interest in becoming an adjunct instructor with Arizona Division of Emergency Management. Although your services may be needed in the future, unfortunately there is no need of instructors with your expertise at this time."

—Contents of the autosigned rejection form letter sent to me in June 2006 from the State of Arizona, Department of Emergency and Military Affairs, Division of Emergency Management, Director of Training and Exercise.

Whatever labels you choose to slap on it—urban, suburban, city, or town survival—this book will help you become more self-sufficient during times of turmoil in rural or populated areas. There are several different types of self-reliance survival training available from schools, books, videos, the Internet, and more. Whether your interest lies in learning about modern outdoor survival, long-term survival, primitive living, ocean and water survival, escape and evasion, wilderness living, homesteading skills, urban survival skills, or others, all have certain themes in common.

"The GREATEST griefs are those we cause OURSELVES."
—Sophocles

The first and most obvious survival skill is keeping yourself alive in the face of a life-threatening emergency. Regulating core body temperature, keeping it at 98.6 degrees F (37 degrees C), is a prime concern. In fact, the easiest way to die in the outdoors is by succumbing to "exposure," a generic term the media uses for someone failing to thermoregulate his or her body's inner core temperature. Statistically, one meets their maker through either *hypothermia*, low body temperature, or *hyperthermia*, high body temperature. As a general rule, all short- and long-term survival scenarios, whether in the mountains, the deserts, the oceans, or the city, must deal with combating environmental temperature extremes and their deadly affect(s) on the human body.

One obvious difference in the genres of survival training is an element that is often overlooked by both the survival instructor and the student. This difference is the role or nonrole a third party will play in your game plan to stay alive. This third party is most often a Search and Rescue (SAR) team of some kind. While some of the training these teams receive is similar from country to city, each team will have specialized training depending upon the environment in which they spend most of their time. While a modern outdoor survival plan—such as what to do when the 4x4 breaks down in the mountains—should have signaling for rescue as a major component on what to do, homesteading skills, such as growing a garden and canning the surplus, would have little need for a SAR component.

The term "urban survival" conjures up a number of images. For some it means surviving man-eating zombies, for others, guns, guns, and more guns or a twisted hybrid story smacking of Mad Max, Armageddon, and/or a collision course with Earth by an asteroid.

Many years ago, I trained a group whose "guidance" at the time warned them of planetary devastation from a direct hit by an asteroid. Their training coincided, strangely enough, with the movies *Sudden Impact* and *Armageddon*, whose plots involved this very calamity befalling the Earth. Meeting their needs was a bit tougher than most survival courses, as their intention was to survive an epic pounding of the planet in which more than 90 percent of humans were dead ducks. One enterprising student from this tribe bought a brand new Hummer vehicle for the occasion and had it equipped with extra fuel tanks on the roof. I always wondered how he planned to get the fuel and where he thought he would drive to.

People have very different opinions on what is needed during an urban survival scenario. The Hummer man gave little thought in his planning to water, shelter, food, or anything other than barreling over a scorched-earth wasteland in a 4x4 renowned for getting incredibly crappy gas mileage. And he bought the Hummer after my training, even though I'm most certain I never mentioned the advantages of a Hummer when confronting the end of the world.

"Nothing Endures but CHANGE."
— Heraclitus

This book will focus upon:

1. Identifying and recognizing what human beings truly *need*, physiologically and psychologically, to live during short- and long-term emergencies.

2. What supplies would be needed by your household should you be unable to resupply your family with material goods from a conventional store.

3. How to improvise many of your needs from local surroundings to increase your family's self-reliance and comfort: physically, mentally, and emotionally.

4. Reinforcing intention number one above, freeing your family from their self-limiting, slavelike mindset to life's endless "wants," thereby complicating your emergency preparedness plan.

Although I offer basic parameters, *exactly what brand of stuff and how much you choose to have on hand is your job.* After reading this book, assess your family's differences with the Joneses across the street, across the nation, and the world, and decide what works best for you. Variables such as the geography, terrain, and climate where your home is located will factor in, as will everything else; the number of people in your family, ages, medical problems, mobility issues, your surrounding support network or the lack thereof, access to potable water, and on and on. I'll address as many of these variables as possible but there is no way to cover them all.

There are books in every genre that have the word "complete" in the title; the complete book of cooking, the complete book of golf, or the complete book of survival, and so on. The thought that any book is a complete reference to anything is, of course, nonsense, and nothing more than wishful thinking by the author, marketing "spin" by the publisher, or both. This book, like any other, is not complete in its solving of every little problem that could threaten your family's welfare. Although I'm giving this book my all in containing information that I think is relevant to your survival, reading and preparing your home based on its advice DOES NOT GUARANTEE YOU'LL LIVE. There are two scenarios that offer up the most variables of anything on the planet. One is human nature, and the other is Mother Nature, both of which will rear their heads during your survival ordeal. There is no amount of instruction in any book, video, or DVD that will guarantee you'll live through a life-threatening emergency. If someone is guaranteeing your safety after buying their product or taking their course, they are lying to you. Variables equal the unknown, and the unknown equals fear. The easiest and cheapest way to reduce the variables in your survival plan (or life) is to keep things simple.

Resist the temptation to copy verbatim from this or anyone else's book or opinion on how they feel things should be done. Giving away your power to anyone else infringes upon the hallmark of a self-reliant mind-set, which in the end will have you mentally on your knees feeling like a dependent victim to your current and future situation. This book is simply meant to provide you with solid details and ideas to strengthen your family's resolve and bottom line during an emergency. It is your job to get your butt out into the world and do what you think needs to be done for the welfare and safety of your loved ones. In short, study this information and then dare to think for yourself. Everyone who is able to walk and talk can take part in the preparation as well, so hopefully the challenge won't completely rest within your hands.

The **FOUNDATION** of Your Self-Reliance . . . and **TRUST**

"You've got to do your own growing, no matter how tall your grandfather was."
—Irish proverb

In its purest form, self-reliance is just what it implies. To literally be self-reliant is to be able to rely upon yourself for all of your needs. Typically it's a matter of whom you trust, as you're betting that whatever entity you put in front of the word "reliant" will come through for you and yours when the chips are down. If everyone were truly self-reliant, our global economy would collapse, as everyone would be able to provide for themselves everything that was required. No form of sales, trade, or barter would be needed as all people would be self-contained completely within their self-reliant little worlds. The problem is, life doesn't work that way.

So how about if we were all family-reliant instead? This hearkens back to tribal times, in which all of our ancestors took care of their own. For the most part, small hunting and gathering societies had small, close-knit families. If you had too large a family you would literally eat yourself out of house and home.

The founding families of the pioneer movement in the good old USA were family reliant, pushing out into unfamiliar wilderness with a covered wagon full of kids and some hope. Generations back, having lots of kids meant something as the more hands on deck a family had, the more stuff could get done around the homestead for the survival of all.

Even today, lower-income, close-knit families rely upon each other to weather the storms of city living, and team up to help support the family. Grandma lives in the back room, Uncle Fred lives in the living room, and mom, dad, and the kids sleep in the other room. Each part gives what they can for the benefit of the whole. This is a very common practice in Arizona and other states where immigration from Mexico and other Latin American countries is high. In dozens of countries around the world, the family unit is highly esteemed, and there is no stigma attached to having Uncle Fred living near the sink.

If not family reliant, we could be town or city reliant, putting our faith in the belief that city officials will ultimately bail us out of our misery when a crisis appears. How about being state reliant? Hopefully the governor and his or her underlings in the state's bureaucracy will feel just as strongly about your family (and everyone else's) as you do to fend off the demons of civil distress. We could even ponder for a moment about the virtues of becoming federal government reliant. We could hope and trust that the government, in all its wisdom and power, would see fit to keep us safe and sound, protected from all harm.

"There are always those who think **THEY KNOW** what is your responsibility **BETTER THAN YOU DO.**"
—Ralph Waldo Emerson

If you grew up with one of the good history books in school, instead of the sanitized versions, you would have read how, many decades ago, the U.S. government had a little problem with all those damn Indians hanging around. They would get in the way of mining, mess with settlers, chuck arrows at the military, and generally be a pain in the butt toward our goal of "manifest destiny" for the white man. They were hard to find, too, as they just ran off into the hills or the prairies, seemingly completely self-reliant upon the landscape in which they lived.

PARASITES AND TRUE PARASITES: A METAPHORICAL LOVE STORY

Para·site (par' ə sit´) *n.* 1. one who lives at others' expense without making any useful return

In the wild world of nature, the Earth is filled with various types of parasites. Each living kingdom has its share, from plants, to fish, to insects, animals, and humans. The very nature of a parasite's lifestyle revolves around the concept of it being dependent on external circumstances to live. Some parasites are more adaptive than others and when their host dies, they drop off, migrate, search, or simply wait until another host appears. Although they are parasitic, they retain some semblance of the will to live and expend a certain amount of energy to feed once again. These organisms are called *parasites*. Other parasites, when their host dies, they die too. These organisms are called *true parasites* for they can't survive without their host.

In our twenty-first-century world, most modern human beings fall under one of these two categories. Our "host" might be government welfare, an uninspiring yet financially rich lover or spouse, the "security" of the big corporate job, controlling parents or family members, the gifted credit card (for emergencies only, of course), or a number of other modern-day methods of being "kept," guaranteed to slowly rob you of your personal power, motivation, character, and ultimate self-worth.

Be easy on yourself. We can't help but be parasitic to a certain extent. However, for survival purposes, the old adage "don't put all of your eggs into one basket" still rings true. Strive to become more conscious about who your hosts are and gently work for greater freedom. This sidebar is not meant to have you secretly scheming or brooding about your current situation, socially, financially, or otherwise. It's simply meant as a reminder to be conscious as to who or what seems (and I do mean seems) to govern your world.

A bunch of folks in Washington got together and decided that the best way to get rid of these Indians was to take from them their way of life. Just eliminate the buffalo, and whatever else they needed to live free, and pretty soon those savages would be crawling on their hands and knees for help! The idea worked like a charm, and the blankets contaminated with smallpox didn't hurt the cause either.

Overall, once proud and independent Native American tribes across the nation were reduced to a pitiful, dependent existence, forced to live on disease-infested, starvation-prone reservations that popped up across the country. With their physical independence destroyed, their emotional and mental independence died too in the form of apathy and hopelessness. This type of planned injustice seems to happen anywhere a group of people ultimately feels threatened by another group's independence. Unfortunately, it's still happening the world over.

While all agencies—local, state, and federal— hopefully do the best possible job to safeguard the needs of you and your loved ones, it all boils down to whom you trust the most to get the job done right—and to get it done right the first time. Think about this when you're tempted to pass the buck, and your personal power, to someone else. Ultimately, your safety is not the government's responsibility; it's yours. The emergency response chain is only as strong as the weakest link. Make sure the weakest link is not you.

"The nine **MOST TERRIFYING** words in the English language are, '**I'M FROM** the **GOVERNMENT** and I'm here **TO HELP.**'"
—Ronald Reagan

Like a Rock . . .

As stated above, any chain is only as strong as its weakest link. The hallmark of every successful survival outcome is still proper preparation and, of course, a little bit of luck. The majority of people composing our modern civilization are standing on one leg. They lack stability and balance in times of change. They have become unduly dependent on the illusion of the infrastructure surrounding them. Pull the plug or turn out the lights and all hell breaks loose in their world, for they have no backup plan, nor do the majority care or even consider the need to have a plan.

Our anchor generation, the grandparents and great-grandparents who knew how to grow a garden, store food, and make water safe to drink or where to look for it in the first place, are leaving the planet at an accelerated rate. The majority stood firmly upon two legs, as they were intimately acquainted with the skills and supplies necessary to support their lives and those whom they loved. Whether they lived in an urban or rural location, people had a much keener sense of what it took to "keep their ass alive" in the short- and long-term scheme of things. This wisdom was the product of a full-body experience called "taking responsibility for their lives" and originated from the very core of their being.

My grandparents on both sides of the family were dirt poor. Both lived in rural South Dakota and grew up during the Depression. In their early years, all of my grandparents lived on farms, relying upon nature, good weather, lots of work, and friendly neighbors to get by. My grandfather on my mother's side bailed hay with his tractor until he was eighty-three years old. He quit when his tractor rolled on

top of him while negotiating an embankment. I remember him saying that he figured it was a sign he should "retire for a bit."

In my grandparents' time, being prepared was just something you did and was
considered good old common sense. Nobody thought you were paranoid for stock-
ing up on vital supplies; in fact, you were expected to do so. Those in need could
be a burden to their neighbors after the next tornado, blizzard, or lightning storm
rocked the surrounding prairies, causing havoc throughout the state. Nature hasn't
changed much, and if anything, She seems a bit more ticked off. Those who are wise
still stock plenty of emergency gear when getting to town is not an option, even for
the heartiest four-wheel drive.

I grew up around amazing vegetable gardens, fruit trees, root cellars, canned
goods, hunting, fishing, and what my family still calls "that good old pioneer spirit."
It was a time when simplicity ruled and people helped other people because they
wanted to, not because they felt they had to. It is in this spirit that I write this
book on urban survival. Self-reliance is a good thing. It founded this and every other
country, town, and tribe on the planet. Bothering to relearn some of these forgotten tidbits of common sense will fill you and your family with newfound happiness,
independence, and freedom.

"OPPORTUNITY is
missed by most people
because it is DRESSED
IN OVERALLS,
and looks like WORK."
—Thomas Edison

THE ANT
AND THE GRASSHOPPER

"A little knowledge that acts is worth infinitely more than much knowledge that is idle."
—Kahlil Gibran

I've included this classic Aesop fable, albeit slightly modified, for reasons that should be obvious. Are you an ant, or a grasshopper? If you purchased this book, there's no doubt that you possess strong ant tendencies. *Remember, however, that you're not a true ant until you put these pages into action.*

Are you an ant wannabe? Do you constantly talk about the brown stuff hitting the fan, but do little or nothing to address your talk, preferring instead to crank up your headphones and dance?

Due to the nature of my profession, I know plenty of ant wannabes. They wail and gripe about Armageddon, the Hopi Indian prophecies, the end of the Mayan calendar, the return of Jesus, Elvis, or the mother ship, Y3K, the New World Order, black holes, plague epidemics, depleting ozone, judgment day, earth changes, killer asteroids, and exploding, dying, or newly created suns. After they have talked at me, ant wannabes typically end their monologue with a coy look and the phrase, "Well, when the end comes, I know where I'm headed . . . haw-haw." Where they're really headed is straight into my stew pot, so I hope their unwanted visit brings them prefattened.

Ant wannabes, be warned, your less-than-positive actions are contributing to the mass hysteria of the planet. Please shut up, calm down, and do something useful with your time instead of needlessly scaring others. In addition, nothing could be more obnoxiously insulting and arrogant than assuming you will be welcome to take shelter and eat the food of anyone who has bothered to prepare as they saw fit while you spewed negative words and did nothing. Helping those who have been trying to be self-reliant and found themselves caught in a tight spot by a twist of fate is another thing altogether. When the talking stops, people show you who they are and what they feel is important by where they devote their action, time, and money.

If you're a dyed-in-the-wool grasshopper, but a friendly ant gave you this book, and you're even skimming the pages herein, congratulations! You may be cultivating ant qualities, even if by the motivation of curiosity alone.

THE ANT
AND THE GRASSHOPPER

In a field one summer day a Grasshopper was hopping about, chirping and singing to his heart's content as he listened to his headphones. An Ant passed by, bearing with great toil a sack of whole wheat, a jar of honey, a container of powdered milk and a shaker of salt he was taking to the nest.

"Why not come and chat with me," said the Grasshopper, "instead of toiling and moiling in that way?"

"I am helping to lay up food for the winter," said the Ant, "and recommend you do the same, bub."

"Why bother about winter?" said the Grasshopper. "We have plenty of food at present."

But the Ant went on its way and continued its toil. When the winter came, the Grasshopper had no food and found itself dying of hunger, while it saw the ants distributing the food supplies from the stores they had collected in the summer.

Then the Grasshopper knew: It is best to prepare for the days of necessity.

PREDATOR vs. PREY: A Clue into Your SURVIVAL PSYCHOLOGY

"It has been said that doubt and fear are the parents of all human habits, and the rest of the human habits are their children."
—Pearl Dorris

What happens to you externally is only a reflection of what goes on internally, so all true self-reliance begins with you, how you relate to yourself and the others in your world. Sound too groovy? If deep down inside you think you're a schmuck, do you really expect others to view you in a different light?

Predator animals, of which humans are included, prey on the weakest of the species. In the realm of human nature, there are plenty of weaknesses to choose from. In the animal kingdom, if wolves gang up on a robust, healthy bull elk, the chances of them sustaining life-threatening injuries are high. Any injury threatens the wolves' survival, as injuries impede future successful hunts. Predators, whether animal or human, are masters at reading the body language and subtle nuances of their prey. The mugger on the street will mull you over as potential prey much the same that a lion does a gazelle. No words or sounds need be uttered. You're either a suitable target or you're not.

THE WART ON TREVOR

"If you can't convince 'em, confuse 'em."
—Harry S. Truman

At this writing, there's a lot of talk and attention given to fighting the Wart on Trevor. The more we talk about it, feeding our energy into it, the bigger the Wart seems to become. This in turn generates more fear and anxiety. Similar to the above-mentioned strategy for urban preparedness, in order for any plan to have lasting affects, we must deal with the root cause of the problem itself. Dealing with only the effect of an issue puts us into a defensive, reactionary position. It causes a situation of frustration and powerlessness. We can curse and swat at flies all day long but if we refuse to go after the cause, and clean the crap out of the corral, especially the one in our own backyard, we had better get used to swatting. One of the most successful ways to deal with the cause of a problem is to be honest with yourself and your situation.

After much prompting, Trevor eventually showed us his Wart,

and for the first time, allowed us to illustrate a cross section of his Wart. While many over the years have tried dealing with the Wart itself, few have considered dealing with the root cause of the Wart on Trevor. Several have tried attacking the Wart on Trevor as the sole means of ridding it from the world but were shocked to find that instead the Wart simply diversified and grew bigger.

One of the reasons that the Wart on Trevor is so scary is that it's unpredictable, representing the *unknown*, which provides fertile ground for growing *variations*. Variations are the hallmark of all survival scenarios and can quickly bear the fruit of *fear* if left unchecked. Forrest Gump said it best, with my modification, "Survival situations are like a box of chocolates, you never know what you're gonna get." This innate variation is what demands that you learn to realize, and the sooner the better, what you and your family truly need to live.

"In this world there is always DANGER for those WHO ARE AFRAID OF IT."
—George Bernard Shaw

Predation doesn't simply happen on an individual level. It can happen to groups, organizations, or entire towns and nations. When individuals or events spread fear, whether it's based in reality or not, over time, this fear erodes personal power. Very rarely are practical solutions given to alleviate the fear, as very often nobody knows the true source of the fear. Doubt creeps in at first, causing one to question his or her support system and safety. Questioning can be a good thing if it leads to empowerment and action. But too many times the questioning gives way to the giving up of one's personal power. The end result is we'll do almost anything to feel safe again, including giving up personal freedoms and liberties. We willingly turn our lives over to others, giving them virtual power of attorney to do what they think is best for our welfare. Like cows in a slaughterhouse, this is a very powerless and dangerous place to live.

One of the factors that will determine whether you become dinner for a predator is your ability to recognize the difference between your *needs* and your *wants*. This is true for an individual, a family, a tribe, a nation, and a world. Visit a developing nation anywhere on Earth and you'll quickly notice that human beings have very few true needs. But mess with those needs and all hell breaks loose. Knowing the needs to short- and long-term survival helps you to focus upon the non-negotiable items required for your safety. This makes the monumental (and impossible) task of trying to prepare for countless emergency scenarios manageable. After your basic needs are covered, everything else on your preparedness list is fluff.

Today's world seems to be filled with the hidden horrors of the unknown. Whether actualized or not, little is being done to educate people on what is needed to live through a crisis. When a person understands what is needed to live, this wisdom grants them full empowerment to then do something about their situation in order to help make sure that their needs are fulfilled. How they go about doing what they think is necessary is their business. Some needs are non-negotiable, such as safe water to drink, food to eat, and shelter to regulate body temperature. Other needs are specific to an individual, like certain medications or items that foster a psychological calmness or peace of mind. Winnowing your family's needs from its wants is arguably one of the most important tasks to be accomplished on your journey toward independence.

You **ARE** what you **EAT**, and **THINK, FEEL, SPEAK, ACT,** and **FOCUS** your **ATTENTION UPON**

"There is not one destructive thing that can reach you or your world of action except you feed your Life Energy into it by the Power of your Attention."
—Saint Germain

True students of survival, and life, recognize that their inner worlds must be brought into order before their outer experience of life follows suit. If your mental and emotional worlds are filled with fear, doubt, and chaos, how can you expect to have happiness and the calm feeling of centered self-reliance in your life? The feeling and activity of true self-reliance comes from within you and cannot be bought. Being able to consciously project confidence, to truly *feel* it, is fairly easy when you have your bases covered. There is stability, a certain unshakability that comes from becoming more self-reliant in your life, physically and otherwise. You're much harder to knock off balance, literally and metaphorically, as you're anchored within something larger than yourself. You've taken the time to assess what makes you tick, physically, mentally, emotionally, and otherwise, and have chosen to educate, self-correct, and strengthen yourself in the areas of your life where you feel a void. The more you initiate inner honesty and improve upon yourself, the less you will feel off balance when chaos seems to rock your world.

It's been said that the personal initiations required to become a self-fulfilled, happy individual occur right here in everyday life. There is no need to force open the flower, as the teacher appears when the student is ready. How we handle our present learning

> **THE FEELING AND ACTIVITY OF TRUE SELF-RELIANCE COMES FROM WITHIN YOU AND CANNOT BE BOUGHT.**

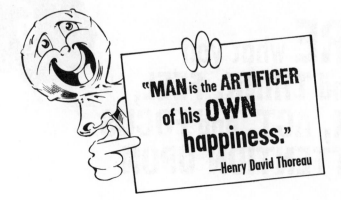

> "MAN is the ARTIFICER of his OWN happiness."
> —Henry David Thoreau

experience dictates the next, and so on down the oftentimes painful road toward self-discovery.

Consciously Taking Back Your Power ... the Road (Not Well Traveled) to True Self-reliance

"THERE ARE TWO WORLDS WHICH RUN PARALLEL TO ONE ANOTHER.
ONE IS THE WORLD OF CAUSE; THE OTHER IS THE WORLD OF EFFECT!"
—EL MORYA

Continually dealing with the effect of some negative action, instead of exploring its cause, is a drag. It puts one on the blaming defensive, and creates excuses and justifications for crappy experiences. In other words, a person gets sucked into the quagmire of victimhood, relinquishing his or her power to the appearance world of physical vision and all of its seeming limitations. *You are the creator of your reality.* There are no excuses and there is no escape from the energy you use in your world that paints the picture of what you experience around you.

Through the Law of the Circle, those who send out criticism, condemnations, and judgment attract much more misery than they originally doled out, as negativity gathers more of its kind through mutual attraction on its return trip back to the sender. As the law is impersonal, those who choose to send out happiness, abundance, and harmony are likewise the recipients of much greater joy and supply. Continued honest, quiet introspection into your life will reveal the truth of this, that the ramifications of our own behavior can be our greatest obstacle to happiness.

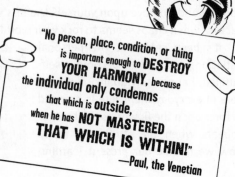

> "No person, place, condition, or thing is important enough to DESTROY YOUR HARMONY, because the individual only condemns that which is outside, when he has NOT MASTERED THAT WHICH IS WITHIN!"
> —Paul, the Venetian

The creative faculties given to humanity, through free will, are the powers of *attention, thought, feeling, speech,* and *action.* How you choose to use them, through your power of qualification, shapes your life experience on this planet. You qualify the otherwise clean slate of an experience with your chosen perception, as no two people view the same experience in quite the same manner. Using the creative faculties can and will take you into the streets of despair or into the mansions of so-called heaven. *What you choose to put your attention upon, you become.* This happens automatically as your life force rushes out to meet whatever thing or condition you choose to focus upon, and its quality rushes back into your world to act. If you see a certain condition, and make the conscious or subconscious choice to *accept* what you see into your feelings, you make it real for you. You invite the external appearance, in whatever form it may appear, to take up residence in your consciousness, thus out-picturing or manifesting itself in your physical life. This

happens regardless of whether the appearance you have drawn to you is a positive or negative quality. This happens regardless of your belief or lack of belief that what you're reading is true, just as the sun doesn't require your belief to rise each day.

"Change **YOUR THOUGHTS** and **YOU CHANGE YOUR WORLD.**"
—Norman Vincent Peale

How many times have you or someone you know been lost while driving around the city, looking for an elusive destination? Before the person becomes "lost," of course, he is completely sure that he knows where he is going. He has convinced himself with his powers of attention, thought, and feeling that the correct destination is right around the corner, or the next corner, or maybe the next. He is lost within his own reality, created by his own bias and, human nature being what it is, with its fierce desire to be right, supports the illusion of his act(ion). No amount of arguing or proof to the contrary can convince the lost person that he is lost, although it's painfully obvious to others.

Once your attention is drawn to something or someone, whether in the outer world, or to a quality within yourself, you will have thoughts and feelings regarding the appearance you witness. Every thought you think and feeling you feel are tangible forces. Almost everyone has had the experience of having their hair stand up on the back of their neck when caught in a creepy situation—"bad vibes," we might call it. Thoughts and feelings are not abstract things and you are accountable for all of them—good and bad—at some time in your experience. They contain much power and are stamped with your essence, so to speak, so the owner of the thought or feeling is always known. Those who think their bad intentions are a dirty little secret are fooling themselves because eventually their negative intentions will return to them with much more of the same.

Like attracts like, so if you choose to think negative thoughts, and energize those thoughts with negative feelings as they leave your consciousness, they eventually return to you with more of their kind. Other negative thoughts and feelings will attach themselves to yours, thereby gaining momentum. You will have much more negativity to deal with on their return flight back to you, their creator, than you originally dished out. Some have called this the action of cause and effect, "what comes around goes around," or "what you sow, you also reap."

To bring a structure into the world, the architect puts his attention toward a certain goal or idea. This mental concept, or thought-form, is the "cup" of the idea the architect wishes to have manifest. Having the cup, thought-idea, or blueprint, the architect then fills the project with his feeling. This emotion or feeling energizes or clothes the thought-form, eventually causing the desired manifestation to appear. All of this requires energy from the person. The home you live in was nothing more than a focus of attention and thought upon a piece of paper long before it came into the three-dimensional world. The line on the paper (one dimensional) became the illustration of your home (two dimensional), and with much feeling, effort, and energy, became the three-dimensional house you enjoy.

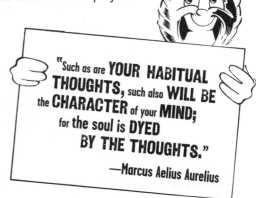

"Such as are YOUR HABITUAL THOUGHTS, such also WILL BE the CHARACTER of your MIND; for the soul is DYED BY THE THOUGHTS."
—Marcus Aelius Aurelius

Through your attention, thought, and feeling, you govern your world. This experience can be harmonious or otherwise. No one, and I mean NO ONE has power over you and your world but you. The conditions that you experience in your life are your creation, your "self" with a small "s" projected out into the world generated by your attention, thought, feeling, speech, and action. From second to second, you experience nothing but your own inner state of consciousness.

When people look upon a forest in the wilderness, they all have different opinions about what they see. Some see the trees competing for light, all jockeying for the best position to tweak the most sunlight possible at the expense of the other trees and shrubs. Others see decay and death from rotting vegetation that litters the forest floor. Still others see the forest as pure harmony and order, everything in its place, all of nature cooperating with itself in one perfect expression.

Likewise, the tree in the forest remains a tree, yet people have varying opinions on how they view the tree. For some it means so many linear feet of lumber; for

others, a home for wildlife; while others simply see the tree as beautiful. Just as the forest and tree are viewed as having different qualities, so, too, do people look at life through different-colored glasses. More than likely, the forest could care less and the tree goes on living contented within its "tree-ness."

Trevor's Rose-Colored Glasses

"'WHERE MY ATTENTION IS, THERE I AM.' THAT MEANS YOUR LIFE IS ACTING THERE, AND 'WHAT MY ATTENTION IS UPON, I BECOME.'"
—MIGHTY VICTORY

The qualified use of our attention, thought, and feeling, coupled with the powers of the spoken word and our actions, create the world we live in. This creation, or colored perception, corresponds with our emotions and how we view the world around us.

The close-up illustration of Trevor's rose-colored glasses shows how self-generated limitations color our perception. Think of the left lens as being a three-dimensional sphere, like an onion, each outer layer temporarily hiding or partially obscuring the other inner layers of awareness underneath. From the outer layer of guilt, to the inner layer of joy, each level of awareness contains a certain amount of energy

and directly affects biochemical neurotransmitter changes within the brain. The closer to the center you move, the more energy you have, thus the more tools and inspiration you have to deal with problems. Much research and many studies of quantum physics have proven this to be so. The concept is rapidly approaching the mainstream school of thought and has even been featured in the major motion picture *What the Bleep Do We Know?* Where your attention is, there you are, and what you think and feel, you become, as your psychology affects your physiology.

As one exercises self-control and consciously governs his or her thoughts and feelings, replacing the negative with the positive, the outer spheres are transmuted and all that is left is joy, illumination, and beyond. The glasses

"HAPPINESS is
an ATTITUDE OF MIND,
born of the simple
DETERMINATION
to be happy UNDER ALL
outward circumstances."

—J. Donald Walters

have no "filter," no color to alter one's perception, and all human-caused limitation ceases to act and is transcended. The spheres are not static and can interpenetrate each other, to a point. Where there is joy, there is no guilt or anger. Yet one can easily experience guilt and anger together.

These perceptions become self-perpetuating within the individual. If you ask a person experiencing grief what the world is like, he will see the world as a sad place. The attention, thought, and feeling of sadness is projected out onto the world and bounces back to the senses, resulting in a change of perception. The projected sadness, before it makes its return trip to the sender, gathers more sadness, thus justifying to the person that this is indeed a sad world—like attracts like. The result reinforces the person's emotional state, so now, with even greater intensity, the person sends out and experiences the world as sad.

If you choose to see the world as a fearful place, and fearful things happen, you might say, "See, I told you so, it's a fearful world." Such reactions prove that the little self, ego, or personality is right, and the personality loves to be right, as it strengthens its validity in the world of the person. Reflexively, the intellect justifies any position the person holds. It rationalizes and defends the quality to make it sound sensible. Conversely, a person experiencing happiness sees the world as a happy place, and is rewarded with more of the same. This self-created projection happens throughout the emotional spectrum of the spheres of influence.

> **"MOST FOLKS** are about as happy as they **MAKE UP** their minds **TO BE."**
> —Abraham Lincoln

The minute someone *demonstrates courage and tells the truth,* she has moved within the spheres of influence to a point where her inner world changes and the person begins to have an increase of her personal power and integrity. While the negative feelings have not all disappeared, the person has greater energy to handle nasty situations. She is no longer living in the world of victimhood. When someone will not acknowledge or tell the truth, she lives within her own creation of lack and limitation. Without truth, unconditional love is not possible, as people are ruled by their own selfishness, in which other people are merely objects to satisfy their needs and wants.

As we progress more and more into the center of the sphere, we become aware that happiness is something that is generated from within us, and we are no longer affected by the limitations of the outer world. We are empowered and consciously take full responsibility for ourselves, deeply aware that we create our own reality every second. Such is the incredible power, and responsibility, of our qualified attention, thought, and feeling—which *always* precede our speech and actions.

Within the outer spheres of Trevor's rose-colored glasses, people avoid us, as we're an energy parasite, sucking at others in an attempt to get our needs met. It's what you *have* in the material world that counts for people seeing through these glasses. Toward the middle of the sphere, we are tolerated and it's the status of what you *do* in the world that counts. At the center of the sphere, people seek us, and it's *who you have become* as a person that matters—and it's all due to the quantity and quality of the energy given off by the individual.

The Creative Power of the Words "I AM"

"I AM IS THE CREATIVE WORD; THE INITIAL WORD THAT PROVIDED CREATION AND FROM WHICH ALL CREATION SPRINGS."
—A. D. K. LUK

The two most powerful words in the English language are the words "I AM." The use of the words "I AM" denote individualized being. Upon using these two words, you decree into your world anything that comes after them, whether positive or negative. When used, they draw forth and release more energy into your world to perform the act or thing you desire. Their power of creation happens regardless of your conscious use of the words. They don't even need to be physically spoken; thinking or feeling the words "I AM" will also have an effect in your life.

Think about these two words for a moment. Within them is the proof that no one outside of yourself has any power over your life. Absolutely *no one else can say the words "I AM" for you*. Only you can say those words to define what you want to enter into your life. When you use "I" or a form of it such as "me," "myself," "my," or "mine," *never* use a negative word or statement after it. When you become aware of the creative power of these words, you will notice throughout the day how many times you and your loved ones think or say negative things after them. After the words "I AM" come the habitual, unconscious phrases such as "not good enough," "not rich enough," "not pretty enough," "not healthy enough," or whatever. Notice how people will affirm their misery, lack, and sickness with the use of the two creative words. And, because the power of manifestation within them acts regardless, they get what they ask for: more misery, more lack, more sickness, and more painful experiences in life. Why? It doesn't take any more effort to say positive things after the words "I AM" than it does to say negative things. Even if you don't believe what you say

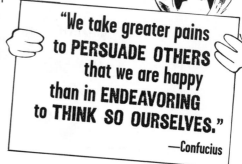

"We take greater pains to PERSUADE OTHERS that we are happy than in ENDEAVORING to THINK SO OURSELVES."
—Confucius

at first, because you have temporarily accepted in your feelings that the physical appearance world rules your life, fake it until you make it. I AM perfect health. I AM rich, filled with abundance and supply. I AM the success I wish to be. I AM perfect harmony and fearlessness.

Once you change the subtle habits of decreeing negative things into your experience by your thoughts, feelings, and conversations, you will begin to see a positive change in your life. You might whine at first that nothing is happening, that no change is taking place, that this was all just a bunch of BS. After having said "I AM stressed" thousands of times, how can you expect things to shift after saying "I AM perfect relaxation and harmony" a few dozen times? If your life seems to be crap and you specialize in affirming how crappy it is, you've already proven that this stuff works! Like everything else in the world, you get out of it what you put into it. Even if you're enjoying your low self-esteem for whatever reason, and couldn't possibly affirm anything positive about your pathetic life, at the very least STOP thinking and saying negative I AM statements! Soon, when some of the negativity has been neutralized from your not giving it so much power, you will gather the strength and courage to actively make positive "I AM"

statements. Eventually the habit will grow, and affirming positive things in your life will become a part of your everyday conversations, both externally with others and inside your head.

Knowing that by using the words "I AM" you force into your physical life whatever statements you put behind it, why would you say anything negative after these words? People's habits are powerful, and most of the world has strong, oftentimes subconscious habits about thinking they're wormlike losers. Many of us have that soft spot that loves to be self-pitied and affirm how shitty things seem to be in our lives. Habit is accumulated energy that has been charged with a certain desire. Get over it and stop being a victim of circumstances that you have created in your life. Gently but with great firmness and determination, demand that positive habits replace unproductive ones. Don't fight the negative habit and give it any more power than it already has. Simply focus your attention on what you would rather have, hold it there with unwavering conviction, and support its certain manifestation with positive "I AM" statements. Negative habits will dissolve when they are no longer being fed by your powers of attention, thought, feeling, spoken word, and action. Thus, change your habits and you will change your life.

Your Responsibility to Life

"WE ARE WHAT WE REPEATEDLY DO. EXCELLENCE THEN, IS NOT AN ACT, BUT A HABIT."
    —ARISTOTLE

To put the above teachings into practice regarding the goal of this book, it's important that you *don't* focus your attention upon disaster and chaos. This is not denial; it's common sense in dealing with the impersonal Law that shapes all of our lives. Don't focus your attention on lack and limitation. Don't focus your attention on survival situations and fear. *Don't focus on things that you don't want in your life*, as "where your attention is, there you are."

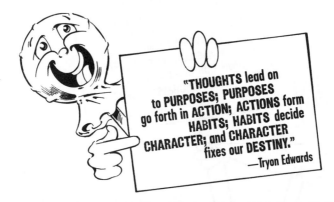

"THOUGHTS lead on to PURPOSES; PURPOSES go forth in ACTION; ACTIONS form HABITS; HABITS decide CHARACTER; and CHARACTER fixes our DESTINY."
—Tryon Edwards

This book is meant to encourage you to take a joyous, positive, proactive stance about your family's preparedness. This is a book about creating a positive mind-set and self-reliant skills that contain the energy, courage, and confidence to shatter doubt and fear. I'm not saying that you won't be scared in an emergency—you will be—but don't compel fear into your experience by dwelling on doomsday scenarios so common in the world.

I'm not saying that ignorance is bliss, either. Pay attention to enough of the world news to keep in the loop regarding important information for the welfare of your family, but keep your focus riveted on the positive. Do not get bogged down in the negativity happening in the world. If you find yourself enmeshed in the chaos again, gently yet firmly switch your attention to something positive without beating yourself up. Once you make the act of dwelling on the positive a *habit* through repetition and refuse to give in to negative influences, the gathered momentum will make it much easier to stay peacefully centered in the face of emergencies. It takes the same amount of effort to think about something positive as it does to think about something negative. Yet the energy return you get by dwelling on the positive far outweighs your initial investment; increased positive energy will assist you in all aspects of your life. In summary, preparing for a disaster doesn't mean you should help create one with your powers of attention, thought, feeling, spoken word, and action.

The Attitude of Gratitude

"MAN TAKES THE GIFT OF A NEW DAY TOO LIGHTLY."
—KUTHUMI

There is a powerful force that you can use to keep your feelings positive and attract to you all that is required to be happy. This force is the self-generated feeling of gratitude within the individual. All of us, at one time or another, have indulged in the destructive, self-centered activity of self-pity. We whine and pout that we are

"I AM still DETERMINED to be cheerful and HAPPY, in whatever situation I may be; for I have also learned from experience that the greater part of our happiness or misery DEPENDS UPON OUR DISPOSITIONS, and NOT upon our CIRCUMSTANCES."

—Martha Washington

not good enough, not pretty enough, not rich enough, not whatever enough, to ever be happy and complete. We do our complaining in heated homes, with full bellies, having almost everything we truly need, while an unexplained force beats our heart and allows us to breathe.

Many people have become numb to what they have and how fortunate they are. While rarely acknowledging the source, we take for granted the abundance in life we receive, and we have a selfish expectation that it will and should always be there for our use. All of us have done so and all of us have experienced the repercussions of "you don't know what you have until it's gone." People who enroll in my longer field courses on primitive living skills and survival skills find out quickly how very challenging it is to get one's needs met from the wilderness. In short, we almost always get our asses kicked and return to civilization with great humility. At the same time, my clients' feelings of gratitude go through the roof. They are filled with thoughts and feelings of thankfulness and truly FEEL, some for the first time in their lives, how fortunate they are, and how very little a human being needs to be happy. Using simplicity and blunt truth, Nature has retaught them to honor what they have and generates within them inner gratitude and appreciation, along with greater personal strength and insight.

The magic of gratitude is that it attracts more abundance into one's life. The very power of heartfelt gratitude freely poured out to the world in acknowledgment for all the gifts you enjoy initiates more wealth. Like attracts like, remember? If you're feeling down in the dumps, put your attention back onto the things in your life that you're thankful for. Hold your attention there and you will feel better as you'll instantly begin to generate uplifting feelings of gratitude and appreciation. The average American will have hundreds of people, places, and things for which they are truly thankful. The vibration of gratitude, and all productive feelings, are tangible, positive forces that will help keep you shielded from many troubles in the first place.

Why am I rambling on about this "esoteric hippy stuff" and not talking about what kind of food

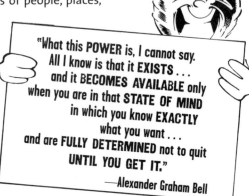

"What this POWER is, I cannot say. All I know is that it EXISTS . . . and it BECOMES AVAILABLE only when you are in that STATE OF MIND in which you know EXACTLY what you want . . . and are FULLY DETERMINED not to quit UNTIL YOU GET IT."
—Alexander Graham Bell

and ammo to buy? Please wake up and accept your eventual freedom! Dealing with the *cause* of an emergency is far superior to dealing with its effect. *You are your most important survival tool!* The prevention of emergencies begins with your life and how you choose to use your powers of attention, thought, feeling, speech, and action. Your ultimate safety and security lie in the right use of these powers. You are the master of your own world, so stop complaining, blaming, justifying, and passing the buck. Refuse to buy into other people's fearful nonsense! Refuse acceptance of their limitations. It is only their opinion and *it has no power!* Most of all, refuse to live within a self-generated world of limitation and victimhood. Cowboy up, gently yet firmly correct your self-limitations, and own your power! Psychological self-reliance is truly the cake upon which all preparedness gear is but icing, and you know what happens when you eat too much icing. Survival scenarios are 90 percent psychology and, to a large extent, your psychology dictates your physiology, in which lies the chemical cocktail called stress and fear.

Gettin' HAMMERED
by STRESS and FEAR

"It's not stress that kills us, it is our reaction to it."
—Hans Selye

Estimates claim that nearly 40 percent of Americans will be exposed to a catastrophic event during their lifetime. As you can imagine, such an estimate would be much higher for developing countries around the world. Low-level stress and anxiety will be guaranteed during disasters, and while not yet manifested as full-blown fear or panic, they will psychologically and physiologically affect the body in much the same way.

During and after a disaster, people will display a wide variety of bodily responses: from extreme courage or panic, to disbelief, to total apathy, as they try to process and make sense of the chaos. Survivors (and ultimately their rescuers who may become "secondary victims" from working long hours under hellish conditions) will display various types of physical, emotional, cognitive, and behavioral changes that are decidedly different from their normal mannerisms. Acute feelings of loss, whether the loss is a loved one or a beloved physical object, will play themselves out on the screen of the human psyche in many ways. Some survivors may numb out. They are often called the "walking wounded" and appear dazed and confused, while others seize the moment and exhibit altruism in their assistance to others. Like Forrest Gump's box of chocolates, "you never know what you're gonna get" with your loved ones' behavior after a major catastrophe. Even the most psychologically tough, professionally trained disaster experts are no match for the extremes of what can happen during and after a major calamity. Because of this fact, many emergency response personnel, both civilian and military, have mandatory "debriefs" after traumatic events.

After the disaster has passed, loved ones may exhibit headaches, sleeping problems, apathy and depression, moodiness and frustration, anger, changes in appetite, guilt, isolation, and the feeling of being completely overwhelmed and

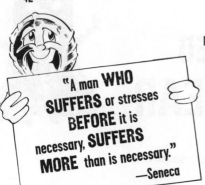

powerless. Children will especially be influenced by the chaos. They strongly depend on daily routines for normalcy in their lives. They may revert to behavior from their earlier years such as bedwetting, thumb sucking, or having nightmares. They may cry and scream and become clingy, or withdraw altogether into isolation. It's also been reported that some children disassociate from the experience completely, pushing the disaster entirely out of their memory.

UNIVERSAL REACTIONS TO TRAUMATIC EXPERIENCES

Physical Reactions:
Headaches
Dizziness
Nausea
Stomach upset
Constipation
Diarrhea
Teeth grinding
Fatigue
Jitteriness
Hyper responsiveness
Disrupted sleep patterns and nightmares

Mental Reactions:
Confusion and disorientation
Loss of memory
Denial
Inability to make decisions
Lack of concentration

Emotional Reactions:
Shock
Fear, panic, and extreme anxiety

Depression, apathy, and sadness
Crying and screaming
Feeling overwhelmed
Guilt
Numbness, denial, and a feeling of unreality

Behavioral Reactions:
Isolation and withdrawal
Irritability
Extreme talkativeness or silence
Increased or decreased eating patterns (binging/fasting)
Suspicion and paranoia
Destructive behavior to self and others
Increased smoking, alcohol, or drug use
Easily agitated and argumentative
Change in sexual needs or functioning

Although the focus of this book is mostly physical in nature, concentrating on the goods required to maintain life in the physical form, I have stated several times the supreme importance of maintaining your psychological health. No physical supplies or skills matter if you're a psychological wreck. *After a traumatic experience, it is very important that your family take the time to talk about how they're feeling. Talking with each other* will relieve stress and help everyone know that they are not alone in this predicament. As you communicate with each other, *listen without blame or judgment.* The last thing survivors need is another helping of guilt or more "what if?" scenarios floating through their heads. If you're a lone survivor, either at the start or the finish of a calamity, search out others for communication. Keep busy and stay active but not at the expense of cloaking your feelings that should be shared with others. Take care of your body; give it rest, feed it, and keep it well watered. Survivors that seem hell-bent on saving the world can implode from self-generated stress unless forced to take a break. Any tribe is only as strong as the weakest link, so everyone must watch out for the welfare of everyone else.

Kids are especially vulnerable to survival stresses. Don't let children fall through the cracks and allow you, or them, to ignore their feelings. Talk with them about their feelings and *listen* to what they say. Give kids as much information as they can understand about the emergency: how it happened, that it's over, and that they are now safe. Spend extra time with them and hug and touch them often, reassuring them that the situation is over. Kids will watch you like a hawk to see how you react to an emergency. If you BS them, they will quickly pick up on it, so be honest, but *you must also demonstrate a commanding presence to make them feel like you have things under control ... even if you feel that you don't.*

Men and women deal with stress differently, and some of the results may surprise you. Don't let mom or Aunt Martha mother everyone else at the expense of her own health. Dad and Uncle Pete may come from a generation that expected men to tough it out and not talk about their feelings. During the Great Depression, it was often my grandmother who kept the hope fires burning as my disheartened grandfather slumped at the barren kitchen table, head in his hands. Be as supportive, tolerant, and loving as you possibly can in this time of strain for the entire family. When everyone knows they're on the same page by having the courage to share like feelings after a disaster, the stress can be carried upon many shoulders, not just a person or two.

Posttraumatic Stress Disorder

Posttraumatic stress disorder (PTSD) is often thought to only involve combat veterans, but nothing could be further from the truth. PTSD affects hundreds of thousands of people and can be experienced by anyone (research has shown that more females are affected than males) who has undergone or witnessed life-threatening events such as serious accidents, disasters, violent assaults, or war. In fact, 10 percent of the U.S. population has been affected at some point by clinically diagnosable PTSD. In essence, PTSD is a powerful physical and emotional response to reminders of a traumatic event, the effects of which may last for weeks, months, or even years after the initial event.

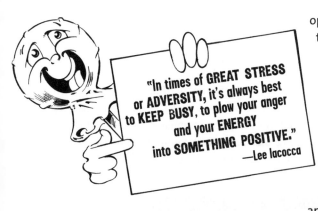

"In times of GREAT STRESS or ADVERSITY, it's always best to KEEP BUSY, to plow your anger and your ENERGY into SOMETHING POSITIVE."
—Lee Iacocca

People at greater risk for developing symptoms of PTSD are those who were "in the middle" of the disaster itself, had multiple stressors at one time, and/or have a past history of trauma. Recent traumas may also trigger old pain and unresolved fears. Events such as direct threats to life, exposure to grisly deaths or maimed bodies, extreme destruction and loss, lack of family support, and the effects of fatigue, hunger, thirst, and sleep deprivation during an extended catastrophe will hammer a person's ability to function.

The symptoms of PTSD can occur years after the traumatic event but usually appear within three months after the incident, and fall into three distinct categories: *reliving, avoidance,* and *hyperarousal.* Reliving refers to "flashbacks" of the past disaster that come up unexpectedly in a person's life. These flashbacks can be mild or severe and can heavily influence an individual's normal lifestyle. Some flashbacks can be so intense that the person will think they are living through the experience all over again during waking hours. Nightmares are also very common. Avoidance is common in people with PTSD, and they will often avoid building or maintaining close relationships with friends or family. They will also go to tremendous lengths to avoid situations that resemble the initial trauma. People with PTSD may have trouble working out their anger, grief, or fear, which can continue to affect their behavior without their being aware of it. People affected may also become hyperaroused and feel constantly threatened by their initial trauma. They may have trouble remembering information, a difficult time concentrating, and a hard time sleeping. Their "fuse" may be short and they may get angry or reactive with little or no provocation.

"That which does NOT **KILL ME** MAKES ME STRONGER."
—Nietzsche

Statistically, half of those with PTSD recover within three months without formal treatment. People who feel they can't regain control of their lives and who have persistent behavioral changes for more than a month should consider seeking professional mental health assistance.

The Physiological Fear Factory

"WE CAN BE AFRAID OR WE CAN BE READY, AND AMERICANS ARE NOT AFRAID."
—FORMER SECRETARY TOM RIDGE, DEPARTMENT OF HOMELAND SECURITY

During *any* traumatic emergency, be it in the backcountry of Idaho or downtown Chicago, *you will be scared*. Get used to this truth now, and the effects of anxiety and fear will be far less paralyzing when they happen to you and those you love.

While the body's initial response to fear has saved countless lives since time began, the long-term stress of fear and the damage it does to the human body has been clinically proven for decades.

FIVE FACTORS DICTATING THE SEVERITY OF AN SNS TOTAL-BODY TAKEOVER

- ➲ Severity of the perceived threat
- ➲ Time available to respond
- ➲ Personal confidence in skills and training
- ➲ Level of experience in dealing with the threat
- ➲ Amount of physical fatigue combined
  with present anxiety

When the brain perceives a "threat to survival," the *sympathetic nervous system* (SNS) goes nuts by immediately releasing loads of stress hormones—called adrenaline or epinephrine—into the circulatory system. This reflex action to stress happens automatically and is virtually uncontrollable. The chemical cocktail is the basis for the body's fight-or-flight mechanism and is characterized by several factors, including an increased heart rate and cardiac output, higher blood pressure, and increased blood sugar. Blood is diverted from organs to the larger muscle groups, resulting in increased strength capabilities and enhanced gross motor skills while the breathing rate accelerates, thereby transporting greater amounts of oxygen to the newly recruited muscle fibers. At the same time, sweating increases to cool the muscles. Minor blood vessels in the arms and legs constrict to reduce bleeding from potential injuries, digestion ceases, and muscle tremors take over. The pupils dilate, reducing depth perception, while axillary muscle performance takes a nosedive, creating blurred vision. And, as if this isn't enough, the field of sight narrows, producing tunnel vision. To a greater or lesser extent, time appears to pass more slowly, called the *Tache-psyche* effect, allowing for increased reaction time to the perceived emergency.

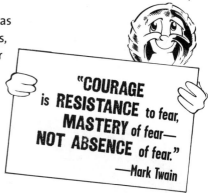

"COURAGE is RESISTANCE to fear, MASTERY of fear— NOT ABSENCE of fear."

—Mark Twain

Researchers have spent years figuring out why stress deteriorates performance in combat soldiers, ultimately linking an elevated heart rate to the poor execution of fine and complex motor skills. They found that a heart rate of 115 beats per minute or faster severely compromised fine motor skills. When the heart rate exceeded 145 beats per minute, complex motor skills began to suffer. In contrast, in times of high stress, gross motor skills were relatively unaffected! That's one more reason to keep your family's preparedness plan and the items you choose to store simple in design.

Once the physiological chaos begins, the SNS rules the body with an iron fist, controlling all voluntary and involuntary systems until the survival threat has been eliminated, personal performance takes a dump, or the *parasympathetic nervous system* (PNS) regains control. The more freaked out you or your family members become, the more the SNS takes over your world. Before busting down the door in the middle of the night, police officers on a raid routinely experience low levels of SNS activity, resulting in increased heart rate and respiration, muscle tremors, and a heightened sense of anxiety. Being rushed by a hungry, one-eyed, one-armed flying purple people eater and its pet Zygot, however, will cause very high levels of SNS action due to the qualities of in-your-face potential death coupled with decreased response time. Such circumstances cause extreme failure of the body's visual, cognitive, and motor-control systems.

Additional problems surface when one realizes the body's physiological response to extreme stress and the PNS payback occur as a result of the demands placed upon it. The SNS mobilizes body resources to deal with the perceived survival scenario. It is the body's "physiological warrior," instantly heading to the front lines for battle regardless of your opinion. The PNS deals with your body's digestive system and its recuperative processes. It is the physiological equivalent of the body's nurturing caretaker, accomplishing everyday tasks for the present and future.

When your body is subjected to stress, the natural balance between the two nervous systems goes down the tubes and the physiological warrior starts to raise hell (fight-or-flight mechanism). As the body's energy is redirected to ensure its survival, its caretaker is thrown into battle as well and nonessential PNS activities suddenly take a dump, sometimes literally. As a result of PNS shutdown, thousands of World War II veterans admitted to urinating or defecating in their pants during combat operations.

How **FEAR** Affects Your **BODY**

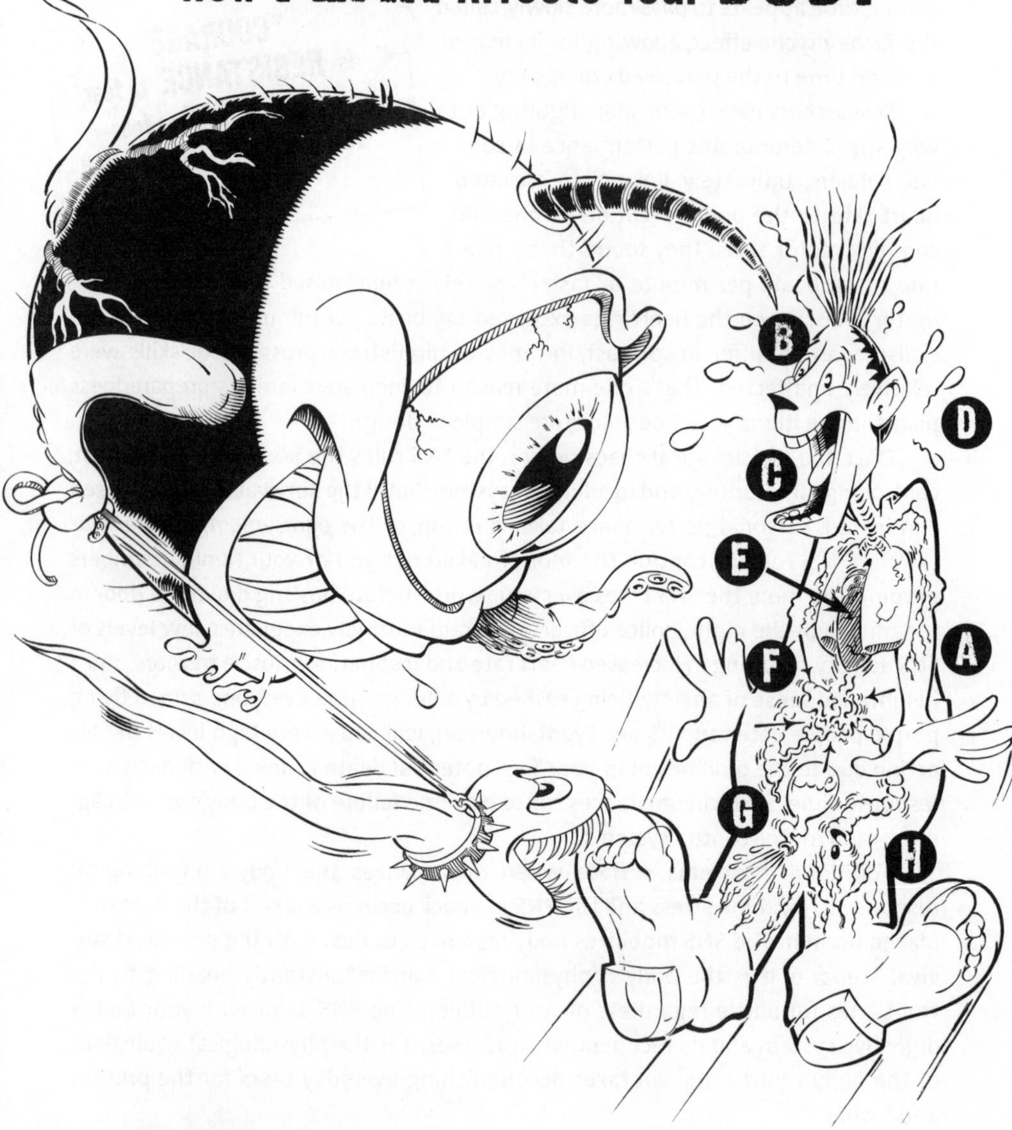

A: Constricted Minor Blood Vessels
B: Dilated Pupils
C: Increased Breathing Rate
D: Increased Sweating
E: Increased Heart Rate Dumps Adrenaline
  into Circulatory System

F: Digestion Ceases
G: Loss of Bowel Control
H: Blood Diverted to Larger
  Muscle Groups

PHYSICAL AND PSYCHOLOGICAL FEAR FACTORS

While the reactions to fear and stress or anxiety are largely the same, anxiety is usually not as intense as fear and persists for a longer length of time, leading up to a specific threat or fear. For example, listening to an emergency radio broadcast of an approaching tornado will stress you out and make you anxious. Feeling your house shake violently down to its foundation when it strikes will cause fear.

Physical symptoms of fear:
Increased heart rate
Shortness of breath
Tightness in chest and throat
Dry mouth, higher-pitched voice, stammering
Increased muscular tension, trembling, and weakness
Sweaty palms, hands, soles of the feet, and armpits
Dilated pupils
Butterflies in the stomach (hollowness),
    feeling faint, and nausea
Oversensitivity to noise

Psychological symptoms of fear:
Shock, numbness, denial, helplessness
Confusion, forgetfulness, and the inability to concentrate
Irritability, hostility or passivity, stupor
Talkativeness leading to speechlessness
Restlessness
Panic, flight
Feelings of unreality, social withdrawal,
    and depersonalization
Sadness, crying, sighing
Auditory and visual hallucinations
Disrupted sleep and appetite

PSYCHOLOGICAL SYMPTOMS of FEAR

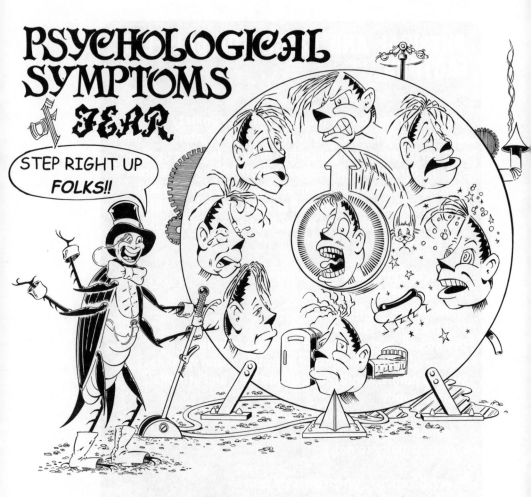

STEP RIGHT UP *FOLKS!!*

It's a lot of work for the body to maintain such an intense state of alert. At the end of the crisis, the PNS demands attention and the physiological payback commences in the form of feeling amazingly exhausted on all levels. But there's more. An urban survival situation is a *continuous* roller coaster of ups and downs, thus the hapless survivor is a slave to repeated chemical cocktails of intense adrenaline spikes and their PNS paybacks. Bit by bit, the body's once-natural and useful response to danger starts to chemically wear the survivor down, pitching the person into a state of immense physical, emotional, and mental exhaustion. In summary, human beings have three primary survival systems: visual, cognitive processing, and motor-skill performance. Under stress, all three go to hell in a handbasket.

The physiological responses to fear can be broken down into four crucial factors for the survivor:

1 *Fear inhibits your metabolic process.* Your body produces heat by digesting the calories in the foods you eat. If this is impaired, your body has a harder time regulating its core temperature in your frigid living room when the gas heat shuts off. Thus, the onset of hypothermia or low body temperature can manifest much more rapidly. By metabolizing food, your body creates energy that can be used to create a warmer microclimate in your home, help a neighbor gather and split firewood, or dig a sanitation trench in the backyard.

2 *Fear impairs your circulation.* Basic first-aid training stresses the importance of the ABCs (airway, breathing, and circulation). Your circulatory system is how your body feeds itself, delivers oxygen to cells, eliminates waste products, and keeps itself warm and cool. In cold temperatures, blood flow is the primary means by which your body maintains its peripheral temperature, which is automatically restricted by the SNS's response to stress. Compromising circulation puts your odds for living into a serious tailspin in both hot and cold climates. In addition, your circulatory system may already be impaired due to dehydration.

3 *Fear impairs your good judgment.* Good judgment is your number one tool for preventing or dealing with a survival predicament in the first place. *Poor judgment calls, without a doubt, are the hallmark of every single fatality during an emergency.* Occurrences such as auditory exclusion, tunnel vision, irrational behavior, freezing in place, and the inability to think clearly have all been observed as by-products of survival

"**MEN FEAR DEATH** as children fear to go in the **DARK;** and as that **NATURAL FEAR** in children is **INCREASED BY TALES,** so is the other."
—Sir Francis Bacon

stress. Do all you can to chill out and calm yourself
and your family, redirecting your energies away from
the fear factors.

4 *Fear impairs your fine and complex motor skills.*
Although these phenomena have been observed
and documented for hundreds of years, and formally
studied since the late 1800s, there is very little
understanding by researchers as to why stress
deteriorates performance.

There are three generic classifications of motor movements or skills involving coor-
dinated action from your body. They are *gross, fine,* and *complex motor skills.* Gross
motor movements signify action involving the larger muscle groups of the body,
such as the arms and legs. Running, jumping, pushing, pulling, and punching are
some examples. Fine motor skills involve some type of "hand-eye" coordination,
such as threading a needle or using a cell phone. Complex motor skills comprise
a whole string or series of motor movements, such as performing cardiopulmonary resuscitation (CPR) or changing a tire. The problem lays in the fact that fine
and complex motor skills deteriorate rapidly under stress. Highly detailed activities,
such as striking and lighting a paper match in the wind to ignite a camping stove,
become nearly impossible to perform under psychological pressure and the physiological flow of adrenaline, rendering all but the simplest of tasks out of the question. Once the proverbial bullets start to fly, the survivor stops thinking with his or
her forebrain, the part that makes us human, and instead depends on the "mid" or
mammalian brain, the primitive part of the brain that's unrecognizable from that
of an animal.

"FEAR is only
AS DEEP AS
the MIND ALLOWS."
—Japanese proverb

In contrast, gross motor skills are performed very well under extreme stress and are easier and quicker to learn, often taking just a few minutes of practice to begin forming a motor pattern. For this reason and others, purchase or make survival gear that is simple in design—gear that can be operated using gross motor movements. For example, pay a few extra bucks when purchasing a camping stove and get the model with the push button or turn-dial spark lighter instead of having to fumble with a match. If the spark lighter wears out or breaks, you can still use a match to light the stove. Unfortunately, much survival training ignores this fundamental truth by continuing to promote complex, detail-oriented skills and behaviors that have little application in a real-life emergency. These training mistakes are many times responsible for a person's failure to use what he or she has learned when faced with a scary situation.

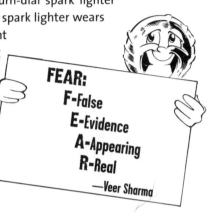

FEAR:
F-False
E-Evidence
A-Appearing
R-Real
—Veer Sharma

It's long been a cliché that fear kills, and now you know why. Knowledge and practice is power. The more training you have dealing with situations that could jeopardize your family's life, the more efficient you'll act if placed within that situation.

Helpful Hints for Dealing with and Controlling Fear

Reading other people's true survival stories is all the proof you'll need that when the going gets tough, the tough get going. Throughout history, people have dealt with and surmounted virtually every possible fear imagined. For optimal results in the field or the city, work at cultivating the following tips until the behavior becomes a natural, automatic reaction.

Controlling Fear in Yourself

⊃ *Be prepared.* Accept the fact that a survival situation could, in fact, happen to you and your family and plan accordingly. Aside from physical practice, being prepared involves advanced planning, cooperating and communicating with loved ones, mental and physical conditioning, discipline, and an intimate understanding of the emergency gear you propose to have on hand.

⊃ *Get the family together and train!* Accepting that a deadly scenario could happen is not enough. Learn all that you can about urban survival and what your body can endure. Recognize and understand what your reactions to fear will be. Practicing skills builds

confidence and strengthens a "can do" attitude regarding your tribe's ability to survive.

⊃ *Don't run from fear.* When you're afraid, take a step
back from the fear and just notice it. Ignore the urge
to analyze, judge, criticize, evaluate, or try to figure
it out. Stepping back provides emotional space and
reduces much of the charge around the fear energy.

⊃ *Stay aware of your surroundings.* Learn to recognize
the early warning signs of dangerous situations. Gain
knowledge to reduce the perceived threat of the
unknown.

⊃ *Stay constructively busy.* Conserving energy as a
survivor is key, yet do all that you can to make your
situation more comfortable, reducing difficulties that
encourage fear. Staying busy keeps the mind off fearful circumstances and gives you a sense that you're in
control of your destiny.

⊃ *Keep your imagination in check.* Stick to the known
facts by separating the real from the imagined.

⊃ *Adapt to your surroundings.* Prepare yourself to think
and act instinctively, like an animal, without judgment over your actions. In a sense, if you can't beat
fear, join it. Formulate plans B, C, and D before they're
needed but don't become attached to any of them.

⊃ *Discipline yourself to think positively.* Even when talking to yourself, strive to use positive "I AM" statements, such as, "I AM going to make it out of here
with my family" and "I AM going to be rescued."

⊃ *Adopt a positive survival attitude.* Keep things in
perspective and focus your attention firmly upon the
goal of keeping you and your family alive and safe
until rescued.

⊃ *Ask for help.* Whether you're currently walking upon a
spiritual path or not, it's never too late to start.

⊃ *Use humor.* Kind humor transforms crummy attitudes.

⊃ *Remember your survival priorities.* If you need to get
out of dodge to avoid the full brunt of a disaster, do
so. No possession is worth more than your life or the
lives of those you love.

Controlling Fear in Others

⊃ *Be a positive example.* Maintain a calm presence and
keep control, even if you feel out of control; inspire

courage, hope, faith, and the willingness to keep trying. This is especially important around kids.

◐ *Maintain discipline.* Work toward finding and maintaining order and harmony within your family and
throughout your neighborhood in a gentle yet firm
manner. Search out people's strengths and assign
them focused tasks to assist the group. Giving people
things to do lessens feelings of helplessness and takes
their mind away from the current situation, while giving them a sense of control regarding their destiny.

◐ *Exercise positive leadership.* Be firm, determined, confident, compassionate, decisive, honest, and humorous.

◐ *Stay alert for early signs of fear in others and, when
recognized, deal with them immediately.* Knowing
how the people in your family react to and deal with
stress is priceless. Be intuitive to the needs of others
and offer whatever support you can. Remember that
one rotten apple can spoil the bunch.

◐ *Cultivate teamwork and mutual support early on.* Perhaps no other experience on Earth will require such
a tightly knit and supportive family for success than
the survival situation. The group that initiates and
maintains a positive mental and emotional outlook,
putting all of its efforts and concerns into the
welfare of the entire tribe, is an extremely
powerful force for staying alive.

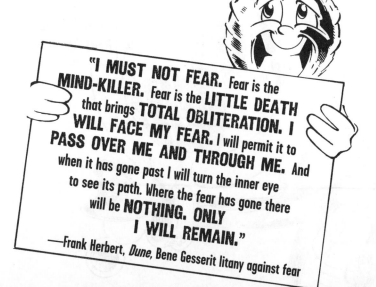

"I MUST NOT FEAR. Fear is the MIND-KILLER. Fear is the LITTLE DEATH that brings TOTAL OBLITERATION. I WILL FACE MY FEAR. I will permit it to PASS OVER ME AND THROUGH ME. And when it has gone past I will turn the inner eye to see its path. Where the fear has gone there will be NOTHING. ONLY I WILL REMAIN."

—Frank Herbert, *Dune*, Bene Gesserit litany against fear

The Art of **CREATIVE COOPERATION** and **PERSONAL RESPONSIBILITY:** Daring to Think for Yourself with an Open Heart

al-tru-ism (al´troo iz´əm) *n.* unselfish concern for the welfare of others
—Merriam-Webster's Collegiate Dictionary

Recent natural disasters, such as Hurricane Katrina in the United States, have proven how far we have to go in the realm of emergency planning, cooperation, and, most importantly, taking personal responsibility for our own welfare. Local, state, and federal agencies couldn't seem to pass the buck quickly enough for the initial embarrassing, inept response to the hurricane. As people lay dead and dying, some of my finer countrymen and women were busy arguing about who should have done what. People in the midst of the

devastation were quick to hand out blame as well, as if taking personal responsibility for their welfare were an alien concept. It was painful to witness.

Over the years, Americans in particular have been all too willing to squander their hard-earned independence and freedom for the illusion of feeling safe under someone else's authority. The concept of self-sufficiency has been undermined in value over a scant few generations. The vast majority of the population seems to look down their noses upon self-reliance as some quaint dusty relic, entertained only by the hyperparanoid or those hopelessly incapable of fitting into mainstream society.

Many people demand outright that someone else think for them, practically throwing themselves at individuals and organizations who will act on their behalf so as to avoid making a personal commitment to their lives. Taking responsibility for oneself has been sacrificed upon the altar of dependence upon others, and insurance companies, corporate health care systems, politicians, banks, and anyone else who stands to make a profit are all too willing to keep up the illusion. This is **not** holding to the spirit upon which our dear country was founded.

> **"FEW THINGS CAN HELP** an individual more than **TO PLACE RESPONSIBILITY** on him, and to **LET HIM KNOW** that **YOU TRUST HIM."**
> —Booker T. Washington

The Rainbow Family: An Example of Selfless Service without the Hierarchal Headache

"WE GOVERN OURSELVES, RATHER THAN EACH OTHER,
BY OBSERVING THE CONSENSUS OF PEACEFUL RESPECT."
—RAINBOW FAMILY MEMBER

Through the haze of self-induced conformity and powerlessness, there have always been those who have bucked the trend and refused to give up their personal power, ideals, and freedom. We typically call them rebels or other labels thrown about by the mainstream media.

One such group is known as the Rainbow Family of Living Light. My rationale for using this, at first glance, "fringe hippy group" as an example should be obvious to those versed in the art of true survival. Unless you have ample *altruistic planning* and *cooperation* to complement your preparedness, you are not prepared, and a *Lord of the Flies*-type nightmare scenario can quickly come to fruition. Unless you are willing to toe the line and do your share in a group crisis—possibly much more than your share—for the benefit of the whole, you might not survive your emergency. Unless you are committed to the welfare of your tribe by having a healthy respect for taking care of your own needs, you're dead weight. In tribal societies the world over, if you were repeatedly a pain in the butt and refused self-correction and responsibility, you were either killed or banished. Centuries ago, going it alone usually meant death. In a strict survival sense, if the single foot protests and will not move and walk forward at the expense of the body as a whole, it must be cut off to save the organism.

I have witnessed the greater Rainbow Family effectively manage more than 20,000 people, some with altered states of consciousness, within a remote wilderness setting, needing no outside assistance whatsoever. Perhaps even more astonishing, they did so using no formal inner hierarchy, as the Rainbow Family has no designated leadership.

According to the Rainbow Family's unofficial Web site, the Family didn't begin at any specific time and has never existed as a formal organization. To quote one source, "In many ways, it is a fundamental human expression: the tendency of people to gather together in a natural place and express themselves in ways that come naturally to them, to live and let live, to do unto others as we would have them do unto us." There are no membership qualifications or fees or dues of any kind. The gatherings are nonaligned both spiritually and politically. They are noncommercial, everyone is welcome, free of charge, and there are virtually no rules other than one of peaceful respect.

The Rainbow Family's unconventional leadership style was initially honed from hard lessons learned at the many megaconcerts and gatherings of the late 1960s and early 1970s,

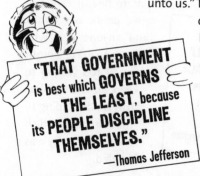

"THAT GOVERNMENT is best which GOVERNS THE LEAST, because its PEOPLE DISCIPLINE THEMSELVES."
—Thomas Jefferson

where skills for coping with and caring for the feeding of tens of thousands of people at a time were necessary.

Rainbow "leadership" has no individual leader. There is no leader/follower decision-making process or hierarchy. All decision-making power takes place at a main council that is open to all. All individuals hold equal power and all decisions are made only by unanimous consent. Although tedious at times, this method makes it impossible for authorities, individuals, groups on a power trip, or others with a self-serving agenda to intimidate or manipulate individuals to the disadvantage of the greater tribe.

The council works for the best interest of the whole. Decisions from past councils are weighed to carefully consider the effect of any new proposal, following the self-governing tenets of the Cherokee Indian tribe in eastern America, which made no decision until the effects of that decision were considered for seven generations into the future. The Gathering itself is a participatory workshop in self-government.

Individuals called "focalizers" take the diverse energy among the Rainbows and bring it into a sense of one-pointedness. They offer direction and get people working together. Focalizers are not placed over the group or elected in any way. They are followed, according to one Rainbow person, "because the people trust them, feel they have wisdom, find their own feelings expressed through them, and expect success from following them." If the people lose confidence in a focalizer, he or she is simply no longer followed. Although the focalizers try to facilitate the consensus of the Rainbow Tribes on a local and national level, things get done in the Rainbow world by the voluntary effort, personal responsibility, communication, and cooperation of individuals—*altruistic participation is the key*.

"The people's **GOOD** is the **HIGHEST LAW.**"

—*Cicero*

Donations of money or goods come from individuals through kind offerings and elbow grease. Money required to purchase food, medical supplies, postage, photo-copies, and other things comes from two main sources: the Magic Hat (direct donations on-site at a gather-ing) and Rainbow Benefits. For medical emergencies, CALM (the Center for Alternative Living Medicine) is always open and is also the Rainbow Family healing arts center. True to dealing with the cause and not simply the effect, their treatments focus on getting to the root of disease, not merely temporary remedies. CALM is staffed with people from diverse backgrounds such as ex-military field trauma soldiers to regular doctors, nurses, EMTs, and herbal medicine and touch healers.

For many Rainbow people, the following four attributes are hallmarks of the Rainbow way of life and are a matter of pride at gatherings:

- ➲ **Be self-reliant.**
- ➲ **Be respectful.**
- ➲ **Keep the peace.**
- ➲ **Clean up after yourself.**

When things get out of control, the Rainbows have their own formal security force called *Shanti-Sena* (which means "peace doers" in Sanskrit) formed of individuals with much experience in the art of mediation. However, everyone is encouraged and expected to *be* Shanti-Sena. In other words, self-governance of human appe-tites and desires and a basic altruistic outlook for fellow Rainbow folks eliminates a lot of unnecessary drama in the first place. They work to deal with the cause rather than the effect of an issue. The motiva-tion is for an individual or group gathered around an incident to focus upon and work toward a peaceful resolution for all.

Many other groups work for the common good of the Rainbow Family Tribe, including the Legal Liaison group, dedi-cated to modern legal matters; All Ways Free, the Family news-paper that compiles essays, stories,

"**GOOD PEOPLE do** not need laws to tell them **TO ACT RESPONSIBLY,** while **BAD PEOPLE** will find a **WAY AROUND THE LAWS.**"

—**Plato**

letters, poems, and art; Co-Operations, who conduct most of the day-to-day business; Supply, which takes in all food and materials donated to the many kitchens; Front Gate, the group that greets several thousand attendees with the common mantra, "Welcome home"; Bus Village, for those who come in campers or live-in buses or vans either part time or year-round; Kid Village, a place for children to find other children as well as for nursing

"A MAN will FIGHT HARDER for HIS INTERESTS than for HIS RIGHTS."
—Napoleon Bonaparte

moms and pregnant women, or those who need a babysitter; and the Trading Circle, where various crafts are traded for other goods—no money allowed.

Whew! And after the gathering is over, the amazing clean-up party commences, in which the camp is drawn inward from the perimeters to one central camp. Campsites and kitchens are dismantled, compost pits and latrines are filled and covered, logs, rocks, and branches are scattered, campsites are strewn with grass and leaves, fire pits are put out and cleaned, hard-packed ground is broken up with a pick and shovel, bare spots are reseeded, and potential erosion areas are shored up. All traces of the Rainbow Family presence are removed and the site is returned to its natural state.

The Art of Consensus Decision-Making

"IF YOU GET TO THINKIN' YOU'RE A PERSON OF SOME INFLUENCE,
TRY ORDERIN' SOMEBODY ELSE'S DOG AROUND."
—OLD COUNTRY SAYING

True consensus decision-making revolves around an environment of trust where everyone suffers or gains alike from the decision. It's ancient in its design and hearkens back to our early ancestors who lived in small tribes or clans. In many tribes of many cultures, the head man or woman was the one who set the example by working the hardest and giving the most back to the clan out of altruistic generosity. Those leaders were "elected" and followed for their natural talents, honesty, and leadership abilities—not for how much money they could raise from self-serving donors.

While decisions will not always meet with everyone's complete agreement, many decisions can be made acceptable so that everyone is at least willing to go along with the choice. In essence, a single person's proposal will naturally change as it becomes everyone's consensus. Consensus decisions are based upon a willingness to drop individual "will" in support of the larger family or scheme of things. The individual agrees to get out of the way of the process for the greater good of the whole.

All participants should pay attention and gently watch the process unfold. It's the duty of all to raise objections to a consensus that is not in the best interest of the family. Don't take things personally if someone raises an objection to your point of view. It's not the person raising a concern that blocks the consensus, but the concern itself, once all participants recognize it as everyone's concern.

Consensus decisions enable the group to take advantage of all of the members' ideas, which in combination can create a higher-quality, better-thought-out decision, in comparison to hiding behind an unexplained vote or a single-person decision. As everyone present is a conscious part of a consensus decision, all are more inclined to own and honor the decisions made and act upon them for the betterment of the whole. Beware of people who actively try to find a decision that is acceptable to everyone, thereby dominating a group's discussion by trying to make

TYPES OF GROUP DECISIONS

- ⮑ *Unanimous agreement:* All participants agree with the decision.
- ⮑ *Majority decision:* More than half of the participants agree or are willing to accept the decision.
- ⮑ *Pure consensus:* All participants accept the decision even though they may not completely agree on the specifics involved. All are still willing to go along with the choice for the good of the group.
- ⮑ *Working consensus:* The decision is accepted by the participants whose cooperation is necessary to make the decision work.

"Of course we HAVE HEADMEN! In fact, we are all headmen. EACH ONE OF us is HEADMAN OVER HIMSELF."
A !Kung (Bushman) of the African Kalahari desert, from the book *Life Without Chiefs*

everyone else go along with them. Watch also for individuals who attempt to cow you and others into saying you accept a decision, even when you don't.

The consensus decision-making model is most effective when pooling knowledge is desirable, and when the total acceptance of a decision is necessary to effectively implement a plan. Thus, consensus decision-making may *not* always be appropriate for the situation at hand. Often other kinds of decisions will need to be made based upon single individuals with the most pertinent experience or by a group vote. However, when a consensus-based decision is likely to produce the best result, people will need to know how it works.

Steps Taken to Assist in Reaching a Consensus Decision

"WE, THE PEOPLE ..."
—PREAMBLE TO THE CONSTITUTION OF THE UNITED STATES OF AMERICA

To be a part of a consensus decision, everyone concerned must:

- *Be informed about the issue at hand.* The more information everyone has regarding the topic of discussion, the more able they will be to make educated decisions. Ignorance is not bliss.
- *Be willing to listen to others' ideas and try to understand their position, viewing differences of opinion as helpful rather than harmful.* The art of listening is just that, and it must be consciously practiced. Remind yourself that a group-friendly, altruistic goal is what consensus decision-making is all about. Be willing to shut up and truly hear people for what they have to say. After all, someone else's opinion, a view that you never considered, might save your life.
- *Be able to describe your position, without arguing, so that others may understand your view.* As simply as possible, describe your point of view. Imagine you're instructing a skill to a child: keep your words concise, simple, and short. Hold in check the ego's love of being right and trying to convince everyone how great you and your point of view are. Don't try to change people's minds. The wisdom or otherwise of your stated position will speak for itself and people will change their own minds or not.
- *Be rational.* Remember Spock on *Star Trek*? Supercharged emotions will be common under stress, but they will kill altruistic group decision-making. If you can afford to do so, wait until emotionally charged people have a chance to chill out and settle down.

Be like the hawk rather than the mouse, seeing all
things from high up, the big picture fully exposed.

➲ *Be part of the process from the beginning.* You are
making decisions that will affect the health and
safety of loved ones. Pay attention, don't interrupt,
leave your ego at the door, and participate from start
to finish. If there are unresolved disagreements you
consider important, steer clear of the temptation to
back down and change your mind just to avoid conflict. Giving in to the pressure of the group will likely
make you pout and feel resentful in the future. This
pent-up bitterness might later consciously or otherwise sabotage the decision to the peril of all concerned. At the same time, don't be stubborn and use
the rationale of what I just wrote to be a jackass and
attempt to selfishly get your own way. Use balance in
all things. For heaven's sake, drop the petty bullshit
and get along! You're still alive, so be grateful and
do whatever you can to pull your own weight and
reduce survival stress and friction within your family,
city, state, and nation.

DEFINING Your Urban SURVIVAL PRIORITIES

"Always bear this in mind, that very little indeed is necessary for living a happy life."
—Marcus Aurelius

What one wants is not always what one needs. The effects of modern civilization and the luxuries it offers intoxicates the senses and makes the task of deciding what your family needs difficult. It's virtually impossible to focus on what is required as the mind is pulled this way and that with the pure overstimulation of Madison Avenue and all the crap they say you must purchase to become a fulfilled and happy human being. After all, the easiest way to sell your wares is to appeal to a potential consumer's fear, ego, or ignorance.

As mentioned earlier in this book, our town, to its credit, had several town meetings regarding the Y2K crisis. I attended every meeting that I could, fascinated with the public display

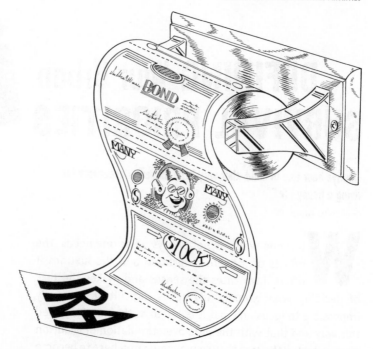

of disaster preparation and human drama. The majority of these town meetings consisted of a panel of several individuals. Each person represented a key element of what most people thought was important if the grid went down. There was the guy from the power company, one from the water department and sanitation treatment plant, a communications person, a representative from one of the local grocery stores, a couple of people I've since forgotten, and a financial planner. After each gave their monologues, the real fun began and the panel was open for questions from the fidgety, sweaty audience. In all the town meetings I attended, more than 85 percent of the questions were directed toward the financial planner! To hell with food, water, having a safe place to take a dump so the kids don't die of dysentery, or finding out if Aunt Mabel's dead in Duluth, Minnesota, as long as our investments are safe—silly, silly people. At the very least, if your investments are on paper, you'll have something extra to wipe your butt with. Enjoy!

"Any **INTELLIGENT FOOL** can make things **BIGGER, MORE COMPLEX,** and **MORE VIOLENT.** It takes a touch of **GENIUS**— and a **LOT OF COURAGE**—to move in the **OPPOSITE DIRECTION.**"

—Albert Einstein

THE PREPARATION GAME (CHECK OFF ALL FIVE FOR FANTASTIC FAMILY FUN!)

➲ *Physical Preparation.* Survival scenarios are synonymous with physical stress and unique sanitary conditions. Sleep deprivation, dehydration, and hypo- and hyperthermia can compound other limitations. Maintaining a proper level of physical fitness, health, rest, and hygiene is strongly recommended.

➲ *Mental and Emotional Preparation.* Self-confidence is the key and is the result of proper prior planning, skills practice, strong family cooperation and communication skills, personal belief systems, and your overall experience with stress and doing more with less.

➲ *Materials Preparation.* Have on hand the right equipment for the job (maintained and in proper working order) and know how to use it. Having backup equipment for critical goods is wise in case of theft, loss, sharing with others, accidents, or breakdowns.

➲ *Dangerous Scenario Preparation.* Weird stuff happens. Mentally play out possible disaster scenarios with your family (and neighborhood if possible), including rendezvous points, leadership roles, and relevant environmental and civic emergencies. If this is done successfully, the end result should be a happier, calmer, and more centered family unit—not a bunch of anxiety-ridden, paranoid people freaking out about how many ways there are to die.

➲ *Spiritual Preparation.* A strong grounding in a Presence larger than oneself is an extremely powerful force and imparts the gift of a positive, holistic, eagle's-eye view of the current situation and life in general.

Note: Outside of an ever-changing Mother Nature and urban or suburban landscape, the proverbial wild card lies in human nature and how it reacts to stress. Make every effort to get to know the other people in your tribe before crisis strikes.

Sacred Simplicity

You are directly responsible for your life. Through free will, you are the directing intelligence through your heart, and what you think, feel, and hold your attention to is what you become. One of the most challenging things you may need to accomplish is to psychologically download into your loved ones the power of doing more with less. Your entire survival plan—from physical preparation to riding out the storm itself and helping your neighbors along the way—can be made easier by keeping your outlook on the situation as simple as possible. The fewer moving parts the better, in your mind and in your toilet. Moving parts, literally and figuratively, leave options for elements of the unknown—the origin of fear—to breed and manifest.

Americans in general, but especially my generation and younger, are spoiled rotten. We are incredibly self-centered and used to getting our own way, and we have a tantrum if we don't. A big crisis is our e-mail being down for a day. Many have moved far from center on what life is all about and what is truly required to live and be happy. If you or someone you love is a slave to materialism, it can jeopardize your survival plan. If a loved one can't live without their hairdryer or other luxuries after the grid takes a dump, they're in for a rude awakening—as are you. The lack of electricity might cause them to have an emotional meltdown during an emergency. I strongly recommend that you have a family powwow about basic values as they pertain to the grid coming down and the lack of conveniences that will occur. It's best not to have this conversation around a single lit candle during a blackout—don't learn to swim when the boat is already sinking.

The quickest way to find out what you need to live in any situation is to go without. If you sat down anywhere in the world with only the clothes on your back, you would quickly conceptualize what is needed for your survival from your current environment, or you would die. In fact, the priorities of your survival would come to you. First, you would seek to eliminate whatever condition brought discomfort to your body. If it's too cold or too hot, you would need shelter. After this challenge was met, another would surface that would require attention and so on down the line. Mother Nature, coupled with the fact that you

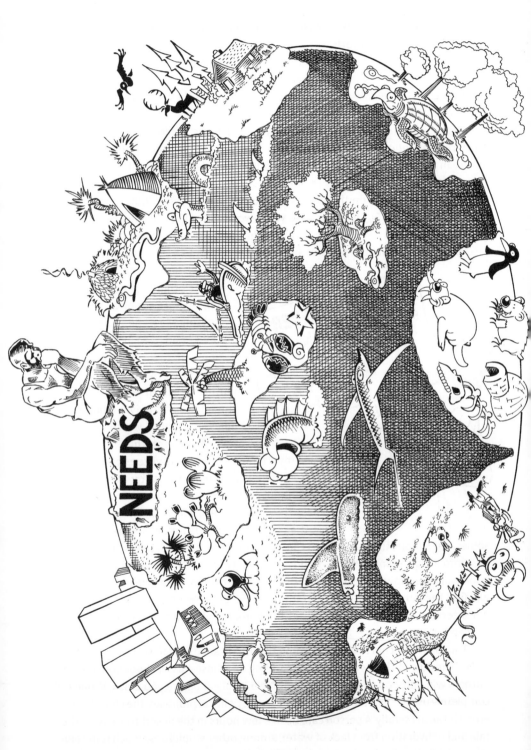

possess a physical body in a physical world, mandate what is required for your overall survival and comfort.

In like manner, the tens of thousands of homeless people living on the streets around the world deal with life the same way, at least at first. They find out quickly what is needed to live through discomfort, improvising their needs from their surroundings. As being uncomfortable is a drag, they take their destiny a step further and seek to get their needs met before the need arises, exploiting the concept of *advance preparation*. Many homeless people are extremely good at procuring from an urban environment what is needed to live. Their lack of amenities has honed their awareness about what is required to sustain life. Am I saying that you have to live in the woods or on the streets to figure out what your family needs during troubled times? No. But it would give you a worldview on gratitude and appreciation that you would never forget. In any event, I've done both so you don't have to.

For most urbanites, life can be broken down into a few precious categories of physical needs. They are as follows: clothing, sleep, water, shelter, food, sanitation and hygiene, lighting, first-aid, communications, and transportation. The order of their importance will be dictated by your current and future situation. Pay no mind to the "gods" of survival who preach endlessly about which category is more important than the others. While I myself preach about the virtues of regulating body temperature via clothing and water in an outdoor survival scenario, both take a backseat to first-aid when one realizes they have a tree branch sticking out of their leg. While the contents of this list may look harmless and somewhat simple, the human ego can mess it up in a heartbeat and turn a simple idea into a nightmare of things to buy and events to fear. In the coming pages this book will cover how to deal with all of the above categories, as well as others. You will find the job of preparing your family for the unknown much easier if you first pay attention to what is known about the human body and the priorities required to keep it alive.

The following chart hammers home the importance of your survival priorities. I call it "The Rule of Threes or Fours." Depending on whose survival book you read, the authors will differ on the increments of time involved before you croak. While not completely useless as a teaching tool, much like political promises, the chart is full of errors if taken literally. A person can die in a few hours in the desert from hyperthermia and dehydration from lack of water, among other stupidities, which is in seeming contradiction to the chart to the right. In like fashion, if I tell nicotine-addicted

The Rule of Threes or Fours

If you ...	You could be dead in ...
Panic	3 to 4 seconds
Have no oxygen	3 to 4 minutes
Have no shelter	3 to 4 hours
Have no water	3 to 4 days
Have no food	3 to 4 weeks
Fall apart as a group	3 to 4 months (or, of course, weeks, days, hours, or minutes)

students in my courses that they can't smoke for the next several days, I might see the "fall-apart-as-a-group" statistic go down the tubes in a few hours. What this chart does accomplish, however, is to plainly illustrate what will statistically kill you first. This wisdom allows you to intelligently compile a preparedness checklist for what will befall you, sooner or later, without becoming a slave to another's opinion. Three tons of canned food and ammo stashed in your garage doesn't mean much if you die from hypothermia in your on-the-grid house, featuring electric space heaters, while in the midst of a several-day, mid-January power blackout.

In addition, the chart illustrates the all-important role that psychology plays in all emergency scenarios. Panic—the bane of all—thrust into a survival situation must be dealt with first and throughout your ordeal. How many watts of power your generator puts out is irrelevant if you're too scared stupid to fire it up. Like anything else, training, practice, and proper advance preparation will serve you well in your family's time of need. The very fact that you're still plowing through this book is a testament to your wanting to know more and take the bull by the horns in your family's self-reliance and independence. Notice also how all of the items listed in the chart with the exception of group dynamics, to a greater or lesser extent, involve keeping your body's inner core temperature at 98.6 degrees F (37 degrees C)!

"MOST OF the LUXURIES, and many of the so-called comforts of life, are not only NOT INDISPENSABLE, but POSITIVE HINDRANCES to the ELEVATION OF HUMANITY."
—Henry David Thoreau

How much stuff
DO YOU NEED . . .
and for HOW LONG?

"The more you know, the less you need."
—Australian Aborigine saying

The average modern wilderness survival scenario lasts approximately seventy-two hours, or three days, before rescuers find you dead or alive. In contrast, our hypothetical urban survival scenario has no set time limits. Eventually, we're assuming that local, state, and federal emergency management agencies will bail us out of our predicament . . . but the question is, when? In a wilderness survival emergency, only you and the company you keep are screwed. Meanwhile, back at the ranch, the grid is up, the power is on, people are commuting to work, and the burgers are sizzling on the grill at the nearest fast-food joint. Nothing has changed, and the ordered chaos we call Urbania chugs along just swell.

Imagine if all of your modern-day niceties "hiccupped" for a short while and failed to function on cue. Better yet, picture the services and conveniences that you take for granted each day coming to a screeching halt for an unknown period of time. It's obvious from past disasters around the world, human caused or otherwise, that local emergency response personnel are hopelessly understaffed. As noble, selfless, and hardworking as those emergency teams are, they always require assistance from other towns, counties, states, and sometimes nations. All of this takes time to accomplish, and time is one commodity that may be in high demand if you don't take care of the simple, basic needs that your family will have *before* the crisis happens.

> **HOW MUCH SURVIVAL STUFF YOU HAVE IS DIRECTLY PROPORTIONAL TO WHAT YOU FEEL THREATENS YOUR HOME, AND HOW LONG THE EFFECTS WILL LAST.**

How much stuff does your family need to store for an emergency and how long will it take until help arrives? The short answer is, how would I know? Once you've decided for your family *what* is required for their survival and comfort, you can progress to the all-important *how much* is required. How much survival stuff you have is directly proportional to what you feel threatens your home, and how long the effects will last. In other words, how much you store is a custom decision that must be made by you and

"He who **DIES** with the most toys is, nonetheless, **STILL DEAD.**"
—Anonymous

your family. Factors that will help you reach a rational decision are included below. While certainly not all-inclusive, these points detail the lion's share of variables that should influence your decision on how much preparedness gear to have around the house. For the curious or desperate, my boilerplate advice for most urban areas is to have a minimum two- to four-week supply of what's needed to function without outside help of any kind.

Enough is Enough: Determining How Much To Store from the Store

The following points will help you fine-tune how much preparedness gear your tribe might need. Supplement the list with family meetings, facts on the ground about your unique situation, and common sense.

- ⮑ *The number of family members in your tribe, including pets.* Obvious enough, yes?
- ⮑ *The number of children, elderly, and special-needs members.* The young and the old have different needs. These differences fall into many categories including nutrition, entertainment, healthcare and first-aid, sanitation, and mobility. Specialty items catering to either group can be easily overlooked when buying and storing regular supplies. In most instances, these specialty items can be improvised, yet in some cases, a shortage of needed items may cause your family member's death. Take a serious look at what little Jimmy and Grandpa Joe truly need for their survival and purchase more than what's needed for your worst-case scenario. Likewise, people with disabilities or who use special medications may frequently have their medical needs overlooked.
- ⮑ *The proposed duration of your emergency, imagined or otherwise.* My crystal ball broke a long time ago.

This is the wild card that no one can escape, *knowing how long the emergency your family must endure
will last.* Pay attention to the other points in this list,
make an educated guess regarding what types of
emergencies could be the most prevalent for your
home turf, plan and prepare the best that you can,
have faith, and be happy.

➲ *Realistic opportunities to resupply your stock.* A common thread in most urban survival scenarios is the
limited ability to purchase more goods. In a realm
where living off the land means commandeering
the 1986 Cutlass Supreme from the supermarket to
the discount store, your self-reliance will last as long
as the last item on the shelf, or the capacity of your
gas tank. Travel may be impossible (not to mention
dangerous) due to clogged freeways and streets. Even
if your grocery store is located down the street, don't
expect to come home with bacon and eggs during an
emergency.

➲ *Rationing supplies as opposed to continuing your normal, "nonemergency" lifestyle.* Failing or refusing to ration your supplies and switch your family into "conservation mode" will have dire consequences for your stored goods over longer emergencies. Around the globe, case histories regarding survival situations are loaded with examples of people blowing through limited supplies in short order. The reasons for doing so are endless, as are the ways in which the offending parties died.

One of the most famous cases of survival involved the Uruguayan rugby team whose plane crash-landed deep within the Andes mountains. Search planes were sent out to locate the missing plane almost immediately. A few days into their ordeal, the survivors spotted a plane overhead that seemed to circle them and acknowledge their location. In celebratory glee, they proceeded to consume all of their known food and drink while putting a serious dent into the group's stash of cigarettes. Days

"Civilization is a LIMITLESS multiplication of UNNECESSARY NECESSARIES."
—Mark Twain

later, on a dying radio, they heard that the rescue
mission to locate them had been called off. In fact,
the survivors hadn't been seen at all, as the top of
their plane was white and had crashed at an elevation in which snow covered the ground year-round.
Before their ultimate rescue, the group remained on
the mountain for more than two months, forced to
eat the bodies of their dead friends and relatives in
order to live.

➲ *Having a neighborhood support group as opposed to
going it alone.* So-called American independence has
done damage to our sense of community. Do you
know your neighbor? Do you care? The average 1800s
American mountain man died when he was between
thirty-four to thirty-seven years old. Mountain men
were not living off the land without survival tools.
They possessed several horses and mules, bags of
flour and other dried staples, rifles, knives, traps, fire-
starting methods, intimate knowledge of the landscape they were working within, potential friend-
ships with native peoples, guts, determination, and a
serious sense of adventure. Do you have any guesses
as to why they died so young?

A friend of mine who teaches primitive living
skills put together a "primitive living" experiment on
her land. Several people, all well versed in the hard
skills it takes to live from the land, joined her for the
event. For months prior, each prepared what they felt
would be required to give them a fighting chance.
They dried deer and elk meat, made baskets, buckskin
clothing, extra footwear, hunting and fishing implements, pottery cookware, shelters, and on and on the
list went. When the experiment finally commenced,
more than 75 percent of the people washed out before the first week was over, many due to headaches
suffered from caffeine and nicotine withdrawal! My
friend ended up alone with her eight-year-old daughter for the next several weeks.

Regardless of her knowledge and the fact that
she was on her own turf, she was unable to advance
beyond eating and using the stores she had initially
prepared for the experiment. She couldn't gather
enough new calories to break even with what she

started with, let alone store a surplus for the coming weeks. This trial was conducted in late summer in northern Montana, a land where calories were not going to get any easier to find as autumn hit and winter followed.

As she recounted her experience, she stated that the reason she failed to make any progress toward a self-sustaining lifestyle was because she had to do everything herself. In the case of the mountain men, doing everything alone flat wore them out, leaving them more susceptible to the dangers of their daily life. In other words, they died young from the sheer harshness of their solitary lifestyle. For all of you rugged individualists out there, take heart and listen to the wisdom of the tribe. Consider creating a support system with like-minded individuals who live nearby.

- ➲ *Climate and season.* Cold and hot weather each have their variables that tax human survival. Frigid temperatures will cause your body's metabolism to spike and burn through calories like crazy, depleting your food stores more quickly than usual. Hot weather will cause you and your family to suck down your water supply in short order. Be sure to update and rotate certain stored items to meet the challenges of the changing seasons.
- ➲ *The geographical location of your home.* During the summer of 2005, America suffered her largest disaster nightmare to date as Hurricane Katrina slammed into Louisiana and Mississippi, devastating the coastline and completely obliterating entire towns from the landscape. Thousands died and tens of thousands were displaced. Built below sea level, the city of New Orleans, the Big Easy itself, was under several feet of water. On the sixth day of the disaster, countless people, dehydrated, short or out of food, and very scared, were still waiting to be rescued from partially submerged homes and apartments. For God's sake, if you live in or near geographical areas that are especially vulnerable to some kind of unique tragedy, please take the necessary precautions to deal with your area's worst-case scenario. In New Orleans, knowing how to disinfect water for drinking

could have literally saved dozens of lives, and it can
be done for as little as one dollar, or with trash and
know-how for free.

➲ *Your ability to improvise your needs directly from your
environment.* Many communities are more suburban
than urban. Many more are flat-out rural. If you have
a creek running through your backyard, hooray for
you, provided that you have the ability to disinfect
the water when the bodies float by. If wildlife regularly wanders around your home, you have options
that others do not. If the back lot of your property is
wooded, you have access to supplies valuable to your
family's survival; if your kitchen window looks out
over a vegetable garden, all the better. After gleaning
the necessities for survival from common sense, this
book, and other sources, peruse your immediate area
to discern which tasks and needs can be improvised
directly from your environment. Remember that simplicity and doing more with less are important keys
to your family's survival.

FINDING OUT What You'll MISS around the House BEFORE IT'S GONE

"He who does not economize will have to agonize."
—Confucius

Assuming that you live in a metropolitan area, as 80 percent of our nation does, a large part of your survival plan will focus upon your home. If you're living on "grid power," provide fun for the entire family by finding the main breaker and turning it off. (Tell your family first what you're trying to accomplish). Folks living in apartments or other places where the neighbors would frown upon your little game can simply duct tape switches and appliances as reminders that they no longer work. Try this exercise some evening and see if you and your family can sense the feeling that someone has you by the groin. Most families quickly realize that their world as they know it can be brought to a standstill in the blink of a breaker. Like Alcoholics Anonymous, the first step in the healing process is to realize that we have a problem. But in this case, we're not powerless to do something about it.

Another cool exercise to find out how much power and fuel your family uses is to compile a list. The list should include all major appliances or items that require electricity or fuel such as propane or natural gas that your family uses on a daily basis. For example, the word "refrigerator" stands for the refrigerator, the word "television" represents the television and so on. Each time a family member uses an item on the list, they put a check mark beside the item. This method is more effective if everyone writes down the amount of time the item was used. If the television is checked off, write down how long you watched TV after the check mark. Using the check mark system allows family members to at least see how many times an appliance has been used (as they put the check mark by the appliance before they use it), in the event they forget to jot down how long the appliance was on after the fact. You might

SUNDAY POWER & FUEL USE	Fridge	Kitchen & Be Lights, Lights	living room lights	TV	radio	Stove	microwave	washer/dryer	hot water	toast
	24	½ hour	1 hour	1 hr.	½ hr.	1 hr.	5 min.	1 hr.		6 2 hrs. min.
		1½ hrs.	2 hr.	3 hrs.	½ hr.	1 hr.	10 min.	2 hrs.		
		2 hr.	½ hr.	½ hr.	1½ hr.					5 2 hrs. min.
		½ hr.								
		= 24 hrs.	= 4hrs.	= 3 hrs.	= 4½hr.	2 hr.	2½ hr.	15 min.	3 hrs.	
Grand Total Family Power use for Sunday ≈ Approx. 49 hrs.										

BREAKER ON OFF

also have a list for items that are used every week or two. If your family is honest with itself, it won't take long to pick out the high-use items. Extending the exercise a full week, photocopying the original checklist so that each day has a fresh page upon which to record your day's consumption, will give you a good average to work with regarding your family's fixation with its furnishings.

Next, have a family meeting (remember consensus decision-making, if applicable) and carefully look over the high-use items in the household. What stuff has the most check marks beside it and how long was it used? Decide for your family what are non-negotiable, high-need items. I would recommend breaking this into two parts. The first list should have items that dictate the very survival of your family. In essence, your family would die in a long-term survival situation without these items. Anticipating the duration of your family's mock survival scenario is paramount to what and how many supplies you will need. Only you know if more supplies will be required for your situation.

Part two includes items that, while not truly needed for base survival, would be nice to have around to keep the kids from crawling up the walls. This list might include a few high-use items from the main list that add to the family's sense of calm by promoting psychological comfort. If television is prominent for your tribe, and you don't have a small, battery-operated TV (as if full programming would be up and running in a serious emergency), consider instead the ultimate goal of TV. While it can provide information, TV typically provides entertainment, but so do board games, and with fewer moving parts and less energy consumption.

Listing what your family actually uses each day and how long they use it will hammer home the truth about what they deem important in your household. Without this written evidence, you will be far less likely to accurately assess your family's needs and wants, and what will push their buttons when they are deprived of the furnishings they love so much.

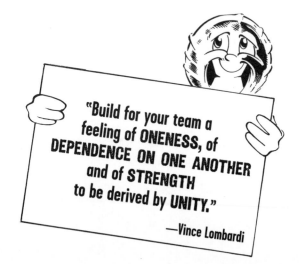

"Build for your team a feeling of ONENESS, of DEPENDENCE ON ONE ANOTHER and of STRENGTH to be derived by UNITY."

—Vince Lombardi

PART 2

HAND CANDY

Gimme SHELTER!

"If design, production, and construction cannot be channeled to serve survival, if we fabricate an environment—of which, after all, we seem an inseparable part—but cannot make it an organically possible extension of ourselves, then the end of the race may well appear in sight."
—Richard Neutra, *Survival Through Design*

The optimum ambient temperature in which human beings are able to maintain core body temperature without stress is 79 to 86 degrees F (26 to 30 degrees C). Although the modern home now serves many purposes, physical and psychological, a home used to have one main priority. It matters not if your home is a mansion or a shack for this purpose. Both the mansion and the shack are simply shelters, and a shelter's main purpose in the past was to act as an extension of clothing to help thermoregulate the core body temperature of its occupants. I don't care how much money you've dumped into your shelter to compete with the Joneses, if it's too hot or cold inside, you'll be miserable. This almighty god called "room temperature" is a phenomenon so common and taken for granted that its importance to comfort and happiness has been completely overlooked by modern urbanites. It's only when the invisible switch of room temperature clicks off that people realize how dependent on the grid they have become.

According to Tony Brown, founder and director of the Ecosa Institute, Americans use more than 30 percent of the country's total energy budget to heat and cool their homes. This wasteful blasphemy should hammer home the point that stabilizing the inner temperature of the home ranks high on the list of priorities for all Americans. It's a blasphemy because there are many alternative building and common-sense options for builders and homeowners alike that severely reduce or all but eliminate the need for heating and cooling the home with outside resources. The Ecosa Institute is a sustainable design school for architecture students that teaches alternative methods of design, construction, and energy efficiency. It is part of the growing tide of people worldwide who know there are better options for building smart, efficient homes without pillaging the land. Imagine how much freer this nation and the world would be if common-sense building alternatives to promote energy efficiency were actively promoted by the world's governments. What if we eliminated even half of the above percentage of our nation's energy dependence by simply building or modifying current homes to make better use of free energy sources and conserve the ones they use? Luckily, we don't have to wait for status quo politicians who seem to be more interested in keeping their job than doing their job.

The Self-Reliant Freedom of Good Design

"MY PRECEPT TO ALL WHO BUILD IS, THAT THE OWNER SHOULD BE
AN ORNAMENT TO THE HOUSE, AND NOT THE HOUSE TO THE OWNER."
   —CICERO

In a modern outdoor survival situation the most common way to die is to succumb to *hypothermia*, low body temperature, or *hyperthermia*, high body temperature. Knowing this, and knowing that this country has become a slave to foreign energy in order to have a comfortable living room, I wanted to design a home that would thermoregulate its own core body temperature, and I have. While my home looks unconventional, the basic concepts that I've incorporated to achieve energy freedom are orientation, thermal mass, and insulation. These common-sense concepts can be applied to any home regardless of the materials it's constructed from or how it looks.

It's winter in the high desert as I write this, and last night the thermometer outside read 9 degrees F (minus 13 degrees C), a bit colder than typical and, ironically, part

of the same storm system that left 500,000 people without power in the Midwest. Regardless of single-digit temperatures, my home remained a cozy 72 degrees F (22 degrees C), and it did so without using *any* conventional energy resources. I have no heating bills of any kind and I don't burn wood. My home is heated entirely by the free clean energy of the sun, a phenomenon commonly referred to as "passive solar." Along with orienting my home solar south, I have the proper square footage of windows to match the square footage of my home so that it doesn't under- or overheat. These windows let in shortwave radiation from the sun that soaks into my stone floor during the day. At night when outside temperatures dip, the stone floor, which is a great conductor of the sun's energy, re-radiates the stored sunshine, or heat, as long-wave radiation that keeps the house warm. Insulation and thermal mass help retain the heat throughout the night. The process starts anew the next day. Even though my home is dependent on the sun for heat, it's designed to retain this comfort for several days of cloudy weather or storms.

In the summertime, when outside temperatures hit triple digits, I enjoy inside temps in the high 70s (approximately 25 degrees C). I have no cooling bills of any kind. A simple roof overhang designed for my window height and latitude keeps the higher summer sun's rays from hitting the stone floor. My windows and doors are situated to take advantage of the prevailing weather patterns and the cooler nighttime breezes. In fact, the entire front of the house is a huge parabola that acts as a scoop to harness the dominant southwestern weather systems for optimal natural free ventilation when required. Once again, thermal mass and insulation keep out hot temperatures while maintaining the cooler inside environment.

I've utilized an open floor plan that allows natural light from the sun to reach all rooms of the house, even though my house is underground. This eliminates the need for artificial lighting of any kind until it gets dark outside. The wall paint is impregnated with mica, which is highly reflective of natural or artificial light, thereby increasing the light value. Hundreds of pieces of shattered mirror line a vertical skylight that reflects sunlight into a back room that has no windows of its own.

What electrical lighting, appliances (including a microwave, washing machine, and computer), and tools that I require are powered by a self-contained solar system. A carport to shield vehicles from the summer sun doubles as a rain catchment surface, which funnels thousands of gallons of potable water into a holding tank that gravity feeds into the house. My hot water comes from the sun as well, which heats up water-filled panels and the salvaged inside of a conventional water heater that's painted black. Although much of the time I use a small, two-burner, propane-fueled stove for cooking, my solar oven cooks everything from lentil soup to chocolate cake for free. Regardless of my frequent stove use, by paying attention to fuel consumption as outlined in the creative cooking chapter, I can make my barbeque grill-sized propane tank (twenty-pound cylinder) last more than a year and a half. And it costs less than thirteen dollars to fill.

The rooms in my home are a series of parabolas, one of nature's strongest shapes, thus my home was built for a fraction of the cost of traditional earth homes that require massive infrastructure to hold up the weight of the earth. The shape of my roof is, of course, arched, like the top of an igloo, so even though grass and flowers grow on the roof, it doesn't leak, as there is no flat surface for water to collect. The precipitation that does hit the roof is directed by earthen contours and berms toward waiting fruit trees that are heavily mulched with compost, sand, and stone to conserve water. The earth acts as thermal mass, helping to slow down fluctuations in temperature, and the grasses on the roof not only stabilize the earth from erosion, but act as insulation, especially during the hot summer months when they shade the roof from the sun. The hot-season native gramma grasses require no water other than rain and also provide forage for the wild desert cottontail rabbits (which I hunt for food) that live on my roof.

In short, my off-the-grid home thermoregulates its own inner temperature in hot and cold weather extremes, self-ventilates, lights itself during daylight hours, and provides supplemental meat for the table, all for free, and all with very little activity on my part. It does so because I researched and implemented the virtues of good building design and paid strict attention to the natural world of my particular building site.

Most homes are dependent boxes plopped down upon a landscape in which little or no thought was given as to how the landscape operates, except to take advantage of the pretty view. Did I mention that I have a pretty view, too? Because nature is so often ignored when building footprints are laid out, the homeowner pays the price for the builder's ignorance each month in heating and cooling bills. And more than a quarter of energy expenditures within the United States goes to pay for this nonsense.

While it might be impractical to retrofit your home to take advantage of these concepts, one of my friends did, and it has completely changed the comfort level of his mountain log home. New homebuilders have the option of researching what alternative building methods will work for their geographical life zone, and I encourage them to do so. The little extra effort and thought you put into the design of your shelter will save you loads of time, headaches, and money over the years. With the precarious nature of petroleum supplies these days, your super-energy-efficient home will have a healthy resale value when compared to the common oil-guzzling or natural-gas-consuming box. While giving you instructions on designing a self-reliant, energy-efficient home is out of bounds for this book, mentioning that it's

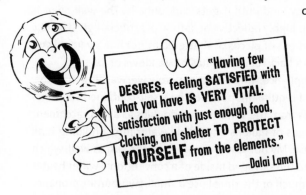

"Having few DESIRES, feeling SATISFIED with what you have IS VERY VITAL: satisfaction with just enough food, clothing, and shelter TO PROTECT YOURSELF from the elements."
—Dalai Lama

entirely possible to do so is not. Ultimate self-reliance comes when one prepares to mitigate the cause of problems instead of fiddling around with the effects.

The Art of Regulating Your Core Body Temperature: An Ignored yet Critical Competence

Hypothermia: (From the Greek *hypo*, meaning "under, beneath, or below," and the Greek *therme*, meaning "heat.") Hypothermia occurs when your body's core temperature drops below 98.6 degrees F (37 degrees C).

Hyperthermia: (From the Greek *hyper*, meaning "over, above, or excessive," and the Greek *therme*, meaning "heat.") Hyperthermia occurs when your body's core temperature rises above 98.6 degrees F (37 degrees C).

As stated earlier, the main intention of your home or any shelter is to help thermoregulate your core body temperature during periods of outside temperature fluctuation. Still don't believe it? In simple terms, if it's too hot outside, you retreat into the house to enjoy the air conditioning. If it's too cold outside, you withdraw inside to thaw out by the heater.

If a catastrophe brings down the power grid, unless you have alternative ways to heat or cool your home, *you may be subjected to extreme outdoor temperatures inside your home.* Dozens of people die in America each year, in their homes, due to lack of thermoregulation. In the late summer of 2003, Europe was heavily hit by a major heat wave in which tens of thousands of people died. The ensuing drought caused crops to fail and thousands of acres of countryside to burn in forest fires. Nearly 20,000 people died in Italy; 2,139 in the United Kingdom; 7,000 in Germany; and 14,802 in France—all within a few weeks. As France does not normally have very hot summers and most residences are not equipped with air conditioning, people were unaware of how to deal with the onslaught of high temperatures. Due to the rarity of the event, French officials had no contingency plan for a heat wave and the crippling effects of dehydration and hyperthermia. To complicate matters further, the heat wave occurred in August, a month in which many French citizens (including governmental physicians and doctors) are on vacation.

Closer to home, obnoxious summer heat waves in Chicago alone have killed more than a hundred people in just a few days from hyperthermia and dehydration. Hundreds more die each year across the nation as drought cycles increase and temperatures climb. Likewise, winter weather and hypothermia go on a killing spree as snow and ice storms knock out power, snarl traffic, disrupt communications, and delay aid to hundreds of thousands of people without heat. Far from needing radically cold temperatures to do its work, the majority of deaths from hypothermia occur when air temperatures are between 30 and 50 degrees F (minus 2 to 10 degrees C).

The term "exposure" is a generic term often used by the media to describe deaths due to *hypothermia* or *hyperthermia.* Both are, by far, the unspoken causes of death that in silence and without fanfare go about killing the unprepared en masse around the world. Please realize that many of the skills and concepts presented in this book are directly or indirectly related to helping you achieve and maintain a normal core body temperature for your survival. The following information on body temperature regulation is extremely important, so don't space out and go on auto-pilot when you read it. The most efficient way to prepare for and mitigate a disaster is to know its cause.

Thermoregulation: Your Body's Nitty Gritty for Both Country and City

In humans, core body temperature alternates in cycles throughout the day. While daily activity is responsible for some of this cycling, the body's *circadian rhythm* accounts for the majority. Inner body temperatures are lower in the early morning, around 97.9 degrees (36.6 degree C) with the late afternoon high being approximately 99.3 degrees (37.4 degrees C). Age is also an important factor, as some thermoregulatory responses are not fully developed until after puberty. People in their sixties and older will be subject to less sweating in reaction to heat and a reduced vasoconstrictor response and shivering in response to cold. While body temperature regulation between men and women is similar, there are several subtle differences in females. Females have a smaller blood volume, lower hemoglobin concentration, smaller heart and lean body mass (less muscle means less shivering), a greater percentage of total body fat, greater surface area to mass ratio, a higher body temperature set point for sweating, and geometrically thinner extremities, to name a few.

Primary Body Core
98.6° F (37° C)

"Shell" of Skin
92° F (33.3° C)

Secondary Body
Core Areas

Females also have the added difference of monthly temperature variations relating to menstrual cycle, pregnancy, and menopause.

Fluctuations in core body temperature, high or low, of even a few degrees can severely compromise your ability to survive. To control its inner temperature, the body must be able to sense a change in environmental temperature and respond accordingly. To do so, in part, the body is equipped with *warm* and *cold receptors* located in the skin, spinal cord, muscles, and brain that begin physiological changes to quickly deal with temperature extremes. Many variables contribute to the development and severity of hypothermia and hyperthermia including a person's age, sex, health, nutrition, body size, hydration, physical exercise, exhaustion, duration of exposure to wind and temperature, wetness, medications, intoxicants, and prior adaptation to heat or cold. The core body temperature is thermoregulated by the physiological responses and reflexes of *vasoconstriction, vasodilation, shivering,* and *sweating.* Aside from basic physical necessities such as an unobstructed airway, breathing, and circulation, thermoregulation is of prime importance for your short- and long-term survival.

Temperature regulation in humans represents the balance between *heat production* from metabolic sources such as digesting a pizza and exercise, and *heat loss* from respiration and evaporation (sweating) and the physics of radiation, convection, and conduction. Once hypothermia develops, the heat deficit is shared by two body compartments, the shell and the core. Your outer skin or "shell" consists of .065 inches of skin and has an average area of 2.2 square yards. This means that on average your shell accounts for only 10 percent of your total body mass. The rest of it is considered "the core." In other words, when your body senses a drop in core temperature, it burns through an enormous amount of calories and puts a dent in your stored food supply.

Human beings suck in their ability to physiologically adapt to *cold* environments. Temperature regulatory mechanisms act through the autonomic nervous system and are largely controlled by the hypothalamus. The hypothalamus responds to stimuli from nerve receptors in your skin, which is the largest organ in your body. In a cold environment, body heat is conserved first by the constriction of blood vessels near the body's surface (vasoconstriction), keeping the majority of blood (heat) in the core. The body thus uses the skin and underlying fatty layer as insulation. The one area of skin that doesn't constrict blood flow when the outside temperature gets cold is the scalp, which likes to remain at a fairly constant temperature regardless of outside extremes. This is one reason why the head and neck area loses (and gains in hot temperatures) a tremendous amount of heat.

In its attempt to regulate temperature, the body changes blood flow to the skin. When blood vessels are dilated wide open in hot weather, the body can circulate more than four quarts of blood every minute—in the skin alone. In cold weather, blood vessels constrict the skin's blood flow to an amazing 99 percent of the former, a mere 0.02 quarts per minute! Ironically, when temperatures continue to drop, blood vessels in the skin dilate (vasodilation), and if temperatures drop further, the blood vessels alternate back and forth between dilation and constriction in the body's attempt to ensure that the skin remains undamaged from the cold. The result is your red nose, ears, hands, and other appendages in the wintertime. If outside temperatures continue to plummet, however, surface blood vessels constrict continuously to protect the core.

Second in the body's response to cold are uncoordinated waves of muscle contractions more commonly referred to as *shivering*. Shivering utilizes small parts of the skeletal muscles called motor units, which contract at around ten to twenty times per second and can increase your metabolism fivefold! The energy needed for shivering comes from fats and simple sugars (carbohydrates) and can be used up quickly if not replaced with extra food. Shivering *decreases* when carbon dioxide levels raise (as in a poorly ventilated home or emergency shelter), when the oxygen in the air becomes thinner (extremes in altitude), and through the use of alcohol, which impairs the shivering response.

Since blood vessels are essentially the pipes your body uses to heat itself by forcing warmed blood throughout your body, ingesting substances that dilate surface blood vessels is stupid. Purposely constricting blood vessels is also a bad move whether through nicotine use, dehydration, or tight clothing. Dehydration slowly turns your blood into ketchup, making it that much harder for the heart to circulate the sludge around in order to keep inner temperatures stable. Low temperatures also change the composition of blood, making it thicker by up to 21 percent, by increasing the number of particles such as platelets, red blood cells, and cholesterol.

When it's *hot* outside, heat must be lost by the body to maintain a proper core temperature. Brain cells are particularly sensitive to high temperatures. Increased surface blood flow through dilated vessels, especially in the arms and legs, works at dissipating extra heat by exploiting the major surface areas of the body as well as avoiding the insulating properties of subcutaneous fat. Once again, if your blood turns to ketchup because of dehydration, this activity is severely compromised. The increased surface blood flow and the wonders of evaporative heat loss through increased sweating are the main tools your body uses to stabilize its inner core when outside temperatures soar.

Cellular Chaos

Your body's 50 billion cells have permeable membranes, or "walls," consisting of lipids or fats. Through these membranes cells make and break bonds at precise rates, maintaining such levels as our sodium and potassium balance. These membranes, being composed of fats, are very sensitive to changes in temperature.

When your core body temperature drops, proteins within the cells start to clump, causing holes, while water in and around the cells freeze to form jagged ice crystals that shred the delicate membranes. Conversely, as the core overheats, cell membranes begin to lose their elasticity and can actually melt. With cell membranes damaged, precision rates are altered and once-pristine body systems fall into a state of unregulated pandemonium. *Fluctuations in core body temperature literally cause chaos on a cellular level, chaos you can see in the uncoordinated signs and symptoms of hypo- and hyperthermia.*

In summary, living in **cold temperatures** without insulated clothing and footwear, lying on uninsulated ground (conduction), or wearing weather-dampened or sweated-out cotton clothing (evaporation) in the wind (convection) while being unable to improvise a heat source (radiation) can all cause death by hypothermia.

Conversely, in **hot temperatures,** *radiation* from the sun (directly and reflected from the ground and particulate matter in the air) can heat up *conductive* ground surfaces in excess of 150 degrees F (65.5 degrees C). This in turn helps produce heated *convective* winds capable of *evaporating* sweat obscenely fast with little cooling effect for the body. Add in the effects of *metabolic heat* produced by digging a sanitation trench in the backyard at noon, and you have a serious setup for dehydration, hyperthermia, and death.

Knowing the Signs and Symptoms of Hypothermia and Hyperthermia

A "sign" is a behavior you see in someone else while a "symptom" is a behavior someone else sees in you. Notice that the psychological signs and symptoms of hypothermia and hyperthermia are very similar, involving disorientation and poor coordination. These similarities are no accident and offer vital clues into a person's physiology at the time. *In city or country, recognizing the signs and symptoms of hypothermia and hyperthermia in yourself and others is critical as they are the body's warning signals that things are getting out of whack on a cellular level.* The majority of people dead from exposure had ample early warnings that were ignored. These warning signs are your second chance to immediately manipulate your internal and external environment in whatever way you can to prevent further heat loss or gain.

Heinous Hypothermia: The Signs and Symptoms

Early Signs and Symptoms
⊃ Core temperature 95–96 degrees F (35–35.5 degrees C)
⊃ Shivering
⊃ Decreased awareness
⊃ Unable to think or solve problems
⊃ Apathy
⊃ Confusion
⊃ Skin pale and cool to the touch
⊃ Numbness (stinging pain)
⊃ Loss of dexterity

Advancing Signs and Symptoms
⊃ Core temperature 93–94 degrees F (33.9–34.5 degrees C)
⊃ Obvious shivering
⊃ Stumbling

➲ Deterioration of fine and complex motor skills
➲ Little or no effort to protect oneself
➲ Unaware of present situation

Advanced Signs and Symptoms
➲ Core temperature 91–92 degrees F (32.8–33.4 degrees C)
➲ Intense shivering
➲ Difficulty walking
➲ Thick or slurred speech
➲ No effort to protect oneself
➲ Skin appears ashen gray and cold
➲ Possible hallucinations

The Death Zone
➲ Core temperature 87–90 degrees F (30.6–32.2 degrees C)
➲ Shivering comes in waves
➲ Unable to walk
➲ Speech very difficult to understand

   If the core temperature continues to drop, shivering will cease, breathing and
   pulse will appear absent, and the skin will become blue in color. Death will
   quickly follow.

Hideous Hyperthermia: The Signs and Symptoms

There are three levels of environmental heat illness recognized by the medical profession. Listed in order of severity, from bad to worse, they are *heat cramps, heat
exhaustion,* and *heatstroke.* There are two types of heatstroke, *classical heatstroke*
and *exertional heatstroke.* Classical heatstroke generally occurs in out-of-shape,
sedentary older folks who decide to weed the garden or mow the lawn at noon in
July. Exertional heatstroke happens after intense physical activity in a hot environment, especially during periods of high humidity, which prevent the cooling power
of evaporation. During this type of heatstroke, despite earlier beliefs, the victim
may still be sweating heavily, as the sweat glands are usually still active at the time
of collapse. Heatstroke is extremely serious and can be avoided by *paying attention*
to the signs and symptoms of heat cramps and heat exhaustion.

Signs and Symptoms of Heat Cramps
➲ Core temperature 99–100 degrees F (37.3–37.8 degrees C)
➲ Thirst
➲ Irritability
➲ Profuse sweating
➲ Headache
➲ Dizziness
➲ Nausea, vomiting

- Decreased appetite
- Generalized weakness
- Spasms of the voluntary muscles and abdomen after exercise and exertion in a hot environment

Signs and Symptoms of Heat Exhaustion
- Core temperature 101–102 degrees F (38.4–38.9 degrees C)
- Excessive thirst
- Profuse sweating
- Headache
- Dizziness
- Nausea, vomiting
- Generalized weakness
- Decreased appetite
- Disorientation
- Confusion
- Cramps
- Weak, rapid pulse with shallow, rapid breathing
- Cool, pale, moist skin
- Decreased awareness or unconsciousness

Signs and Symptoms of Heatstroke
- Core temperature 103–106 degrees F (39.5–41.1 degrees C)
- Disorientation
- Confusion
- Hot, flushed, potentially dry skin (classical heatstroke) or hot, flushed, sweaty skin (exertional heatstroke)
- Signs and symptoms of shock
- Rapid, bounding pulse or rapid, weak pulse
- Initial deep breathing, rapidly progressing to shallow breathing, followed ultimately by no breathing
- Dilated, sluggish pupils
- Delirium
- Little or no effort to protect oneself
- Unaware of present situation
- Seizures
- Stroke
- Coma

If elevated core temperatures remain constant or continue to rise, the Grim Reaper will take you out to lunch.

How Your Body Loses and Gains Heat

Humans are incredibly vulnerable to temperature extremes. Like a motor vehicle, the body has very limited temperature parameters in which it will "run." If these limits are breached, the vehicle runs worse and worse until it finally stops running altogether. Regardless of where you live on this planet, you are susceptible to certain physical laws that dictate how your body loses and gains heat from the environment. It matters not if your environment is the deep woods of Alaska or an apartment in downtown Tokyo, the laws of nature described below will be enacted. By recognizing and understanding the following general physics involved in heat loss and gain, the survivor can intelligently assess virtually any situation placed before them and, one by one, manage the problems. Knowing these simple laws in advance allows the wise person to prepare accordingly and mitigate potential breaches to thermoregulation before they happen.

Conduction

Conduction is the transfer of heat (energy) through direct contact with an object, including hot or cold air against the skin. The direction of heat flow is always from a warmer to a cooler temperature. If you touch a surface that's less than 92 degrees F (33 degrees C), you will lose heat through conduction. If the object touched is warmer than 92 degrees F, your body gains heat. Substances vary in their thermal conductivity quite radically. Water has twenty-five times the conductivity of air while muscles possess nearly twice the tissue conductivity of fat. Under normal conditions, conduction accounts for approximately 2 percent of the body's heat loss for a standing person.

"It is in the **SHELTER** of other people that the **PEOPLE LIVE.**"

—Irish proverb

Convection

Convection is the transfer of heat (energy) through currents in air and liquids and can be either forced or natural. Convection has within it many variables including density, surface shape and temperature profiles, flow dynamics, conductivity, and specific heat. An example of forced convection would be rolling down the windows of a moving car or sitting in front of a fan. Natural convection happens when density changes in heating or cooling molecules next to the body cause them to move away from the body itself. This "boundary layer" effect is caused by slower-moving molecules directly against the skin produced by radiant heat given off by the body. This layer is only a few millimeters thick and is the equivalent of a constant, three-mile-per-hour wind.

Classic convection experienced by everyone is the "wind chill factor," which causes existing outside air temperatures to feel much colder then they actually are. The effects of wind chill are directly responsible for thousands of deaths all over the world. In contrast, hot desert winds can feel like a hair dryer on the skin, and suck away evaporating sweat so quickly you might not think it's hot because you're "not sweating." Sweat evaporating from the skin at such an accelerated rate does little to help cool the body.

Researchers have found that under neutral conditions as much as 40 percent of the heat loss from a naked human body stems from convection! Add wet clothing and/or strong winds to the scenario and the percentage climbs dramatically.

Radiation

Radiation is the act of losing or gaining heat (energy) through, well, radiation. There are two types of radiation we're concerned with. Terrestrial, or *long-wave* radiation, emanates from fire, a human body, or just about anything else on the planet having a temperature greater than absolute zero or minus 460 degrees F (minus 273 degrees C). Radiated body heat is truly the emission of electromagnetic energy in infrared wavelengths of which the body is both emitting and receiving. Curling up in the fetal position reduces your radiant heat loss by 35 percent when compared to a person standing with arms away from their sides. Radiant heat loss is a force to be reckoned with as it accounts for around 45 percent of the total heat loss from a nude body in neutral conditions. Surfaces that are good at absorbing radiation are also good at giving it off.

Shortwave radiation emanates from the sun and varies in its intensity according to the time of day, altitude, latitude, surface reflection, atmospheric pollution, ozone levels, and season. Most ultraviolet radiation bathes the Earth at midday, 80 percent between the hours of 9 a.m. and 3 p.m. and 65 percent between 10 a.m. and 2 p.m. Radiation from sunlight can heat a person in three ways, directly on the skin, reflected off particulate matter in the atmosphere, and reflected off the ground, and, unlike long-wave radiation, it is absorbed to a greater extent by darker-colored clothing and skin pigmentation. In hot climates, all can lead to dehydration and hyperthermia if not properly managed.

HOW Your Body GAINS Heat

DESTITUTE DON   **BODY TYPE:** Larger surface-area-to-volume ratio superior at eliminating excess heat

A: Direct Solar Gain (Radiation)

B: Breathing through Nose Limits Water Loss (Respiration)

C: Hot Wind (Convection)

D: Reflected Particulate Matter Solar Gain (Radiation)

E: Nicotine: Diuretic, Constricts Blood Vessels, Increases BMR

F: Insulation from Hot Ground (Conduction)

G: Ground Reflected Solar Gain (Radiation)

H: Alcohol: Diuretic, Impaired Judgment, Increased Blood Viscosity

Destitute Don loses heat through:

I: Increased Heat Loss through Wet Clothing (Evaporation)

HOW Your Body LOSES Heat

TED THE TRANSIENT   BODY TYPE: Larger volume-to-surface-area ratio superior at minimizing heat loss

A: Cold Wind (Convection)

B: Alcohol: Diuretic, Impaired Judgment, Increased Blood Flow to Skin

C: Increased Heat Loss through Wet Clothing (Evaporation)

D: Insulation from Cold Ground (Conduction)

E: Reduced Insolation (Incoming Solar Radiation)

F: Water Loss through Breath (Respiration)

Ted the Transient gains heat through:

G: Food (Metabolic Heat)

H: Fire (Radiation)

Evaporation

Evaporation is the act of losing heat (energy) through the conversion of a liquid to a gas. The principal way your body loses heat in a hot environment is the evaporation of water, in the form of sweat, from your skin, as well as a small amount of evaporative cooling gained from exhaled moisture. To get the job done humans have 2.6 million sweat glands, more than any other mammal. Staying in wet, sweaty clothing after overexerting in winter cold will place you one step closer to death through increased hypothermia.

Respiration

Respiration is the act of losing heat (energy) and water vapor through the respiratory surfaces of the lungs by breathing. The air you inhale must be humidified by the body to saturation in order to be used efficiently. When this vapor is exhaled, the resulting evaporative heat loss at high altitudes can rival sweat as a cooling factor. More typically, however, respiration heat loss is minor when compared to the others above. A tremendous amount of water can be lost through the breath, especially in extremely cold temperatures. Cold, dry air breathed into warm, moist lungs pulls out as much as two quarts of water daily in minus 40 degree F (minus 40 degrees C) temperatures. In some instances, the same conditions destroy the cells lining the respiratory tract.

Critical Clothing

In a **cold weather situation**, the simplest means of staying warm is to trap your body's metabolic heat by using insulation or dead air space in the form of clothing, adding or subtracting layers as changing temperatures dictate. In addition, physical exercise, fire craft, shelter, and calorie-rich foods all help to keep the body's core temperature at a lively 98.6 degrees F (37 degrees C). Cold muscles work more slowly and with less efficiency, greatly retarding the ability to perform seemingly simple tasks for survival.

Conversely, in a **hot weather situation**, indigenous peoples wear long, flowing woolen robes in extreme desert temperatures for a reason. Your skin is the largest organ of the body, and if you burn it, you severely compromise your body's ability to cool itself as even moderate sunburn causes a decrease in the responsiveness and capacity of the sweat glands. Clothing is the easiest method to use to protect your skin from direct solar radiation from the sun, as well as radiation reflected off particles in the atmosphere and the ground. The most important factor in determining how a fabric will repel ultraviolet radiation is the tightness of the weave, followed by its color and whether the fabric is wet or dry. Specialized, sun-protective clothing is becoming more common and manufacturers have developed various strategies to keep out the sun's rays including tightly woven nylon, chemically treated cotton, cotton/synthetic blends, clothing bonded with ultraviolet-radiation-absorbing devices, and chemical shields added to laundry detergents.

In hot weather, when ambient temperatures are near or above normal body temperatures, to limit heat loss through vasodilation, your body relies on one main mechanism to cool itself called sweating. Sweat is 99 percent water with a pinch of sodium chloride (salt) and potassium and is the only way your body cools itself when subjected to elevated external temperatures. The conversion of a liquid to a vapor requires a certain amount of energy or heat, called the *heat of vaporization,* and is directly responsible for wicking away the high temperatures that threaten to kill you from hyperthermia. Even though sweat contains only a paltry 1 percent sodium chloride, long-term sweating without the ability to replenish that salt poses serious physiological problems, which is a major reason to store salt as part of your food storage program. People acclimated to hot weather produce more sweat, but with a lower concentration of lost salts.

Sweat glands are found in the skin in concentrations from 650 to 4,000 per square inch and occur most abundantly on the forehead, scalp, face, neck, front and back portions of the trunk, and the top of the hands and forearms. The face and scalp alone account for 50 percent of the body's total sweat production! In fact, the

A TRIED-AND-TRUE ACRONYM FOR WEARING WINTER CLOTHING IN BOTH CITY AND COUNTRY!

C = keep yourself and clothes CLEAN
O = avoid OVERHEATING
L = wear clothes LOOSE and in LAYERS
D = keep DRY

only skin areas that don't have any sweat glands are the lips, nipples, and external genitals. Sweat via evaporation cools the skin and, with it, the blood flowing through it. The cooled blood returns to the body's core via the veins where it picks up more heated blood and returns it to the skin's surface for cooling. Any liquid evaporating from the skin will work to cool the body, so don't be shy about soaking your clothing in scummy, nonpotable water, although make sure it's free from chemicals, pesticides, and other skin irritants.

High water-vapor pressure, more commonly referred to as *humidity* of 70 percent or higher, severely restricts the evaporation process. Regardless of how much water you have available, if your body can't rid itself of excess heat you risk dying of dehydration and hyperthermia. Personal humidity levels close to the body's surface may elevate by wearing poorly ventilated clothing, as it reduces airflow over the skin. High humidity levels cause sweat to simply drip off the skin instead of evaporating. People in humid environments commonly experience the need to towel off several times after a shower or bath due to these elevated humidity levels. Be forewarned! *Hot temperatures combined with high humidity levels are voracious killers and are responsible for summer heat waves that wipe out hundreds of people.* Not only does proper clothing insulate you from the heat and cold, it also allows the sweat upon your skin to evaporate *slowly* and *efficiently*, making maximal use of whatever water you already have within your body.

The Layering System

Using the layering system, clothing for both hot and cold environments can be categorized into three sections: *base layer, insulation layer(s),* and *environmental layer(s).* Base layers are used against the skin, trapping air close to the body. They should be made from a fabric that insulates while transporting (wicking) water vapor away from the body and should be nonirritating and nonconstricting. Insulation layers are added or subtracted as outside temperatures warrant between the base and environmental layers. The environmental layer protects against outdoor elements such as wind, rain, snow, sun, and brush and should be lightweight, durable, loose fitting, wind and water resistant, and able to easily vent excess moisture buildup. *Water-resistant* and *waterproof* fabrics are two different concepts, as the former "breathes" to a certain extent to let generated body moisture escape. The latter is a *vapor barrier* and, although useful in some applications, requires advanced thought and the right conditions to be used successfully. Telling the difference between the two fabrics is easy. Put your hand on the outside of the material. Put your lips to the fabric and blow on the fabric from the inside out. If you can feel the air from your breath on your hand, it is water-resistant material.

All clothing systems for any climate involve dead air space or *insulation.* Clothing insulation is measured in *clo.* Technically, one clo is equivalent to the amount of insulation needed to keep a seated person comfy in an air temperature of 70 degrees F (21 degrees C) with a relative humidity of less than 50 percent, and an air movement of .2 miles per hour. Simply put, a common business suit provides one clo of insulation. Insulation is much more effective when worn in several thin layers as opposed to one thick layer, as this allows you to adapt not only to changing temperatures by taking off or putting on clothing, but the air space between the layers of clothing insulates as well while adding no weight, bulk, or cost to the user. The layers should resist moisture accumulation, and increase in size so as not to constrict the body when worn on top of one another. They also need to be easy to put on and take off and pack in case of a pending evacuation.

Your clothing, especially the extra clothing you pack in a bug-out kit (a portable emergency kit containing vital gear when needing to evacuate an area, see page 409), should be adaptable to all types of circumstances. Your clothing should block the sun's ultraviolet rays, keep you both warm and cool, and also be bug-resistant, quick drying, durable, and nonrestrictive. The layering method allows you to add or subtract layers of clothing at will in response to your increasing or decreasing metabolic output and the environmental temperatures at hand. This ability to fine-tune your wardrobe helps minimize sweating-out your clothing through overexertion. Insulation filled with frost and water does little to keep you alive, thus venting excess moisture in cold conditions is of paramount importance. Actively venting excess perspiration from clothing and moderating physical activity in the first place has several advantages. Your clothing insulation layers stay drier and warmer when activity ceases, clothes remain cleaner longer, and you achieve a lower metabolic rate, which conserves precious energy and water. *The ideal scenario in the cold is to regulate clothing layers and activities to allow you to operate at peak performances without wasting water and energy to sweating or shivering.*

In hot climates, clothing protects you from direct radiation from the sun, hot winds, and scorching ground temperatures. Loose layers of the appropriate material grant protection from the sun and increase airflow while slowing the evaporation of sweat for superior cooling. *The ideal scenario in the heat is to regulate layers and physical activity to allow you to operate at peak performances without wasting energy while achieving protection from the sun and making maximal use of your sweat for cooling.*

Properties of Clothing Materials

The type of material your clothing is made from can directly affect your ability to successfully thermoregulate your core body temperature. The following are brief descriptions of the more common fabrics that have withstood the test of time. The properties described below are just as applicable for blankets and sleeping bags.

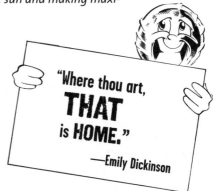

"Where thou art, **THAT** is HOME."

—Emily Dickinson

Cotton

Cotton is *hydrophilic*, meaning it transfers sweat from your skin to the material itself, thus it's horrible at "wicking" wetness away from skin. In fact, cotton loves moisture and will become damp simply when exposed to humid air. Once wet, it feels cold, loses 90 percent of its insulating properties, is a drag to dry out, and wicks heat from your body twenty-five times faster than when it's dry. Because of this, *wearing cotton clothing in the wintertime is a death wish.* Yet, in scorching summer deserts, it's my fabric of choice for precisely the same reasons. Cotton also has decent abrasion resistance and blocks out a reasonable amount of UV radiation from the sun.

Polypropylene

Polypropylene resists absorbing moisture as it's *hydrophobic*, meaning it transfers moisture from the skin across the fabric itself to other clothes or the air so it actually dries from the inside out. This quality makes it great at wicking sweat away from the skin, thus it's popular as a base layer with outdoor recreationists. Polypropylene feels soft and is relatively cheap and easy to care for. Wear it for a few days in a row however, especially if you exercise, and you will reek something awful, especially in a confined shelter. Being synthetic, polypropylene easily melts to skin when exposed to heat so be careful around fires, candles, stoves, and other heat sources. Polypropylene's most insidious disadvantage, ironically enough, comes from its superior wicking abilities. It wicks moisture away from the skin so well that the wicking action uses more body energy (calories) from the survivor than other fabrics. Because of this, polypropylene should only be worn when there are ample food supplies and when energy losses are not critical.

Wool

As wool is animal hair composed of hollow cells that trap air, it's a poor conductor, thus an exceptional insulator. Its natural crimp and elasticity contribute to its superior insulating properties. Wool is *hygroscopic*, which means it readily absorbs moisture but suspends the water vapor within the fiber itself. While any moisture in wool or other fabrics decreases its insulation value, wool can absorb 35 to 55 percent of its weight in water before "feeling" cold and wet. Although it's tedious to dry out, wool retains more heat as it dries than synthetics. This fact, combined with a slower wicking rate, allows wool to use less body energy than polypropylene.

Various breeds of sheep produce various types of wool so not all wool is garment quality. A wool fiber under magnification looks like a heavily barbed spear tip. Aside from allergies, cheap wool and poor manufacturing techniques will cause wool to itch like crazy when in contact with your skin. Wool is inherently flame retardant and won't melt to your skin when exposed to heat sources so it's safer and more forgiving than synthetics if you are using fire to dry out damp clothing. A real boon to the urban survivor is the fact that wool is able to neutralize many types of acids and chemical bases, helping to prevent the buildup of germs. On the down side, wool is bulky when compared to synthetics, thus requiring more space in your shelter or bug-out pack.

Polyester

Polyester is by far the most widely used material in clothing. Polyester pile fabrics, common in backpacking and camping stores, are good insulators, can absorb a fair amount of water without feeling cold, and are hydrophobic. The fibers themselves can be woven into many different thicknesses providing both insulation and wind-stopping abilities in a product that is more compact than wool.

Nylon

Nylon, especially rip-stop nylon, is tough stuff and is commonly used in the design of environmental layers from coats to jackets of all kinds. Tight weaves work well at repelling wind and water and can be made waterproof through various coatings available at outdoor stores, albeit at the expense of breathability. Nylon is also extremely compact and lightweight and the little water it does absorb evaporates quickly. Your environmental layer is critical, as a wind of merely nine miles per hour can reduce the effectiveness of your clothing's insulation by 30 percent. In addition to the wind chill, mixing wet clothing along with the "bellows" effect produced by walking and your clothing insulation can be compromised an unbelievable 85 percent!

Down

Down's compressibility, loft, and weight-to-warmth ratio are legendary—when it remains dry. Unfortunately, down is hydrophilic and sucks even more than cotton in cold, wet environments, losing virtually all of its insulative properties, and it is a booger to dry out.

To summarize, the gross motor skill art of putting on and taking off layers of clothing to regulate body temperature is amazingly simple, requiring very little practice, calories, and water from the survivor. Knowing the virtues of clothing is truly a family-friendly survival skill in which all can participate, from the very young to the very old. In short-term cold-weather survival, the divine simplicity of layering correctly even eliminates the necessity of firebuilding, which is a fine and complex motor skill that requires plenty of physical dexterity and prior training, precious time, calories and water from the survivor, dry tinder and adequate fuel, an ignition source, a safe spot to build, and constant monitoring. In a pinch, it's possible to improvise insulation from nature depending upon the environment. Leaves, pine needles, dry grass, plant fibers, moss, and other material may be available. Urban landscapes as well will present several options for improvised insulation such as the stuffing in chairs, sofas, vehicle seats, carpeting and carpet pads, and others.

Alternative Shelters

Unfortunately, your home may be completely or partially destroyed after a major disaster. This would be everyone's worst nightmare, even during temperate weather, but imagine the destruction happening when it's very hot or very cold outside. Thus the need to have some kind of alternative shelter should rank very high on your survival list. Major earthquakes in other parts of the world have happened during the peak of winter. Many people who had initially survived the quake itself died from hypothermia due to a lack of shelter.

If your home experiences a disaster, check for structural damage before entering the home, if you choose to reenter it at all. Make sure it's not in danger of collapsing. Ultimately, this inspection will need to be done by a professional. Some members of the family, especially kids, might not want to go anywhere near the house if they have been traumatized by the disaster, for fear of the house collapsing or triggering some other kind of nightmare. If you do decide to reenter your home, make sure to turn off any outside gas lines and let the house air out for several minutes to remove potential escaping gas. When entering the home, don't use open flames as a light source. Instead, use a battery-operated flashlight or some other nonfuel-burning light source.

If you live in a hot or cold environment, the primary motive for your shelter should be the thermoregulation of your core body temperature. Even temperate locations get chilly after rains or in the evening hours. Now that you're hip to the physics of how your body loses and gains heat by convection, conduction, radiation, evaporation, and respiration, don't place your alternative shelter in a dumb spot. Consider your shelter as a "body" as well as it, too, will be subject to the same laws of physics. If you attempt to shelter your shelter, so to speak, you'll get more bang for your buck as you'll gain more comfort with less effort and save wear-and-tear on your shelter. It's very common in the Southwest to see amazingly intact Indian ruins that are hundreds of years old. Without exception, the better-preserved ruins were built under basalt overhangs or in caves, thus the native person's shelter was sheltered.

> ## UNDERSTANDING AND COOPERATING WITH THE LAWS OF PHYSICS THAT GOVERN HEAT LOSS AND GAIN WILL ALLOW YOU TO ASSESS THE OPTIONS YOUR IMMEDIATE ENVIRONMENT HOLDS AND MAKE INTELLIGENT DECISIONS ABOUT WHERE AND HOW TO CONSTRUCT A MAKESHIFT SHELTER FOR YOUR FAMILY.

Anytime you can utilize a structure that is pre-existing, you will save calories (energy/food), water, and time. All are *very* precious commodities during a survival situation. While in the wilderness you may choose to modify a pre-existing group of boulders for shelter; in urban and suburban environments, thousands of shelter options exist just waiting for you to take advantage of them. Understanding and cooperating with the laws of physics that govern heat loss and gain will allow you to assess the options your immediate environment holds and make intelligent decisions about where and how to construct a makeshift shelter for your family.

Every shelter on Earth manifests itself as one or both of the following categories: a *protective barrier* and/or an *insulative barrier*. A nonpermeable protective barrier can shield the user from rain, wind, and sun, but it has no insulation value in itself. An example of a protective barrier would be a tarp, a wind-breaking jacket, teepee, or the roof of your house. An insulative barrier is composed of dead air space and excels at trapping and stabilizing the radiant temperature of an object. Insulation in your thermos can keep the cocoa hot or the Kool-aid cold. An example of an insulative shelter would be crawling into a pile of leaves, wearing a loosely woven wool sweater, or hanging out in an Inuit igloo. While a fluffy wool sweater is wonderful to insulate you from cold outdoor temperatures by trapping the metabolic heat created by your body, it sucks when it's windy as the wind blows right through the unprotected insulation. By forcing in colder outside air, the wind blows away the boundary layer of heat that was trapped next to your skin. By putting on a wind-breaking jacket (protective barrier) over the fluffy sweater (insulation) one can achieve comfort. You could wear several fluffy sweaters that would eventually act together as a protective barrier, but, of course, it would impede your mobility and you would look like the Michelin man. My wickiup described below, much like the above-mentioned igloo, was composed almost entirely of insulative materials. I simply used a lot of these materials and stacked them on top of each other to allow my "insulation" to shed rain or wind. Your house features the protective barriers of a roof and walls, while having insulation (fiberglass or foam) added between the protective barriers. Two protective barriers side by side but not stuck to each other will create a small amount of insulation due to the dead air space created. This dead air space can be enhanced by adding other improvised insulation as explained in the improvised sleeping bag section coming up. *What is required to shelter your tribe, whether it's a protective barrier, insulation, or a combination of both, will depend on what aspects of conduction, convection, radiation, evaporation, or respiration threaten to kill your family.*

Tarps

A *tarp* is a piece of waterproof or water-resistant material with *grommets* (circles of metal or plastic) anchored around its perimeter that allow it to be tied and suspended in many different configurations. Depending upon the need of the survivor, tarps eliminate, reduce, or enhance convection and radiation. If folded up many times for use as a sleeping pad or something else, they can also help minimize conduction.

There are few shelters that offer more multiuse options than the tarp. Lighter-weight tarps, like many backpacking tents, are extremely portable in case your crisis forces you to hit the road. Tarps can be set up in a number of ways, depending upon the weather and climate needs of the moment. They can be strung up to repel blistering summer sun or shield their occupants from driving winter wind and snow. They can be used as a ground cover (if the ground is rough, you might accidentally put holes in your tarp) or to collect and hold rainwater for drinking. Tarps can be folded to create an improvised backpack to carry everything from firewood to babies. In short, the tarp is a miracle membrane that repels wind, snow, rain, and excess sun—virtually any weather condition that Mother Nature can throw at you—and it does so in a lightweight, portable fashion, cheaply, effectively, and with a minimal amount of effort from the user.

I lived in the woods in a cone-shaped brush shelter, or wickiup, for a few years. It was made from blanket load after blanket load of pine needles and debris laid upon a framework of ponderosa pine poles. To shed rain, I kept the angle of my more-than-two-foot-thick walls fairly steep. Working by myself, it took several days to complete. While I would have lacked the insulation value given by the debris, had I used a tarp, my home could have been completed in a few hours. Such is the power and adaptability of any durable, waterproof, protective barrier.

Tarps come in a variety of materials and sizes, from four-by-six feet to ten-by-twelve feet and much larger. You can choose from those made from ungodly heavy canvas to relatively light and compact rip-stop nylon or woven plastic. Even rolls of black or clear plastic can be used with added modified grommets. The weight and bulk of the tarp depends on the thickness of the material and how much is used. To be fair to the canvas junkies, I have an eighteen-foot teepee that weighs less than forty pounds. If spread out on the ground, its material would make a few ten-by-twelve tarps. On the flip side, I've also seen heavy canvas "cowboy bedrolls" that weigh more than ten pounds and cover only one sleeping bag.

What kind of tarp you choose will depend on what you're using it for. Almost every household has a cheapo woven plastic tarp in the garage. It's used for everything from covering the winter woodpile to lying on when you crawl under the car to change the oil. Ultraviolet radiation will eventually eat every tarp (and teepee, and wall tent, and yurt) known to humanity. How quickly it gets eaten depends on the type of material, if it's been treated with a UV-protective coating, the strength of the solar radiation, weather, and how long it's been exposed to the sun, to name a few conditions. What kind of tarp you buy and how much money you'll spend should be determined by how important it will be to your family's overall shelter needs.

Homemade Grommets

Tarps have grommets placed at each corner and along the lengths of each side, an inch or so from the edge of the material. A separate piece of durable cord (rarely included with the tarp) should be tied through each grommet, giving you the design control to set the tarp up in many different configurations. I like to use parachute cord or some other camping store knockoff variety. Don't use poor-quality cord, as it will get easily damaged, especially in heavy winds when your tarp tries to become a kite. Some quality tarps have grommets made from loops of nylon webbing that are sewn directly onto the tarp itself.

Rolls of plastic and even Tyvek® house sheeting can be made into tarps by adding improvised grommets. Although commercial grommet kits are available at the store, you can also wrap a rock or some other semiround object in the plastic itself wherever you need a grommet. To keep it solidly within the plastic, tie the rock off soundly at the base with the same piece of cord that will act as the tie-down. To increase its strength, you may want to double or triple the plastic by folding it before you add the rock. Commercial tarps that inevitably rip out or lose a grommet can be dealt with in like fashion. For smaller space blankets, I've duct-taped corners and pushed a large safety pin through the duct tape for an improvised grommet. Cord can then be threaded through the safety pin for tying off.

Tents

Much like tarps, but without the extreme versatility, tents provide an easy home away from home. They can also be set up within the house if the need should arise. A major advantage to tents over tarps is their supreme ability to *block out bugs!*

Survivors living in a tick-infested or mosquito-laden hell might trade their firstborn child for a tent if no other shelter is available. Don't underestimate the nightmare some bugs can create if you're forced to camp out in the backyard.

Tents come in a wide variety of styles, sizes, and qualities. Some hardcore, two-person mountaineering tents cost hundreds of dollars and are built to withstand near-hurricane-force winds. Some discount-mart tents are so cheaply made that they will rip at their seams with little provocation. You don't need to break the bank when purchasing a tent, but don't buy a cheapo one either. The tent should primarily be considered "survival gear" and reserved for such an occasion, but you may lightly use it for other family outings as well.

"BUILD IT and they will COME."

—Jim Morrison (back from the dead), from the movie *Wayne's World 2*

Some tents look like domes, others like squares, some are triangles, and some are shaped like a geometry class acid trip. The shape you choose should be easy to assemble under stress and durable in crummy weather. Some tents are huge, allowing the entire family to hang out and dance, while others are small enough to have a fart linger far too long. The king-size family tents are nice but not very portable if you're forced to evacuate by foot or by bicycle. Some fancy backpacking tents are incredibly lightweight and are smaller than a loaf of bread when broken down for packing. Analyze your needs and decide which style and size would work best for you.

Space Blankets

Space blankets are not truly blankets at all as they contain no dead air space. They do, however, excel at reflecting radiant energy or "heat" from long- and shortwave radiation. Space blankets normally come in two varieties. The smaller version, when folded, is about the size of a pack of cigarettes. It's extremely shiny and made from aluminum-coated Mylar plastic that supposedly reflects up to 80 percent of your body's radiant heat. Its incredible shine factor also excels at signaling for rescue in full sun. The larger, heavier-duty version, while not as reflective as its smaller cousin, is much more durable. (There is also a new version of a space blanket on the market that is quieter and much more durable than the first type I mentioned. It claims to reflect up to 90 percent of radiation but, if anything, looks a bit less shiny than the former. I have used this version and the older space blanket version side by side with nearly identical results.)

The larger blankets are constructed of a tougher woven material and have grommets in the corners. Some models feature a built-in hood, thereby protecting the all-important head and neck area when worn poncho-style. Although smaller than a tarp, they're useful for shelters, ground cloths, windbreaks, or as a simple body wrap. On summer desert survival courses they are the only shelter I carry, as they work great for escaping sudden monsoon thunderstorms and provide just enough reflected warmth for reasonable comfort and sleep despite plummeting nighttime temperatures. Heavy-duty space blankets have only one reflective side, the other side being one of several color choices. Purchasing the blaze orange or red model will serve dual duty as a signal panel to make you more visible to rescuers.

Space blankets have the power to reflect a fire's warmth toward you *or* blistering desert sun away from you, thus they assist in regulating body temperature in virtually all climates. They can be used to line homemade solar ovens for cooking food and disinfecting nonpotable water, and they can be taped over the inside of windows in your home, office, and vehicle to reflect away unwanted solar radiation during hot temperatures. I have reflective bubble insulation, available at most hardware stores, between the roof and the headliner of my vehicle. As short- and long-wave radiation penetrates inanimate objects, the shiny insulation reflects hot summer sun away from the car and helps trap wanted internal heat during the winter months. Space blankets can also be used as liners for improvised insulation nests for cook pots, which are described in the cooking chapter. Being an impermeable barrier (they're a vapor barrier, so know their limitations!), they also shed rain, snow, and wind.

While most smaller blankets are flimsy, noisy in the wind, and too small for many applications, such as covering an entire person, this handy piece of gear reflects radiant heat, is lightweight, compact, easily accessible, cheap, and has many, many uses for the urban survivor.

Wall Tents, Teepees, Yurts, and Such

These guys are basically tents on steroids, and I've owned and spent time in all three. Most are made from heavier canvas that's UV-treated for longer life in the outdoors. Sunforger is a type of canvas that's supposed to be the bomb in sunny weather. My-eight-hundred-dollar wall tent was made from Sunforger canvas. It sported a ten-foot-long rip after being up for less than fifteen months. The particular maker fixed their product for free, minus shipping, and upon looking at my trashed tent, stated that the canvas looked several years old. After telling him my story, and wondering why he didn't keep the lot number for the canvas to identify the poor quality of material, he said he would make it right with me, as repairing bad canvas is a joke. Although it has been nearly four years now, I'm sure he'll follow through on his promise someday. The bottom line on tents that don't support making a fire inside them is this: when it's 20 degrees F (minus 5 degrees C) outside, you will hate life in your tent, no matter how much you paid for it.

My yurt (a Mongolian structure) worked great and I lived in it for three years in a friend's backyard. While these shelters are more expensive and less portable than tents, all of them come with options that allow you to either have a fire inside or install a woodstove for heat.

Teepees are cool but the poles are a hassle and they are extreme overkill for a disaster scenario.

Improvised Tents

So called "tube tents" can be improvised from two fifty-five-gallon drum or barrel liners or large-capacity lawn and leaf bags. Drum or barrel liners are available at hardware or discount stores and usually come in clear or black plastic. These liners are much larger than the usual lawn and leaf bag (thirty-nine-gallon capacity) and are created from a thicker "mil" plastic for a tougher product. Simply cut the end out of one of them and duct tape the two together. Plastic and all other fabrics or materials that are completely waterproof (as opposed to water-resistant) are vapor barriers, thus they don't "breathe" and will collect the moisture exhaled from your lungs and the perspiration lost by your skin. This rising moisture collects on the surface of the plastic and can drip all over you or freeze and drip all over you later when it thaws, thus getting your clothing, gear, and spirits wet. If condensation is a problem, do your best to vent out this moist air however you can. If condensation is a serious problem, you can also vent the end of the tube tent that you're not using as an entrance or completely cut the end out.

Improvised Sleeping Bag

An improvised sleeping bag can also be made from two fifty-five-gallon drum liners and newspaper. The plastic bag provides a protective barrier while the newspaper provides insulation or dead air space. Put one drum liner inside the other and stuff the void between the two barrel liners with crumpled up newspaper or something else that will provide insulation.

Condensation from the vapor barrier you are creating can be minimized by creating a series of small puncture holes in the inner barrel liner with a pencil or pen. This will let some of the water vapor out and into the void between the bags. The exterior barrel liner can be treated the same way, as eventually the newspaper will get soggy from the water vapor.

When making the sleeping bag, it helps to have one person stand up inside the plastic bags,

"No one can say of this house, 'There is **NO** TROUBLE HERE.'"

—Chinese proverb

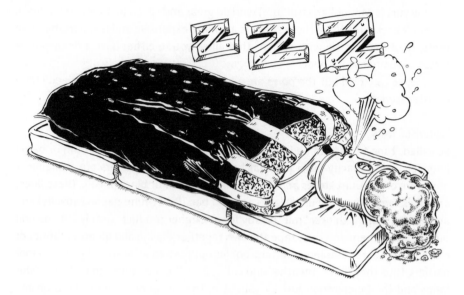

holding them up and apart, while a second person stuffs the void with crumpled newspaper. The "collar" or entrance to the sleeping bag where the two barrel liners come together can be duct taped in key places to hold in the newspaper. Refrain from completely sealing the collar with duct tape as it will breathe to let water vapor escape and allow oxygen in. Also, keep your head out of the bag when sleeping, as a tremendous amount of water vapor is given off by your breath.

Recreational Vehicles (RVs), Trailers, and Automobiles

I have lived in a few vehicles and trailers over the years and there are pros and cons to doing so. Having a house that moves can be handy when needing to evacuate an area, but in certain disasters with high winds they can become a death trap. For those who are inexperienced with building shelters or have a seeming lack of materials with which to do so, these vehicle options, running or not, will provide some semblance of home when conventional housing is not an option.

Be careful during cold weather not to burn fuel inside these improvised shelters where the danger of carbon monoxide poisoning can manifest itself. During times of hot weather without conventional air conditioning, it may be cooler *beside* your vehicle under a tarp that is suspended from the vehicle itself or from surrounding anchor points. Vehicles that can be moved should be relocated under vegetation or other natural or man-made shade sources that will substantially cool down the inner environment of the vehicle itself. You can heat your vehicle in cold weather if you orient the vehicle's main windows to face solar south. RVs, trailers, and automobiles that are not needed by your tribe can be a welcome relief to neighbors who have lost their shelter options in the aftermath of a disaster.

Alternative Heating and Cooling Methods for Your Home

I have stressed repeatedly the need to thermoregulate body temperature along with how much time and money Americans spend to assure room temperature in the home. The "temperature of your room" can be a nasty wakeup call to a lack of preparation when your home is severed from the grid with no options for heating or cooling. The following are choices that will give you greater control in regulating a comfortable temperature when conventional methods fail.

It's Too Cold in the House! The Art of Keeping Your Home Warm

(Warning! There are many heat-producing items that can be brought into the home when it's chilly—and some of them could kill you and your family from carbon monoxide poisoning. The dangers of toxic carbon monoxide appear in detail later in the chapter, so don't skip it. Also, any fuel-burning heat sources pose the risk for **fire danger.** Have a quality fire extinguisher on hand at all times and make sure that it's rotated and replaced or serviced on a regular basis.)

South-facing Rooms: Looking for Naturally Warm Places in the House

My entire home is heated by the common sense of passive solar design. As I write this, regardless of current freezing outdoor temperatures and snow on the ground, sunlight is streaming through south-facing windows and is being absorbed into my stone floor for an inside temperature of 70 degrees F (21 degrees C), with no need for other heating methods. While you might not live in a home that was designed to be heated by the sun, you can certainly modify rooms in your home to take advantage of this free energy source after a grid meltdown.

When it's cold but sunny outside, all south-facing rooms with windows will be warmer than most others. The latitude and seasonality of your location will influence how far south the sun will appear before and after the zenith of the winter solstice. Simply put, the sun will be lower in the southern sky at noon for the winter season. The lowest it will appear is on the winter solstice in late December. After this, the sun will appear slightly higher until it peaks out at its highest point on the summer solstice in June. Along with the proximity of your neighbor's house or garage, trees and vegetation, and other obstructions, the width of the overhangs of your home's roof will determine if winter sunshine enters the windows. In ancient Rome there was a "sun law." It protected everyone from jerks who would have otherwise built a structure blocking sunlight from reaching a residence.

The Romans built their famed bathhouses facing solar south for a reason. Find out which direction your house is oriented. The sun rises in the east and sets in the west. South-facing rooms with windows will heat up during winter months from sunlight entering the window(s). This shortwave radiation from the sun turns to long-wave radiation when it enters the room. Since the wavelength of the radiation has been increased, it has a problem exiting the window, thus much of the heat is trapped within the room. Individuals unknowingly experiment with this

phenomenon during summer temperatures and kill their pet or child by leaving them in the car in direct sunlight with the windows rolled up.

South-facing windows should remain closed but free from drapes or anything else that will impede sunlight from entering the room, including dirty windows. If the sunlight can shine upon an object that has great *thermal mass*, such as a concrete, stone, tile, or brick floor, so much the better. Thermal-mass resources are typically high-density materials that are slow to absorb and release heat. When thermal mass is heated up by sunshine or any heat source, it will store the heat and re-radiate it back into the room during colder nighttime temperatures. Periodically watch the sunlight track across the room during the day and move obstructions such as area rugs, chairs, or tables that prevent the sun from directly striking thermal mass areas. When it gets dark, cover your windows by drawing the drapes to help hold in the stored heat. Extra window insulation can be improvised with towels or bedding hung in successive layers, if desired, for greater dead air space. Remember to uncover the windows the next day to allow spent thermal mass areas to again recharge with solar radiation from the sun.

Marvelous Microclimates: Creating a Home within Your House

When it's god-awful cold inside your home and you lack conventional methods of heating, you will naturally retreat to the warmest room or rooms in the house. In this case, bigger is not better. *Smaller rooms* with good solar gain and insulation are much easier to heat than larger rooms. Rooms with high ceilings will cause the spiders to be comfortable while you freeze your butt off below. When it's cold, think like a squirrel and create a small, cozy microhabitat that effectively thermoregulates core body temperature. The squirrel doesn't care about impressing the Joneses with space and flash. In cold temperatures it builds a nest that allows it to get inside with just enough room to wrap its fluffy tail around its body for added insulation. There is no wet bar, Jacuzzi, or back porch. In cold weather your McMansion is a detriment, not an asset, when it's pulled, kicking and screaming, from the grid and no other power source is available to heat its tremendous volume.

Block off a "warm room" from the rest of the colder house. Close doors or hang blankets in door openings to seal in as much of the warmer air as possible. If you do have an alternate heating source within the room, don't seal it up so tight that you all wake up dead from carbon monoxide poisoning. Make sure that the room has adequate ventilation. Spaces under doors can be chinked with extra clothing or towels to prevent cold air from seeping into the room.

Covering Windows with Space Blankets and Plastic

Long- and shortwave radiation penetrates through objects. If drapes and extra blankets are used for insulation on windows when the sun goes down, space blankets can still be taped on the inside of windows to reflect heat back into the room to help retain warmer inside temperatures.

Don't forget that dead air space (insulation) and reflected radiation are two different things. You can also achieve dead air space by taping clear plastic over the outside of your windows, sort of an improvised storm window. Clear roll plastic comes in a variety of thicknesses, "mils" or millimeters. The thicker you go, the tougher the plastic, but it will also be more opaque. This opacity will cut down on solar gain entering the house from south-facing windows. When I teach students how to make solar stills to gather water in the desert, there is a difference in the amount of radiation that reaches the still (thus creating water) if we use six-mil plastic as opposed to using four-mil plastic. You might consider using six-mil plastic for its durability on windows and openings that don't have any solar gain value and use the thinner-mil plastic on south-facing windows or don't cover them with plastic at all.

Playing House with Sofa Cushions, Blankets, and More

Remember when you were six years old and tore apart the living room furniture to make forts? The concept of many outdoor survival shelters improvised from limbs and leaves is to make a small shelter that can be heated by the survivor's body heat alone. Sofa cushions, extra blankets, sleeping bags, linen, or clothing can be used instead to create sleeping cocoons or smaller shelters within your warm room to help regulate body temperature. After you're done laughing, re-read the section explaining how the body loses and gains heat by conduction, convection, and radiation. With these basic concepts in mind, coupled with your predicament and the resources you have on hand, improve your situation, like the squirrel, by decreasing the surface area and volume of your room. This super-small and insulated fort might only be appropriate for sleeping, but it will be warmer when filled with your family than the room itself. Camping tents can also be set up in homes to serve a similar purpose.

Getting High and Snuggling

The average human body generates 300 BTUs of heat each hour. Mittens, where the fingers are touching and enjoying the radiant heat from each other, are much warmer than gloves, where each finger is forced to heat itself. Get the entire family to sleep next to each other if necessary, and invite the dog and the cat as well. By doing so, you will create a "creature" that has a much larger volume-to-surface area ratio, excellent for staying warm in the cold. Many times on my outdoor courses, modest students freeze their asses off the first night, only to pig pile the second night. Your family can be modest or it can be warm; the choice is yours.

Cold air sinks. Sleeping up higher will put you closer to warmer air, yet use common sense so that you don't fall out of bed and break your neck. Although a floor can be insulated from colder conductive ground temperatures, it's still on the floor where the majority of cooler air pools. After a day's worth of solar gain, if you have a two-story house, see if upper rooms are warmer than the downstairs. Lofts in homes are notorious for becoming blazing hot while the rest of the house stays at room temperature.

Alternative "Fuel Burning" Heating Options

Fireplaces

Many newer homes have faux fireplaces, some with "electric" or gas logs, designed only for looks and ease of operation. Since they are slaves to the grid, these types of fireplaces function only when you have an external energy source. Fireplaces are horrible at retaining heat in the first place, as most of the heat value goes up the chimney, but they certainly beat freezing your butt off. Luckily, the long-wave radiation created by the fire strays far from the source and radiates out into the room, regardless of its inefficiency. The megapolis of Phoenix, Arizona, often has air quality alerts during the winter season, which blissfully isn't much of a season, in which all wood-burning efforts at heating a home are banned. It's doubtful that this law would be enforced in a catastrophe, yet the ability to breathe trumps keeping warm.

If your home has a real fireplace, get it ready for action even if it's not normally used. DO NOT fire up the hearth after years of nonuse or neglect and expect your safety to be intact. Chimney fires caused from creosote buildup, bird nests, squirrel homes, and other odd things can and will burn your house to the ground. Don't risk becoming homeless and further stretch already tapped rescue teams. I'm pleading with you here: if you are even remotely thinking about using your fireplace as an emergency heat source, *have it inspected by a chimney sweep at least once per year!* If you're feeling especially cheap at the thought of hiring this out, consider the pricelessness of your family's comfort and safety during a very scary time. Once your chimney is clean from soot and debris, inspected for leaks to prevent carbon monoxide poisoning and cracks that can let sparks escape into the attic and burn down your home, make sure you have fuelwood on hand to meet your needs and the necessary fire-starting devices to keep the situation lit and burning.

Woodstoves

I adore woodstoves, even the older inefficient models. There is something very satisfying about not being beholden to the grid during cold weather when needing to obtain a comfortable indoor temperature. Some newer models use surprisingly little wood to achieve long-lasting indoor comfort. I have used many woodstoves in a variety of living situations. They are much more efficient than fireplaces, as the metal of the stove itself has more heated surface area for allowing the long-wave radiation produced from the burning fuel to saturate the room. Oxygen levels can be strictly controlled, especially in newer woodstoves, thereby making fuel last longer and burn more completely. Models with electric-powered blowers to increase efficiency should not be counted upon for obvious reasons. Many homes have pellet stoves, which burn prepackaged, combustible pellets instead of regular firewood. Some pellet stoves will not allow their owner to burn anything else if the pellets run out. Find out which boat you're sitting in and have an ample supply of pellet fuel on hand if this is your only option for obtaining heat. Conventional woodstoves have the adaptability to be able to burn anything, from lumber scraps and broken-up chairs and tables to dead tree limbs, a serious asset in a survival situation.

Homeowners who choose to install a fireplace or woodstove after the fact are looking at paying a considerable amount of money. Of the two, it's usually cheaper to install a woodstove, as woodstove pipe goes together quickly as soon as a safe route is created for it to vent to the outside. If your home does not currently have a fireplace or woodstove, and you would like to add one, check around and consult a professional before doing so. If your fireplace or woodstove is not professionally installed, you risk burning down your

"Home is the place where, when you have to GO THERE, they have to TAKE YOU IN."

—Robert Frost

house. Your local woodstove dealer should be able to answer any questions you have about models, installation, accessing firewood, and local regulations regarding the installation and use of your stove or fireplace.

Buying Firewood . . . or Improvising It

All species of wood have different *BTU* counts (British Thermal Units). A British Thermal Unit is the amount of heat required to raise one pint (or pound) of water up one degree F (.556 degrees C) or the energy it takes to completely burn one large strike-anywhere kitchen match. In my part of the country, juniper (*Juniperus osteosperma* and others) and several species of oak (*Quercus* species) are routinely harvested and sold as firewood. Although both make great firewood, oak contains a higher BTU count (approximately 35 million BTUs per cord) and thus contains an energy value greater than the same amount of juniper wood (approximately 25 million BTUs per cord). Because of this energy difference, oak is more expensive. Although our surrounding forests are filled with giveaway dead or dying ponderosa pine trees from bark beetle infestations and drought, it's not a sought-after fuelwood as the BTU count is only 17 million per cord, and the resinous, low-heat conifer creates more creosote than the other woods. When push comes to shove, don't get hung up on these details. For your intentions, all of them will work to heat your house.

Most firewood is purchased in a measurement called a *cord*. A standard cord of firewood is a pile measuring eight feet long by four feet wide by four feet high for a total of 128 cubic feet of fuel, give or take due to the air spaces caused by the size and straightness of the pieces, how they're split, and how the wood is stacked. These differences can cause the total wood volume in a cord to fluctuate by seventy or eighty cubic feet or more.

Several factors will determine how much a cord of wood will cost (if it's available in your area at all). Forest closures due to drought, the species of wood, whether it's split and/or delivered, whether it's "green" or "seasoned" and ready to burn, and the current demand for the product influence the price. If you're buying firewood for a "just in case" emergency, saving money by buying green wood that has been recently cut might pay off. If Murphy's Law hands you a series of minus 20 degree F (minus 5 degree C) temperatures in your living room days after your purchase, you can still get the wet wood to burn by splitting it into much smaller pieces and adding them intermittently to a strong heat base of burning fuel, although it's a hassle. Burning green wood is not optimal; it is harder to start and maintain and it burns with less heat than dry wood, which causes more creosote to build up in the chimney. If you want to gather your own firewood, obtain the necessary permits to access public lands, get your equipment (axes, saws, chainsaws, splitting mauls, etc.) in good working order, and be ready for hard work.

"Seasoning" is a slang term for drying wood until it's ready to burn. Wood is deemed seasoned when its moisture content reaches equilibrium with the moisture in the surrounding air. The requirements for seasoning wood are the same as those needed to dry sliced fruit—good air circulation, sunshine, and dryness. Green wood can be stacked outdoors in a suitable location for about six months in most climates and it should be ready to go. In dry hot climates, it will probably be ready to go in half the time depending on how big the pieces are. Proper stacking, in which as much surface area as possible is exposed to dry, warm air currents will cut down on the drying time. Wood that is seasoned will be comparatively lightweight and have ends with deep "checks" or cracks.

All wood products in the natural world are, in essence, stored energy from solar radiation and photosynthesis. Wood loses this stored energy in one or both of two ways—it can burn or it can rot. If you purchase partially rotten or "punky" wood, you're getting ripped off, as the wood has already lost some of its energy or BTU content to the environment through decay.

Before building your woodpile, set an expendable lumber base (such as an old sheet of plywood) on some elevated material like concrete blocks that will keep your wood off the ground and limit the infestation of termites and other critters. Stacking wood off the ground also prevents the wood from drawing ground moisture, allows air to circulate freely around it, and cuts down on the amount of dirt that sticks to it. Woodpiles stacked against the home, while looking cute and cozy in a country calendar, should be avoided for obvious fire danger. Buy a cheap tarp instead to cover your wood or store it in a strategic, sheltered location that allows you to easily obtain the fuel but doesn't pose a fire risk. Use stakes or end braces built to measure a standard cord to keep the woodpile from collapsing.

Woodpiles are magnets for rodents. Even though the little buggers can transmit diseases and destroy vital equipment, your survival mind-set should be licking your chops at the prospect of raising your own "beef" with little or no effort. Baited mouse and rat traps in proximity

"Home is a **SHELTER** from **STORMS—ALL SORTS** of storms."

—William J. Bennett

of the pile will easily catch the occupants of your rodent ranch. For the scoop on cooking your critters, see page 338. Enjoy!

Fun with Fake Found Firewood

For families without access to natural firewood, check the front and backyard for loose limbs on trees, lumber scraps, old pallets, or a number of odds and ends that are combustible when enough heat is used. Almost any wood product can be burned in a pinch. Avoid burning pressure-treated lumber (it usually has a faint greenish color), as it's filled with toxic chemicals such as arsenic that will off-gas when burned. Avoid burning railroad ties. Particleboard and plywood will smell funky due to the glues that hold them together, and I would refrain from cooking my hot dog over the coals if given a choice, but it will work for general heating needs within the home if that's all you can scrounge. The older the plywood or particleboard the better, as time will have had a chance to mellow out the bonding glues.

If things get super tough, how many chairs do you really need? A few cheap, white-man houses built on some Indian reservations in Arizona were used as fuel, little by little, by inventive occupants who, piece by piece, slowly burned every chair, cabinet, door, wall stud, and porch railing for heat until the home was so uninhabitable that they moved on. Old hunter-gatherer instincts die hard, I guess.

Even fuels that at first glance would seem a waste of time for your fireplace can be modified for longer burn times. In the American West, experiments have been done to create "logs" by tightly binding tumbleweeds (Russian thistle) together. Fuels that would normally combust in seconds last for several minutes after modification. You don't have to ride the range to create your own faux fuel. You can make your own improvised firewood logs by tightly rolling up old newspapers and tying them securely. The tighter you roll the logs, the less oxygen they will receive and thus the slower they will burn when added to an established heat base. Potential family fun for all: the winner with the slowest-burning log gets an extra serving of canned beans.

"Fuel-Burning" Space Heaters (Propane, Kerosene, Coal, Natural Gas, etc.)

Many people in rural or smaller communities have no access to natural gas main lines and use propane gas instead to provide a variety of household needs. It can be delivered by truck to fill large personal storage tanks, or smaller tanks can be brought to the dealer itself to be filled. Although most recognizable on the backyard grill, bottled propane can heat water for hot showers, heat homes, cook food in ovens, and even keep the ice cream cold inside a propane refrigerator. Many recreational vehicles are packed with appliances that run solely on propane.

All fuel-burning space heaters will produce toxic carbon monoxide gas. (We are assuming that electric space heaters are a no-go as the power grid is down.) Many local fire codes do not allow any kind of fuel-burning space heater to be used in an occupied structure unless it has first been "vented" to the outside. *Caution!* Do NOT use your propane or natural gas kitchen stove or oven in an attempt to heat your house for the same reason.

Many people own fuel-burning space heaters that are used in the garage, around outdoor work sites, and such. If you lack any other heat source, the temptation will be very strong to bring it into the house when you start seeing your breath. If appropriate for your family, prepare now for pending chilly home temperatures by having a qualified professional install a modern fuel-burning space heater that's vented to the outside. Read the carbon monoxide poisoning section below about using unvented space heaters. Below are some basic safety precautions to take with any space heater, including electric models.

Space Heater Safety Tips

➲ When using a fuel-burning space heater, open a window to provide adequate ventilation. Never use fuel-burning appliances (kerosene, coal, or propane) without proper ventilation due to deadly carbon monoxide fumes! Although oxygen-depletion alarms are standard on most modern space heaters, these are not the same as carbon monoxide alarms. Wall-mounted, room-vented space heaters that are connected to gas lines are also considered unvented space heaters. *Using unvented space heaters in your home puts you and your family at risk of dying of carbon monoxide poisoning.*

➲ Make sure that your smoke and carbon monoxide detectors are working.

➲ Make sure your space heater has an automatic tip-switch, a cutoff device required on newer models that turns off electric or kerosene heaters if they tip over. Try to purchase a heater that has an automatically controlled thermostat that shuts off by itself when a pre-set temperature is achieved. Make sure it has a guard around the flame area or heating element and only use safety-listed equipment that is labeled with UL or AGA certification.

➲ Keep space heaters at least *three feet* away from everything on all sides of the heater, including walls, furniture, curtains, clothing, and other obvious combustibles.

➲ Do not place anything on top of a space heater.

➲ Place the heater on a hard, level, nonflammable sur-face; do not place it on rugs or carpets, on tables or countertops, or where the heater will be susceptible to being knocked over or block an emergency exit in your home.

➲ Make sure your space heater is in good working con-dition. All space heaters need frequent checkups and cleaning, as a dirty heater is a potential fire hazard.

➲ Use only the proper fuel for each space heater. Never use a fuel in a heater that is not designed to burn that fuel.

➲ Don't store kerosene, gasoline, or other flammable liquids in your home. Use an approved safety con-tainer for storing flammable liquids and store them in a safe location. When refueling a kerosene heater, don't overfill it. If cold kerosene is used, it will expand as it warms up inside your home and may cause the burner to flood, causing potential flare ups. Never fill your kerosene heater while it's burning.

‣ Never leave children or pets unsupervised in a room with a running space heater. Keep young children away from space heaters, as loose clothing may be drawn by a draft into the heater and catch fire.

‣ If you use an electric heater, make sure your home's wiring is adequate for the load and in good condition. Never cover a heater's cord with carpeting or furniture, as this could cause the cord to overheat and start a fire. Avoid overloading the circuit and avoid using extension cords. Use an approved power strip with a built-in circuit breaker. Space heaters should have a polarized AC (alternating current) plug, in which one blade is longer than the other. If the plug should fail to fit into an outlet, contact an electrician to replace the dated outlet. Do not use older space heaters or heaters with cords that are cracked or frayed. Avoid using electric space heaters in the bathroom and never touch an electric heater when you're wet.

‣ Turn off your heater (and unplug, if electric) if you leave the area and before going to bed.

Dangerous and Deadly Carbon Monoxide

Carbon monoxide (CO) is a colorless, odorless, and tasteless toxic gas that is the result of incomplete burning of solid, liquid, and gaseous fuels. This silent monster is responsible for more unintentional fatal poisonings in the United States than any other medium, with most deaths occurring during the colder winter months. According to the Centers for Disease Control and Prevention, more than five hundred people in the United States die each year from carbon monoxide poisoning while 15,000 to 40,000 more visit hospital emergency rooms for treatment. Prolonged exposure to carbon monoxide can lead to neurological damage. The Consumer Product Safety Commission (CPSC) estimates that poorly used space heaters alone kill three hundred people each year and are responsible for more than 25,000 residential fires.

If the grid goes down, the odds of grandpa dragging the barbeque grill into the house for heat or putting the gasoline-powered generator too close to the house will increase. Even yours truly has had close calls with carbon monoxide, so don't get cocky at your family's expense and think it can't happen to you and yours.

How Is Carbon Monoxide Created?

Carbon monoxide is created from a number of sources: leaky furnaces and chimneys; back drafts from woodstoves, fireplaces, gas water heaters and stoves; generators and other gasoline-burning equipment; exhaust fumes from vehicles in attached garages; unvented kerosene and gas space heaters; and tobacco smoke.

Caution! Individuals commonly die from carbon monoxide poisoning in locations where they thought they had adequate ventilation, such as in tents, RVs, and drafty cabins.

People get sick or die each year from carbon monoxide poisoning at Utah/Arizona's Lake Powell when using houseboats for the family vacation. Either folks swim too close for too long next to the idling engines or run poorly vented generators while making margaritas in the close quarters of the boat. Think about the source of carbon monoxide. *If you are burning fuel, and you see an orange or yellow flame, this is a sign that carbon monoxide is being released.* So what about the yellow and orange flame of a candle? Unless you have several hundred burning at once in a poorly ventilated area, don't worry about it. Yellow and orange flames are caused by unburned carbon particles from the combustion process. Although you shouldn't totally drop your guard for a blue flame, it signifies a much more complete combustion process than the former. In conventional, fuel-burning household appliances, oxygen is mixed with the fuel to achieve a more complete burn, thus the blue flame on your kitchen stove. As oxygen supports combustion it raises the temperature of the burning fuel, and the higher heat value burns away the otherwise unburned carbon particles. Speaking of oxygen, carbon monoxide poisoning causes the formation of *carboxyhemoglobin* in the blood, which inhibits the absorption of oxygen in your body. When people breathe in carbon monoxide gas fumes, red blood cells in the bloodstream carry it instead of oxygen to all of the body's tissues.

The Mighty Carbon Monoxide Detector/Alarm

As carbon monoxide is odorless, tasteless, and generally invisible, having a battery-operated carbon monoxide detector is worth its weight in gold. (Although plug-in models are available, they will do you no good if the electrical grid crashes. Check to make sure plug-in models have a battery backup system. Test battery-operated detectors frequently, change the batteries every six months, and have a fresh stash of batteries nearby.) In September 1993, Chicago, Illinois, became one of the first cities in the nation to adopt ordinances requiring the installation of carbon monoxide detectors/alarms in all new single-family homes and in existing single-family homes that purchased new oil or gas furnaces. Carbon monoxide detectors are cheap, easy to install, and commonly available at local hardware and big box discount stores. Although new carbon monoxide detectors should be compliant, make sure your purchased detector/alarm meets the requirements of the current UL standard 2034 or the requirements of the IAS 6-96 standard. Install the detector(s) according to the manufacturer's instructions, and make sure it's not covered up with drapes or furniture. The CPSC recommends that you install a separate detector near every different sleeping area. Carbon monoxide detectors are also available for boats and recreational vehicles. *Test your carbon monoxide detector/alarms frequently per the manufacturer's instructions!* A carbon monoxide detector/alarm does provide added protection, but it's not a substitute for the proper use and upkeep of appliances that can produce carbon monoxide.

The Sinister Symptoms of Carbon Monoxide Poisoning

Early Symptoms (often mistaken for the flu but without the fever)
- Headaches
- Nausea
- Fatigue
- Shortness of breath
- Dizziness
- Muscle pains

Advanced Symptoms
- Disorientation
- Impaired vision and coordination
- Confusion
- Unconsciousness
- Death

The health affects from carbon monoxide depend on the levels of carbon monoxide present, the length of the exposure, and each individual's age and health condition. The individuals most at risk are infants, pregnant women, and people with chronic heart disease or respiratory problems, but everyone, even the family pets, are vulnerable.

What to Do If Poisoned by Carbon Monoxide

If you suspect that you or a loved one has carbon monoxide poisoning, take action immediately!

1 Get out! Move the affected person to fresh air immediately and give supplemental oxygen if available.

2 Contact medical help if available.

3 If the person is not breathing, perform CPR (cardiopulmonary resuscitation) until help arrives.

4 Turn off any combustion appliances.

5 Make sure to ventilate the area of concern by opening windows and doors and leave the house.

6 Make repairs to the cause of carbon monoxide as soon as possible. Don't space out and forget that the area in suspicion is a danger. Remember, carbon monoxide is invisible to you and your loved ones!

How to Prevent Carbon Monoxide Exposure from Occurring

➲ *Check the flame colors of your appliances.* If it's yellow or orange, you have a carbon monoxide problem!

➲ *Check all flues for blockages.* Make sure flues are open, drawing properly, and free from debris such as excess carbon, bird nests, or plants. Flue guards should be installed to prevent critters and debris from accumulating in the first place.

➲ *Make sure your home has adequate ventilation.* All fuel-burning appliances will produce carbon monoxide if they are starved for oxygen.

➲ *Choose the proper size of woodstove.* Hopefully it's certified to meet EPA emission standards, and make sure that all of the doors fit tightly. Fiberglass door gaskets

"You CAN'T be OVERPREPARED."

—Arizona Governor Janet Napolitano, NPR interview on disaster preparedness are commonly available from any commercial stove dealer.

➲ *Check that appliances are installed properly and are serviced regularly.* Make sure that all fuel-burning appliances were installed according to the manufacturer's specifications. Have them inspected, adjusted, and serviced every year. Don't mess around with do-it-yourself machismo if you don't know what you're doing!

➲ *Purchase "vented" space heaters whenever possible.* (Note: The careless use of space heaters is renowned for starting house fires. Never use space heaters on carpeted areas and keep them at least three feet from all combustible materials such as furniture, bedding, and drapes. Don't suspend wet clothing or other articles on or around the heater to dry as they could catch fire. Keep children and pets away from the heater and never leave the heater on when sleeping or leaving the area. If the heater cord or plug feels hot, unplug it and call a repairman to check for problems. Keep an ABC dry powder fire extinguisher in your home at all times.)

➲ *Don't burn charcoal grills or fuel-burning camping equipment in ANY closed environment such as homes, tents, vehicles, garages, etc.* (Note: I use a two-burner propane stove in my home for *cooking* only, a temporary event as opposed to trying to heat the home.)

➲ *Don't leave the car idling in your attached garage even if you have the garage door open.*

➲ *Never use ANY fuel-burning appliances such as clothes dryers, ovens, or stoves for heating your house.*

➲ *Never use fuel-burning appliances in rooms with all of the doors and windows shut, or where people are or will be sleeping.*

➲ *Don't use gasoline-powered tools, generators, etc., indoors.*

It's Too Hot in the House! The Art of Keeping Your Home Cool

North-facing Rooms: Looking for Naturally Cool Places in the House

During summertime heat, recognizing and exploiting cooler microclimates in your house will be necessary to achieve relative comfort and, in a worst-case scenario, will be needed to prevent you from dying of dehydration and hyperthermia. Notice

that this section is directly the opposite of the south-facing room section with a few similarities designed to maintain whatever temperature it is that you're looking for.

North-facing rooms in the home will naturally be cooler during hot weather as direct sunlight never shines within the windows of the room at any time of the year. Even if the room has no windows or openings of any kind, it will still be cooler. If you're unsure of how your home is oriented, every family will have a room that people dread going into during the wintertime because it's damn cold. The chances are high that this room is facing north.

North-facing rooms can be blocked off from the rest of the home to keep the cooler temperature insulated against the onslaught of heat generated from the rest of the house. Close doors or hang up blankets to insulate and block off doorways from the rest of the home and use towels or extra clothing to insulate *above* doorways and higher open areas if needed. *Hot air rises, and cooler air sinks*, thus don't bother stuffing towels under the door. Using the "hot air rises" principle, the entire house can get rid of some of its excess heat through the installation of attic vents.

If north-facing rooms do have windows or openings, they can be utilized to cool down the room at the appropriate time of day. While it may seem counterintuitive at first, I keep all doors and windows in my home *closed* during the daytime in the summer. I open the doors and windows in the evening or at night when it cools down outside. I especially like to open windows that are located high up, as the rising warm air easily escapes. The cooler convective nighttime breezes fill my home all night, bringing inside temperatures down from whatever heat was gained from the heat of the day. To insulate my cooler indoor temperatures from the outside heat, I then close doors and windows the next morning when it starts to warm up outside. Combined with great insulation, orientation, and thermal mass, this simple process works for me as free air conditioning all summer long.

Lay Low and Be Cool

Cooler air sinks. Although insulation such as carpeting or throw rugs works well at retaining hot or cold temperatures, the bare floor of a room, especially if it's a concrete slab, stone, or tile, will be much cooler than the carpet itself. If it gets really hot inside and you're forced to lie on the floor, the resulting heat loss through conduction will be greatly increased if you lie on the bare floor itself without any insulation blocking the transfer of heat. Mattresses can be taken off of their box springs and put on the floor, as can sofa cushions, to make an improvised bed that maximizes lower cooler air.

I fondly remember living in my yurt in the summertime. I would often lie naked on the cool floor when forced to endure yet another summer day in Arizona in a fabric shelter in direct sun with no insulation. The yurt itself was set up on a circular platform constructed of sandstone, 2x4s, and plywood. As my shelter location was on a slight slope, the height of the sandstone wall varied and there was a crawl space underneath the plywood. We cut an opening in the floor, and then covered the opening with a piece of plywood, which I could take off to allow the cooler air from underneath to make its way into the lowest part of the yurt. Even so, some days still sucked and were hotter than hell. Regardless of crummy circumstances, which are all temporary, buck up and maintain a positive attitude as best you can.

Many homes have basements or other built-in underground storage rooms for garden produce. All will be wonderfully cool when compared to the rest of your home.

Wet and Wild

When a liquid changes into a gas (evaporation), the process uses heat or energy. Many times on cross-country desert survival courses, my students use extra water to wet down their clothing. Clothing covering the head, neck, and torso areas respond the best to being wetted down, as these areas possess the most sweat glands. Don't be shy, wet down your clothing or the sheets on the bed when things get smoldering in the house. When wet, cotton clothing and sheets allow for the best loss of heat from your body compared to other materials. Back in my yurt days, I often wet my clothing down with water to stay cooler. In certain conditions, wet clothing on a body excels at losing heat much more effectively than being naked.

The mass production of air conditioners for homes didn't begin until the 1950s. Regardless, Phoenix, Arizona, was the territorial capital of Arizona in 1899, with a population of 5,444 hardy souls who knew how to sweat their butts off in desert summer heat. Early Phoenicians used basic tricks such as insulation, thermal mass, and orientation, just like we do, or should do, to stay cool. They also soaked down sheets with water and hung them from their porches, doorways, and as dividers between rooms. Cooler nighttime breezes would become even cooler when passing through the wet sheet, similar to the soaked burlap "box cooler" my grandmother used to have. It consisted of a wooden framed box, which held the food, surrounded by a layer of burlap. On top of the burlap-coated box was a metal container with tiny holes in its base. My grandmother would fill the container with water and it would slowly seep out the holes throughout the day so as to constantly keep the burlap wet—perfect low-tech evaporative cooling. Creative and liberal use of this concept can make unbearable high temperatures bearable in a pinch. Many urban desert neighborhoods employ swamp coolers on their homes for the same effect.

Horrifying Humidity

Many of you reading this live in locales that are hot and humid. Humidity is a true killer, and when it approaches 70 percent or more it completely impedes the body's evaporation process. High humidity levels will make many of the water tricks in this book useless when trying to "make nice" with hot outdoor temperatures. *As the body's main cooling mechanism (the evaporation of sweat) is ineffective during periods of high humidity, it is extremely important that you monitor your behavior and don't do highly physical tasks during the heat of the day.* If it's already hot outside, and your sweat won't evaporate due to high humidity, and you create excess metabolic heat by working like a crazy person during the hottest part of the day, you're asking for trouble.

Going Under Cover

Obviously, it's hotter to stand in the sun than in the shade. *Any* shade allowing protection from direct solar radiation will drastically make your living environment cooler. Rooms not oriented to the north, yet featuring plenty of overhead shade cover from trees, buildings, or whatever, may be cooler inside than the sun-beaten roofs of exposed north-facing rooms, especially if you have crummy insulation in your attic or ceiling. Pay attention someday to how and when the summer sun pummels your home and make mental notes for the future. Tarps, opaque rolls of plastic, blankets, or other shade-producing items can be strung up over parts of your home to eliminate some or all direct sunlight. Along with the created shade, the dead air space produced between the tarp and the house acts as bonus insulation from hot temperatures. Think of your home as a body similar to yours. If it stands out in direct sunlight all day long, it will be much hotter than if it has access to shade. It's very common in the desert to see mobile homes with entire carports erected over the mobile home itself for the same benefit. This is the same reason that many ancient Native American tribes in the Southwest built stone-stacked pueblos under natural rock overhangs. If your house is cooler on the outside, you will be cooler on the inside.

Covering Windows with Space Blankets

I've mentioned this several times but now I'll get specific. Taping a space blanket to the inside of your home's window will reflect away direct shortwave radiation from the sun, as well as hotter long-wave radiation from the boiling outside environment. Smaller, more reflective space blankets will be easier to use for this application than the heavier grommeted type. In truth, while the shinier the material the more it will reflect, any reflective surface can be used. Tape up tinfoil if that's all you have, but keep the foil flat and neat and don't scrunch it up, thereby eliminating some of the tinfoil's reflective value, and put the shinier side out.

Whatever you use, the reflective surface should be taped onto the window itself if possible, yet done so in a way that will allow you to remove it when necessary without ripping up the material. If the reflective surface is hung or taped a few inches away from the window itself, radiation will heat up the space between the reflective surface and the window. This heat gain will eventually leak into the room.

SUPER SIMPLE SUMMARY

- ⮑ Your home's (or any shelter's) main purpose is to help thermoregulate your core body temperature in hot and cold temperatures.
- ⮑ Avoiding *hypothermia* (low body temperature) and *hyperthermia* (high body temperature) is a major factor in your survival. Know the signs and symptoms of both for yourself and others.
- ⮑ Being properly dressed by having adequate clothing and staying hydrated by storing and drinking sufficient water are the easiest ways to thermoregulate core body temperature and stay warm or cool during temperature extremes.
- ⮑ Your body loses or gains heat from the environment through *convection* (wind and moving water), *conduction* (touching a hot or cold object), *radiation* (shortwave radiation from the sun and long-wave radiation from everything else), *evaporation* (sweating), and *respiration* (breathing). Pay attention to the same

physics when improvising or setting up an alternative shelter such as a tent, tarp, or RV.

◷ Your home could be partially or completely destroyed during a disaster. Check for structural damage before entering the home. If you choose to reenter, make sure it's not in danger of collapsing. Ultimately, this inspection will need to be done by a professional. If you do decide to reenter your home, turn off any outside gas lines and let the house air out for several minutes to remove potential escaping gas. When entering the home, don't use open flames as a light source. Instead, use a battery-operated flashlight or some other nonfuel burning light source.

◷ Have portable, alternative shelter option(s) that are easy to set up under stress such as a tent or tarp in case you need to evacuate your home or your home is damaged in a disaster.

◷ In Cold Weather: Maximize the warmest room(s) in the house and isolate it from the rest of the colder home. As a general rule, smaller south-facing rooms with windows will be warmer on cold, sunny days than other rooms in the house. Direct sunlight hitting thermal mass areas such as a concrete floor will re-radiate more heat at night than the same floor covered with a throw rug. Close and insulate under doors with extra clothing or towels, cover windows during nighttime hours with clear plastic and /or space blankets, and make group "sleeping forts" to maximize body heat. Remember that warm air rises, and sleeping next to a family member will be warmer than sleeping alone.

◷ For your safety and maximum efficiency, woodstoves and fireplaces should be serviced yearly by a professional whether they have been used or not. Have an adequate supply of firewood or pellets on hand, stored in a safe location away from the house.

◷ *Danger!* Beware of deadly carbon monoxide fumes when using *any* fuel-burning heating source indoors such as fireplaces, woodstoves, or propane, kerosene, natural gas, or coal-burning space heaters. *All yellow and orange flames produce poisonous carbon monoxide.* Install battery-powered carbon monoxide

detectors and alarms near all rooms where people will
be sleeping.

- ⊃ Space heaters should be vented to the outside and
  kept in good working order. Keep all heaters at least
  three feet away on all sides from all combustible
  materials. Use caution with space heaters around children and pets and store all fuels in approved containers safely away from the home.

- ⊃ In Hot Weather: Maximize the coolest room(s) in the
  house and isolate it from the rest of the hotter home.
  Look for north-facing rooms, draw window blinds,
  and utilize space blankets or tinfoil to keep out the
  sun. Close doors, insulate higher openings in rooms
  to keep out rising hot air, and create shade wherever
  possible. Open windows at night to let out trapped
  heat and let in cooler nighttime air and close them
  again before outside temperatures rise. Cooler air
  sinks, so go low and wet down clothing and/or sheets
  that can be hung between rooms or in doorways to
  increase evaporative cooling.

- ⊃ Beware of high humidity levels when it's hot outside.
  Humidity levels of 70 percent or greater severely impede the evaporation of sweat from your body. Wait
  for cooler early morning or late evening temperatures
  before doing heavy physical exercise.

WONDERFULLY Wet and Wanted WATER

"Many of the wars of this [twentieth] century were about oil,
but the wars of the next century will be about water."
—Ismail Serageldin, former World Bank Vice President, 2000

For short- and long-term survival, virtually nothing will eclipse the importance of potable water for you and your loved ones. Ignore this fact and you will meet death. Over dramatic? I wish it were. *Water is a biological necessity down to the cellular level.* It is not an optional item. It is general knowledge that water accounts for nearly two-thirds of the human body's total weight. Research has shown that the older we get, the drier we become. Floating around in the womb, overall body water content is more than 80 percent. As infants, our body water content drops to around 73 percent. In young adults, the body contains roughly 65 percent water, 70 percent in the muscles and 50 percent in fat deposits. Between forty and sixty years old, water content drops to 55 percent for males and 47 percent for females. After sixty, the rate drops even further, 50 percent for males and 45 percent for females.

Water has several amazing properties, including the fact that it's an excellent solvent. Water dissolves a remarkable number of inorganic and organic molecules. When dissolved, molecules break apart to form a solution. Living activities on a cellular level take place either dissolved in fats or water. Water has a high heat capacity, meaning it requires a lot of energy to heat it up, or cool it down, so it can handle a wide variety of outside temperature fluctuations within the cell before problems arise. The water in your blood helps the circulatory system get rid of excess heat, or distribute heat to wherever it's needed during the cold. Digestion and metabolism are water-based processes, and water lubricates the joints and helps eliminate waste products from the body as well. Water is even required for the simple act of breathing, as the lungs need

"CHILDREN of a culture BORN in a WATER-RICH ENVIRONMENT, we have NEVER REALLY LEARNED how IMPORTANT WATER IS to us. We UNDERSTAND IT, but we DO NOT RESPECT IT."
—William Ashworth

moisture to oxygenate blood and rid the blood of excess carbon dioxide. Nearly 70 percent of the Earth's surface is covered in water. It is therefore no exaggeration to say that water is life itself.

In desert climates, temperatures can be so hot and dry that people don't seem to perspire. Since they're "not sweating," they underestimate how hot the outside temperature really is, thereby reducing the urge to drink. The truth is revealed by putting your hand on your skin for a minute or two. Lift your hand and you'll find it's sodden with sweat, proof enough of the body's desperate attempt to keep the brain and internal organs cool. In extreme hot temperatures, unprotected skin instantly loses moisture. The skin is the largest organ of the body, and directly responsible for the evaporation of sweat, thereby helping to keep your inner temperature at a comfortable 98.6 degrees F (37 degrees C).

A person at rest, *doing nothing*, loses from two to two and a half quarts of water every day. If your home is located in a hot part of the country, be forewarned that you and your family will use much more water than this. Some of this water loss, about 600 to 900 milliliters, happens simply to keep our skin supple and healthy and is called *insensible perspiration*. In extreme hot temperatures, it's possible to lose a gallon of water an hour in sweat. That's an unbelievable 8.3 pounds! This heinous fact should make apparent that the "standard survival recommendation" of carrying one gallon of water per person per day in the desert is completely bogus. When living, recreating, or traveling in hot temperatures, I recommend at least three gallons of water per person per day, more if the terrain, temperatures, or activities undertaken are extreme. Seeing as how the average American *individually* uses 116 to 220 gallons of water *every day*, with some wealthy communities in my arid state using in excess of 400 gallons per person daily, it isn't hard to see our gross neglect regarding the importance of conserving this precious fluid. (Note: The average African family uses about five gallons of water each day.) Pitifully, the National Drinking Water Alliance estimates that up to 50 percent of the water that families use could be saved by implementing simple conservation methods like low-flow shower heads and low-flush toilets.

For every quart of sweat you lose, your heart rate raises about eight beats per minute, your cardiovascular system becomes more stressed, and your cooling system declines. In other words, before dehydration kills you, it greatly impedes your physical and psychological performance.

Deadly Dehydration

Seventy-five percent of Americans are chronically dehydrated. Thirty-seven percent mistake the thirst mechanism for hunger pangs. Lack of hydration is the number one trigger of daytime fatigue. If you live in an arid region or one with oppressively high humidity, you know how tough it is to remain hydrated. Doing so takes a lot of work! Although at times it's hard to remember to drink, and then to drink enough, it is critical for your physiology and psychology that you remain maximally hydrated.

Dehydration is deadly in hot and cold weather. When the blood in your circulatory system loses water, it gets thicker. Thick blood circulates more slowly and is harder for the heart to pump, and in regard to temperature regulation, it hinders the body's ability to lose excess heat or circulate needed heat. When the volume of blood and extra cellular fluids decreases, water is literally sucked from the cells, causing them to shrink, thereby damaging cell membranes and the proteins inside.

HOW YOUR BODY LOSES WATER

Factors Inside the Body	Body Water Loss	Factors Outside the Body

-Physical exertion
-Certain medications
-Illness (fever)
	Increased sweating	-Hot temperatures
		-Direct short- or long-
		  wave radiation
		  (sunlight/fire)
		-High humidity

-Physical exertion -Illness (fever) -Breathing through mouth	Increased respiratory loss	-Low humidity -High wind speed -Cold temperatures
-Hypothermia	Increased urine loss	-Diuretics: alcohol/coffee/ tea/certain medications
-Diarrhea -Vomiting	Increased bowel and stomach loss	
	Increased insensible perspiration	-Hot temperatures -Low humidity -High wind speed
-Bleeding	Increased blood loss	
	Increased digestive loss	-High protein, fat, and sodium diet

Platelets actually stick together in the blood due to a lack of plasma. The result is an increase in the naturally occurring salts in the remaining body fluids. Normal body fluid has a salt concentration of 0.9 percent. In contrast, urine contains 2 percent salt, plus toxic urea, while seawater has a whopping 3.9 percent. Many researchers feel that rising salt concentrations within the body are responsible for the punishing side effects of dehydration.

Exposure to cold weather without protective clothing or some other way to remain warm increases urine production. When surface blood vessels constrict from the cold, reducing the circulatory system and increasing blood pressure, pressure sensors in the body perceive an increase in volume and stimulate urine production. To make things worse, when outside temperatures fall, so does your kidneys' ability to concentrate urine, and the end result is that you lose even more water.

Body functions are *severely* limited if you lose 10 percent of your weight due to dehydration, yet physical, mental, and emotional impairment is manifest with the slightest loss of water, especially in the heat. Losing just 2 percent of body weight in water compromises your overall judgment by 25 percent and severely limits physical endurance. Being outside in temperatures of 100 degrees F (38 degrees C) or more will cause you to lose another 25 percent. To summarize, if you live in hot temperatures and are a quart and a half low on water, you are operating at *half* the person you usually are! In Arizona and other arid parts of our nation and world, this is a very common occurrence. The water in your body affects your circulation, metabolism, good judgment, and overall attitude, just like the emotion fear.

How Much Water?

So how do you know if you have enough water in your system? Thirst should *never* be an indicator of when or how much to drink. Being thirsty is a sign that you're already a quart to a quart and a half low. To make matters worse, somewhere down the line in Dehydrationville, the thirst mechanism stops working altogether.

The best way to tell if you're maximally hydrated is the color of your urine. It should be as clear as the water you drink, with no color whatsoever. Certain medications

Pee Rules:
Clear,
Copious,
and
Frequent

and vitamins, especially B vitamins, color urine. The volume and frequency of urine produced by someone who has been drinking copiously are other hydration indicators, although not as reliable as color. Using the three together will provide the most effective guesstimating as to when and how much you and your family should drink.

There is no adaptation to dehydration. Military personnel have learned the hard way that "being tough" is not an acceptable substitute for water. Astute military commandeers have recognized for years that when personnel operate in hot temperatures, *even when abundant water is readily available,* soldiers will not drink enough water to avoid dehydration *unless they are forced to drink.* This oddity is called "involuntary dehydration" and I experience it all the time with students on my survival courses. Think about it for a minute. When you are thirsty, meaning that your body is already a quart or more low on water, you have the urge to drink. To allay your thirst, you drink a few swallows of water and, *voilà,* you're no longer thirsty, but your body is still dehydrated and will continue to grow more so unless you force yourself to drink a quart or more of water. If you live in hot temperatures, drink more water than your body seems to want. Watch your family like a hawk, especially older people, small children, and babies for the signs and symptoms of dehydration. It only takes one person to compromise the whole group. Exotic methods for procuring water such as solar stills are notoriously unreliable and can hasten your death.

"THE CRISIS of our diminishing WATER RESOURCES is just AS SEVERE (if less obviously immediate) AS ANY WARTIME CRISIS we have EVER FACED. OUR SURVIVAL is just AS MUCH AT STAKE as it was at the time OF PEARL HARBOR, or THE ARGONNE, or GETTYSBURG, or SARATOGA."

—Jim Wright, U.S. representative, 1966

Signs and Symptoms of Dehydration

Early or Mild to Moderate Dehydration
- ⮑ Headache
- ⮑ Irritability
- ⮑ Dizziness or lightheadedness
- ⮑ Excessive thirst
- ⮑ Nausea / loss of appetite
- ⮑ Dry mouth, cracked lips
- ⮑ Mild disorientation and confusion
- ⮑ Fatigue / lethargy
- ⮑ Decreased urine output / dark-colored urine
- ⮑ Muscle weakness
- ⮑ Flushed, dry skin

Late or Severe Dehydration
- ⮑ Extreme thirst
- ⮑ Very dry mouth, skin, and mucous membranes
- ⮑ Severe confusion and disorientation
- ⮑ Severe muscle cramping in the arms, legs, back, and stomach
- ⮑ Lack of sweating
- ⮑ Convulsions
- ⮑ Fainting
- ⮑ Bloated stomach
- ⮑ Heart failure
- ⮑ Sunken dry eyes with dark rings and few or no tears
- ⮑ Dry, wrinkled skin with a lack of elasticity
- ⮑ Rapid and deep breathing
- ⮑ Low blood pressure
- ⮑ Rapid, weak heartbeat
- ⮑ Delirium, unconsciousness, and death

Situations or People with a Higher Risk for Dehydration

Infants and Children
Worldwide, diarrhea-induced dehydration is the leading cause of child mortality. Children are especially susceptible to dehydration due to their smaller body weight, higher turnover of water and electrolytes, and lower sweating capacity.

Elderly
Older adults are more susceptible to dehydration due to a less acute sense of thirst and a reduced ability to respond to temperature changes and internal water

conservation. Older people may also forget to drink and may have chronic illness or dehydration side effects caused by medications.

Sick People or People with a Chronic Illness
Fever, diarrhea, and vomiting seriously dehydrate the body. (It's estimated that, globally, diarrhea causes 4 million deaths per year.) The higher the fever, the more dehydrated you'll become. Having a simple cold also enhances dehydration, as you feel less like drinking. Chronic illnesses such as diabetes, kidney disease, cystic fibrosis, adrenal gland disorders, alcoholism, and others further dehydrate the body.

Living at High Altitudes
High altitudes of 8,000 feet or more cause dehydration, as the body attempts to compensate for the elevation by rapid breathing (lost water vapor in the breath) and increased urination.

Exercise
Increased physical exertion causes the body to sweat. High humidity levels increase sweating and decrease the evaporative cooling of sweat. Humidity levels of 70 percent or greater impede the sweat/evaporation process altogether.

Hot/Dry and Cold Weather or Climates
The hotter the outdoor temperature and the drier the climate, the more the body will sweat to preserve its core body temperature. Cold, dry air pulls water from the body's warm, moist lungs at a frightening rate, up to one quart per hour in minus 40 degrees F (minus 40 degrees C).

Cramped Quarters

Close, cramped locations, common in survival shelters, use more metabolic water from survivors as water exhaled from the breath increases.

Increased Urination

While this is the result of some diseases, diuretics such as coffee, tea, alcohol, and some blood pressure medications cause increased urination and/or perspiration.

Burn Injuries

The skin is the largest organ of the body. Third-degree or large first- or second-degree burns cause extreme fluid loss from the body.

Pregnant or Breast-feeding Women

The Institute of Medicine recommends that pregnant women drink ten cups of water per day. Breast-feeding moms are encouraged to drink about thirteen cups. Reread the other above factors and adjust your fluid intake accordingly, regardless of these recommendations.

HARDCORE HYDRATION

In the middle of the seventeenth century, on the border of England and Scotland, Carlisle Castle became home to the last siege of an English castle when Bonnie Prince Charlie's Jacobite garrison tried in vain to hold off the Duke of Cumberland's Hanoverian army. The defeated Scottish Jacobites were held in the dungeon of the castle, now known for its "licking stones." These licking stones were created by the dying Jacobite prisoners in their desperate attempt to get water. The castle walls were made from damp sandstone in which the prisoners literally licked pockets into up to four and five inches deep with their tongues looking for moisture to stay alive. The imprints of the captives' tongues are visible within the castle walls to this day. Any survivors were brutally executed on nearby Gallows Hill.

"When you **DRINK THE WATER**, remember **THE SPRING**."

—Chinese proverb

High Protein, Fat, and Sodium Diets

Those who eat large amounts of the above food types, as most Americans do, will use more of their body's water to break down and process the nutrition.

What about Electrolyte Solutions?

In my book *98.6 Degrees: The Art of Keeping Your Ass Alive!* I shared the four main techniques for quick, maximal hydration. They are listed below. Although these techniques are in no particular order in regard to their importance, take a close look at number three.

Four Factors for Accelerated Maximal Hydration

1. *Adequate volume*
2. *Temperature*
3. *Minimal salts, carbohydrates, and sugars*
4. *Carbonation*

Drinking fluids containing salts, carbohydrates, and sugars causes the stomach to hold this water in order to digest the nutrients contained within it. In essence, the presence of nutrients in your water causes your stomach to treat your water like food. After all, the stomach and small intestine absorb nutrients from whatever you put in your mouth; that's their job. For the fluid you drink to be absorbed in order to stave off dehydration, it must reach your large intestine. The more foodstuff water possesses, the longer it hangs out in the stomach and small intestine digesting.

A barrage of sports drinks exist on the market, many backed by big-money advertising campaigns. While they have their merits (including flavoring funky-tasting-and-looking water after it's been disinfected), all contain a fierce amount of salt, carbohydrates, and sugar. While electrolyte replacement can be an issue in long-term survival, it pales in comparison to dying of short-term dehydration. Electrolyte solutions can and will be abused by people assuming that if one scoop is good, three must be better. My hometown fire department stopped using dry electrolyte replacements altogether as they were getting sick due to the fact that they lacked the water in their systems to process the excessive electrolytes being ingested. In addition, sports medicine colleges around the nation have completed study after study on hydration and most flat-out recommend plain old water. Of the many electrolyte replacement solutions tested, most all were successful at increasing hydration simply because they tasted better than straight water, thus the subject tended to drink more and more often. If you or the kids insist on using colored, sugary, electrolyte replacement solutions, consider diluting the overall concentration with added water, and beware the scores of bees and yellow jackets that will flock to the sugary brew. Don't lose sight of the fact that the most important factor is drinking a lot of water, even if it's laced with trace nutrients.

Stay away from all alcoholic products, as alcohol increases dehydration by eliminating more fluid from the body through the kidneys than the quantity of liquid you originally consumed. After all, alcohol is a toxin, and your body requires eight ounces of plain water to neutralize one ounce of alcohol.

Dehydration and Sickness in Kids

There are times to use electrolyte solutions, and one of these times is with sick children. It wouldn't hurt to have on hand oral rehydration solutions such as Pedialyte or Ricelyte for infants and children who have diarrhea, vomiting, or fever. If you can, check with your doctor first to see if this is advised. Oral rehydration solutions are available at most drugstores. Check the shelf life to see how long they'll keep. Most adult dehydration caused by diarrhea, vomiting, or fever can be improved upon by drinking more plain water. Fruit juices and sodas can make diarrhea worse. In a pinch, use the following homemade oral rehydration solution for any family member who may need more than simply water to rehydrate a sick body.

Handy Homemade Rehydration Solution

- 1/2 teaspoon salt
- 1/2 teaspoon baking soda
- 3 tablespoons sugar
- One quart (liter) of room-temperature potable water
- Mix the above ingredients in the quart of water and don't fudge this recipe. *Be sure to measure the ingredients accurately!*

Bogus Bottled Bubbly?

Bottled water can be up to 1000 times more expensive than regular tap water and it may not be as safe. That said, commercially available bottled water might very well be what you store for your preparedness plan. In 2003, Americans spent more than $7 billion on bottled water that on average cost more than one dollar a bottle. Many bottlers claim that their product originates from some faraway spring or ancient glacier. If true, it's hard to say how many resources were squandered in the bottling and transportation of that liter of water from the French mountains, not to mention the estimated 1.5 million tons of plastic that are used to bottle 89 billion liters of water each year.

As if that's not obscene enough, many of these exotic waters have turned out to be bogus. A few years ago, the National Resources Defense Council (NRDC) conducted a four-year study that tested more than 1,000 samples from 103 brands of bottled water. The results? You guessed it: the researchers discovered that 25 percent or more of bottled water is really just tap water in a bottle. Sometimes the water was "purified" by reverse osmosis or some other means, and sometimes it wasn't. It gets worse. Under the same NRDC study, eighteen of the 103 bottled water brands tested contained "more bacteria than allowed under microbiological-purity guidelines."

Bottled water is actually defined as a "food" under federal regulations and thus sits under the wings of the Food and Drug Administration (FDA). The Environmental Protection Agency is responsible for municipal water supplies, or tap water, and is required to uphold much stricter standards. Unlike bottled water companies, the EPA requires that local water treatment facilities provide users with a detailed description of the tap water's source, and the end results of any testing, including violations in contaminant levels. You might remember getting one of their little letters in the mail, profiling your water in minutia. While municipal water companies are required to test for harmful pathogens several times per day, bottled water companies are required to do so only once per week. I could go on about the testing differences. In addition, one-fifth of the brands tested positive for synthetic chemicals like *phthalate*, an unsafe chemical that finds its way into the water from the plastic container itself. The end result is that bottled water companies are not bound by the same standards as municipal water systems, thus they have the option of providing your family with water of a lower quality than you now receive from your kitchen faucet.

Storing Water for a "Rainy Day"

Storing water involves having water-safe container(s) in which to put water for future use. Not all containers are made from materials that you can safely store water in. If you don't have regular access to water sources where you live, stored water will be vital to your survival, both short and long term. Indigenous peoples used a fascinating variety of items to store and transport water such as gourds; seashells; ostrich eggs; animal stomachs, bladders, and intestines; bamboo segments; pottery; tightly woven baskets; and wooden containers hollowed out by fire. You will never fully appreciate how precious your virtually unbreakable, plastic camping water bottle is until you use one of these items on a cross-country field course. I routinely use gourds as canteens on some of my primitive living skills courses, and the stress involved in making sure they don't drop or bang into something and break is intense. You have but limited space within your body to store one of the most prized commodities for your survival. Having several modern, quality water containers, both fixed (due to their size) and portable, will be a *huge* asset to your peace of mind and potential survival. While you should be fully prepared to use modern container options, it should not weaken your adaptation muscles as to what could be used in your neighborhood to store and transport water in the event that your regular containment options are destroyed, stolen, or lost.

Whatever containers you choose to store your water in, make sure they have tight-fitting lids to keep out debris and critters. Massive plastic water tanks, for

WACKY WATER FACTOIDS

TA-DA!!!

- Of the 1,700 million square miles of water on planet Earth, all 326 million trillion gallons of it, less than 0.5 percent is potable.
- Ninety-eight percent of our planet's water is composed of ocean.
- Two percent of the Earth's water is fresh but locked-up in the form of glaciers (for now).
- 0.36 percent of the planet's water is found underground.
- Only 0.036 percent of the Earth's entire water supply is found in our lakes and rivers.
- Each day, the sun evaporates 1,000,000,000,000 (one trillion) tons of water.
- The human brain is 75 percent water.
- Human blood is 83 percent water.
- Human bones are 25 percent water.
- One inch of rain falling on one acre of land is equal to about 27,154 gallons of water.
- Groundwater can take a human lifetime just to traverse one mile.
- If the entire world's water were fit into a gallon jug, the freshwater available for us to use would equal only about one tablespoon.
- Over 90 percent of the world's supply of freshwater is located in Antarctica.
- One drip per second from a leaky faucet can waste 2,000 gallons of water per year.
- If all plumbing fixtures in the United States were replaced with water-conserving fixtures,

we could save 3.4 to 8.4 billion gallons of water a day.

- The average toilet uses five to seven gallons of water per flush. A shower uses five gallons per minute.
- The average bath uses about thirty-six gallons of water.
- An average American residence uses 107,000 gallons of water per year. (146,000 gallons per year in some Arizona communities.)
- The United States uses about 346,000 billion gallons of freshwater every day, including water used for irrigation, industry, fire fighting, and street cleaning.
- Americans use five times the amount of water that Europeans use.
- Two-thirds of the water used in an American home is used in the bathroom.
- Less than 1 percent of the water treated by public water systems is used for drinking and cooking.
- The average person spends less than 1 percent of their total personal expenditure of money for water, wastewater, and water disposal services.
- Water expands by nearly one-tenth of its volume when it freezes.
- Frozen water is 9 percent lighter than unfrozen water, which is why ice floats.
- Drinking adequate amounts of water can decrease the risk of certain types of cancers, including colon cancer, bladder cancer, and breast cancer.
- Drinking adequate water can significantly reduce joint and back pain.
- Adequate hydration can prevent and alleviate headaches.
- Seventy-five percent of a chicken is water.
- Ninety-five percent of a tomato is water.
- Seventy percent of an elephant is water.

"Water has become a **HIGHLY PRECIOUS RESOURCE.** There are **SOME PLACES** where a barrel of **WATER COSTS MORE** than a barrel of **OIL.**"

—Lloyd Axworthy, foreign minister of Canada, 1999

example, have a few openings that are completely sealable and a manhole-type cover that has a one-way vent, thereby allowing the tank to "breathe" and compensate for air pressure changes. If your containers, both large and small, are not sealable, you will have all sorts of thirsty critters try to horn in on your supply, especially if you live in an arid environment.

I collect rain, and one of my catchment basins is a plastic fifty-five-gallon drum that's open to the air. Along with rain, it commonly collects rat poop, bird droppings, and other weirdness, but I don't care as it's reserved for watering specific vegetation. Some of the more heinous things it collects, especially during the hotter months, are swarms of bees looking for a drink. While we get along fine so far, they could be a problem around small children.

Warning! It is not uncommon for bees to fly into open drinking containers of water. If your container is opaque, you will not see the bee when you take a drink. The bee could sting you in your mouth or throat and possibly cause a potentially fatal allergic reaction called *anaphylactic shock*. If your airway becomes occluded due to swelling caused by the sting, and you don't have immediate access to medical intervention, you will die. This scenario is especially common with opened soft drinks, as bees love sugary water. Deaths due to bee, wasp, and yellow jacket stings kill hundreds of people each year in the United States alone, so pay attention and consider using only transparent containers for drinking.

How Much Water Should I Store?

How much water you store depends on the variables already discussed and your opinion. At the bare minimum, *store at least one gallon per person per day.* If you live in an arid climate store as much water as you can, at least *three gallons per person per day.* The primary motive for storing and using this water is your family's hydration (thermoregulation), with cooking and sanitation close behind. Don't forget that pets will also require water. Rural and suburban families that own livestock, horses, or other large animals should plan accordingly for their needs. Most animal owners will know how much their animals drink during hot and cool weather—if not, pay attention the next time you water them.

Keep internally hydrated, but otherwise use water sparingly, and strictly ration your water with regard to sponge baths and the like. While most conventional emergency preparation information advises you to be independent and prepared for three days or seventy-two hours, be independent with water for at least one week, two weeks if possible, and three or four if you can manage the space and expense. Having "just enough" of any life-giving, precious resource leaves zero room for the variables that will happen after a disaster that will impact your stored supply. Never put all of your eggs in one basket and have, at minimum, two places in which you store your family's emergency water. These locations should be out of the sun and cool, if possible—away from toxic chemicals, gas containers, and other garage or closet household items that could permeate through some water containers and affect the quality of the water. Water should also be stored at your place of work and in each vehicle.

Water is fairly heavy, 8.3 pounds per gallon, and is not compressible, so the space that it takes up is the space that it takes up. Since water is so heavy, containing large amounts requires very well-made containers. There are many different containers available and all of them have their pros and cons. Before storing water in smaller preused containers, wash them first with dish detergent. After rinsing, disinfect the inside of the container with one teaspoon of household chlorine bleach per quart of water. Swish the mixture around and let it sit for a few minutes, rinse well, and you're ready to use it for water storage. Look at the following list of the most common water storage containers, and decide which containers or combinations of containers work for you.

Common Types of Water Storage Containers

Plastic

There are many advantages to using plastic containers. They are extremely common and they come in a large variety of sizes and shapes, from one-quart, backpacking-style water containers to massive tanks capable of holding thousands of gallons. They are durable, corrosion resistant, repairable, lightweight when empty, and relatively cheap. Opaque models will inhibit algae growth and come in non-attention-grabbing colors such as forest green and black.

Some disadvantages are that plastic will eventually deteriorate from ultraviolet rays from the sun, may burn/melt with sufficient heat, and will easily absorb and retain odors. Naysayers claim that all plastics eventually leach harmful chemicals into stored water.

Small Plastic Containers

There are many small plastic containers to choose from and all give you the option of easily transporting water. Due to their smaller size, usually under a gallon, they double as a convenient drinking container suitable for young children and older people alike. For long-term storage, look for containers that are made specifically for potable water or other liquids. This doesn't mean you should use a plastic container that housed paint thinner in its last life for even short-term use, so please, use common sense.

Liter Pop Bottles

These containers are tougher than hell, commonly available, easy to drink from for small children and the elderly, and store easily. I've had clients use them on rough, cross-country survival courses, and I'll admit, they can take some abuse. Almost all lack any useful opacity so they will breed algae if exposed to light for any length of time. This same trait makes them wonderful containers to use with the ultraviolet radiation "SODIS" water treatment method explained later in this chapter.

"Camping Style," One-Quart/Liter-Capacity Water Bottles

Your local camping and backpacking store will have a varied array of *quality, one-quart/liter-capacity water bottles* that can take extreme abuse. A common make is Nalgene. I wrap each Nalgene with two rows of duct tape that support a parachute cord loop with which I use to carry the bottle. The duct tape is supremely multiuse and has served me well for many tasks, from preventing blisters on feet and repairing rain gear to anchoring a splint made from a willow branch for a shattered patella. Six years ago, one of my Lexan plastic Nalgenes was run over by a truck hours before a film shoot with an Ohio news station (it's a long story). Other than a few abrasions, it's fine and I use it to this day. The older-style plastic Nalgenes, usually whitish in color, will degrade over time. I have had this type of plastic bottle shatter like glass when dropped. The weak link with Nalgene bottles is the plastic cap, as it's made from a softer plastic in order to grip and seal the container. I have had these caps shatter when my bottle was dropped. You can buy caps alone, they're about two dollars, and the wise person will pick up at least an extra cap per bottle.

Zipper-lock Freezer Baggies

I love zipper-lock freezer bags. Buy a name brand as there is a difference in quality and make sure to purchase "freezer" bags as they're thicker than standard zipper locks. Quality quart- and gallon-size freezer bags will hold their quantity in water, sealed in a standing position, without bursting open. As the quart-sized bag holds a quart and the gallon-sized bag holds a gallon of water, zipper-locks work well when using halogens such as iodine or chlorine to disinfect water. These bags have a very wide, flat mouth and can skim water from ground areas such as shallow puddles that other containers can't. They can also be scrunched up and reopened inside

water-bearing areas to collect liquid that a quart bottle won't fit into. They are the everyday, urban version of the ultimate collapsible water container and have zillions of uses. Emergency zipper-lock water containers can be beefed up with duct tape on the outside to improve their durability against abrasions and punctures. Freezer bags also show promise when used as a container to disinfect water by ultraviolet radiation.

Juice Bottles
Plastic or glass juice bottles should be thoroughly washed and dried before use. However, even after multiple washings, you may smell and taste a hint of papaya or whatever type of juice the container originally held—the plastic containers will retain the smell and taste the most.

Bleach Bottles
Chlorine bleach bottles that housed regular sodium hypochlorite 5.25 or 6.0 percent without added phosphates or scents are durable and well suited for water storage jugs. They are opaque as well, unlike most juice bottles, and thus are more attractive for long- term water storage in which algae might be an issue.

Milk Jugs
Although superior to an animal stomach, milk jugs and gallon water containers from the grocery store both suck for storing and transporting water. Although I have used both for temporary purposes, both the container and the lid are too flimsy. Compared to the other types of containers available to you, milk gallons

degrade quickly when exposed to the sun, especially here in the Southwest. Use these only when you have no other option.

Collapsible Containers, Both Large and Small

Plastic or rubber collapsible water containers provide water containment without the bulk of the container when empty. As mentioned, water is not compressible and requires a certain amount of volume when stored. This, of course, means that empty water containers will still be a space hog, using up room that might be at a premium for your family, especially in that efficiency apartment. The weak link of many collapsible containers is the thin, folded, or pleated plastic or rubber itself. The movement of the plastic/rubber creates weak areas within the plastic/rubber, which later leads to leaks. Many years ago there were quality containers being made, but from my modern experiments, most of the commercial options are crap. For this reason, don't have the bulk of your water storage containers be the collapsible variety.

"Camping Style," Five- to Seven-Gallon Jerry Cans

On my outdoor courses, I use plastic jerry cans a bunch. Most come with a cap and a funnel-like adapter that allow for easier pouring. Other caps convert into a spigot that allows you to open and close it as needed without formally capping the entire container. Some are cheaply made and others are not. Get the thickest plastic you can find and expect sooner or later for the caps and spouts to break. These are usually sold separately, like the caps to the Nalgenes, so pick up extras.

These containers are going to be heavy when full, from forty to fifty-six pounds, so limit their use to storing or transporting water for short distances. While all models have a built-in carrying handle, some designers had a clue and built in two handles, one at the top and the other toward the bottom. This allows for easier pouring and for two people to tackle the job of lugging the thing around. On some dry-camp field courses, I have my students carry full jerry cans to our base camp. The average carry distance for two healthy young males, depending on terrain and air temperature, is about a quarter to a half a mile before they want my head on a stick.

Fifty-five-Gallon Drums (Yes, This Is Considered a Small Container)

New or preowned fifty-five-gallon drums or barrels are extremely common on many survival supply Web sites. While all of them sold for storing water should be made from food-grade plastics, double check before ordering. Food wholesalers and restaurants might be another place to score some containers, although no doubt they will need cleaning and may reek of their former contents until the end of time. One of my fifty-five-gallon drums was a former home for olives. It has smelled of olives for more than seven years but I don't care as I don't use its water for human consumption. Even so, the smell is purely cosmetic.

Some have tried the following method to eliminate the infamous "pickle bucket stink" from their containers. First, wash the hell out of the inside of the container with dish soap. Next, use a paste solution of baking soda and hot water and scrub it some more and/or fill the container up with hot water and dissolve into the water a cup and a half of baking soda, stir it up good, and let the solution sit for a few days. Empty it out (hopefully on some thirsty plants) and fill it again with water and this time add a cup and a half of chlorine bleach and let it sit for a few days. Chlorine evaporates so seal the bucket as it sits. If your container doesn't have a cover, consider not wasting your time with it as it will be inferior for storing water anyway due to infiltrating debris and critters. Do this process during hot weather as it will slightly expand the plastic and allow greater access to more of the "pores" that hold onto the odor. Empty the container and let it dry with the top off. If this doesn't work, get used to the smell of pickles.

When filled with water, a fifty-five-gallon drum would herniate the Incredible Hulk if he tried to move it, so figure out where you want it before you fill it. Be careful about putting them in older homes with sketchy wooden floors or on second-story floors or higher as they will weigh more than 450 pounds when topped off. Some retailers sell cool little pumps that fit on top of the drums that allow your family to pump out the water. Other people cut into the bottom side of the drum and install a spigot. Others don't mind opening the top and using a pot to simply scoop out water, or they use a garden hose to siphon off the contents. Obviously, due to their great size, fifty-five-gallon drums are meant to store water in a static location. Even so, when mostly empty, they aren't that bad to move around and are relatively convenient and cheap for most homeowners to own a few.

Large Plastic Containers
In the Southwest, plastic water storage tanks of all shapes and sizes are a normal part of life. Many people, especially in rural areas, either haul their own or have water delivered to their homes via commercial water trucks. The most common tank size for home use is 3,000 gallons, due to its manageable size (approximately 95 inches by 105 inches), and the fact that water trucks usually hold 1,600 to 2,000 gallons. If you have the space, and choose to purchase a large-capacity plastic tank, choose one that is opaque (as most are) to inhibit algae growth and choose a low-key color such as black or dark green. Larger tanks come with an opening near the bottom, one near the top, and a manhole-type cover that allows for smaller folks to climb into the tank, if needed, for cleaning or repairs. Additional holes can easily be added wherever you like.

In the many years that I've had my tank, I've never had a problem with algae or anything else. Before I got around to capping off one of the top holes, a bird flew into the tank without my knowledge, became trapped, and died in the water. We drank the nondisinfected water anyway and watched the bird slowly dissolve until only the skull remained. Skittish guests refused to drink and brought their own water for months, thereby saving a great deal of water. I'm not recommending the dead bird trick as a way to be cheap with your water but it does demonstrate and affirm water being the ultimate natural dissolver when given sufficient time. My own mother still refuses to drink the water some seven years later.

Any clear container left filled with water and exposed to direct or indirect sunlight will in time grow algae. This bright green slime coats the inside of the container with surprising rapidity. While I'm no algaeologist, the varieties that I have dealt with over the years have given me zero problems. When a thin layer of it decides to separate itself from the side of my water jug, I simply consider the stuff free food and drink it down. Other people, perhaps not

WHAT ABOUT ALGAE ANYWAY ?

surprisingly, have been vocal with their objections to sharing my jug. Although it's typically the stuff you can't see floating around in water that causes the problems, I understand their protests. If your family freaks out about their greenish-looking bottles, help to prevent algae growth in the first place by making clear bottles opaque with covers or paint. Also, keep them out of direct or indirect sunlight and change the water inside often. If algae takes over your bottle, it will be nearly impossible to get out without mechanical scrubbing, which is difficult to accomplish in many containers with tiny openings. The easiest way to get rid of algae is to add a couple of tablespoons of bleach to the bottle along with a little water. Shake it up a bit, let it sit for a few minutes, then come back and shake it some more until the algae breaks off and/or dissolves in the chlorine solution. Rinse the bottle out and you're back in the good graces of your fussy family. Rotate your stored water supply every six months to a year whether it was used or not.

Some suggest that chlorine be added to large amounts of stored water that sit for a long period of time, but I have never found the need to do so. I'm drinking the same water now that

I added to my tank fourteen months ago (without adding any fresh water) and it's fine, sans any means of disinfection. While I cover how to use chlorine to disinfect smaller quantities of water on page 167, adding chlorine drop by drop to a 3,000 gallon water tank would have the same effect as being forced to listen to one Menudo song. For those who insist on adding chlorine bleach to large amounts of stored water, sans Menudo, the recipe is as follows.

HOW TO DISINFECT 1,000 GALLONS OF WATER WITH CHLORINE BLEACH

I went straight to the source of water disinfection information for this one and talked with Rick Pinney, water superintendent for the city of Prescott, Arizona. He kindly spent nearly an hour with me on the phone going through complex math formulas that had me close to cutting my wrists. In the end, he took pity on my anemic math skills and just gave me the answer. Thanks, Rick!

The following is used to treat 1,000 gallons of nonpotable water with sodium hypochlorite 5.25 or 6 percent to achieve a concentration of one parts per million. If you're wishing to disinfect more or less water, do the math.

The following dosage is given in three different measurements that all equate to the same amount. Choose whichever *one* works best for you.

Use 1/3 cup chlorine bleach per 1,000 gallons of water

Or

2 1/2 ounces of chlorine bleach per 1,000 gallons of water

Or

14 1/2 teaspoons of chlorine bleach per 1,000 gallons of water.

Although larger cylindrical plastic tanks are not meant to be buried, I have mine buried in sand a few feet so the pipes running to the house aren't susceptible to damage from freezing temperatures. For purely emergency use, a family can pick the proper tank location (the company who sells you the tank should be able to supply you with how to prepare the ground for the size you purchase), attach a valve to the bottom opening, fill the tank with water, and fill smaller containers as needed without the headache of freezing pipes.

While these tanks are fairly UV resistant, they will take a beating in direct sunlight over the years. That said, I've seen tanks that have baked in the Arizona sun for more than a decade and they look brand new. If an idiot shoots at your tank, or it is somehow damaged short of a gaping hole, plastic tanks can be repaired by the use of a plastic rod of material that is simply melted into or over the leak.

Glass Containers

There are some advantages to using glass containers. Potentially harmful chemicals cannot leach into the water from glass. Water doesn't pick up weird tastes from glass and glass does not absorb odors. Ultraviolet rays from the sun have no effect on glass and glass containers will last almost indefinitely if not damaged.

The disadvantages to glass containers are pretty obvious. They are breakable (and the resulting mess can cause serious injury) and nonrepairable. They are heavy compared to plastic. It is rare to find any glass containers over a one- or two-gallon capacity. Algae will grow in them unless they are painted or covered. They are noncombustible, but they may crack or shatter with enough heat. They may crack if exposed to freezing temperatures when filled with water.

Small Glass Containers

Small containers of a gallon or two are about all you'll find, the most common being those that held apple juice. Look over the advantages and disadvantages of the various containers explained and decide whether glass fits with your water storage plan.

Galvanized Metal

Galvanized metal containers have some advantages. They are durable, repairable, noncombustible, and are commonly available (especially in rural areas) in a wide variety of sizes.

The disadvantages are that they are expensive and heavy, even when empty. They will eventually corrode and the reflective metal is highly visible unless it's painted. The zinc coating may also present a health problem. Because of the zinc, aquaculture folks won't use galvanized containers to raise their fish; they use plastic.

Small Metal Containers

Before plastic, metal buckets, milk jugs, and coolers were common. I have adapted old metal milk jugs for back-country water containers and have always had the problem of eventual corrosion and rust— and drinking flakes of rust is a drag. Although you can sand and paint the inside with some sort of paint that's nontoxic, it's a

"**IN THE END,** our society will be defined not only by what **WE CREATE** but by what **WE REFUSE TO DESTROY.**"
—John Sawhill

lot of work, and work you're destined to repeat if you use the container for long-term water storage. The most practical household application for storing water in metal containers is to fill extra cooking pots and pans.

Large Metal Containers

Many ranches and farms in the West use massive galvanized metal tanks that hold the results of the neighboring windmill. These can be purchased in a variety of sizes for home use as well. Check the pros and cons of plastic and metal and decide what's best for you.

Wonderful Water Storage Containers You May Already Have at Home

Important Note: Know where the water intake valve to your home is located. If there are reports of broken water or sewer lines in your area, or if you're recommended to do so by the authorities, you will need to shut off this valve to prevent contaminated water from entering your home. **For those living in apartments or other places where accessing a water intake valve is slim, recognize that the water coming into your home after a disaster may be heavily contaminated with sewage, dangerous chemicals, or other substances that could make you ill or kill you.**

Bathtubs

While many newer homes and apartments have opted out the bathtub in favor of a shower, the vast majority of households have this ready and willing container ready to fill. In an emergency, your hydration will far outweigh how you look and smell so buck up and fill it to the rim while you can. Watch the kids for accidental drowning and keep the water as clean as possible. It's doubtful that any tub is clean enough to drink from but that's not the point. You can always disinfect the water later for drinking.

Swimming Pools, Jacuzzis, and Hot Tubs

All of the above contain a bonanza of emergency water. No matter how nasty the water, waterborne pathogens can be killed with the methods explained in this book so be thankful you have something to disinfect. Added chlorine eventually evaporates over time and loses its punch so don't worry about superchlorinated water. If you've added chemicals to your pool or spa, check with the manufacturer to see if you're out of luck to use the water as drinking water, even with disinfection methods. If it isn't suitable for drinking or cooking, you can always use it for keeping clean and other hygiene needs.

The Back of the Toilet

The back of your toilet, NOT the bowl, will have water that should be potable after disinfection, just to be on the safe side. Do not use water that has been chemically treated or that appears "blue."

Sinks

As the average U.S. household turns on its faucets an average of seventy times each day, leave at least one sink free for washing, cooking, and the like. I have been in some homes that have massive kitchen sinks that could bathe an eight-year-old. If this is you, hubba-hubba, store what water you can! To use the existing water trapped in your pipes, find the highest faucet in the home and turn it on (and leave it on for this exercise) to let air into the pipes. Water should then freely drain from the lowest faucet in the house.

Water Beds

Water that has been sitting in your bed since the turn of the century may have become a toxic cocktail. Check with the manufacturer to see what kind of plastic or rubber your bed is made from, and if it imparts noxious chemicals into the water over time. Fungicides added to the water may also make it unsafe to use as drinking water. If not suitable for drinking, even after disinfection, it's always a welcome commodity for hygiene and sanitary needs.

Water Heaters

Many homes are equipped with old-style water heaters that store forty gallons or more. These can be accessed and drained if need be for potable water. Be sure the

"When the **WELL IS DRY,** we know the **WORTH OF WATER.**"

—Benjamin Franklin

electricity or gas is off and open the drain valve at the bottom of the tank. Turn off the water intake valve at the tank and turn on a hot water faucet in the house, lower than the water heater itself if possible. When the crisis is over, remember to refill the tank with water before electricity or gas is hooked back up to the heater. The water found in *hot water heaters* such as those designed for heating entire homes should **not** be used for drinking water.

If you have the money and the opportunity, consider purchasing an "on-demand" water heater. This little gem, popular in Europe for years, heats only the water you're using at the time. If you're a wasteful slob, this means you could take an everlasting hot shower. If you're a responsible human being, you'll save immense amounts of energy, i.e., money, over time as the water heater is not constantly turning on and off to keep those forty gallons of water hot for your next use.

Ice Cubes and Liquids in Canned Goods
Although miniscule, the water from melted ice cubes is potable and should be utilized. The average household also has many types of canned goods that contain large amounts of liquid such as canned fruit, tomato juice, and fruit juices. None of these, however, should be thought of as replacing water to combat dehydration. Although many canned vegetables contain water, they are typically laced with sodium and should not be thought of as drinking water. It should be saved along with the vegetable to be used to cook the contents of the can or consumed directly from the can with the vegetable itself.

Radiators in Vehicles
DO NOT drink water from radiators or use it topically on the skin or clothing to increase evaporative cooling. The chemicals in antifreeze can be lethal inside the body and irritating outside the body.

Collect, Collect, Collect Your Water!
There are approximately one million miles worth of city and county water pipelines and aqueducts in the United States and Canada—enough to circle the earth forty times. If your only access to water is through these pipelines, or a private well in which the pump runs off grid power, you won't have any idea if and when your spigot will run dry, so start collecting water the instant that you are able to do so in a disaster situation. Although it will seem like a hassle to have containers all over the house filled with liquid, you will eventually use them up. Use the containers first which are the biggest inconvenience to have filled with water. *If you live in an arid region or are dependent upon "grid water," I can't possibly overemphasize the importance of gathering and storing every possible drop of water that you can.* I don't care how much food, ammunition, firewood, and flashlight batteries you have stored, *if you fail to have an adequate supply of drinking water, you and your loved ones will die.*

Making Your Water Safe to Drink: The Art of Water Disinfection

"AFTER A MAJOR CATASTROPHE, POPULATIONS ARE PARTICULARLY VULNERABLE TO WATERBORNE
DISEASES, AND OUR ABILITY TO PRODUCE LARGE QUANTITIES OF SAFE WATER AND PROVIDE ADEQUATE
SANITATION QUICKLY HAS BEEN CRUCIAL IN ENSURING THAT THESE COMMUNITIES WERE NOT SUB-
JECTED TO A SECOND DISASTER."
  —MARKKU NISKALA, SECRETARY-GENERAL OF THE INTERNATIONAL FEDERATION OF
  RED CROSS AND RED CRESCENT SOCIETIES IN RESPONSE TO THE DECEMBER 2006 TSUNAMI

For centuries various means have been used to make water safe to drink. A couple
of recorded methods date back to 2000 BC. One states that water must be exposed
to sunlight and then filtered with charcoal. Another, that nonpotable water must
be boiled and then have a piece of copper dipped within the water, seven times no
less, before finally being filtered. The actual mechanisms of disinfection, however,
through the knowledge and destruction of otherwise unseen dangerous pathogens have only been around for a hundred years or so.

There are more than 58,900 public water supply systems in the United States.
Approximately 85 percent of U.S. residents receive their water from public water
facilities while the remaining 15 percent supply their own water from private wells
or other sources. It wasn't until 1974, when the Safe Drinking Water Act (SDWA) was
enacted, that public drinking water supplies were protected on a federal (national)
level in the United States. Today, potable water meets over a hundred different
standards for drinking water quality. That said, others argue that there are more
than 2,100 known drinking water contaminants that may be present in tap water,
including several known poisons.

It doesn't matter how plentiful water is if it's unsafe to drink. Disasters of all
types are notorious for fouling whatever drinkable water a community had and
making it a challenge for emergency response personnel to disinfect or deliver
potable water to the population. I remember vividly the news footage of hundreds
of people begging for water from their rooftops during the aftermath of Hurricane
Katrina while New Orleans stood submerged in, well, water. Waterborne, diarrheal
illnesses took their toll as norovirus, *Salmonella,* and *toxigenic* and *nontoxigenic V.
cholerae* were confirmed among Katrina evacuees.

Even in good times, the Centers for Disease Control (CDC) receive notification
of more than 4,000 cases per year of illness due to drinking water contamination.
Water can be contaminated by organic and inorganic substances from land erosion;
the disintegration of minerals, rotting vegetation, and rotting animal and human
bodies; earth- and waterborne biological pathogens; industrial chemical pollutants; and microorganisms from animal and human waste.

There are many ways to disinfect nonpotable water, but I'll limit my how-
to writings to the most common household methods. The term "water disinfection" means killing or removing the pathogens or bugs that make us ill. While its
usage is technically associated with chemical halogens like iodine and chlorine,
it can be applied to filtration and heat as well. The term "water purification," as
preached in the majority of survival books and elsewhere, involves the removal

WANTED

BACTERIA

PROTOZOA

PARASITES

VIRUSES

THE FEARSOME FOUR
DEAD OR DEADER

CONTACT SHERIFF

of organic and inorganic chemicals and particulate matter and deals with how water *looks*, *tastes*, and *smells*. It has nothing to do with the art of eliminating harmful microorganisms that will have you barfing up a lung and filling your pants with excrement. Severe diarrhea can significantly increase your body's fluid loss, up to twenty-five quarts (liters) in a twenty-four-hour period! Death from dehydration caused by diarrhea is one of the biggest killers of people worldwide, especially infants and small children. Estimates are that, worldwide, 28,000 to 68,000 people die *each day* from diseases caused by contaminated water and unhealthy conditions.

There are four families of critters that cause us gastrointestinal grief: protozoa, parasites, bacteria, and viruses. Some of these creatures mean business and can make you very dead if not dealt with sooner or later. For our purposes, all of these creatures, especially the viral variety, are measured in microns. They are thus extremely small and can't be seen with the naked eye. It's usually what you *can't* see in nonpotable water that hurts you, not the stuff that may be visibly swimming around doing the backstroke. This is an important realization, as your family may scream bloody murder if they have to drink safe water with "stuff" swimming in it, and yet blissfully chug down clean-looking water that's laced with harmful waterborne pathogens. In regard to the halogens described below, the various harmful microorganisms have different rates of resistance to being killed. The easiest for halogens to kill are bacterias; the most difficult, parasitic ova and larva. As both are "invisible," it really doesn't matter, other than reminding you to use caution when treating your water.

Tincture of Iodine 2%

Iodine is a chemical halogen available in many forms including 5–7 percent solution, 10 percent solution, tablets, crystals and 2 percent tincture. Although I prefer the 2 percent tincture, regardless of what form you choose it must remain in contact with the water for a certain period of time in order for it to kill the pathogens. The amount of contact time required varies in regard to the water's temperature and pH, how strong the iodine solution was made, the type of microorganisms that are present, and the quantity of nitrogen compounds and particulate matter found within the water. Of the four families of waterborne pathogens, iodine kills them all with the exception of the protozoa *Cryptosporidium parvum*, which infects many herd animals including cows, goats, sheep, deer, and elk.

"MUDDY WATER,
let stand—
BECOMES CLEAR."
—Lao Tzu

HOW TO DISINFECT ONE QUART OF NONPOTABLE WATER WITH TINCTURE OF IODINE 2%

5 to 10 Drops

TEMPERATE
+
CLEAR
=
30 MINUTES

WICKED TIN
WALLOP
THE
CAT

Dribble disinfected water through threads before drinking

In most situations, I use five drops of tincture of iodine 2 percent per one U.S. quart of water (there are four quarts to a gallon), although as many as ten drops per quart may be used. (Note: A liter of water is just a bit more than a quart but I've never found the need to add more iodine or any other halogen to compensate for this.) For most water sources, let the five drops sit for thirty minutes before drinking. The medical books say twenty minutes, but I like to add in the extra protection of more time. This next point is critical, so pay attention. *If the water you are about to disinfect is NOT clear and temperate, you will need to add more iodine per quart and/or let the iodine sit longer before the water is safe to drink.* Turbidity or water's "cloudiness" is caused by suspended particulate matter such as clay, silt, plankton, and other microscopic organisms and is often the reason some water tastes and smells ghastly. Funky-looking surface water is a common occurrence in many locales and contains ten times the organic carbon content of aquifer groundwater. Waterborne pathogens can absorb into or already be imbedded within the floating matter to such an extent that organisms in the center of the chunks are somewhat protected from disinfection methods. Iodine is a halogen and will readily bond to the nitrogen compounds, organic and inorganic, present within the water's turbidity. These nitrogen compounds, commonly referred to as pond scum, tamper with the halogen's ability to kill pathogens and require either more sit time for the water to disinfect or adding greater amounts of halogen, or both.

Filtering out water turbidity decreases the number of microorganisms present in the first place, while decreasing the amount of iodine needed to disinfect the water. Doing so also makes your water look and smell a lot better. Water clarity can be improved by simply letting it sit or by straining it through a piece of clothing, bandana, paper towel, coffee filter, or any tightly woven material.

Iodine and halogens, in general, are very *temperature* sensitive, and take longer to do their work when water is cold. Thus, the colder the water the more contact time is required in order to successfully eliminate bad bugs. For extremely cold water let the five drops sit for two to three hours or longer if possible. To cut down on the sit time you can also add more iodine, up to ten drops per quart, although this will make the water taste strongly of iodine, and it's not exactly a kid-tested and mother-approved flavor. Having several water containers will let you stagger your disinfection times by treating some while drinking others. This allows the disinfecting water to sit for long periods of time by using less iodine, thus conserving the precious substance and making your disinfected water taste a whole lot better.

The pH of the water being disinfected is also a factor. Halogens form several compounds, each with different disinfection rates, by oxidizing in water. How well each compound works is determined by pH. In general, the optimal pH for halogen disinfection is 6.5 to 7.5. The more alkaline the water, the greater the dose of iodine is required. If water is extremely alkaline or acidic, it's usually too nasty to drink anyway, so don't be overly concerned with the water's pH.

If the water you're disinfecting is highly suspicious and difficult to filter, *add more iodine* rather than just prolonging the contact time. When dealing with extremely questionable water sources, both the color and the taste of iodine-treated water can be used as rough indicators for the proper disinfection amount. Under these circumstances, if the iodine taste created makes the kids complain even louder and the contents of your container appear yellow to light brown, you've successfully achieved 0.6 parts per million or greater, which is what you want.

In summary, strain or filter the water to be disinfected if necessary through a piece of cloth to get rid of organic and inorganic matter. For heavier particulate matter, you can also let the water stand for several hours in a larger container such as a five-gallon bucket. Next, add no more than ten drops of iodine per U.S. quart or liter (I use five drops per quart or liter). Give the container a little shake. If the water temperature is fairly temperate, let the solution disinfect for thirty minutes. If the water is cold, increase the iodine's disinfection time. Before drinking, partially unscrew the lid of the container it is in and turn the container upside down, thereby allowing treated water to dribble down the threads. It only takes a drop of water containing pathogens to get ill. This action also flushes out any untreated water that may have been hiding in the threads of the container. By the way, if you flavor water to make it more palatable and the flavoring contains vitamin C (ascorbic acid), it will neutralize the iodine (and its nasty taste!) before it does its killing. Wait thirty minutes or longer after disinfecting before adding the flavoring! A few years ago, zinc brushes were available to rid the water of its iodine taste and could be found at most camping stores.

Liquid tincture of iodine 2 percent has a much longer shelf life, up to several years longer, than the compressed iodine tablets on the market. Iodine tablets, available at most camping stores, are relatively expensive and very susceptible to heat, light, and moisture degradation. If you choose to use the pill form, or that's all you have, the directions for their use should be on the bottle, usually two tablets per quart of water. Tincture of iodine 2 percent comes in its own unbreakable, one-ounce plastic bottle with a built-in cohesion dropper inside the cap, and retails for under two bucks. The bottle is typically tinted or opaque, giving the iodine greater protection from light sources. Circle the bottle with brightly colored tape for better visibility and write "Iodine" in permanent marker on its surface to minimize misunderstandings. The tincture is widely available and can be purchased at most discount pharmacies. If the pharmacy doesn't have any in stock, they should be willing to order some. Make sure to purchase the reddish-colored iodine as the drops from the "denatured" or clear iodine are hard to see hit the water. Another advantage of iodine 2 percent is its use as a topical wound disinfectant. When I was a kid, my skin was stained with iodine a good part of the time due to an assortment of scratches, cuts, abrasions, and punctures. In short, this compact, lightweight, cheap, easily available, globally effective, multiuse, extended shelf life, handy-to-use product is worth its weight in intestinal parasites for the urban and suburban survivor and outdoor enthusiast alike.

WARNING! If you look closely at the bottle of tincture of iodine 2 percent you will see a skull and crossbones with the word "poison" written underneath. In the early 1900s, iodine was used to disinfect entire town water supplies. The U.S. Navy

"Water is the **MOST NEGLECTED NUTRIENT** in your diet **BUT** one of the **MOST VITAL.**"
—Kelly Barton

AND YOU THINK YOU GOT PROBLEMS?

- ⊃ More than 1.1 billion of the world's people don't have regular access to clean water.
- ⊃ One billion people must walk three hours or more to obtain drinking water.
- ⊃ In Mexico, 15 percent of the population must haul or carry water.
- ⊃ Nearly 2 percent of U.S. homes have no running water.
- ⊃ More than 2 billion people on earth do not have a safe supply of water.
- ⊃ Today, at least 400 million people live in regions with severe water shortages.
- ⊃ There are more than 70,000 known water pollutants.
- ⊃ Nearly 10,000 children under the age of five in developing countries die as a result of illnesses by using impure water.
- ⊃ Worldwide, waterborne diseases cause approximately 15 million deaths each year.

has performed multi-month studies on unknowing shipbound sailors in which extreme amounts of iodine were added to the ships' drinking water. So far, nobody has reported a problem or sired a kid with three heads. Prison systems as well have performed their patriotic duty by secretly experimenting on hundreds of inmates with no problems being reported. Regardless, *iodine is recommended for short-term use only, no longer than thirty days*. The halogen iodine does have the following contraindications so know your family's medical history before using it. **Do NOT use iodine water disinfection methods of any type if you are pregnant or have a known allergy to iodine or a thyroid problem**.

10% Povidone–Iodine Solution

Most everyone has this product in their home first-aid kit, more commonly recognized under the trade name *Betadine*. 10 percent povidone-iodine replaced tincture of iodine 2 percent as a topical wound disinfectant largely because povidone doesn't sting when it's applied to a wound. (Tinctures contain alcohol, which causes the stinging.) Povidone itself is nontoxic and was used as a blood extender during World War II. Regardless of the larger number—10 percent as opposed to 2 percent —use eight drops of 10 percent povidone-iodine per quart or liter of water instead of five drops. For a maximum dose, similar to using ten drops of tincture of iodine 2 percent instead of five, don't use more than sixteen drops of 10 percent povidone-iodine per quart of water. Buy the generic version of this product, not the trade name, at the

INGENIOUS IMPROVISED EYEDROPPER

To use the halogens iodine and chlorine you'll need to measure them in drops (or gtts) to disinfect your water. The easiest way to do this is to have an eyedropper attached with a piece of string to the gallon of bleach, or rubber-banded or taped to the one-ounce bottle of iodine. (Most iodine bottles usually have a built-in dropper based on cohesion on the inside of the cap.) If you don't have an eyedropper, or lose the one you had, you can easily improvise a dropper from a spoon and a piece of paper.

Make a strip of paper three or four inches long and a quarter inch wide. It can be torn or cut with scissors so don't get fancy about it. Then, take an ordinary kitchen spoon, fill it halfway with iodine or chlorine, and place most of the paper in the spoon with about an inch overhanging the tip of the spoon. The strip of paper will saturate with the halogen, and with the spoon slightly tipped, will draw by capillary action, drop by drop, the halogen down the strip. If you want more drops faster, slightly increase the tilt of the spoon. If you're the visual type, check out the picture in the photo section.

grocery or drugstore to avoid paying high prices. Other than the variation in the dose, follow the same guidelines as used for 2 percent tincture above.

Chlorine Bleach: Sodium Hypochlorite 5.25 and 6%

Chlorine, like iodine, is a halogen that is commonly used to disinfect water. Sodium hypochlorite ($NaOCl$) was initially tinkered with in 1785 by the Frenchman Berthollet, who first used it to bleach cotton. It has a pH of about 11 and is relatively unstable. It's widely used for a variety of purposes in many industries such as agriculture, chemical, glass, food, paper, pharmaceutical, and waste disposal.

While in the past iodine was used to disinfect town water supplies, chlorine has taken its place. Hypochlorite was first used to disinfect water to help combat cholera epidemics in London in 1854. It was used much later as a routine water treatment, initially in Belgium in 1902. Here in the United States, its first use in disinfecting city water happened in Jersey City, New Jersey, and Chicago, Illinois, in 1908. While the water treatment plant guys and gals use the big chlorine guns, we common folk have access to sodium hypochlorite 5.25 and 6 percent, otherwise known as chlorine bleach. For water disinfection purposes, buy bleach without added phosphates, dyes, or perfumes. It's commonly available at practically every supermarket, drug, and discount store in the nation, and if you purchase the generic brand, will cost less then two dollars for a gallon. This gallon will treat hundreds of quarts of nonpotable water while sanitizing your emergency potty, help you dispose of a corpse, clean your sink, bathtub, shower, and floor, as well as assist in removing the bloodstains from your shirt after fighting the neighbor over limited emergency supplies if you fail to act on the advice given in this book.

Short of drinking bleach outright, or using ridiculous amounts when disinfecting water, its toxicity is limited. It is corrosive and will stain clothing so keep it in an unbreakable container and use it with care. Hypochlorite solutions will eventually lose their chlorine over time as the active chlorine evaporates at a rate of 0.75 gram per day from the solution. Heat disintegrates it, as do air and sunlight, certain metals, and other things not normally found in a household. Thus *rotate* your sodium hypochlorite stock because when it has been stored for a long time, it becomes inactive. Store it in a cool area in an opaque, airtight container. Stay on the safe side with the potency of your chlorine and replace your gallon of bleach every year, whether you've opened it or not.

Since it is a halogen, like iodine, chlorine will readily bond to nitrogen compounds, organic and inorganic, present within the water. These nitrogen compounds, or pond scum, mess with the halogen's ability to kill, requiring either more sit time for the water to disinfect or greater amounts of halogen. Strain your water first through a bandana or some other article of clothing or let the water sit for a few hours in a five-gallon bucket to let the unwanted stuff settle to the bottom. This is especially important when using chlorine bleach, as organic matter bonds with the chlorine itself, actually changing its chemical makeup into something called *chloramine*, which does nothing to disinfect your water. Chlorine also doesn't work well with alkaline water and doesn't like being physically jostled, like being bounced around in a backpack. These are the main reasons I don't like it for disinfecting water in a wilderness setting, although I know people who are allergic to iodine and choose to use chlorine.

Important Note: I have seen conflicting data from reputable medical and chemical engineering sources regarding sodium hypochlorite's effectiveness against *Giardia Lambia* and *Cryptosporidium*. Some say it doesn't work and some say it does. Keep this in mind when using this halogen when these two critters are suspect.

Disinfecting Water with Chlorine Bleach

To use chlorine for disinfecting *clear* and *temperate water*, add two to four drops of chlorine bleach per U.S. quart. Give the container a little shake and let it sit for thirty minutes. Slightly open the cap, dribble some disinfected water down the threads, and smell the water. IT SHOULD SMELL LIKE CHLORINE. If it doesn't, add another drop or two of bleach and let it sit for another thirty minutes. As stated above, chlorine is sensitive to the temperature of the water. For cold water, either add another drop or two of chlorine and/or let the water sit longer, two to three hours or more, in order for it to properly disinfect. As a side note, normal tap water contains about 0.2 to 0.5 ppm (parts per million) of chlorine, swimming pools contain 1.5 to 3.0 ppm, and hot tubs 3.0 to 5.0 ppm.

Attention! When using iodine or chlorine to disinfect suspect water sources, if in doubt, *add more halogen and/or let the water sit longer.*

Filters

The first water filter was developed in 1685 by the Italian physician Lu Antonio Porzo. The filter consisted of both a settling and a sand filtration unit. Later, in 1746, French scientist Joseph Amy received the first patent for a filter design which used filters created from wool, sponges, and charcoal. It was used in households as early as 1750, and the trend seems to have continued.

Today many homes have water filters under their sinks to make municipal water taste and look better. Backpacking and camping stores are chockful of por-

table water filters that are designed specifically to screen out harmful waterborne pathogens. Most of them accomplish their task in the same way, by having some sort of filter material that physically "filters out" the bad bugs. Some water filters are large and, while semiportable, are designed for the stationary disinfection of large volumes of water for group expeditions. A few water filters are massive and are enjoyed by entire communities. The first U.S. water plant utilizing filters was built in 1872 in Poughkeepsie, New York. Other water filters are gravity fed and are ideal for use in the home. They can be purchased at many hardware stores and home building supply centers. Simply add the water in question into the catchment basin in the top, and it slowly percolates through the filters, screening out whatever pathogens the maker claims . . . you hope. If you purchase a filter of this type, make sure its intention is the filtering out of harmful pathogens (or chemicals), not simply prettying up how the water appears.

A filter's effectiveness is typically rated in *microns*. Different pathogens are different sizes, and the more expensive filters filter out the smallest, or those of the tiniest microns, in size. Viruses are so dinky that many will not be caught by any filter. To compensate for this, some manufacturers offer the option of a screw-on, iodine-impregnated post-filter that disinfects your water after it's filtered. As some water filters are expensive and can run more than two hundred and fifty dollars, the reader might wonder why people don't simply use iodine that costs less then two bucks and can disinfect wounds as well. My answer is, buyer ego or ignorance and effective marketing. If you have a known allergy to iodine, that's one good reason to use a filter (without the iodine post-filter), but you will still be at the mercy of most viruses. Currently, this is not a big deal in the United States, but it is a serious concern on your visit to India. Make note that after a disaster and the potential contamination of potable water sources with poor sanitary practices, dead bodies, and God knows what else, viruses can make a roaring comeback in your sleepy little town.

Although an important part of your survival plan is the creation of potable water, water filters offer up only one use, violating the credo of multiuse gear. Most are expensive, and all backpacking varieties are mechanical, and mechanical things have many moving parts, which can and do fail under use. I have seen more than one brand-new water filter choke in the field, much to the dismay of its owner. In the Southwest, where many rivers and streams look like chocolate milk due to sediments, filters can clog within minutes. They then go through a vicious cycle: cleaned, clogged, cleaned, clogged, etc. A filter is usually operated by pumping a knob or lever with the hand, and the more clogged a filter becomes, the harder it is to operate. I have witnessed people in a sweaty lather trying to coax their filter to poop out a quart of water. If you have the time and the container, pour gathered water into your trusty five-gallon bucket to allow sediments to settle. Lighter foreign objects can be skimmed off the top. Many backpacking filters have a foam float attached to the gathering hose that allows you to adjust where it's stationed in the water so you're not sucking dirt off the bottom. All but the most expensive water filters will need their filters changed on a regular basis so buy spares. Even the more expensive ceramic filters will eventually wear out from repeated cleanings so factor this into your family's preparedness plan.

Some filters claim to filter out certain amounts of radioactive material, heavy metals, and other chemical contaminants. The problem with these claims is, how are we to know? The people who have the real money to invest in whether any disinfection method works as claimed, be it a filter or halogen, are the medical community and the military. My local laboratory charges more than one hundred dollars to inspect for *each* pathogen that may or may not be present within questionable water.

All in all, I do appreciate filters for their convenience, but don't limit your water disinfection strategy to its mechanical mercy. One of the main advantages of filtration for certain types of gathered city water is that it is bound to remove at least some pollutants.

Filtering Toxic Chemicals, Heavy Metals, and Pollutants

Killing organic waterborne pathogens is one thing, filtering out toxic chemicals, heavy metals, and other pollutants is an entirely different matter. A simple Web search will pull up dozens of water filter options that deal with waterborne pathogens and/or chemical contaminants. Many can be installed under the kitchen sink or attach to the water faucet itself.

Whole-house water filters are the parents of their kitchen-sink kids and can be quite complex. Many households use both, as whole-house systems filter water from where it enters the home but do nothing about potential lead contamination in the house's plumbing system. Most whole-house water filters use a four-stage filtration system to remove harmful contaminants from water. The first stage removes sediments in the water that may clog the remainder of the filter, reducing its effectiveness. The second stage utilizes a chemical process called water atomization that alters the molecular structure of chlorine and turns it into harmless zinc

"FILTHY water CANNOT BE WASHED."

—West African proverb

chloride. The third and fourth stages of filtration involve filters made from bituminous-activated carbon and coconut-shell activated carbon that filter out chemicals, pesticides, and other pollutants.

The Environmental Protection Agency (EPA) has two definitions for devices that filter out undesirable stuff from water. For an item to technically be called a "filter," it must be capable of a "4 Log" contaminant reduction, meaning at least 99.99 percent of the water's contaminants are removed. For an item to be called a "purifier," it must be capable of a "7 Log" contaminant reduction, meaning that 99.99999 percent of all contaminants are removed. Thus a purifier is one thousand times as effective as a filter. A 4 Log filter is probably sufficient for many conditions and, of course, will be cheaper to purchase than a purifier, but the choice is yours. In any event, the old adage "better safe than sorry" goes a long way when one of your most critical resources for survival (water) is unfit to drink.

Unfortunately, almost all in-line filter options count on things being normal in Urbania to function—ample water pressure being the most obvious. When the power grid is down, those who rely on grid power won't have the electricity to provide the pressure needed to run water through the pipes and filters in their homes. The best option is gravity, and there are several smaller gravity filters on the market. These usually consist of a cylinder in which nonpotable water is poured into the top and allowed to settle over time through the filtering membranes to the bottom where it's drained off and ready to drink. In my home, I don't need pressurized water entering the house, as I placed my water storage tank higher than the house so gravity could do the job. I had to special order a particular faucet valve, as almost all on the market require pressurized water lines to operate, but that was the only oddity required.

The membranes in all filters and purifiers will eventually clog and need cleaning or replacement. Because of this, it's wise to have an extra one around the house. Most replacement filters are not cheap, but the quality of the filter should be why you purchased the unit in the first place—not for how pretty it looks in the kitchen. The life of the membrane can be increased dramatically if nonpotable water is carefully filtered beforehand or at least allowed to settle, thereby eliminating all visible signs of particulate matter. If you're going to invest in a costly home-based water filter or purifier, you want it to concentrate on screening out harmful pathogens, chemicals, pollutants, and heavy metals, not the pond scum you were too lazy to screen out beforehand.

Hopeful Homemade Filters?

A few high-buck water filters claim to screen out almost anything undesirable. Some with reusable filters even claim to screen out radioactive radiation, but how to clean the radiation out of the filter remains a mystery. As with all things self-reliant, it's your job to research which water filter or purifier is best for your family. Don't buy cheap crap, but at the same time take a careful, skeptical look at what manufacturers claim, even with the successful independent test data that a few have.

Military survival books and others usually include a homemade water filter that can be made with improvised items in the field. I have seen illustrations using the leg(s) from a pair of pants, or two containers filled with various makeshift filtering materials. Some of these materials, such as carbon from a fire and sand, have been used for thousands of years for the same purpose.

So let's say you tie off the bottom of one or both legs of a pair of pants. Then you hang the pants and fill the void within the legs with layers of carbon, sand, and maybe polyester quilting, such as from a mattress pad. You pour water into the top of the pants and let it slowly gravity filter through the layered materials to drip into a waiting clean container below. Now what? Is the water safe to drink? Is it free from toxic chemicals, nitrates, pesticides, pollutants, and garbage that the other water disinfection methods won't eliminate? How can you visibly know for sure when dealing with contaminants that are invisible to the naked eye? When will the damp and dark filter material start to breed weird microorganisms that will then find their way into your filtered water?

"ALWAYS DRINK upstream from the HERD."
—Old farmer's quote

I don't know anyone who has used any improvised filtering method who has had the resulting filtered water tested for the effectiveness of its methodology. Even if it were effective, there is no guarantee that the results would be identical the next time due to tremendous variables. If your family has no other option, by all means, improvise whatever you can to make your water safer to drink. But don't exclusively rely on the sketchy methods presented in many survival books for the safety of your family—especially when you have a choice!

Boiling

Boiling is hands down the oldest means of disinfecting water. You'll need a container, the water in question, and a heat source. Although almost any fireproof container will work for conventional boiling, it helps to have a container that's suited for the job. A great multiple-use pot is two to four quarts in capacity, stainless steel, with a tight-fitting lid and bail (handle). I can't say enough about this simple yet masterful piece of gear. You can use it for many things: melting snow or ice for water, cooking dinner, making coffee, storing other survival gear, digging, etc. The next time you see a cable channel show documenting rare indigenous peoples hidden away in some remote jungle, check out what they have for "white man" gear. As the camera pans over the village, you'll probably spy steel machetes and a metal pot or two, traded for God knows what. The natives are masters of their environment and can make fire from sticks and rope from plants, but ahh, that steel edge and that shiny thing that can be put straight onto the fire without burning up . . . wow, now that's worth having. Are you laughing yet? Then try leaving all of your metal containers behind on your next camping trip—without bringing your prepackaged fancy camping food. Metal containers have truly revolutionized the world, just one reason why they appear on my "Really Cool, Gotta Have It, Multiple-Use Stuff" list in a future chapter.

The tight-fitting lid, or some improvised lid if one is not available, will save you fuel (as the water will boil quicker) and water (that would be lost through evaporation), both time-precious commodities. The bail or handle allows you to easily carry the pot or hang it from a branch or wire for improvised backyard or back alley business. Stainless steel is tough and safe to use long term for water or foods without the potential health risk of aluminum.

There's a lot of bogus garbage on the Internet and in books about how long to boil your water to make it safe to drink. Heat works exponentially over time to kill pathogens. Dairy farms don't boil milk, they pasteurize it. South of the border in Mexico, if you're unfortunate enough to get stuck drinking tap water, people in the know recommend that you at least drink water from the hot side of the faucet, after letting it cool down, of course. At sea level, water boils at 212 degrees F (100 degrees C). Even if you only have enough heat to get your water up to 180 degrees F (82 degrees C), spend the several minutes it takes to let it cool down, especially with a lid on the pot, and the heat will still kill all harmful pathogens. Armed with this knowledge, you can better understand why I'm *not* recommending that you boil the hell out of your water for a half an hour or more. I explain more about the pasteurization process after this segment.

Disinfecting Water by Boiling

To disinfect your water by boiling, fill the pot with water and put the lid on. If you don't have a lid, improvise something such as setting another pot on top. Put the pot over your heat source and simply *bring it to a boil*. This action alone will kill all pathogens, as some species die as the water is being heated up. If you live at elevation, or are dealing with truly sketchy water, let the water boil for a minute or two. When water boils, the level of oxygen dissolved in the water decreases, making it taste "flat." After the water cools, its taste can be improved by aerating it by pouring it back and forth between two clean containers or shaking it vigorously in a closed container with air space.

After the water has boiled, turn off your heat source or take the pot off the fire and leave the lid on until it cools. Again, this continued "free heat" further guarantees that all nasty critters will die. When I hardboil eggs, I bring the water to a boil using another pot for a lid, shut of the heat, and let the eggs cook for several minutes in the scalding water. Over time, this saves a lot of fuel while achieving the same results. While some of you might be wondering when I'll get a life, harboring a conservation mind-set now will make the transition over to an emergency scenario with limited supplies that much easier and less scary. You'll also do the Earth a favor, and save money so you can work less at the job you hate. After the water has cooled sufficiently to drink, you're ready to hydrate. You can use nonpotable water for cooking as well when bringing any food source to a boil. There is no need to boil water, making it safe to drink, and then reboiling it again for eight minutes when cooking the survival pasta.

While boiling destroys the waterborne pathogens that we're concerned about, it takes effort to continually boil water for drinking, especially if all you have are smaller containers. For those living in hot climates, with no air conditioning because the grid collapsed, the last thing you will want to do is boil water. This procrastination will lead to further dehydration. Boiling requires a heat source, and heat sources need fuel to burn. Fuel—whether it's white gas, propane, or the busted-up kitchen table—might be hard to come by. The heat produced from burning fuel can also burn down your house, garage, or town without proper care as to where the heat source is created and managed, and having the know-how and tools to properly extinguish a blaze if things get out of control. In other words, boiling to disinfect water takes a lot of energy and responsibility, so the "drop, drop, fizz, fizz" convenience of the before-mentioned halogens should be a viable option for every household.

Pasteurization

Contrary to poplar belief, it is not necessary to boil microbiologically contaminated water to make it safe to drink. I wrote about boiling because it does work, and may be more valid than other disinfection methods under certain circumstances. Also, some of you may feel super-paranoid about trusting the pasteurization process (if you're a milk drinker, get over it). Also, contrary to what many people believe, it is usually not necessary to distill water to make it safe to drink. I cover distillation next, as many of the water disinfection methods outlined herein, including pasteurization, will not help if water is brackish or chemically contaminated.

While *sterilization* kills all of the organisms in the water, pasteurization kills only those organisms that cause harm to humans. Pasteurization involves heating water to 149 degrees F (65 degrees C) for six to twenty minutes, or to a higher temperature for a shorter time. (Note: There was some contradiction in my research into how *long* the water being pasteurized must remain at the peak temperature of 149 degrees F. Whichever time you decide to use, six or twenty minutes, remember that you will not be swilling down water at that temperature anyway and that the water will continue to disinfect as it cools to a manageable drinking temperature.) Pasteurization kills all bacteria, viruses, and parasites, such as *Giardia, cryptosporidium, endameba,* the eggs of worms, *shigella, cholera, salmonella* bacteria and those that cause typhoid, the enterotoxogenic strains of *E. Coli,* Hepatitis A, and rotavirus, to name a few.

A standard glass thermometer can be used to accurately measure when the correct temperature for pasteurization is achieved, as will another device available from many solar cooking businesses online or elsewhere. This option is the Water Pasteurization Indicator (WAPI). A prototype was first developed in 1988 by Dr. Fred Barrett, who worked for the U.S. Department of Agriculture. The present WAPI device was developed by Dale Andreatta and other graduate engineering students at the University of California at Berkeley. The device itself consists of a polycarbonate tube that's sealed at both ends. The inside of the tube is partially filled with a blue soybean fat that melts at 156 degrees F (69 degrees C). To use, the WAPI is placed inside the water container being treated with the fat end up. It's easy to tell when the water reaches 156 degrees F because the highly visible fat melts and runs to the bottom of the tube. The WAPI is durable and can be used many times, and can be placed in a solar oven, cook pot, or over a stove or fire. Heating water to the pasteurization temperature rather than the boiling point can reduce the energy required by up to 50 percent, saving fuel, time, and water.

Distillation

While the above-mentioned water disinfection techniques work well at killing organic waterborne pathogens, *they will do nothing to remove other potential containments from water such as heavy metals, salts, and chemicals.* Distillation requires boiling water for many minutes and catching the resulting steam. The Seri Indians in northern Mexico desalinate seawater by boiling it in fifty-five-gallon drums.

"WATER IS H_2O, HYDROGEN two parts, OXYGEN one, but there is also a THIRD THING that makes water and NOBODY KNOWS what that is."

—D. H. Lawrence

They wrap a wet, cool rag around a copper pipe exiting the container, which cools down the escaping steam that is then caught in a waiting container. This method is extremely fuel intensive, yet dying of dehydration trumps deforestation. Although tedious and a fuel hog, distillation gives survivors a much better chance of removing suspected dangerous contaminants from gathered water.

For small-scale water distillation, fill the largest cook pot you have halfway with nondisinfected water. As the water will need to be boiled for several minutes, there is no need to disinfect it beforehand. This cook pot should have a lid or one that's improvised that will conform to the following directions. The lid will be put on the pot *upside down* to allow for its resulting convexity to direct trapped steam, as it cools and turns to water droplets, toward the center of the lid. Before putting on the upside down lid, attach a smaller, heat-resistant container such as a cup or bowl to the lid's handle using wire or string so that it hangs right side up inside the pot without touching the water. This cup or bowl catches the directed water droplets from the lid. Boil the water for as many minutes as required to fill the attached cup or bowl. The resulting water that drips from the lid into the cup or bowl is distilled and should be free from waterborne pathogens and other contaminants. Although making a water distiller may be a pain in the butt, once it's made, it can be used many times. Water can also be distilled after being disinfected by other methods for those who are dealing with extremely nasty water or who simply want added protection.

The SODIS Water Treatment Method:
Using Free Ultraviolet Radiation from the Sun

In 1991, research for the future SODIS water treatment method was undertaken by SANDEC (the Department of Water and Sanitation) at the EAWAG (Swiss Federal Institute for Aquatic Science and Research). They conducted wide-ranging laboratory and field tests to develop and refine for general use the Solar Water Disinfection Process (SODIS). Their extensive testing revealed what some of us desert rats have suspected for years, that the ultraviolet radiation from intense sunlight shining through a nonopaque container filled with nonpotable water will irradiate and kill undesirable waterborne pathogens, rendering the water safe to drink. In truth, the inspiration for using radiation from the sun to kill pathogens in nonpotable water started to develop in India as long ago as 2000 BC.

For the past decade, SANDEC has been providing information, technical data, and advice to local institutions and more than twenty developing countries worldwide. Currently, the SODIS method is used to treat the daily drinking water of more than two million people around the world. Studies into the effectiveness of the SODIS program have shown a reduction in dysentery by 20 to 50 percent. For developing nations, further benefits were achieved by combining SODIS with handwashing programs.

You as a reader are aware by now that many hundreds of thousands of people die each year in developing counties from dysentery and disease caused directly or

indirectly from contaminated water. My hat goes off to the people at SANDEC and EAWAG and many other organizations for their work in solar water disinfection; they are spending time and money to truly make a difference in our world, a difference that can be owned and operated by the people themselves, not corporations.

SODIS does not completely sterilize water of all critters, as it's primarily used to inactivate the pathogenic microorganisms that predominantly cause diarrhea. When the SODIS bottle is exposed to the sun, other harmless bacteria present in the water may keep growing. The SODIS method does not produce sterile water, as drinking water does not have to be sterile. Laboratory research has shown that many bacteria, viruses, and protozoa are eliminated including, but not limited to, the bacteria *Escherichia coli (E.coli), Vibrio cholerae, Streptococcus faecalis, Pseudomonas aerugenosa, Shigella flexneri, Salmonella typhii, Salmonella enteriditis,* and *Salmonella paratyphi;* the viruses *bacteriophage f2, rotavirus,* and *encephalomyocarditis virus;* the protozoas *Giardia spp.,* and *Cryptosporidium spp.;* and the yeasts and molds *Aspergillus niger, Aspergillus flavus, Candida,* and *Geotrichum.*

In a nutshell, the SODIS method involves filling up a clear, plastic, one- to two-quart container with nonpotable water. This bottle is then put into direct sunlight, on the roof of a house or elsewhere, for several hours until the ultraviolet radiation from the sunlight disinfects the water for drinking. While there are several specifics to the methodology to ensure success, and I write about them below, this data can also be found on the SODIS Web site at www.sodis.ch/.

Finding and Using Containers Compatible with the SODIS Method

Concentrated sunlight (ultraviolet radiation) is the name of the game so stay away from containers with more than a one- or two-quart (or liter) capacity. Don't use large containers!

Ultraviolet radiation is reduced by increasing water depth. The more surface area-to-volume ratio you can achieve, in other words, the more of the sun's rays that can shine through the smallest "thickness" of water, the better the method will work. Although clear soda bottles are not optimal for the SODIS method as they have a small area for exposure to sunlight, they are common and readily available in most towns and cities. (See comments on using plastic bags below.)

Use only newer, clean, clear plastic containers with lids. These containers should be in good shape, not old, dinged, and scratched up ones that will block UV radiation. In like manner, opaque, tinted or colored plastics will block the necessary radiation from the sun and should *not* be used for SODIS. Older clear containers and colored plastics can be utilized, if clean, to store water that has already been treated in the newer clear bottles. All plastics break down and age when exposed to the sun, thereby reducing their transparency for maximum UV radiation. This breakdown transforms plastic materials into *photoproducts.* SODIS laboratory and field tests showed that the resulting photoproducts were generated only at the outer surface of the bottles. No photoproducts or additives (UV-stabilisators) were observed leaching into the water itself. For the length of most urban disasters, sun-weakened bottles won't be a problem, as the SODIS people recommend that you retire all containers used for SODIS after one year of continuous daily use.

Research carried out in Canada at Montreal's Brace Research Institute (BRI), in collaboration with international colleagues, found that plastic bags are the best material for solar water disinfection. Heavy-duty freezer bags, as mentioned, will hold either a quart or a gallon of water sealed and will lie flat in comparison to soda bottles when full, thus exposing more water to greater concentrations of UV radiation. While this departs from the SODIS method of plastic bottles, plastic bags, although far less durable, may be a viable option for you. Any labeling printed on the bag should be turned down so as not to impede solar radiation. Be careful of hot, conductive surfaces as they may deform and melt the bags.

A note about glass: While clear glass bottles can be used, glass is thicker than plastic and will block some of the UV radiation and add time for the water to heat up. Glass containers are also heavier when empty and can be easily broken. Tests done with improvised large containers made with window glass did not work, as the glass did not transmit enough UV radiation. Many windows on the market have UV inhibitors to keep your couch and chairs from fading in the sun.

If possible, use plastic bottles made from PET (Poly Ethylene Terephtalate) instead of those made from PVC (Poly Vinyl Chloride). PET bottles provide a greater transmittance of UV radiation as they contain less UV stabilizers, are readily available, and are cheap, durable, and contain fewer additives than bottles made from PVC. PET containers can be distinguished from PVC containers by burning a sample. PET will burn easily, the smell of the smoke is sweet, and the flame goes out slowly. PVC is difficult to burn and the smell of the smoke is strong and nasty. Bottles made with PVC will also have a blueish glimmer.

If you use bottles that are longer than they are wide (soda bottles, for example), be sure to lay the bottles down on their sides, thereby exposing maximal surface area to the sun while creating a minimal amount of water depth. If the bottles are laid onto a reflective/conductive surface such as metal corrugated roofing or some other like surface, the water temperature will be increased. Don't forget about the physics of convection, radiation, and conduction as learned from the shelter chapter. The key to SODIS being effective is maximum ultraviolet radiation, and to a lesser extent, heat. Try whatever types and combinations of reflectors, conductive surfaces, and protection against cooling breezes it takes to maximize radiation and heat into the water, especially in marginal solar gain locales or during the winter. People living in really hot climates should watch out that the bottles don't start to deform from too much heat. Desert ground temperatures exposed to summer sun, let alone metal, can reach more than 140 degrees F (60 degrees C). Each year, Phoenix, Arizona, has several contests where gung-ho participants see who can cook an egg on the pavement the quickest. Experiment in your locality to see what works.

When the bottle(s) are filled with water, place them on a surface that will get *full sun* during the hours needed for treatment. Avoid areas that will become partially shaded at some point during the day. Southern exposure niches for the top half of the planet work well at having the most available sunshine during the winter months. Protect the bottles from cooler convective breezes and enhance reflective radiation if necessary. Do NOT place the bottles on flammable materials such as grass, cloth, straw, or hay, thinking you'll insulate the bottle from heat loss. The water in clear bottles can condense the sun's rays like a magnifying glass and quickly set fire to combustible surfaces.

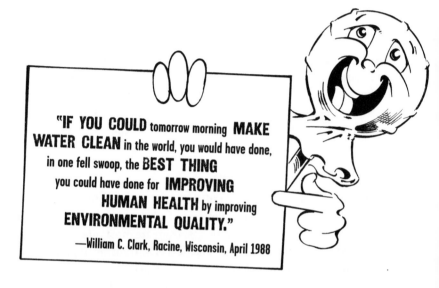

"IF YOU COULD tomorrow morning MAKE WATER CLEAN in the world, you would have done, in one fell swoop, the BEST THING you could have done for IMPROVING HUMAN HEALTH by improving ENVIRONMENTAL QUALITY."
—William C. Clark, Racine, Wisconsin, April 1988

What Type of Water Can I Treat with SODIS?

Any microbiologically contaminated water, even water that may have contacted human feces, is suitable for SODIS. The entire purpose of SODIS is to improve the microbiological quality of water through ultraviolet radiation and heat from the sun.

IMPORTANT! *Any* suspended particulate matter (turbidity or "pond scum") in the water you gather will impede the ability for sunlight to fully penetrate the water in the bottle, thereby reducing UV irradiation and how hot it will get. *Water put into treatment bottles should be as clear as possible.* Filter the water through coffee filters, a clean cloth, or a bandana to remove any floaters and particulate matter from the water. Nonpotable water can also be left to sit for several hours in a larger container to let particulate matter sink to the bottom and/or be skimmed off the top. On the SODIS Web site, they offer a test that will tell you if the water has too much turbidity to be used without filtering first. They recommend you fill the bottle with the water in question and put the bottle on top of a piece of paper with words that have letters about 3/4 inch high (1.5 centimeters). Next, with the lid off, look down through the bottle to the paper at the bottom and see if you can read the words through the water. If you can, the water is ready to treat with no need for filtering. Water treated with SODIS also tastes good, as oxygen levels within the water are not reduced, as they are with boiled water. After the water has been treated, don't make the mistake of pouring it into "dirty" containers that will recontaminate the water!

Oxygen is important for killing waterborne pathogens, as sunlight forms highly reactive molecules such as free radical oxygen and hydrogen peroxide that help in their destruction. The earlier SODIS method involved shaking the partially filled bottle vigorously to aerate the water before filling the bottle fully and setting it in the sun. Further research has determined that under normal conditions, water from creeks, wells, ponds, and rivers contain more than three milligrams of oxygen per quart, which is more than sufficient to get the job done without further aeration.

Water that has been contaminated with chemicals or pesticides should not be used, as solar radiation will do nothing to remove the contaminants. For this problem refer back to filtration and distillation.

Optimal Climate and Weather for SODIS

The SODIS method requires UV radiation and elevated temperatures to work. For the "techies," sunlight with wavelengths of 315–400 nanometers (nm) on the ultraviolet range of the electromagnetic spectrum are most effective at destroying bacteria (of which colorless plastic or glass excel at transmitting). To treat your water, expose the bottles to direct sunlight for at least *six hours* if the sky is cloud free and totally clear, to up to 50 percent cloud cover. Although not recommended by SODIS, if the sky is "50 percent" cloudy, I would increase the time that the bottles sit by an hour or two or more (why not?). If the sky has 100 percent cloud cover, UV intensity is cut to 30 percent or less and the bottles should be exposed to the "sun" for *two consecutive days*. During days of continuous rain, don't use SODIS, as it's not reliable. But who cares, get out there and gather the rain! In regard to the water temperature, the SODIS people claim that if the water reaches at least 122 degrees F (50 degrees C) for one hour it's pasteurized and ready to drink. The locations where SODIS is most effective lie between the latitudes of 15°N/ S and 35°N/ S, the latter being the best—areas of semiarid land with high solar radiation, limited cloud cover and rain, and 3000 hours of sunshine per year on average. The second best location is between the equator and latitude 15°N/ S.

SODIS does have a few limitations. It doesn't work for treating large amounts of water in one container and it requires suitable weather conditions (high solar radiation) for effectiveness. While you folks in Washington state and Maine might be out of luck, you all have an abundance of firewood, so boil away. People in desert regions oftentimes lack the needed fuel resources, so it all works out in the end.

Disinfecting Your Family's Water: One Super Sacred Responsibility

No water disinfection method is perfect. With all disinfection methods, *always* err on the side of being conservative. The ten minutes you refused to wait for your water to properly disinfect, or got lazy with your boiling, could cost you days or weeks of unnecessary time on and around the toilet. If you're in the middle of disinfecting water with halogens, get distracted from the job, and when you return can't remember which containers are safe to drink, *disinfect the entire batch over again.* You might invent some way to clearly mark the containers that have been disinfected with colored tape, string, or another method. The person or persons responsible for disinfecting the family's water should take their job very seriously. Screw up with this one, especially with limited medical help after a crisis, and you could help slowly kill a loved one with dysentery.

Finding Emergency Water in an Urban/Suburban Setting

"THESE ARE UGLY DECISIONS, BUT YOU EITHER DRINK WATER OR YOU DIE."

—PETER BEATTIE, PREMIER OF QUEENSLAND, AUSTRALIA, ANNOUNCING THAT DUE TO THE COUNTRY'S WORST DROUGHT ON RECORD, THE STATE WOULD START USING DRINKING WATER CONTAINING RECYCLED SEWAGE WATER

If your home front runs dry, there are several places to look for water in an urban setting. Now that you know how to disinfect the stuff, you must broaden your views about drinking water that, before the disaster happened, you wouldn't have gone swimming in, let alone drink. A point that needs to be clarified about most of the disinfection methods we have talked about so far is that they are for killing organic, living, waterborne pathogens. Contaminants from chemicals and pollutants will be very common in urban and suburban water sources, and boiling, iodine, and chlorine bleach will *not* remove them! If ingested, any of these contaminants can make you sick, or in concentration, kill you. Only commercial filters specifically stating that they deal with chemical contaminates and/or the distillation method give you a shot at screening out these unwanted particles.

Explore your alternative water options now. The next time you walk, bike, or drive through your neighborhood, keep your eyes open as to what you could use as an emergency water resource. Keep in mind that post-disaster, "public" water resources will become hot spots and magnets for others who may also have run out of water. History has proved that human nature can get ugly during times of crisis so find as many water options as you can. *Never* put all of your self-reliance eggs into one basket. Remember that water is very heavy at 8.3 pounds per gallon, and moving it around by hand if vehicles are benched due to gas shortages will be a challenge.

The following list highlights water options you may have in your area. I have beaten you over the head for several pages about how important water is to your survival. The ultimate responsibility lies with you about "reconning" or exploring and locating safe water options that you and your family might utilize during troubled times.

Streams

Ahhh, running water! Many of you reading this chapter have been shaking your head in wonder at my fanatical stance on water as you have it running everywhere within your neighborhood. Good for you, for you are truly blessed. Being from the high desert, I can only dream of the luxury you have, but I've seen pictures in magazines.

Streams vary in size from a trickle to a current that would wash away your SUV. If you have a stream winding its way through your community, find out where it starts. How many miles downstream are you from the source? And what exactly, or who, is upstream? Find out now if there's a major (or minor) chemical plant or chicken farm along its banks. During the Bosnian and Croatian conflict, families fled their homes to camp at nearby mountain streams. The families upstream used the stream for everything, including going to the bathroom. Families downstream became ill with dysentery and many babies and young children died as a result of poor sanitation practices. With or without poop in the water, the common assumption that water running briskly over rocks and aquatic plants disinfects itself is utter nonsense.

After reading this book, you will be worlds ahead of the general populace about what is needed to survive a disaster and the responsibility this means to the natural world. But you mustn't assume that the rest of the population won't be shitting in the stream above you; I tell you now that they will be. Our disinfection techniques can deal with those pathogens, but they can't deal with the gene pool dropout who dumps weed killer into the stream in order to create an empty container. Unfortunately, you are at the mercy of your neighbors when dealing with these types of water supplies. Just because the water looks clean doesn't mean that it is. I apologize that I have no way of telling you how to assess the quality of your water from chemicals or pollutants other than many heavily polluted urban streams will have obvious, nasty-looking, multicolored water. Streams and rivers are commonly used as dumping places fostered by our out-of-sight, out-of-mind mentality regarding sanitation. After an extreme disaster, you may see anything and everything floating past your home, dead bodies and all.

Know your stream, and ultimately, your neighbors. For those of you who have been active in your community protecting above-ground water resources and enjoying their beauty, your efforts just may save your life. *Treat all above-ground water sources with caution, no matter how pure they seem, and disinfect accordingly.* That small, picturesque Rocky Mountain stream running through property where no one lives above you can still have a dead cow or elk decomposing in the middle of it. If you feel good about using your stream for drinking water, follow the before-mentioned water disinfection techniques and keep hydrated.

Rivers

As rivers are basically streams on steroids, and travel farther through more variables of people and places, they are susceptible to more contaminants. While some may argue that the larger volume of water compensates for this—and they're partially correct, remember the "small" dead bird in my "large" water tank?—there is no way

A SPECIAL CAUTION ABOUT "HUMAN-MADE" LAKES AND PONDS

I'm not certain why, but man-made ponds are very common in the Southwest desert, especially around golf courses and more affluent communities. Many urban planners, and I use the term "planner" loosely, should be hung by their toes for using scarce water resources for the titillation of their pocketbooks and for the residents who should have remained in Minnesota if seeing surface water is what they crave. These pretend ponds are typically ringed with unsustainable, water-hogging vegetation from grass to weeping willow trees that are unsuited to the climate and ground conditions as well. As these plants would die within weeks without continuous care, cared for they are, and volumes of chemical fertilizers and toxic pesticides are used to keep things looking electric green. The problem this presents should be obvious, as rain runoff and leaching flush these toxins directly and indirectly into the fake pond. If an insane developer's wet dream is on your family's emergency water hit list, pay close attention to the factors just discussed. Golf courses are notorious for dumping extreme amounts of fertilizers and pesticides onto the greens so be forewarned. Although potentially pricey, many towns have water-testing services. Do your homework, make your decision, and disinfect the water the best that you can.

to accurately assess this for the common homeowner. Know your river(s), use common sense when gathering water from it, and disinfect the water accordingly.

Natural Lakes and Ponds

Many communities have lakes and ponds within their midst, whether natural or artificial. There are no natural lakes within the entire state of Arizona, and yet we have several "lakes" as the result of the damming of natural rivers and streams, Lake Powell being one of the most massive. If naturally produced, lakes and ponds usually spawn from underground springs, rain runoff, or snowmelt. Where the water comes from and what type of earth it's sitting on will give you general clues as to its potability. There are a few ponds in the West that are contaminated with naturally occurring arsenic from the ground. They're not difficult to spot as they have absolutely no life growing within them, and frequently sport the bones of small mammals on their banks who have attempted to use the toxic tea to slake their thirst.

Due to the fact that the water in lakes and ponds is somewhat stagnant, especially in smaller ponds, the water may have some type of nitrate contamination or be corrupted by organic and inorganic substances from land erosion, the disintegration of minerals, rotting vegetation, and earthborne biological pathogens, as well as the usual industrial chemical pollutants, and microorganisms from animal and human waste. It all depends on the history of your pond or lake, so know the water source as accurately as you can.

Lakes and ponds are not typically used as dumps, as are streams and rivers, because there is no current to take away the offending idiots' refuse, but don't assume there's not something weird under the water ten feet from the bank. No matter how innocent the water looks, disinfect all water for human consumption via the methods described earlier in this chapter.

Fountains, Goldfish Ponds, Wishing Wells, and Other In-town Water Oddities

Urban areas are blessed with many unlikely places to find water. Simply make a mental note of where yours are located, decide whether they would be a likely candidate for consumption after disinfecting, and enjoy.

Random Water Spigots

As a troubled and trashy teen I lived on city streets for a spell and finding water proved to be a challenge. I quickly learned that most urban and suburban buildings have water spigots that can be found at some point around their perimeter. Gas stations, office buildings, department stores, and dozens of other buildings and their owners need water to wash down loading docks, clean supplies and equipment, water ornamental vegetation, etc. Several of these outdoor faucets have their handles removed, as the owners are tired of vagrants using their turf as a watering hole. Some of these functionless faucets simply require coaxing from a pair of pliers and you're back in business. Keep in mind that you're technically taking water from someone else, so be discreet, use caution, and watch your back. Since almost all of these spigots are hooked up to municipal water supplies, they should not be depended upon during or after a crisis. CAUTION: The water from some of these spigots may not be potable (or at least that's what you may be told when you wish to fill up a canteen). As with all things improvised, if you find yourself flying by the seat of your pants, assess the priority of your needs while minimizing damaging variables, and keep your attitude positive.

Harvesting Rain

I love collecting rain, especially here in the desert. Harvesting rain, although fairly simple at first glance, is the subject of many books. One can harvest rain by creating swales or "speed bumps" directly on the ground for catching rain runoff for percolation into the earth, thereby creating a water bank for thirsty plants, or harvest rain directly from rooftops, among other places. At minimum, many people in arid parts of the country choose to put a collection container under a gutter

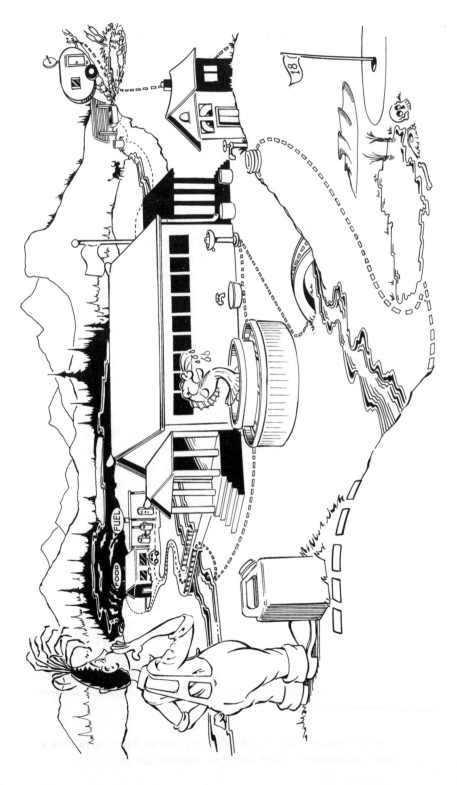

"ALL the water that WILL EVER BE IS, RIGHT NOW."
—National Geographic, October 1993

or divert gutter water onto needy vegetation.

When catching rain from conventional rooftops, many factors will influence its potability including, but not limited to, the *type* and *cleanliness* of the gathering surface, airborne contaminants, and the storage container it's collected in. Certain toxic materials used for roofing may wash off into the storage tank during rainfall. Leaves, dust, bugs, and bird, mouse and rat poop, among other garbage present on your roof, will also wash off into your storage container if roof washers are not employed (various types of roof washers divert the first five or ten gallons of rain into a separate container allowing the roof to wash off with the first part of the rain.) Extreme contaminants in the air (remember toxic rain?) can also be present that would influence your caught water's potability. Of course the most extreme would be radioactive fallout. As already discussed, water must also be stored in the proper container.

I had a client from Ohio who claimed his entire neighborhood caught water from conventional, asphalt-shingled rooftops, which funneled rain into aboveground cisterns hidden by shrubbery. He caught the rain, which supplied all of his family's needs and pumped it directly into his home, using no filters whatsoever—and the man was a physician. Ironically, your home's roof might supply you with all of the emergency water your family would need during a crisis. Check what type of roofing your house has and research whether it's recommended as a safe surface for gathering water for human consumption. Remember the above snippet from the doctor who took my course and realize that companies will be conservative with what they tell you for fear of lawsuits. If push comes to shove, short-term contaminants in water do not override dying of dehydration.

To figure out how many gallons of rain you could collect from your roof in a year, first measure the outside dimensions, or true "footprint," of your roof to determine its surface area. Heavily sloping roofs don't matter, as they catch no more rain than flat roofs. Next, find out what the annual rainfall is for your area—my high desert is twelve inches, which we will use in this example. To find the gallons per cubic foot, we'll take the above information and multiply it by 7.48. The formula to use is as follows:

Surface area, or footprint, of gathering surface x annual rainfall x 7.48 = gallons of rain (on average) collected per year.

Let's try a sample equation using a hypothetical twenty-by-forty-foot roof (800 total square feet) in an area with twelve inches (one foot) of annual rainfall: 800 x 1 x 7.48 = 5,984 gallons per year.

If you get eighteen inches per year, multiply by 1.5, if you get twenty-four inches of rain per year, multiply by two, and so on.

Because some of the rain will be lost to overflowing gutters, wind, evaporation, and seepage into the roofing material itself (with the exception of metal roofs) multiply the above number by 0.95.

5,984 gallons x 0.95 = 5,684 gallons of rain per year.

Keep in mind this tremendous amount of water was gathered upon a very small surface area using annual rainfall calculations from the desert! Take the time to do the math for your roof's footprint, coupled with your annual rainfall, and you will be astounded at the number of gallons you could gather from your home. With a little bit of effort, this free, life-giving substance can be directed into large-capacity water tanks for the enjoyment, and survival, of your family.

Some people who lack conventional roofing materials because of their lifestyle choice (teepees, wall tents, etc.) use other nonpermeable barriers to collect rain. Tarps and sheets of plastic can be suspended above the ground to catch large volumes of water that is then directed into waiting containers or garden areas. I once collected more than forty gallons of rainwater in one storm by finding a natural hole in the ground that was located within a small wash (arroyo), which I then lined with plastic. Grommeted tarps are much more durable and easier to hang than plastic sheets but any nontoxic, nonpermeable barrier is worth considering for catching and holding moisture.

Melting Snow and Ice

Depending on where you live and the time of year, melting snow and ice can provide emergency water for your tribe. For the Uruguayan rugby team that crash-landed high in the Andes Mountains in the 1970s, their only option for water during their seventy-plus day forced stay came from ice and snow. They created this water daily by placing highly reflective metal panels salvaged from the downed aircraft at a slight angle facing the sun. The panels heated up from the sun's rays and were dusted with snow throughout the day, which melted and funneled down to waiting containers.

Newly fallen snow contains more than 90 percent air, thus it contains less water than snow that has been around for a few days or weeks. This high air content and minerals present within the snow are the main reasons people complain about bad-tasting water and scorched pans when trying to melt snow. To effectively melt snow, start with a small amount in your metal container before you put it on the heat source. As this amount melts, add a bit more snow. The more water you have in the pot, the more snow you can add as it will dissolve the snow. I have

THE *WHEN ALL HELL BREAKS LOOSE* 2008 "YOU'RE KIDDING ME" AWARD WINNER!

Our winner is real-estate developer Richard Mladick of Mesa, Arizona!

Oblivious to a current statewide drought emergency (ongoing since 1999), Mladick's brainchild is to construct a 125-acre mega-water park in the middle of the Sonoran desert. The park would offer a fake ocean capable of generating surf-sized waves for surfing and boogie boarding, a snorkeling pool, a scuba lagoon, white-water rivers for kayaking, phony beaches, and more. To achieve the 50 million gallons of water needed to initially fill its artificial oceans and rivers, the park will suck up water from depleting underground aquifers. Being located in the hottest, driest metro area in the United States, the park will use 100 million gallons of groundwater each year, enough to support 1,200 people in the Mesa area. Pitifully, 65 percent of those who voted in the 2007 election in Mesa approved the water park, thereby granting the project an estimated $35 million in tax incentives.

When queried about his project, Mladick said he wanted to create the kind of lush environment he remembers from growing up in Virginia Beach, Virginia, and surfing in Morocco, Indonesia, Hawaii, and Brazil. "I couldn't imagine raising my kids in an environment where they wouldn't have the opportunity to grow up being passionate about the same sports that I grew up being passionate about."

Apparently unaware that he can simply move back to Virginia or take his kids on a surfing vacation, and in the interest of saving Arizona from Mr. Mladick's dream, I am offering to fly Mr. Mladick and his offspring one-way to the lush environment of their choice. Congratulations, Richard!

tried packing a pot full of snow and putting it on the wood stove, but it takes a lot longer for the snow to melt, thus using more fuel, and it can scorch the bottom of the pot. If you have water to spare, put an inch or so in the pot before adding any snow and let it heat up, as this will assist in melting the snow when it's added. If you feel your snow turned to water is unsafe to drink, simply boil it per the disinfection section. Follow the same strategy for melting ice, which will contain much more water value than snow. Gather snow and ice from clean areas and don't eat yellow snow.

Unless you use the Uruguayan rugby team's melting method, or have the time and space to bring large amounts of contained snow or ice into some part of your house to slowly melt, transforming ice and snow into water will require fuel and a suitable container. If fuel is in short supply, you will once again have to prioritize your needs. Think ahead and always try to kill two birds with one stone, such as melting snow for water on or around the woodstove that is keeping the family warm and cooking their food.

SUPER SIMPLE SUMMARY

- ⊃ Water is a biological necessity down to the cellular level. Without it you will die. Thus, if it's not readily available from your environment, storing potable water for the entire family, including pets, is of prime importance.
- ⊃ Dehydration adversely affects your physiology and your psychology. Many factors increase the risks for dehydration such as chronic illnesses, living at altitude, exercise, hot and humid weather, cold and dry weather, pregnancy and breast-feeding, and being either very young or very old.
- ⊃ Thirst is *never* an indication of adequate hydration. Your body is maximally hydrated when your urine is clear. Lesser indicators are how often you pee and how much you pee. Vitamin B and certain medications will color the urine regardless of how hydrated you are.
- ⊃ It may be necessary to strongly encourage family members to drink to avoid becoming dehydrated, especially during very hot or cold weather. Most people will not drink enough water on their own to stay hydrated.
- ⊃ If you choose to use them, electrolyte and rehydration solutions should be used with caution. Don't over-use them as they can make you sick in concentrated quantities. First try to alleviate the dehydration with adequate quantities of plain water.
- ⊃ For families without access to natural water sources, plan ahead by storing potable water in containers. Store a *minimum* of one gallon of water per person per day. If you live in an arid environment, storing three gallons of water per person per day is highly recommended. Don't forget about pets and realize that your

stored water will also be used for cooking and sanitation needs. There are many types of water storage container options. Choose what works best for your family, don't store them all in one location, and remember to store water at the office and in vehicles as well.

➲ If applicable, beware of contaminated water entering your home after a disaster from the municipal water intake pipe attached to your house's plumbing system. Know where the shutoff valve is and pay attention to local emergency broadcasts about if and when to turn off the water supply entering your home.

➲ Fill as many preexisting water storage containers, such as bathtubs, extra sinks, and pots and pans, as you can with potable water. Know how to access other water options such as hot-water heaters and the backs of toilets.

➲ Nonpotable water should be disinfected before drinking using a method such as household chlorine bleach, iodine, boiling, filtration, pasteurization, distillation, or UV radiation. For water sources suspected of being contaminated with chemicals and pollutants, use the filtration and/or distillation methods.

➲ As a general rule, use *great caution* when disinfecting nonpotable water sources for drinking. *If in doubt, re-treat the water in question!*

➲ Scout your neighborhood *now* for possible alternative emergency water sources in case your home runs dry. Streams, rivers, ponds or lakes, fountains, and random water spigots may be available. Don't reduce your survival options by having only one alternative source of water. Use extreme caution when using man-made sources of water such as artificially created ponds at golf courses. Such water sources can be laced with chemicals and pollutants.

➲ Harvest rain whenever possible using a variety of nontoxic, nonpermeable materials such as the roof of your home, or suspended tarps or plastic sheeting. Disinfect rainwater before drinking using the described disinfection methods.

➲ Melt snow and ice for water. Ice contains much more water than snow by volume.

➲ Don't use nonpotable water to wash dishes, brush teeth, prepare food, or make ice.

FAMILIAR yet Fantastic FOOD

"Thou shouldst eat to live, not live to eat."
—Socrates

While food is not a priority in a short-term survival scenario, which lasts on average seventy-two hours or less before you are rescued, for an extended emergency it's a must-have commodity. Food is a hotly debated item in survival and everyone has their opinion about what you should have on hand and how much. As psychological stress is such a huge part of every survival scenario, knowing where your food is coming from and having enough for your family will do wonders for everyone's peace of mind. Consider storing a few snacks in your car and office as well.

In a nasty, long-term crisis in which you are unable to resupply your cupboard, you will be forced to ration your family's food. Take the mind-set *now* that your survival rations, in their truest sense, are just that, THEY ARE RATIONS; and rations are to be rationed. Beware, as the Earth's history is full of fools who willfully chewed through their survival supplies in short order, their deaths being the only proof of their bad planning. If you want to live high on the hog for a few days, purposefully storing and eating gourmet supplies at the beginning of your ordeal, that's your choice, but be able to get down and dirty with a food supply that is supernutritious and easily stored and rationed, at the expense of taste if need be. Much about your food storage strategy, of course, revolves around the wants and needs of your family.

The Big Three: Macronutrients in Food

Foods contain three macronutrients: carbohydrates, fats, and proteins, along with trace amounts of micronutrients such as minerals and vitamins. Each type contains a certain amount of kilocalories (kcal) or units of food energy and metabolizes or "burns" differently within the body. Fats contain the greatest amount of kilocalories at a whopping 9.3 kilocalories per

gram. Carbohydrates come in second with 3.79 kilocalories per gram, and then proteins with 3.12 kilocalories per gram. Each kilocalorie is equivalent to 1,000 calories and is the quantity of heat required to raise the temperature of 1 kilogram of pure water 1 degree C. One pound of body weight equals around 3,500 kilocalories. At 280 kilocalories a pop, that's nearly thirteen Snickers candy bars!

The largest energy reserves are found in the largest parts of the body, principally muscle (around 28 kilograms) and fat (15 kilograms). On average, a healthy body contains a storehouse of energy: around 1,200 kilocalories of carbohydrates, 24,000 kilocalories of protein, and 135,000 kilocalories of fat. As stated earlier, the burn rates of macronutrients, how their kilocalories are metabolized by the body, vary. Just as adding various types and sizes of firewood to a fire influences the burn size and time duration of the flame, so the three macronutrients influence the body in much the same way. Fats, as an example, like larger fuelwood, contain the most calories per gram, but also require more oxygen to oxi-dize their components down for metabolism by the body. Simple sugars (carbohydrates), like hard candies, act the same as smaller kindling wood and don't contain many kilo-calories, but they break down very quickly and thus are metabolized by the body very fast. Putting kindling-size wood on a fire will produce a huge flame in a heartbeat but it's short-lived.

"FOOD is an important part of a BALANCED DIET."
—Fran Lebowitz

Almost everyone at some point has "hit the wall," as an athlete would say, having burned up their available carbohydrate supply. Eating a few simple sugars and carbohydrates might be all that's necessary to jump-start your body's system. If your survival tasks become extremely physical, working at less than 60 percent of your maximum exertion level uses more fats than carbohydrates, thus helping to prevent blood glucose depletion. This physiological rule is one that aerobics instructors use to their advantage in helping clients lose fat while they maintain the energy needed to keep exercising during their class. If the weather is cold and available body carbohydrates are drained, heat production starts to fail and you become hypothermic much easier. In this situation, you *must* eat simple carbohydrates to tap into your body's remaining fat reserves.

Subjecting your body to cold weather without the protection of adequate clothing or shelter will cause your body to burn more calories. In other words, having adequate clothing or shelter for the climate and season will make your emergency food supplies last longer. Not only what you eat, but also *how* you eat can affect your body's thermoregulation in cold weather. Eating smaller, more frequent meals increases the body's metabolism, thereby burning more calories for digestion, a process referred to as *diet-induced thermogenesis*. This thermal effect of food, or "TEF" principle, increases your metabolism, which in turn increases the amount of calories burned. These increased calories produce more internal heat for the survivor when needed.

As already mentioned, if your survival situation goes long term, survival rations, in their truest sense, should not be considered substitute meals. Their main focus is to provide the survivor with sugar in order to minimize catabolism and dehydration in order to increase survival time. Ideal survival foods, provided

POTENTIALLY PROBLEMATIC PROTEINS

Proteins are not ideal survival foods in hot environments for several reasons. If water is scarce, proteins should be avoided, as the metabolism of protein depletes body water stores. Protein metabolism produces urea, a toxic compound excreted by the kidneys. The more protein you eat, the more water the body devotes to the production of urine in order to rid the body of urea. Eating quantities of protein in a limited-water situation hastens death through dehydration long before starvation. However, in long-term survival scenarios where starvation is a possibility, the body consumes protein anyway by cannibalizing muscle tissue. Unlike proteins, the metabolism of carbohydrates and fats, to a certain extent, contribute to body water stores up to twelve to seventeen ounces per day depending on the type of diet. Furthermore, the metabolism of protein produces a higher metabolic rate, thus using more energy and creating more heat. Use common sense and adapt to your particular situation. Proteins are a wonderful thing in cold, low-elevation environments with plenty of available drinking water.

there's adequate water to drink, consist of mostly fats and carbohydrates. While fats are packed with calories they take time for the body to metabolize into the simple sugars or glucose required for energy. In addition, fats are not well-tolerated as an energy source at high altitudes. If you live at altitude, store extra carbohydrates in the place of some fats and proteins, as carbohydrates are already partially oxidized and thus require less oxygen from the body—up to 8 to 10 percent less—to convert into energy. *More than any other nutrient except water, a reduced carbohydrate intake depletes muscle glycogen stores, decreasing your endurance.* For short-term survival (one to three days), a lack of calories is not nearly as important for performance as a lack of carbohydrates. Simple sugars and carbohydrates provide fast energy as they metabolize very quickly and are required for the body to be able to access its stored fat deposits. For the long term, however, if not accompanied by certain complex carbohydrates and proteins for stabilization, this quick source of energy leaves your body just as quickly, resulting in the infamous "sugar crash."

The *Glycemic Index* (GI) was developed in 1981 and is a numerical system for measuring how fast carbohydrates in various foods trigger a rise in blood sugar or glucose. Foods containing high amounts of fats and proteins don't cause blood sugar levels to rise nearly as much as those containing carbohydrates. In essence, the higher the GI number, the greater the blood sugar response. In general, a GI of 70 or more is high, 56 to 69 medium, and 55 or less is low. Until the early 1980s, scientists assumed that only digested simple sugars produced rapid increases in blood sugar levels. In truth, many simple sugars don't raise glucose levels any more than some complex carbohydrates, as not all carbohydrates act the same when digested. Foods producing the highest GI response include several starchy staples that folks commonly eat including breads, breakfast cereals, and baked potatoes. Even table sugar is low on the GI list in comparison. Low-glycemic foods include beans, barley, pasta, oats, various types of rice, and acidic fruits among others.

Consuming food with a high GI will cause your blood sugar to go through the roof. In response, your pancreas releases insulin in an attempt to combat your body's rising sugar levels. Ingested proteins contain *glucagons* that swim around the bloodstream trying to stabilize the blood sugar, helping to prevent the crash your body experiences by consuming simple carbohydrates or sugars alone.

In summary, the three macronutrients found in foods—proteins, fats, and carbohydrates—contain different amounts of calories and metabolize at varying rates within the body. The savvy survivor should store foods containing all three macronutrients. In addition, it would be wise to have on hand a one-size-fits-all, portable, quick, no-cook combination food source containing simple sugars and carbohydrates that jump-starts the body's glucose levels immediately. This same food source should also possess longer-burning carbohydrates for short-term energy and fats for sustained, long-burning energy. Proteins, with thought given to their disadvantages, should be present as well, thus stabilizing simple sugars and carbohydrates, helping to prevent the "crash," as well as providing the body with extra, long-burning fuel.

Foods including all macronutrients will give you the greatest bang for your buck, metabolizing in succession sugars, carbohydrates, proteins, and finally fats. Native American people knew the advantage of combining foods for maximum energy and performance all too well as their rugged lifestyles demanded the most from their bodies. They developed "pemmican," a staple that possessed all three macronutrients: berries for simple sugars and carbohydrates, meat for protein, and fat for fat. All three elements were prepared and mixed together to create the ultimate indigenous trail mix.

Your Basal Metabolic Rate (BMR): Defining How Much Feed You Truly Need

Your *basal metabolic rate* (BMR) is the amount of calories you burn at rest doing absolutely nothing. It is the bare minimum number of calories or energy your body needs to sustain the life process: respiration, circulation, cellular metabolism, glandular activity, and the maintenance of core body temperature. BMR requirements vary widely based on age, sex, muscle and bone weight, and height, so pinning down how much calories you burn sitting on your butt can be a challenge. The four main physiological factors that influence the burning of calories for BMR are as follows:

1 *Being male.* Men and boys burn more calories simply being men than women do being women.

2 *Your age.* Young people burn far more calories than middle-aged or older folks.

3 *Muscularity.* More muscles require more nutrients, even at rest.

4 *Tall people.* The more body one has, excluding fat, the more nutrition is required to keep the body idling.

The biggest calorie burners or those who eat the most food are young, tall, muscular men or boys—ask any mom. Statistically, tall women will burn more calories than shorter women and so on. Make no mistake about it, if you go by the serving size posted on the labels of foods, they will not have taken these variations into account—how could they? If your household plans on feeding several large teenage boys during a crisis, plan on storing much more food.

The following BMR worksheet can be photocopied and filled out by each member of your tribe. This will give you an estimate of how many calories will be required to feed your family when they are *doing absolutely nothing*. However, being inactive is not a typical daily survival activity so the worksheet also has an activity level option that will increase the daily amount of calories required for that person depending upon which activity level they choose. This will give you an estimate of the active caloric needs of each family member, a more true representation of what they are burning right now in the bustle of daily life. Other factors such as illness and weather conditions will also influence how many calories your body uses. Cold weather without proper shelter or clothing will dramatically increase the amount of calories your body burns in order to thermoregulate its core body temperature.

Basal Metabolic Rate and Active Caloric Needs Worksheet for Guys and Gals —Harris-Benedict Equation

Women

Your height in inches: _____
Multiply by 4.3 = _____ = A
Your weight in pounds: _____
Multiply by 4.4 = _____ = B
Your age in years: _____
Multiply by 4.7 = _____ = C

Men

Your height in inches: _____
Multiply by 12.7 = _____ = A
Your weight in pounds: _____
Multiply by 6.2 = _____ = B
Your age in years: _____
Multiply by 6.8 = _____ = C

Plug in the above information into this formula to estimate your BMR:

Females: A + B + 655 − C = _____ is your basal metabolic rate per day.
Males: A + B + 66 − C = _____ is your basal metabolic rate per day.

As your BMR is simply the amount of calories you burn doing absolutely nothing, choose one of the following options regarding your activity level and add it to your BMR number as indicated below.

Sedentary to lightly active: (active less than 30 minutes 1 or 2 days per week at minimal intensity)
Multiply your BMR number above by 1.3 = _____ calories you need per day

Moderately active: (active for 30 minutes 6 to 7 days per week at moderate intensity)
Multiply your BMR number above by 1.4 = _____ calories you need per day

Very active/athletic: (active for 60 minutes 6 to 7 days per week at a high intensity)
Multiply your BMR number above by 1.5 = _____ calories you need per day

The active caloric needs are the amount of calories you burn each day being you, doing all of the activities, work or play, that make up a day in your life. Life sucks without enough calories and you may be obliged to share some of your stored food with others so choose a calorie number on the high side.

If you're curious about the breakdown of carbohydrates, proteins, and fats of your *daily energy consumption* based upon your active caloric needs, use the following formula.

Protein = (Your active caloric needs) _____ multiplied by 0.15 =
_____ calories,   divided by 4.0 = _____ grams of protein

Carbohydrates = (Your active caloric needs) _____ multiplied by 0.55 =
_____ calories,   divided by 4.0 = _____ grams of carbohydrate

Fat = (Your active caloric needs) _____ multiplied by 0.30 =
_____ calories,   divided by 9.0 = _____ grams of fat

Factors That Will Determine What You Choose to Store and Eat

⊃ **The type of food your family prefers.** Your choice of emergency food should be linked as closely as possible to the realities of your pending disaster. In

"The food here is **TERRIBLE,** and the portions are **TOO SMALL.**"
—Woody Allen

other words, if you and the kids love steak at every
dinner, think again about how that stored steak will
look after six days without the freezer working due
to a power outage.

➲ *How long your supposed "emergency" will last.* There
are many forms in which you can buy your beans:
canned, freeze-dried, dried whole, and dehydrated
into a powder, to name a few. Each form will have its
advantages and disadvantages in regard to its shelf
life and palatability, or in other words, how long it
will store before it gets nasty, or at the very least,
becomes virtually nutrition free.

➲ *The age and health of your family members.* Dietary
restrictions of one kind or another are very common. Grandpa Joe and his dentures will not be happy
campers when he attempts to eat leathery lentils
that were either stored too long or undercooked because of lack of water, fuel, time, or ability. Bouncing
baby Francine will be equally unimpressed at your
meal plan. Take time to research family members
who may have certain food allergies; an allergic reaction can range from an annoying inconvenience to
killing your loved one. I don't care what the emergency food company phone representative said about
their company's one-size-fits-all food storage plan
being the best, people don't have the same needs.
Think ahead to avoid food preparation hassles and
pissed off family members.

➲ *Your home's ability to store the food of your choice
through variations in temperature, available space,
and location.* While bulk foods such as whole grains
are cheap, they're heavy and take up space . . . a lot
of space if your survival scenario involves weeks of
cooking rice in the backyard. While people can and
have gotten creative with how they've stored their
food stash—five-gallon buckets becoming legs for the
dining room table, for example—it may not be practical for your efficiency apartment on the thirtieth floor.
All stored foods are highly affected by fluctuations in
temperature. If you live in a warm climate, or experience times of the year where it gets warm in your
house, your stored food will not last as long as it will
in a home that achieves a constant, low temperature.

- ⊃ *How big your wallet or purse is.* Many prepackaged emergency or "backpacking" foods, while convenient, are not cheap. You pay for the preparation that goes into that pasta primavera and cranberry-walnut chicken. Large families or those on a budget will be turned off at the pricey cost per meal for these options.

- ⊃ *Pets.* Don't forget about Fluffy and Scrapper when storing food. Like human canned food, canned pet food is a no-brainer to store. Dry dog and cat foods can be stored in the same way as dry human food. If you have finicky pets, they won't be if they get hungry enough. Jillions of unwanted back-alley feral dogs and cats in the country are proof to the fact that animals will eat about anything to stay alive. Although I can't imagine that your family would have any wasted leftover food on their plates after an extended crisis, any leftovers that for lack of safe cold storage can't be saved should be given to Peaches and Fido. I once lived at a radical hippy commune that made their own dog food from scratch. The pets ate like the people, who were all vegetarian. While many will argue that this is not healthy for a dog, and they may be right, the commune dogs were as obnoxiously healthy as ever. Maybe they cleaned up on supplemental mice and rats, too. In a serious pinch, eat the pet food. While it's not for human consumption, neither is the weird stuff written about later in this chapter that humans all over the planet have eaten in dire need. When I was a little boy, like most little boys, I experimented with eating many things. I specifically remember how the dog food tasted that day long ago because my mom whipped my butt when she caught me with my face down in the doggie dish. One morning, years later, I ate a common breakfast cereal and instantly flashed back

> "Give a man a fish and you feed him for **A DAY.** Teach a man to fish and you feed him for **LIFETIME.**"
> —Chinese proverb

to the dog food incident. Yup, one of those popular, "healthy" breakfast cereals tastes just like dry dog food—without the milk.

Junk Food Junkie

Although I love, appreciate, and recognize good-tasting food when I eat it, I'm not attached to the whims of my taste buds. After all, I drank blended tuna fish for years. Although you probably won't choose to get your protein in this manner, when push comes to shove, food is nothing more than fuel for your body. The more food you eat that has the desired nutrition your body demands, the less food you'll require to get your nutritional demands met. Translation, you will need to buy and store less food for your family. Junk food is just that, junk, and you will require much more of it to fuel your body during times of stress. High-quality simple foods, such

as whole grains, possess much more burn time for the buck (and are typically much cheaper than processed foods) and are great additions to any survival pantry. You would require cases of sugary snack cakes to achieve the equivalent in nutrition of a few pounds of whole wheat.

Here's one more thing on the "my food needs to taste good" school of thought. If this last statement is true for you, so be it, but plan now for having the proper culinary training and ingredients required to make your food taste wonderful long after the grid goes down. For hundreds of years, the spice trade was one of the most lucrative on the planet, as our ancestors were all tired of eating bland, crappy-tasting food. Who can blame them? My concern, as a survival instructor, is not how your food tastes, but that you have food to taste at all. I have eaten many things in the wilderness that would make most people vomit, all in the name of survival nutrition, and because we didn't have any other options. My point is this: please don't get too picky with your food if supplies run thin. Necessity might require from you someday that you ingest things that you didn't think were edible. Many, many people all over the earth have been reduced to eating the greatest of all taboos, each other. This book will not include ideas for barbecuing Uncle John, but it will include bare-bones survival fare that is cheap, easy to store for long periods of time, nutritional, and, with a little bit of ingenuity, good tasting.

What About Fasting?

I know many people who have fasted for more than three weeks and they are still breathing air. While hunger is a bummer, especially when combined with the stresses of a survival situation, food-deprived folks can still function for long periods of time. Fasting (deliberately not eating) has been around for thousands of years, and in some world religions it's standard practice. Fasts lasting longer than two or three days use up liver glycogen completely and consume nearly half of the muscles' glycogen stores. After this, if the body is still without food, the body synthesizes glucose through a process called *gluconeogenesis*. Ketone bodies are then formed by the oxidation of fatty acids that are utilized as energy by the muscles and brain. In a normally fed individual, ketone oxidation accounts for less than 3 percent of the total energy bill for that person. Longer fasts produce so many ketone bodies that they provide for more than 40 percent of the body's energy requirements and up to 50 percent of the brain's glucose needs. Eventually, the longer the fast, the less glucose the body uses, therefore reducing the amount of cannibalization the body must undergo to support gluconeogenesis. Fasts lasting more than fourteen days cause the body's basal metabolic rate (BMR) to decrease by 21 percent as the body becomes superefficient with its resources.

WHY BE HUNGRY WHEN YOU CAN BE STONED?

No one likes the feeling of hunger. Its persistent presence gnaws at even the most psychologically hardened souls. If things get bad at your place, consider what others have done to lessen the feelings of lack. Eritrean women are known to tightly strap flat stones to their stomachs to lessen hunger pangs. Mothers in many countries boil water with stones and tell the children that the food is almost ready, hoping they will fall asleep waiting. Let's hope (and prepare) that it doesn't come to this.

Real-life starvation scenarios, such as the Donner Party in which far more women survived than men, show that women may have a metabolic advantage over the guys. As an important side note, medical research has found that ketone production may come to a screeching halt after eating only 150 grams of carbohydrates per day. This means that if you have fasted, and then eat a very small amount of food, you lose your former ketone production advantage when the food is gone. I have talked to people with a lot of field experience who feel this is nonsense, so the choice is yours in how your body may react to the effects of fasting and food.

"When the LAST tree falls, when the LAST river is polluted and when there is NOT A BREATH of clean air left, people will realize YOU CAN'T EAT MONEY."
—Toilet stall door in Canadian high school basement

If you haven't tried fasting, do so. Your family may hate you for a few days but feel free to blame it on me. The best time to find out that you become a raging ass with low blood sugar is not when your food supply is running low. Fasting will give you a broad look at how you and your family, physiologically and psychologically, deal with the stress of a no-calorie meal plan. Unknowns are scary so anytime you can cut down on the fear factor with simple training and hands-on experience, do it with enthusiasm.

The Minnesota Starvation Experiment: A Window into a Hungry Person's World

Wow! My clothes look sloppy! My belt buckle is in the last notch—a decrease of three notches since the starvation began.
—Lester Glick, Minnesota volunteer, March 16, 1945

In the early 1940s during World War II, thirty-six young male conscientious objectors participated in a human semistarvation study for six months conducted by Ancel Keys at the University of Minnesota. The intention of the study was to learn the physiological and psychological effects of semistarvation in the hopes of dealing with the rehabilitation of refeeding civilians who had been starved during the war. As the psychological ramifications of the study were just as important as the physical, all participants were heavily screened for extraordinary psychological stamina. Overall, the participants lost 25 percent of their total body weight in a controlled, clinical setting.

For the first three months of the semistarvation experiment, the men ate normally while researchers documented their personalities and eating patterns. For the next six months, the volunteers were fed half of what they normally ate. The study ended with a three-month rehabilitation time in which the men were gradually refed to prestudy levels. In all cases, the volunteers experienced radically altered physical, psychological, and social changes.

> **I'm beginning to want to isolate myself from the other subjects who are develop-**
> **ing all kinds of weird behaviors ... and the starvation is less than half over!**
> —Lester Glick, June 24, 1945

Predictably, all of the men fantasized about food: in their conversations, read-
ings, thoughts, and actions. Menial tasks during the day were harder and harder
to accomplish as the volunteers' concentration remained solely upon food. As the
experiment continued, and sex drives plummeted, the men smuggled food, made
bizarre mixtures of food which were eaten in long, drawn-out rituals of two hours
or more, and collected cookbooks, menus, and educational literature on food, including basic agriculture. As the calorie cut continued, they hoarded food memorabilia
such as kitchen utensils, hot plates, and coffee makers. The "collecting" progressed
to nonfood items as well, such as old clothes and garage sale junk. Chewing gum
was limited after one subject was found chewing more than forty packages of gum
per day, so much that he developed a sore mouth from the exercise. All achieved
extreme pleasure by smelling food or watching others eat.

> **Books on starvation tell us that hungry people eat clay, wood, bark, unclean ani-**
> **mals, and often become cannibalistic. Yesterday I took the lead out of a pencil and**
> **began chewing the wood. I think about how cannibalism is a terrible option for a**
> **starving person, and try to put it out of my mind, but I can't seem to stop thinking**
> **about it. People are a terrible bore. I don't know what I'd do without my private**
> **room and my stack of cookbooks.**
> —Lester Glick, June 25, 1945

During the refeeding phase, as had been the case for some of the men who had
binged during the experiment, some continued eating to the point of vomiting,
only to start all over again after the vomiting ceased. After three months of normal meals the men still complained of increased hunger after eating. Some men,
whose daily estimate of calories topped 10,000, would start snacking within a half
an hour of eating. After more than five months of refeeding, most of the volunteers reported somewhat normal eating patterns but some continued to eat much
greater portions than when the experiment began.

> **Today Jim and I made a routine visit to a restaurant to watch people eat. We**
> **bought our usual black coffee and directed our attention to a well-dressed lady**
> **who had ordered a beautiful pork chop dinner. She tinkered with the chop, eat-**
> **ing less than half of that wonderful looking tenderloin. She nibbled at the string**
> **beans, embellished with nuts and bacon. Finally she ordered a fantastic coconut**
> **cream pie, which appeared to us as God's prize creation. She pushed off the won-**
> **derful whipped cream on the top, nibbled daintily at the filling, leaving the crust**
> **untouched. What a stupid woman! She paid her bill and left the restaurant, with**
> **Jim and I close behind. Jim stopped her and proceeded to lecture her on world**
> **hunger and how she was contributing to it. She shrieked an exclamation and took**
> **off running.**
> —Lester Glick, July 6, 1945

Most of the psychological changes such as collecting and hoarding continued, as did
the total preoccupation with food. Although the men were chosen for their more

than average psychological stamina, most experienced severe emotional break-down as the semistarvation progressed. Depression, apathy, irritability, anger, and radical mood swings, along with the inability to function overall, dogged the volunteers relentlessly. Anxiety in once-stable men increased as nail-biting and smoking were chosen to combat hypersensitivity and nervousness. Humor between the men disappeared and they became socially withdrawn from each other, visiting friends and family, and the facilitators. The men showed signs of impaired judgment and alertness, along with impaired concentration and comprehension, as well as poor motor coordination, reduced strength, hair loss, decreased tolerance of cold, headaches, added sensitivity to noise and light, ringing in the ears, and spots in front of their eyes. Their body's physiological processes seemed to slow down across the board, from body temperatures to heart rates, including a drop in their normal basal metabolic rate (BMR) by nearly 40 percent. Upon refeeding, those who consumed the most calories also had the biggest gain in their BMR.

> Cannibalism, death through starvation, grass salads, and eating garbage are more than fleeting thoughts. We are told that we are starving so that thousands of starving people might be fed. Such thoughts are fleeting, and I'd give them up in a minute for a few slices of bread.
> —Lester Glick, July 8, 1945

The Minnesota study proved the body's amazing ability to adapt in times of food shortages. In times of dire need, everything, including the sex drive, takes a back seat toward the goal of obtaining more calories. The study should make it glaringly obvious as to the benefits of a well-thought-out food storage plan, and hopefully your ability to improvise gathering calories should your "plan" disappear. I've included the study here not just to encourage you to store food, but to have you realize the psychological, not just physiological, ramifications of a forced low-calorie diet. If your family finds itself with limited food opportunities, and starts acting a bit weird, you will have been forewarned.

Epilogue
A few years ago, sixteen of the thirty-six original participants who were still alive were interviewed. Despite all the hardships and suffering they endured, all of them said that they would do it all over again, saying the study was the most impactful experience of their lives. After the original study ended, many of the participants worked at rebuilding the war zone of Europe, working in ministries and diplomatic careers. Survivors of the study living in Florida still meet regularly. All continue to be strong advocates for human service programs, promoting justice, peacemaking, and concerns about world hunger.

What about Living off the Fat of the Land with Wild Edible Plants and Game?
There is perhaps no quicker way to ruin your day than by putting the wrong thing into your mouth and swallowing it, and I speak from experience. There are many

variables when using wild edible plants and game as part of a survival plan. The more variables a plan contains, the more moving parts there are, the more Murphy's Law is liable to act, and that which can go wrong, will go wrong. Some people reading this have read other survival books in which many wild edible plants were shared. A few of you have taken field courses on wild edible plants taught by knowledgeable and enthusiastic instructors, a few of who are probably friends of mine. I have attended plant walks where the instructor stated confidently to mesmerized students that the instructor could live off the seeds of one plant alone for many months, although they had never attempted

"Hunger is the **BEST SAUCE** in the world."
—Cervantes

to do so for even a day. Some readers will gaze into their backyards or back forty and see endless amounts of wild edible plants: cattails, watercress, prickly pear fruit, and others. Some no doubt feel confident that nature's bounty will be there in their time of need, oblivious to potential drought, flooding, fire, insect infestation, human or animal exploitation, premature cold snaps or warm spells, chemical contamination, dubious nutritional and caloric values, limited palatability, odd preparation requirements for edibility, and seasonal availability. All wild game, both large and small, have their share of challenges, legal and otherwise. Hunting and trapping are true arts and require much practice, the right equipment, and the proper area to be successful. That said, some people in the United States could live on roadkill alone and I do envy you. On the positive side, rats and mice are easy to catch but most of you will quickly exhaust your supply.

I'll let you in on a little survival instructor secret. There is a great yearning by many to live off the land, wild and free, perpetuated by movies, television, outdoor magazines, and all aspects of the media. Whether it was cowboys and Indians, Daniel Boone, Grizzly Adams, or Jeremiah Johnson, the illusion of forever successfully living from the land has long ago been hammered into the human psyche. The concept has reached mythological proportions, containing a certain glamour and mystique equaled only by the romance of martial arts or the Navy SEALs—both highly exaggerated by the media as well. When a survival instructor works with innocent, wide-eyed students eager to place the instructor upon a pedestal and/or the media, whose bottom line is selling a product at the expense of truth, a change can happen. The instructor may start believing his own BS. In other words, you might be taught survival concepts and skills that don't have a snowball's chance in hell of working under the real-life pressures of a true survival scenario. Along with the cool "wild" things you can eat, your survival instructor should also mention the extreme psychological and physiological stress your body, mind, and emotions will be under, and that your fine and complex motor skills, including your cognitive skills, will have gone to hell in a handbasket, seriously compromising your hunting and gathering abilities. But hey, that reality just ain't no fun, and it don't make very good TV neither.

Thanks to Rambo, clueless TV producers and magazine editors, testosterone, and lots of ego there is great pressure for survival instructors to make magic and prove themselves at all costs, including honesty, to be able to pull the rabbit out of the hat regardless of circumstances. History has proved this to be a lie, as many indigenous peoples, depending upon the life zone in which they lived, died young while living off the fat of the land. The truth is, for much of the planet, there isn't a whole lot of fat left, at least not in my area. In summary, closely scrutinize survival teachings through a fierce lens of discretion and realism. Even if you possess the needed training and resources to do so, take a serious look at your situation to see

Beware

the SURVIVAL INSTRUCTOR

if harvesting calories from the land is realistic for your survival setup. Gathering wild plants and animals for food may be the icing on the cake for your survival plan, but I would strongly caution you against it being the "cake." In the end, if you're still determined to "play Indian," be willing to accept death as a possibility.

This snippet is in no way meant to discourage you from learning and practicing what indigenous food resources you have in your backwoods or your backyard. Learn all you possibly can about your area and what type of calories, if need be, can be harvested or hunted. Putting all of your eggs in one basket is not a wise move with any of your family's resources, especially food.

So Glad to Have You for Dinner!

"THE MISFORTUNE OF OTHERS, EVEN YOUR OWN FAMILY, LEAVES YOU COMPLETELY INDIFFERENT WHEN YOU HAVE NOTHING IN YOUR BELLY. YOU ROB RUTHLESSLY; YOU WOULD EVEN KILL."
—HYOK KANG

In our planet's history, famines, both "natural" and man-made, have caused people to literally eat anything they could shove into their mouths. In the twentieth century alone, more than 70 million people died from starvation around the world. If you have the mind-set and the will, history proves that nothing is taboo to eat when extreme hunger knocks at your door. The following true examples, which are just a smattering of scenarios that have occurred, are not meant to gross or bum you out. They are meant to knock you out of American complacency and encourage you to take your food storage program seriously. They are also meant to inspire appreciation within you and your loved ones to be grateful for the food you eat now, and hopefully in the future. Have the "picky eaters" in your tribe read this section twice. Bon Appétit.

Egypt, AD 1200–1202

A drought prevented the Nile River from its annual flooding, preventing people from growing their crops. Approximate death toll was 110,000, due to starvation, cannibalism, and disease.

Europe, AD 1315–1322, the Great Famine

Bad weather and crop failure caused the death of millions of people by starvation, disease, infanticide, and cannibalism. At that time in Europe's history, famines were common and people were lucky to survive to the ripe old age of thirty. It seems that hard times knew no economic boundaries. In 1276, official records from the British royal family, society's wealthiest people at the time, recorded an average life span of thirty-five years.

Ireland, 1845–1849, the Great Potato Famine

Potatoes, the mainstay of the Irish diet, were inflicted with a potato blight that killed the crops. Local grain and livestock were owned by the English, and laws prevented the Irish from importing grain. The combination of crop disease and politics caused the death of 1.5 million people by starvation, cannibalism, and disease.

⬆ Disinfecting, drop by drop, a gallon of water with chlorine bleach using an improvised dropper made from a strip of paper and a spoon.

⬅ Commercial water disinfection products and good ol' household chlorine bleach.

⬇ Disinfecting nonpotable water on the roof using ultraviolet radiation from the sun.

⬆ More in-home water storage options: Fill the sink and access water from the back of the toilet. The washing machine can also be turned on and filled, sans detergent and clothes, if advance preparation allows.

⬅ A smattering of water storage and transportation options. Note the infamous condoms and the heavy-duty freezer bags, gallon and quart size. The weird-looking brown thing in the middle is a gourd canteen.

⬆ An easier way to carry 113 pounds of salvaged water . . .

⬆ . . . another option.

⬆ Various rain catchment systems
⬅ using plastic and metal storage
⬇ tanks.

⬆ B.O. busters. Both the large pressurized sprayer and the hand spray bottle can be painted black or a dark color for better heat absorption from the sun.

🔈 Kitchen containers and bathtub filled with the luscious liquid called water. Harvest and store what you can until the pipes run dry.

STORED FOODS AND COOKING OPTIONS . . .

➲ Pasteurizing nonpotable water in a commercial solar oven.

🔅 Various forms of stored food: (from left to right) Pasta, dried fruit, canned food, MREs (meals ready to eat), freeze-dried and dehydrated food in single-serving foil packets, whole grains and legumes, and dried food in nitrogen-packed #10 can.

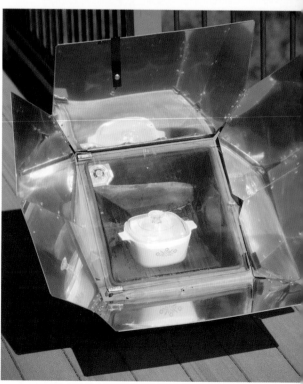

⬆ Cook stove options. The small fold-up stove in front uses hexamine or other fuel tablets for fuel. Notice the coffee-can cook pot on the far left with bailing wire handle and tinfoil lid.

↺ No conventional kitchen stove? Not a problem with a handy dandy two-burner camping stove.

⬆ Preparing to break-in a Dutch oven with its first meal in the backyard.

➲ Picture perfect pots; one sporting a genuinely jamming Ace Frehley (my boyhood hero) rubber ducky. Note the metal loop on the lids for securely tying them down, with or without survival gear inside, when needing to hit the road.

LIGHTING UP YOUR LIFE . . .

1 Bright ideas to light up your life! The blue LED flashlight in the middle has its own solar-panel charger built in, thus it never needs conventional batteries. Note that extra batteries are stored within their original package.

2 Lovable lanterns. The white gas (middle) and propane (right) models smell and get hotter than hell when lit. Use caution, common sense, and serious ventilation if you dare use them indoors. The battery-operated lantern on the left is the only safe lantern of this variety for use indoors.

3 Curious candle collection. The big green one in the back, through a combination of poor design and cheap wax, sucks as the flame tunnels into the candle as it burns, hiding the flame before it finally puts itself out. The "turd"-shaped candles in the front are handmade from beeswax and bear fat with a hand-twisted, two-ply wick made from a dogbane plant (*Apocynum cannabinum*).

4 Two "lights" for the price of one by using a mirror. Horrid, jail jumpsuit orange-colored candles can be bought cheaply in after-Halloween sales.

5 Smaller oil lamps give off a surprising amount of light. "Glass wicks" ensure worry-free operation for years.

6 Oil lamps, just like grandma used.

7 Homemade oil lamp made from a tuna can, cooking oil, and a wick created from a strip of paper towel.

8 Candle lanterns. Notice the homemade one in the center created from a glass food jar, wire for hanging, sand, and a candle.

MORE FUN WITH LIGHT . . .

1 Cute but "ho-hum" chemical light sticks before boiling.
2 Bright . . .
3 Brighter . . .
4 Brightest!
5 Heated sticks kick out a fierce amount of light, at the expense of longevity.

Piece of resin-saturated wood (pitch stick) propped open into four prongs to allow for greater oxygen when lit and burning.

Awesome aboriginal candle. Raw pitch wood (from a conifer) is below. Notice yellowish color at far left.

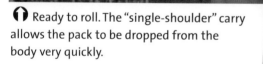 Ready to roll. The "single-shoulder" carry allows the pack to be dropped from the body very quickly.

 The "double-shoulder" carry is similar to a modern backpack. This method is more comfortable for longer treks.

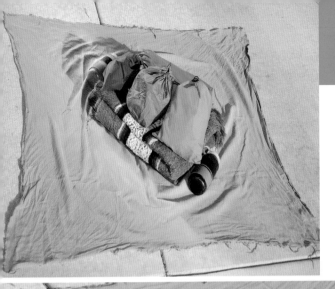

⊂ Improvised fabric backpack with gear.

⊍ When the pack is "closed," this side will be in contact with your body. Stuff sacks allow you to carry odds and ends in an organized fashion without losing them from the pack. Water bottle weight is counterbalanced on either side.

⬆ Long live the wheel! Don't let an addiction to petroleum dumb you down when needing to transport the goods, human or otherwise.

⬆ Help with "getting out of dodge" while keeping your hands free: conventional backpacks, day packs, fanny packs, and portable shelter options (tents and tarps).

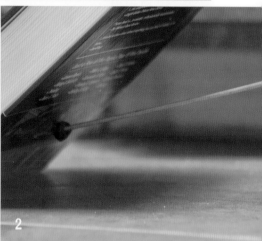

1 "Taking out" the pantry rodent raider. Urban deadfall trap made from a book, two pencils, dental floss, a match, and a shish-ka-bob skewer.

2 Two raisins skewered on bait stick serve as an incentive.

3 Commercial traps set in a rodent run. The mousetrap in the middle, baited with peanut butter, can be modified like the rattrap at right using a piece of whatever to improvise a "death paddle," allowing the animal to trip the trap by scurrying across its surface; no bait needed.

1

1 Five-star survival cuisine: mouth-watering rat on a platter with colorful garnish.

2 Welcome home, honey!

3 You'll dazzle after-disaster dinner guests with your succulent mouse on a stick. Watch 'em beg for the recipe!

4 Eating what bugs you. A hopper-ka-bob, fresh off the grill.

2

3

4

🎙 Got rats? Watch the wee ones squeal with delight when playing fashion with their dolls using the pelts from your kills. Surviving in style for the "nuclear family"!

FIRING THINGS UP . . .

🎙 Light my fire! A few of the more common ways to achieve ignition. Unfortunately, the white-tipped strike-anywhere matches in the Prince-approved purple match safe are slowly but surely disappearing from the market due to federal regulations. Thanks for keeping us safe, guys!

① A bevy of commercial technical tinders and other things that burn. Tinders are typically used to help ignite fuel, wet or otherwise, when using meager ignition sources. Other than my homemade tinder described in *98.6 Degrees: The Art of Keeping Your Ass Alive!*, my favorite is the Fire-Up brand in the middle.

➲ Extreme close-up of using oooo steel wool and batteries to create heat.

➲ Notice the tinder bundle made from juniper bark and dryer lint.

⊍ The "glowing snake" of steel wool at the bottom will be quickly put into the tinder bundle and blown into flame—a harmony of heat/ignition, fuel, and oxygen.

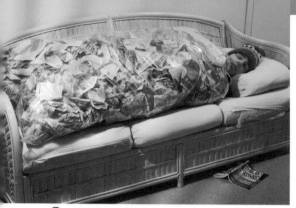

⬆ Robbie Rubbish homemade sleeping bag created from barrel liners, duct tape, and newspaper.

⮕ Keeping in touch with updates from authorities with a hand-crank powered AM/FM radio.

⬇ Emergency potties in the garage ready for deposits. Notice scrap lumber as an improvised toilet seat.

BLOATED BUREAUCRATS

In its 2006 yearly report that measures Americans' access to food, the United States Department of Agriculture (USDA) reported that 12 percent of Americans, some 35 million people, could not put food on the table at least part of last year. Of these, 11 million reported going hungry at times. Regardless of this, the USDA has chosen to phase out the use of the word "hunger" in its reporting, instead choosing to use the term "very low food security." Mark Nord, a USDA sociologist and lead author of the change, said that, "hungry [is] . . . not a scientifically accurate term for the specific phenomenon being measured in the food security survey [and] . . . we don't have a measure of that condition." A panel recommending that the word "hunger" be dropped from the USDA vocabulary said the word "should refer to a potential consequence of food insecurity that, because of prolonged, involuntary lack of food, results in discomfort, illness, weakness, or pain that goes beyond the usual uneasy sensation." Could they be serious? Seeing as how USDA reports indicate that the number of the hungriest Americans, whoops, I mean Americans that apparently aren't yet starving, but who are simply experiencing the "usual uneasy sensation" has risen over the past five years, wouldn't it be a better use of tax dollars to take some action about "very low food security" in our nation? For all the overfed bureaucrats (who doubtfully have ever had a "usual uneasy sensation") who chose to spend their time and our money helping to wipe out the word "hunger" instead of hunger itself, this "Famine" section is for you. It proves that we do indeed have a measure of "that condition" called hunger.

The Great Plains of the United States, 1930s

The United States experienced the worst drought of the twentieth century. The resulting lack of precipitation caused massive dust storms, which dominated the landscape, causing severe health problems while destroying crops and killing livestock. Death toll is unknown. Dust storms destroyed my grandmother's garden several times in a season. As the garden was necessary for the family's survival, she simply replanted, watering the acre-plus garden by hand with a bucket. The subsequent malnutrition and hard labor nearly killed my pregnant grandmother (and my aunt). A couple of times a month my grandfather would bring home "treats" from town, which consisted of two oranges. One orange was split between her two children, the other eaten by my grandmother during the pregnancy of her third child, in which she ate the entire thing, peelings and all.

The Soviet Famine, 1932–1934

The Soviet Famine was initiated by Josef Stalin in an attempt to boost industrialization financed by forced collective farms in which grain production fell by 40 percent. His draconian measures included forbidding peasants to leave the country without permission; expelling, killing, or sending rich peasants to labor camps; and forcibly seizing what little food remained to double grain exports to raise cash for his failed plan. The predicted chaos included a report issued by an Italian consul member in the Ukraine reporting "a growing commerce in human meat" and that people were killing and eating their own children. Astute authorities immediately responded, not with food, but by distributing posters that read: "Eating Dead Children Is Barbarism." Due to a national cover-up forbidding doctors to disclose on death certificates that the deceased had starved to death, numbers for the total dead are sketchy but estimates are at 5 to 8 million people, 10 to 25 percent of the population of the Ukraine.

> When the snow melted true starvation began. People had swollen faces and legs and stomachs. They could not contain their urine . . . and now they ate anything at all. They caught mice, rats, sparrows, ants, earthworms. They ground up bones into flour, and did the same thing with leather and shoe soles; they cut up old skins and furs to make noodles of a kind and they cooked glue. And when the grass came up, they began to dig up the roots and ate the leaves and the buds; they used everything there was; dandelions, and burdocks and bluebells and willow root, and sedums, and nettles . . .
> —Soviet writer Vasily Grossman, recording the spring of 1933

"A crust eaten **IN PEACE,** is better than A BANQUET partaken in ANXIETY."
—Aesop

The Warsaw Ghetto, 1940–1942

Three hundred eighty thousand Jews were confined to a 3.5-mile area that normally housed 160,000. The population eventually reached 445,000 before the Nazis sealed off the area with a ten-foot wall, with the intention of starving all of the inhabitants within nine months. Official food rationing provided 2,613 kilocalories per day for Germans, 699 kilocalories per day for Poles, and 184 kilocalories for Jews in the Ghetto. Tens of thousands died from starvation and disease.

> People of all ages died in the streets, in shelters, in homes, and in hospitals. Nighttime produced a special hazard as even the most courageous or insensitive lost their nerve when, in the darkness of the night, they happened to accidentally

step on some soft object that turned out to be a cadaver. The family commonly removed a body from their home onto the street, after removing all evidence of identity. In that way, they might be able to use the extra ration card for a few days.... Mothers hid dead children under beds for days in order to receive a larger food ration.

—Witness account of life in the Ghetto

Northern China, 1958–1962

Chairman Mao's failed bid to "industrialize" his nation, along with several natural disasters and drought, killed an unbelievable 30 million people by starvation, disease, infanticide, and cannibalism. Desperate families swapped each other's children to eat, thus avoiding having to eat their kin. The pest reduction campaign to protect crops included the entire country beating on pots and pans to prevent sparrows and other birds from landing until they fell down dead with exhaustion. Without the predation of the birds, insect pests multiplied, damaging crops. During the mass starvation, clueless officials doubled the exports of grain and decreased food importation. Although it was the world's largest famine, it was not revealed to the rest of the world until 1981.

On the muddy path leading from the village, dozens of corpses lay unburied. In the barren fields there were others; and amongst the dead, the survivors crawled slowly on their hands and knees searching for wild grass seeds to eat. In the ponds and ditches people squatted in the mud hunting for frogs and trying to gather weeds. It was winter, and bitterly cold, but ... everyone was dressed only in thin and filthy rags tied together with bits of grass and stuffed with straw.... Sometimes neighbors and relatives simply fell down as they shuffled through the village and died without a sound.... The dead were left where they died because no one had the strength to bury them.... The silence was unnatural. The village oxen had died, the dogs had been eaten and the chickens and ducks had long ago been confiscated by the Communist Party in lieu of grain taxes. There were no birds left in the trees, and the trees themselves had been stripped of their leaves and bark. At night there was no longer even the scratching of rats and mice, for they too had been eaten or had starved to death.

—Famine survivor Mrs. Liu recounting the winter of 1959.
Of the 300 people who lived in Mrs. Liu's village, only 80 survived

Biafra (now Nigeria), Africa, 1967–1969

Civil war–caused famine kills 1 million people, leaving another 3.5 million to suffer from extreme malnutrition.

North Korea, 1994–1998

A combination of reduced Chinese and Russian food subsidies, along with the effects of collective farming, flooding, drought, and government corruption, caused an estimated 2 to 3 million people to die of starvation, disease, and cannibalism. Defectors reported the elderly routinely walked out into fields to die, thereby reducing the burden of having to be fed.

Weeds, of whatever kind, were boiled up and swallowed in the form of soup. The soup was so bitter that we could barely keep it down. Our neighbors collected grass and tree bark—usually pine or various shrubs. They grated the bark and boiled it up before eating it. And much good it did them: their faces swelled from day to day until they finally perished. The poorest children lived on nothing but grass, and during class their stomachs rumbled. After a few weeks their faces began to swell, making them look well nourished. Then their faces went on growing until they looked as though they had been inflated. Their cheeks were so puffy that they couldn't see the blackboard. Some of them were covered with impetigo and flaking skin. My friends and I caught frogs and cooked them skewered on bicycle spokes. We also ate grasshoppers, which are delicious fried, as are dragonflies. Grilled, the flesh of fat dragonflies tastes a bit like pork; but you can eat them raw, once the head and wings have been removed. Sparrows and quails ended up in the pot. We caught them with nets set in wooden frames. Other birds, like crows, we fried on a brazier.

—Excerpted from Hyok Kang's book *This is Paradise!*

Depressed? Don't be! Focus on the positive and get off your butt and make sure your family has the food they need for potential emergencies. After all, stored food is a life insurance policy you can really sink your teeth into.

Food Storage Options

Now that you're good and hungry, let's discuss the many options that you have concerning what form your stored food might take. Canned, dried, or dehydrated meals, whole grains packed in buckets, freeze-dried food, and MREs (meals ready to eat) are the more common types of food-storage strategies on the market. All have their advantages and disadvantages. All will, sooner or later, need to be *rotated* to prevent your stock from going bad and/or losing much of its nutritional value. There are extremely comprehensive books on long-term food storage. The Mormons (Church of Jesus Christ of Latter-day Saints) are the kings and queens of doing their homework regarding this and much can be learned from their generations of experience. Check out a Mormon bookstore in your area or search online for other food storage information.

Keep in mind that the focus of many of these books is a long-term storage plan for food that will last one year or more. The task of storing food for such an extended amount of time can seem so complex and daunting that many families throw up their hands in frustration and blow off storing any food altogether. Slow down and breathe. How much food your family should have on hand depends on your family's supposed emergency. Most households, excluding destitute college students, already have an ample supply of food on hand that should last for several days in a pinch. Maybe this is all you'll need for your perceived emergency, or all the room you have to store food in the first place. Knowing you're in an emergency situation will allow you to ration what food you do have, thus making meager rations last even longer. If you want specific lists of stuff to buy for a comprehensive, long-term food storage strategy, research other books whose focus is on providing you with that information.

The Simple Bare-Minimum Food Storage Plan

The average person eats one ton of food each year. If you're not into storing large amounts of food, have on hand at least the bare minimum to get you through a crisis and to remain independent from the bureaucratic and logistical nightmare that will envelop those who failed to have reserve food supplies available. *At minimum, your family should have a two- to four-week supply of food on hand at all times.* This food should require little or no cooking and meet all of your nutritional needs. It should be easy to access, portable in a pinch, and require the bare minimum of preparation and fuss. To implement this type of food storage program, simply buy more food from the store than you normally would, and when you get down to the emergency two- to four-week supply, make a trip to the store. In your mind, your home should be "out of food" when you reach your two- to four-week stock. If you bite into this stock from laziness or whatever, replace it as soon as possible. This extra food should not sit in the closet for months. It should be a part of your regular meal plan and ROTATED normally. In truth, it is not "stored" food at all, simply extra food that you have on hand as part of your regular fare in the kitchen.

I can't emphasize enough that you keep this extra food as simple as possible concerning its preparation. On my outdoor courses, I state in writing that clients should bring simple foods that require NO COOKING. Regardless of this, many still do. Because they didn't pay attention to the instructions, we are at times forced to create a heat source to cook their dinner. This heat source usually takes the form of a campfire, which requires a safe area to build the fire, dry fuel, an ignition source, knowledge of how to make a fire, the constant adding and adjustment of the fuel, hassling with rocks or berms of dirt to suspend a fireproof cooking container that someone happened to pack, water, and lots of time. While the rest of us have eaten our bagels and trail mix or tuna with crackers, the food cookers are still trying to get their water to boil. Don't underestimate how tedious cooking over a campfire can be (assuming you have the materials and know-how to do so), especially under the physical, mental, and emotional strain of an emergency. There are many down and dirty foods that are ready to eat on the spot. For most families, **canned foods** will be the cat's meow as they are widely available, durable and portable, cheap, store well for up to two years, and are easy to open and eat, in the can with a stick if necessary, with zero preparation.

Food Storage Rules of Thumb

There is no perfect food storage plan for every family as there are far too many variables to contend with, from personal dietary preferences and restrictions to global climates affecting storage. Many people waste much of their food storage supply by failing to obey a few simple rules of thumb regarding purchasing and storing food in bulk. Almost everyone interested in the storage of food will agree upon the following rules.

1 *Store only what your family will eat.* This sounds straightforward yet many families buy food, especially bulk items, based solely on price rather than what the family actually eats. It doesn't matter if you get a good deal on lima beans if your family hates them or has never had them. They will surely eat them if they get hungry enough, but why go through the hassle and the dirty looks? In addition, an emergency is not the time to find out that someone in your family is allergic to the new food you just introduced them to.

2 *Faithfully ROTATE what you store.* Depending on what you store and how it's stored, you must continually rotate your food stock. Seasoned food storage junkies frequently refer to the concept of "first in, first out," abbreviated as FIFO. If not already possessing dates from the factory, all containers should be dated as to when they were purchased to easily distinguish the can of corn that's two weeks old from the one that's two years old.

3 *Keep foods stored in the best possible conditions for maximum shelf life.* Heat, light, moisture, and excess oxygen are not friendly toward stored food. A following section will delve more deeply into details. Keep all stored food off the ground. Concrete floors can "sweat" moisture during temperature fluctuations when in direct contact with storage containers so put containers on thin wooden slates instead.

> "To lengthen thy **LIFE,** lessen thy **MEALS.**"
> —Benjamin Franklin

4 *Foods stored in moisture (canned or bottled) should not be stored longer than two years.* After this time these foods will rapidly lose their nutritional value.

5 *Use only food-grade storage containers.* Food-grade containers won't transfer potentially toxic substances from the container itself into the food. If a container does not specifically state that it is FDA approved for storing food, you should contact the manufacturer, especially if the container is plastic. Specify the characteristics of the food you're storing, whether

it's alkaline, acidic, wet or dry, etc., as these qualities may affect the container. Ideally these containers will protect the contents from light, moisture,
insects, rodents, excess heat, and air infiltration.
Check wholesale food companies for containers such
as food-grade plastic buckets, Mylar bags, or metal
containers such as #10 cans with lids. I have picked up
several used three- to five-gallon plastic food containers from restaurants or school cafeterias for free,
so be creative. Grocery stores carry a variety of plastic
containers designed to store food. Glass jars with
tight-fitting lids may also be used.

6 *Keep it simple!* Human beings can complicate anything. Looking at food storage plans in books, on the
Internet, and elsewhere will prove that people are
bound and determined to have just as many culinary
choices after a disaster as they enjoy now. Feel free
to indulge your quest for variety as you see fit, but
*the main intention of variety in your emergency diet
should be the assurance of necessary balanced nutrition for optimal health, not to titillate your taste buds.*
The more elaborate and complicated your meal plan
is, the more time, money, and effort you'll need to
spend to satiate your self-created complexities. If you
insist on having steak at every dinner, you will need
to plan ahead more than the average Joe or Jane in
order to make that happen during an emergency. To
combat the ramifications of a major catastrophe, I
stressed at the beginning of this chapter the importance of treating your stored food as *survival rations*
instead of regular meals. After reading earlier in this
chapter of what people have eaten in times of famine, you might just decide that having beans every
night for a month could be acceptable, appetite fatigue or not. If that's not going to work for your family, that's fine, but don't let your wants interfere with
your needs. If you reject the idea of storing food at all
because it's too time consuming, expensive, or (add
your excuse here)_____, your whining and
whimsy are destroying your priorities for survival! In
times of hunger, you will gladly trade your wishfully
thought of blackened salmon with baby peas for my
bought, stored, and very real plain rice.

Making a List and Checking it Twice

Ideally, your family will make a list of foods that they eat over a specific period of time. This time period is dependent upon your family's opinion of how much food they wish to store. If you think you should have a six-month supply on hand, know how much, and what, your family consumes in that time frame. You can simplify this by keeping track of all food expenditures for one month and multiplying by six, but you will lose some details of your family's food plan by doing so. While the quantities of food consumed might be similar, the variety in your family's diet may suffer by looking at only the small picture. Personally, I don't care if I eat oatmeal every morning for six months, but your tribe might.

How to Store Food for the Longest Shelf Life

Nothing beats the nutritional value and freshness of foods that have just been harvested. My family has grown a garden for years and there is no comparison between a freshly picked tomato to one that has made the long journey to the grocery store and sits lingering in the produce bin. For the majority of families, fresh food will not be an option after a crisis, thus you will need to know how to properly store the food that you purchase for your storage program. If you don't want to mess with a formal storage program, at least don't let your cupboard go bare before resupplying it at the grocery store. Murphy's Law is alive and well and you don't want the grocery store shelves to be stripped due to an emergency the day before you were going to go shopping. The following rules will directly affect how long your stored food will last. The more rules you can check off in your favor, the better your emergency food will keep and deliver prized nutrition and taste during troubled times. Not all households will be able to conform to all the rules but do the best you can for your home environment.

➲ *Keep it cool!* **Although impossible to obtain in most homes, the optimal temperature for storing most foods is 40 degrees F (4 degrees C). The lower the temperature you can achieve, the lower the rate of chemical deterioration of your food. However, if you let foods stored in liquid, such as canned goods or those bottled in glass jars, freeze they can burst or break. For every 18-degree F (10-degree C) increase in temperature, you will lose half of your food's storage life. This means that if you store food in your 72-degree F (22-degree C) closet instead of your 54-degree F (12-degree C) basement, it will last only half as long. If you don't have a basement, north-facing rooms or attached colder porches are another option. Try to avoid locations that have radical spikes in temperature variation. Unless you know your garage has a** year-round cool spot, avoid it. Most garages turn into flaming infernos during the summer months.

- ⊃ *Keep it dry!* Moisture is a huge enemy of stored food. Those who live in high-humidity climates will have a challenge on their hands. The optimal atmospheric humidity level for storing food is 15 to 10 percent or less. At 10 percent humidity, most bugs can't hatch, but you'll be hard pressed to find such an environment unless you live in the desert. That said, even Arizona has times of high humidity, the most notable being the summer monsoon season. Factor your changing climactic and weather conditions into your food storage equation and avoid packing emergency foods for the long haul before, during, or after a rain. If your basement is cool but has mold crawling up the wall due to inherent dampness, find another food storage locale. Beware also of steam or moisture created from water heaters or other out-of-the-way, basement-dwelling appliances. Whenever possible

utilize food storage containers that are moisture-proof and keep them off the ground and away from walls. Using wooden slats underneath and keeping containers from touching interior walls helps prevent the "sweating" that may occur due to temperature differences from the container and the surface it's sitting on or touching.

⮑ *Keep it dark!* Ultraviolet radiation from sunlight and light in general will degrade the nutritional value of food over time, especially fat-soluble vitamins such as A, D, E, and K. Your food storage containers should be opaque, or made that way with nontoxic paint, or wrapped in newspaper, paper bags, black plastic, or put into cardboard boxes with lids to keep things dark. Your storage area as well should be kept as dark as possible. If your stored food shares the closet that you use twice daily, block off the part holding the vittles from light with sheets of cardboard or some other method.

⮑ *Keep it free of oxygen!* Oxygen oxidizes away the nutritional value from your food. Even seemingly moisture-proof containers such as plastic buckets will eventually breathe and allow oxygen and potential moisture molecules to permeate through to the food. Some food companies deal with the excess oxygen by packaging their product using nitrogen, carbon dioxide (dry ice), freeze drying and vacuum sealing, canning, or moisture-absorbing packets (desiccants).

⮑ *Keep it ROTATED!* Frankly, a solid rotational plan will forgive you from many mistakes in storing your food as you will use it up in the order it was purchased—first in, first out—so that it never stays stored for very long. Some companies offer freeze-dried fare and food preserved by other methods that will keep for many years without much thought on your part, but you will pay dearly for the thought they have put into their product. Unfortunately, I have opened more than one "nitrogen-packed in a foil pouch with an added desiccant packet sealed in a number 10 can" survival cuisine product only to have it be rancid after less than two years of storage. If the company guarantees their product can be stored safely for ten years, how do you really know unless you open their

hermetically sealed assumption? Storing what you
use and faithfully rotating what you purchase is the
simplest and safest guarantee that your grub will be
good when you pop the top.

What about Eating "Old" Food?

Foods should be thought of in two distinct ways regarding its eventual spoilage.
Fresh food has both *palatability* and *nutritional value*. While technically all food
starts to lose trace amounts of its nutritional value soon after the harvest, it might
remain palatable or edible long after most of its nutrition is gone. How much nutrition is lost in foods is dictated by how much nutrition the food had in the first place,
how the food was processed, and how it was stored before going home with you
from the store. As explained in the junk food section, empty calories are just that.
Food devoid of nutrition will leave the body starving for nutrients and you will still
feel hungry after eating large amounts of nutritionally empty food. The end result
is that a six-month supply of food that's old will not last six months, as you will eat
more of it to remain healthy and "full."

When the grid goes down, your refrigerator will undoubtedly contain at least
some perishable food. Eat the food in the refrigerator first, and then eat from the
freezer. Save stored foods until all perishables are eaten. In a well-stocked, well-
insulated freezer, foods will usually still have ice crystals in their centers—meaning they are safe to eat—for up to two days. However, use caution. After the 2003
blackout in New York City that left 9 million people without power for up to two
days, an increase in diarrhea was linked to the consumption of meat and seafood
from homeowners' unpowered refrigerators.

Nutritional loss aside, most foods will eventually break down until they look,
smell, and taste like hell. While it's impossible for the layman to know how much
nutrition a food has lost, even little Johnny is capable of spitting out something
that tastes disgusting. Luckily for us and Johnny, food that has lost its palatability is
a great clue that it doesn't contain squat for nutrition either.

Older canned food—provided it's not bulging or leaky, thus indicating toxicity—can be rotated into a fresher food diet to help extend the fresh food. Think of it
as filler that's much better than the Haitian filler of dough balls that are composed
of water, butter, salt, and dirt. One time, I was given a stored five-gallon bucket of
brown rice. Upon opening it, I discovered it was horribly rancid. I decided to experiment with this spoiled food and I ate the rice as a normal part of my diet every day
until it was gone. Other than having a slightly sour taste in my mouth and fierce
flatulence (I was single at the time), I had no problems and went about my extremely
active lifestyle as usual. At the time of this experiment, brown rice comprised half
of my daily diet. Another time, I failed to rotate a large amount of canned tuna fish
and found that many of the cans had slightly swelled up. They were out of date by
two or three years. Being stubbornly cheap and wanting to know what I could get
away with, I saved the cans that had the least amount of swelling and ate their

WHAT'S FOR DINNER?

While nowhere near exhaustive, the following are examples of what people have eaten in times of need around the world. During the civil war in Liberia in the late 1980s, desperate people ate every animal in the national zoo except for the one-eyed lion. While some of the below "food substitutes" can cause diarrhea, which can kill more quickly than starvation, the more open you are to the possibilities of what can be eaten during times of lack, the greater your chances for survival if things get really rough.

⮑ Poisonous mukhet berries. African refugees soak the berries for days to leach out toxins, after which they are ground up. The flour has little nutritional value
⮑ Wallpaper
⮑ Glue from furniture joints
⮑ Rats and mice. In Malawi, children stand on the roadsides selling

- skewers of roasted mice
- Seaweed
- Tree bark
- Grass and weeds
- Obscure plant seeds. In Africa, people excavate anthill and termite mounds to pick out the tiny seeds the insects have gathered and stored
- Corn stalks
- Dirt and clay. The epitome of "dirt poor," impoverished Haitians bake "dough" in the sun made from salt, butter, water, and dirt to make their stomachs feel full
- Dogs and cats
- Horses
- Bugs, bugs, and more bugs. In times of insect infestation and crop damage, people the world over have eaten the invaders, including locusts, crickets, and grasshoppers, which in parts of Africa are called "flying shrimp"
- Poisonous wild cassava. Made edible by pounding and soaking for days
- Mammal bones and raw skin
- Marula fruit seeds. Long after the tasty fruit is gone, hungry Africans crack open the tough seeds with rocks and the impossibly small seeds are scraped out with thin twigs
- Crows, ravens, and vultures
- Other people
- Rawhide and leather, from shoes, clothing, chairs, tables, drums, backpacks, tack from livestock, etc. ad nauseam
- Nearly any living (or dead) creature that flies, crawls, walks, or swims
- Your enemy. During World War II, some Japanese soldiers on the move tracked down, killed, and ate unlucky Allied forces
- Preserved human organs in jars. Due to severe starvation from the combined insults of combat and extreme cold, some from Napoleon's army were reduced to pillaging local medical schools for their next meal

contents, one per day for a period of a few weeks. After I finished each can, I noticed that I felt a bit "off" for half an hour, and then I was fine. I contribute this "off" feeling to my body dealing with the mild amount of toxins that were produced from the old tuna fish trapped inside the can.

I don't like wasting resources, and this includes food. I routinely eat rancid tortilla chips and pull, peel, or push mold off bagels, vegetables, cheese, and other food items. For many years I "dumpster dived" to retrieve a bounty of wasted food and have eaten in alleys where generous restaurants and health food stores left their dregs out for the homeless to feast. I eat the majority of trapped mice and rats at my homestead, not wanting to waste their value and wanting to ever know more and keep in practice about how I would react to extreme foods in times of need. On some of my field courses once-finicky students gleefully eat bugs, rodents, weird plants, flowers, crayfish, frogs, snakes, and anything else we can find. The "five-second rule" for dropped food has never applied in the wilderness.

Sometimes while pushing the envelope in my experimentation with food, I've broken through the paper. I once ate a garden squash that was far too old on the inside, but looked fine on the outside. Another time I cooked and ate beans that I had left for several months in the garden after they had cured. In both instances I was deep in the wilderness, miles away from civilization, and in both cases I wound up power puking and with a bad case of the runs. The extremely painful stomach and hamstring cramps ripped through my muscles, jerking and bending my body like a reed in the wind. The cramps made the physics of trying to go to the bathroom in a normal position awkward to say the least. In both cases the food was "cooked."

After those learning curves, I did some research into how heat affects the pathogens that cause food poisoning. I used to think that I could boil virtually anything, including older roadkill, and that the heat would destroy all of the bad bugs that would present a problem. What I learned in the four-inch-thick medical manual that a physician friend lent me was distressing. Heat does destroy the actual critter, some of which are very reluctant to die. What the heat does NOT destroy, however, is the fecal matter created by the critter. Laboratory studies have been conducted with pressure cookers cooking food for long periods of time, and the food still posed a problem due to the long-dead organism's poop. Some varieties of molds can produce toxic substances called *mycotoxins* which are also unaffected by heat, and those are most likely the culprits that knocked me for a loop in the infamous squash incident. Keep this in mind if you're forced to get creative with really nasty vittles.

I realize pulling a stunt such as eating questionable cans of tuna fish is stupid and potentially deadly, as certain organisms such as botulism and others can kill quickly. What I also realize is many so-called food storage gurus have never had the nerve to experiment in this way. Thus there is very little data about what happens to people when they consume spoiled food. There are too many variables in human physiology and "food physiology" for an experiment such as this to be accurate anyway. Anytime you deal with food that has expired, you risk becoming a victim to food poisoning or at the very least severely reduced nutrition. As my experiments prove, however, there is a gray area when eating some older foods. Use extreme caution when dealing with infants, small children, and the elderly or you could kill a loved one.

Being a survival skills instructor by trade, I'm well versed with how human nature reacts under extreme stress. I decided to include my personal stories above to give you as much information as possible about consuming marginal foods. In summary, I know what you will do if driven by extreme hunger . . . you will open the questionable can.

The Big Four: Whole Wheat, Powdered Milk, Honey, and Salt

Whole wheat, powdered milk, honey, and salt have long been the bare bones "Mormon four" regarding foods that are nutritious and store extremely well. Some authors claim that you can live for very long periods of time on just these four foods. Others say it's bunk. Unfortunately, I can't give you a definitive opinion either way as I have never lived using only these four things for any amount of time, nor do I know anyone who has. Those who scoff at using only whole wheat, honey, powdered milk, and salt for a long-term survival diet ought to have tried to do so. No amount of book research on human nutrition can replace personal experimentation. Even if two people did experiment using the fantastic four as their sole nutrition, whatever result they had does not mean you will experience the same. Many people are allergic to wheat and don't even know it until, of course, they are forced

to eat a diet in which half of the grub is whole wheat. Use common sense in deciding what you will store for your food storage program.

One of the main advantages of the four, especially salt, honey, and even whole wheat if stored properly, is that they will last *indefinitely*, or at least for as long as you'll keep your body. Salt might clump up over time but it can simply be unclumped and used as is. In time, honey will crystallize, especially raw honey, but it can be easily heated to turn itself back into liquid gold. Even nonfat powdered milk, under the authority of actual experience, has been recorded as lasting as long as fifteen years when stored properly in a dry, cool location. Long storage times are important, especially for the insanely busy average American family who doesn't want to dink around with rotating stored foods. Although rotating your food is key to making sure it's loaded with nutrition and doesn't go bad, many of you won't do it. So why not have on hand something to eat besides dirt that has a super-long storage life.

In her book *Passport to Survival* author and kitchen magician Esther Dickey takes the fantastic four to unbelievable levels of culinary creativity. She shows the reader how to separate the gluten from whole-wheat flour to make substitute meat dishes from tacos and burgers to sausage and meat loaf. Esther takes the multiuse magic of whole wheat to new heights as she cracks it, cooks it, sprouts it, steams it, and juices it (wheat grass). The book has dozens of recipes on how to take the four ingredients and first make other elemental ingredients, such as gluten and wild yeast, which can then be used for many other recipes. She even creates all kinds of desserts, from lollipops to cookies and soft ice cream with caramel syrup using only the fantastic four and remedial seasonings. A sample meal in her book reads as follows. For breakfast: waffles with caramel syrup, rolled wheat, and amber tea. For lunch: sausage pizza, gluten cream soup, milk wheat sprouts, and honey taffy. For dinner: wheat "meat" loaf, steamed wheat, pinwheel cookies, and milk. Damn, what a woman! While her book may be out of print, the desire and creativity to do more with less is still available if you have the will.

Whole Wheat

There are several varieties of whole wheat but the *hard red* or less common *hard white* variety have superior storage lives and relatively high protein contents, usually 12 percent. Hard wheats have a higher *gluten* content than soft wheats and are thus superior for making breads. Yet soft wheats excel at making flour for pastas, pastries, and breakfast cereals. Gluten is the protein within the grain that, in dough, traps the gasses produced by the fermentation of yeasts or the reactions of baking soda and powders. These trapped gases cause the dough to rise. The more gluten a grain has, the higher the dough will rise. Not all grains have gluten; rice has virtually none. How much gluten a grain has will dictate to a certain point what you can make with the grain.

Although it's been around for decades, *triticale* is still not well-known to the masses. Triticale has a very high nutritional value and is a hybrid between wheat and rye. The combination brings together the productivity of wheat with the durability of rye, and it can be used in much the same way as both.

Using whole wheat or whole grains in general will be unusual for many people. Many recipes require it being ground into flour for everyday use. High-quality, manual-crank grain mills are worth their weight in gold for any food storage program that includes whole grains and legumes. Stay away from the electric mills for obvious reasons, unless you have a manual-crank mill as a backup. Unfortunately, grains that are ground into flour will lose much of their nutritional value in less than a week. This is the reasoning behind "enriched" flours at the grocery store. Without the added shot of nutritional value, processed commercial flour would be similar to eating spackling as far as the body's nutritional needs were concerned.

Buying Whole Wheat

Whole wheat usually comes in large sacks and can be purchased from wholesale food companies. I bought some from the local health food store so check around. As with all foods for storage, research whom you're buying from and only buy food from reputable companies.

"If more of us valued **FOOD AND CHEER** and song above hoarded gold, it would be a **MERRIER WORLD.**"

—J.R.R. Tolkien

Storing Whole Wheat

Keep it whole until it's needed, and store it like everything else in opaque, moisture-proof, airproof (if possible) containers in a cool/cold, dry, dark area. Although many claim that when properly stored whole wheat can last indefinitely—at least as long as you'll need it in your current body—it's always a smart bet to rotate your food on a regular basis.

Powdered Milk (nonfat)

Powdered milk is a nutritional powerhouse for the survivor and ranks near the top of the nutritional list (eggs being the highest) because it is packed with protein. While you can buy powdered whole milk, the fat it contains will cause it to spoil long before nonfat or skim milk. Nonfat powdered milk is usually available in two forms, instant and regular. While both are nutritionally the same, the instant variety takes up more space than the regular as the instant is less dense and will more easily mix with water. Preparing the milk a few hours in advance of when it's needed will improve the flavor, and so will aerating the water as suggested in the water disinfection section. But it's not worth the risk if you have no means of refrigeration. Powdered milk can be added to a variety of foods to either thicken them or increase their nutritional value and flavor.

Buying Powdered Milk

Instant powdered milk is available at nearly every grocery store. Wholesale suppliers will have large bags that hold many pounds of the product. If this is the way you wish to go, make sure you store it well and in smaller containers to be used one at a time. When powdered milk is opened, its flavor and nutritional content start to break down. Most brands of instant milk are fortified with vitamins, especially A and D, but double-check to make sure. Look for the fanciest Grade A variety you can find, with no artificial colors or flavors. The higher quality means better processing and will typically pay off with an increased storage life.

Storing Powdered Milk

The fifteen-year-old powdered milk written about earlier is not typical, as powdered milks are very finicky to environmental changes, especially moisture, temperature, and light. Take great care to keep it dry, out of the light, and as cool/cold as possible. Vitamins A and D are particularly sensitive to heat and light and will breakdown rapidly at a rate of 20 percent per year, according to some milk producers. Powdered milk usually comes in paper sacks or cardboard cartons and should be immediately taken out and stored in opaque, moisture- and airproof containers. Glass works great as long as it's painted or taped to make it impervious to light. The use of moisture-absorbing desiccants is recommended, as powdered milk sucks moisture (and surrounding odors) out of the air. Properly stored, most authorities feel that dried milk is viable for about two years before needing to be rotated.

Heavenly Honey

Honey has been utilized on planet Earth for a very long time. Spanish cave paintings dating from 7,000 BC depict people harvesting honey from bee colonies. Although the honeybee is not native to America, transported hives found their way to the eastern coast of America by 1622. Today, Americans consume about 500 million pounds of honey each year, more than half of which is imported.

Honeys vary wildly in quality, taste (there are thousands of flavors), colors, and potential medicinal uses. Much commercial honey available at the grocery store is cut with corn syrup. Beekeepers call low-grade honey "crank case oil." To have all of the benefits of honey, you need to purchase straight quality honey. Many health food stores and independent beekeepers sell pure uncut honey. Although it might be more expensive, you get what you pay for. Look for honey that's labeled U.S. Grade A or U.S. Fancy or find a local bee person who sells his or her own. By purchasing honey directly from the source you eliminate the uncertainty of lower-grade honeys or those that are cut with other stuff.

Sweet Medicine

For thousands of years, the ancient Romans, Egyptians, Assyrians, Greeks, and Chinese used honey to treat a variety of wounds and ailments. A combination of

AWESOME ASHCAKES!

So you're stuck with 700 pounds of whole wheat, now what? With a hand-crank food mill, a few other ingredients, and the imagination and wisdom of a chef, your whole-wheat stash can produce a startling array of goodies that are truly delicious. But what if you're a white-trash slob with minimal cooking experience beyond throwing away the boxes from fast-food joints? Fear not; many outdoor survival schools use flour and water to make a simple "cake" in the campfire with a minimum of preparation and cleanup. The end product resembles hard tack from the pioneer days if well cooked. Sometimes after eating the cakes for several days straight my students call them "ass cakes." I remind the precious ones that it's better to have an ass cake than no cake. Anyway, the simplicity of the below recipe can be modified and jazzed up in dozens of ways to please the picky palate.

Ingredients:
➲ Flour
➲ Water
➲ Twig
➲ Coals from a fire

Directions:
1 With twig, mix small amount of water (2 or 3 tablespoons) with flour.
2 Use hands to flatten out dough ball into pancake shape.
3 Throw onto coals of fire.
4 Turn as necessary to keep from burning.
5 Let cool.
6 Eat.

Adding small amounts of water to the flour can be accomplished by making a little depression in the flour and pouring a tiny amount of water into the depression. A twig or something else is then used to stir the water, which will coagulate the flour around the twig. The resulting dough ball can be flattened out like a pancake. Add more dry flour if the cake sticks to your hands, because if it does, it will also stick to the coals in a fire. Toss the ashcake onto fresh coals from a fire (the things that glow red after the fire looks like it's out) and turn it every few minutes until it's cooked. The hotter the coals, the more frequent the ashcakes will need to be turned. Ashcakes can be cooked less for a more doughy texture but will not keep as long as those that are thoroughly cooked due to the extra inner moisture.

The above water recommendation makes an individual ashcake about four to five inches in diameter, depending on the thickness of the cake. For a bigger ashcake simply make a bigger dough ball.

Many things can be added to spruce up an ashcake. While not required, you can add baking powder and soda for a product that will rise to the occasion. You can also mix various types of flour, although make sure to use some that have a high gluten content or the dough balls won't hold together. Turnovers can be made from the dough and loaded with dried fruit, jams, jellies, or whatever you have before they're pinched shut and put on the coals.

low-moisture content, low pH, and the presence of hydrogen peroxide—a by-product produced from the conversion of glucose into gluconic acid—gives honey its resistance to spoiling, as well as its antibacterial and antifungal properties.

Many studies have shown that wounds treated with honey not only heal faster but also scar less. Honey has also been reported as a superior treatment for topical burns and is used as a component in many skin and hair conditioning products. It has also been used to treat stomach ulcers, diarrhea, irritable bowel syndrome, eye injuries, liver problems, coughs, colds, and flu. Although raw foods, including honey, can contain microbes, the potential microbes in honey have never been found to complicate any medical studies, whether adults used it internally or externally.

Honey and Infants

Honey, or any raw foods, should *not* be given to infants, as it takes twelve months for the immune system in a human to fully develop. Although honey won't grow microbes, which are present in many raw foods, a botulism spore can lie dormant within honey. While an adult immune system can easily deal with the microbe levels occurring in raw foods, infants cannot. Gamma-irradiated honey, however, is free from all potential microbes.

Storing Honey

Honey is mostly fructose and glucose. Over time, the sugars separate (mostly the glucose) and cause the honey to granulate. Spun, creamed, or whipped honey has been pregranulated but with particles that are very small. The type of honey as well as how it's stored will dictate when it starts to crystallize. The perfect temperature for honey to granulate is between 55 and 57 degrees F (12.8 to 13.9

degrees C). Although granulated honey doesn't pose any problem other than it being less convenient to spread, it can easily be brought back to its normal state of semitransparency.

Granulated honey can be liquefied by putting the container in hot water. The water should be from 110 to 160 degrees F (43.4 to 71.2 degrees C). If it gets any hotter you risk compromising the flavor and the antibacterial properties that make honey such a good keeper. I have degranulated honey by placing the glass jar in the summer sun for a day. Many types of store-bought honeys are prefiltered and rarely crystallize, as the process requires a particle upon which the crystallization begins and then expands. As with other foods, the cooler it's stored the better, and it should be kept in the dark, away from direct solar radiation. Honey can also be frozen and, according to many beekeepers, doing so for a few weeks will prevent it from crystallizing for up to two years or more. The flavor and some of the medicinal properties in honey do start to disappear over time. Even though honey will technically last your lifetime, it doesn't mean that fresher, rotated honey won't be a superior product.

Sacred Salt

The history of salt is as old as humanity itself. Native Americans in my neck of the woods made a northward, several-hundred-mile journey on foot to visit the Great Salt Lake area of Utah to bring back that oh-so-precious commodity. One of the simple wonders of life is the sodium-potassium balance that continuously navigates back and forth through the lipid membrane of the human cell. Without sodium in the diet, we die. Two of the hardest items to come by in ancient ages for most people were salt and fat. The typical American diet is riddled with both, so much so that low sodium and fat diets appear as far as the eye can see. Maybe it is some memory deep within us that remembers how precious these two things were: is that why we indulge like a kid in a cookie jar for both? What hardy people used to walk for days to mine by hand, we can now buy for nearly nothing at virtually every grocery store in the world. We even throw a form of it called *halite* onto the streets in the wintertime.

Aside from melting snow, salt can be used to preserve animal hides and many types of food, including meats. Russ Miller, the illustrator for this book, has done experiments with salt and raw rabbit meat. He put freshly butchered rabbit layered with salt in an unsealed plastic container, unrefrigerated, for over a year. The meat was not only still good, but it was pliable as well.

Not all salt is created equal and very little of it is made for human consumption. Table salt is by far the most common variety of salt for human consumption and it comes in two varieties, iodized and noniodized. Table salt usually has an additive that prevents it from absorbing moisture and caking up. People that plan to use their salt for pickling and canning might be better off buying other forms of pure salt such as kosher or canning salt without this additive, although both will work in a pinch. There are also a variety of "gourmet" sea salts available at many health food shops. These contain other minerals as well as sodium and should not be used for food preservation if you have a choice in the matter. Rock salts commonly used in homemade ice cream churns are not recommended by the manufacturers for human consumption, but in a pinch, who knows.

As sodium is so important in the human diet, I feel that having it trumps many of the so-called nonedibility of certain salts. On hard-core outdoor survival courses deep in the wilderness, we have commonly broken off a piece of a salt lick put out for cattle. I have personally seen this undoubtedly not-fit-for-human-consumption salt bring students back to life after they have sweated out much of their sodium in the desert heat. Take note that people living in hot climates or doing heavy exercise will lose much of their sodium in the form of sweat, thus will require and crave more salt in their diet. Even though you can get away with using sketchy varieties of salt, table salt and other types that are specifically made for human consumption are so cheap and readily available, why wouldn't you have some on hand for the health of your family?

Storing Salt

As long as you keep it clean and free from dirt or debris, salt stores indefinitely. Salt should be stored in moisture-proof containers, like everything else, in a cool, dark place, although there is latitude in how it's stored. If you're short on cool, dry, dark places for food storage, salt can be put somewhere else as it's fairly forgiving. Although it may yellow over time, it can still be used. One of the reasons salt is such a good preservative is that it draws moisture, even from the air itself, and when it does, it will start to clump up. These clumps can be dried in the sun, a solar oven, or on a woodstove and broken up again for use.

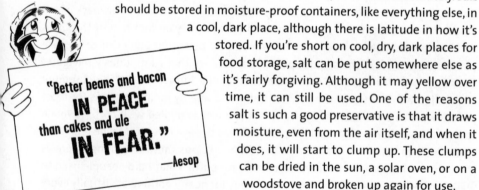

"Better beans and bacon
IN PEACE
than cakes and ale
IN FEAR."
—Aesop

Other Goodies to Store from the Store

Groovy Grains

There are many, many varieties of grains to choose from. If you don't want to eat wheat 24/7, research what other choices you have to tickle your taste buds. Some grains are familiar to the average American and others are going to be found only by the hardcore hippy, deep within the bowels of the neighborhood health food store's bulk bin section. Rice (in its many forms), corn, amaranth, barley, oats (in its many forms), buckwheat, quinoa, millet, rye, teff, and sorghum are some of the more common choices.

While the above grains all have their pros and cons, nutritionally, taste-wise, and in preparation, the long-term storage rules of thumb detailed in this chapter are solid for all of them. Decide which grains your family will eat and if you have the right long-term storage conditions for them in your home.

Luscious Legumes

Legumes are great as most are high in protein (up to 35 percent!) and carbohydrates. That said, any self-respecting vegan or vegetarian knows to combine legumes with other grains to create a complete protein, as grains and legumes alone only contain a partial amino acid profile. As the legume family is one of the largest plant kingdoms on Earth, there are many choices to pick from and most store decently under proper conditions. Some of the more common varieties from the legume family are pinto beans, black beans, fava beans, kidney beans, mung beans, lima beans, soybeans, lentils, peanuts, black-eyed peas, chickpeas, and green and yellow peas (split or whole).

Fats and Oils

Fats contain more than twice the calories of proteins or carbohydrates, making them powerful additions of concentrated energy for any survival diet—although they do require more oxygen in the body to break down and oxidize into usable nutrition. Fats also greatly affect the palatability of foods, and, much like salt, ingested fats are required for life to continue in a human body. This truth has been largely forgotten because fat is so easy to find in the average diet. As everyone knows, low-fat diets abound in America and other affluent parts of the world.

Stories are common of mountain men in the 1800s who ate all the rabbits they could kill and died with full stomachs because the wild rabbits did not contain the fat required to allow the men's bodies to metabolize the meat and absorb fat-soluble vitamins such as A, D, E, and K. The rabbit meat was simply too lean. In another example, some early European Arctic explorers crash-landed their boat upon an ice flow. Many of the men were rescued by traditional Inuit people and given food caught by the natives. When another ship arrived months later, they found that many of the earlier explorers had died. The newcomers at first thought that the marooned sailors had been murdered by the Inuits. It turns out that the Europeans simply died from a lack of fat and nutrition in their diets. The friendly Inuits had fed the Europeans what they ate, but the Inuits ate the entire carcass: fats, internal organs, and all, not just the lean meat. The finicky European sailors had survived the crash in Arctic waters to be killed only by their own refusal to eat the entire animal like the "savage" Inuit natives. When in Rome, do as the Romans do.

Storing Fats and Oils

The problem with fats and oils is they don't store well for long periods of time. They go rancid quickly. Excess oxygen, the main culprit, is eight times more soluble in fat than in water, thus the "oxidation" or spoilage rate is much higher. The less saturated a fat is, the quicker it can go bad. Although it is much more apparent when animal fats become rancid because of the bad smell, vegetable oils still become rancid. Heat and light are also enemies to storing oils and fats. Pay special attention to the laws of food storage with all fats and oils; buy them in the smallest containers as practical and rotate your stock as often as possible. Remember that oxygen is the main factor in fats and oils going bad so larger containers will be repeatedly exposed to excess oxygen as the lid comes on and off. Rancid fats are not healthy to consume in quantity so don't mess around with them if they have gone bad.

Depending on storage conditions, most unopened cooking oils have a shelf life of a year to a year and a half. If you can, keep oils and fats as cold as possible, especially after they have been opened. If the substance freezes, the amount needed can be taken out of the mother container and heated or left out at room temperature. Typically, paler light-colored cooking oils will keep longer than darker-colored oils. Clogged arteries and taste notwithstanding, the best stuff to buy for maximum storage life is canned hydrogenated shortening. Some even contain antioxidant preservatives that will increase the shelf life. If you store an unopened can of this in the right long-term storage location, it may last six to eight years or more. I realize that this type of fat is the bane of all health food nuts, and is being outlawed by some states for commercial restaurant use, but consider what your intention is for having its concentrated, long-lasting calories as a part of your emergency food storage program.

Sweet Tooth (Sugars)

Life without something sweet is a drag. Although honey is multiuse and a great sweetener, it will take some getting used to when used for baking purposes in your solar oven. White table sugar (sucrose), while somewhat white trash, will last indefinitely if kept dry and clean, as sugar inhibits most microbial growth. Brown sugar and powdered sugar are close behind in longevity. Buy a familiar brand from the store and keep it moisture free, in airtight, insect-proof containers. If it does absorb moisture, it will cake up like salt and can simply be broken up and used. Dry sweeteners are more stable than liquid sweeteners over the long haul with the exception of honey.

I like to have a stash of hard candies around for a portable sugar fix on the go. Although they will, like everything else, deteriorate with time, simple hard candies such as peppermints will keep a long, long time and can be bought very cheaply at the end of every Christmas season. The sweetness in hard candies and sweet stuff in general, when used in moderation, can be very soothing on the nerves during stressful situations. It also works great to bribe or shut up kids when nothing else seems to work. Avoid storing candies with nuts or too many ingredients in them as they will spoil rapidly in comparison to straight sugar.

Because of the sugar content, I used to think all candies were invincible to spoilage. Several months back I found the remains of an old stashed survival kit. I went through all the components with great curiosity. I wondered if my opinion had changed over the years on what to store and how to store it. One of the items I found were two Snickers candy bars in a freezer bag. I estimated they had been in my jeep for fifteen years, and had been subjected to temperatures well over 120 degrees F (48 degrees C) to below freezing. As I excitedly unwrapped my archeological find, I found that the chocolate coating had completely vaporized, the peanuts were rancid as hell, and something that I think was caramel and nugget was more or less intact. Of course I ate it anyway and it wasn't bad, other than a slightly funky aftertaste more than likely caused by the rancid peanuts.

Other Cooking Basics

Baking powder, if kept dry in a moisture-proof, airtight container will store for about a year before it loses its potency. It can be tested to see if it's any good by putting a rounded teaspoon into half a cup of hot water. If the baking powder is good, it will bubble like crazy. Most baking powders contain aluminum, except for the Rumford brand.

Baking soda will keep indefinitely if it's stored in an airtight, moisture-proof container. If it's left in the cardboard box, it will last a little more than a year, much less if it's inside your moisture-filled refrigerator.

Yeast is a living organism and needs to be faithfully rotated. The commonly available dried yeast in the foil packets has the expiration date stamped right on the package. If kept in an airtight, moisture-proof container, and as cool or cold as possible, it will keep much longer than the stamped expiration date. It can be tested for potency by mixing a bit of the dried yeast with an equal amount of sugar and putting the mixture into warm water. It should begin to bubble in about six minutes or so.

Spices are, well, the spice of life. The spice trade of centuries past revolutionized the taste buds and the monetary flow of the world. Truly, spices have been so unknowingly important to the nation that some of my friends plan on storing extra spices as a means of barter when the skies fall. Having a variety, or at least a few basic spices, on hand will help counter the dreaded "appetite fatigue" syndrome from setting in on your family. Most spices can be used to cover up bland or bad-tasting foods. There is a reason why standard military-issue MREs come with a bottle of Tabasco sauce.

Spices can be a challenge to store for long periods of time, especially if they are ground up and powdered, which most are. Like other foods they are sensitive to heat, light, oxygen, and moisture. Buy spices that are "whole" if you can, put them into smaller containers if you purchased them in bulk, store them like you would food, and keep your choices simple.

Vinegar comes in many flavors. A common one, apple cider vinegar, will keep indefinitely if stored in an unopened container at room temperature. White vinegar can also be used as a natural cleaning agent around the house.

Insect Infestations

Everyone likes a free meal, especially in the wild world of insects. Grains, legumes, and many other foods can fall prey to serious insect infestations if basic precautions are not taken. I'll never forget the carnage that lurked inside my bag of rolled oats that I foolishly stored in the closet in its original paper sack. I'm not sure what kind of bug it was, but I had perfected a breeding ground for thousands of them—even the neighboring horses wouldn't touch the leftovers.

It's critical that your stored food be bug free, and the easiest way to accomplish that is to make sure the bugs are absent in the first place. Don't buy bulk grains and dried foods from cheap sources or the problem might already be in the bag. Large companies that go through product quickly are a better bet as the food won't sit around as much. With many insects, like my oat bugs, the party seems to happen on the top few inches of food, so look before you agitate the product and hide the evidence.

If you store food in the ways that have been recommended in this book, attracting bugs after the fact should not be a problem. Don't tempt bugs or rodents by being a slob where you have your food stored. Keep things clean. If bugs get out of control in some of your food, get that food out of the house and check to see if other food has been infested.

Some bugs can be eaten along with the food, or the larger varieties sifted out. I don't know how many times I've eaten cereal with weevils in it. I consider it extra protein, as you might, if food is scarce. But the bottom line is, bugs eat your food, and their nutritional value is not likely to make up for the difference in what they have pilfered.

Killing Bugs (and Their Eggs) in Food

Sometimes when the bugs are absent, the eggs are not. One year I harvested native mesquite beans that were a staple food of the desert Indians in Arizona. At first glance the pods looked fine. After a few weeks, the eggs of whatever bugs were within the pods ate away at the goods, unbeknownst to me, and ruined most of the crop. The same thing happened with some pinyon nuts I gathered. Some native peoples used large winnowing-type baskets and hot coals from the fire to parch foods before they were stored.

Freezing and Heating

Cold can be used to kill bugs and their larvae and eggs. If you have access to cold temperatures, large quantities of food such as a full five-gallon bucket can be placed in a freezer at 0 degrees F (minus 17 degrees C) or lower for ten days. If smaller packages of food are used, the days can be lessened to four or five, as the food will require less time to be chilled all the way through. General household freezers are wimpy when needing to achieve seriously low temperatures but many chest freezers can do it. When it comes to killing bugs, the colder the temperature, the better. As the Native Americans have proven, buggy food can also be treated with heat. Most people recommend placing the food in question on a baking sheet into the oven for thirty minutes at 140 degrees F (60 degrees C), a temperature easily achieved by solar ovens. The dictionary definition of "tedious" references processing five hundred pounds of grain that way. Heated food should be eaten within a few weeks of doing so.

"Tomatoes and oregano make it **ITALIAN**; wine and tarragon make it **FRENCH.** Sour cream makes it **RUSSIAN;** lemon and cinnamon make it **GREEK.** Soy sauce makes it **CHINESE,** garlic makes it **GOOD.**"
—Alice May Brock

Molds and Bacteria

Mold can affect *any* type of food, including "dry" foods such as grains and legumes where enough moisture (humidity) and warmth are present. Of course there are fungal strains as well that grow in the refrigerator, as anyone who has opened forgotten leftovers can attest. Notice that hearty molds can infect foods with high sugar or salt contents as well (both excellent preservatives), even when refrigerated. Who hasn't looked in the bottom of a jar of jelly and seen mold or trimmed a piece from a cured salted piece of meat? Not all molds are bad for human consumption, but the ones that are can nearly kill you or at the very least make you extremely sick. As I mentioned with my squash incident, some molds produce toxic mycotoxins, which are produced around the root of the mold itself, so they can be deep within the food itself. Like skin cancer, superficially trimming the surface of the mold will not get the part that's deep within the food. Worst of all, fungal mycotoxins last for long periods of time and are *not* destroyed by heat.

Here in the arid Southwest, we marvel at the rare occurrence of mold and mildew, throwing parties in honor of its extraordinary mustiness. Those of you who live in humid climates are unimpressed and are probably well versed in how to deal with invading mold and mildew. Keep your food storage areas clean. On countertops, refrigerators, and other food storage surfaces, mold can be eliminated with an assortment of household disinfectants such as our beloved chlorine bleach solution. Many "hard" foods such as potatoes, apples, and cheddar cheese can be trimmed of mold. Cut away the infected area along with an inch or so of the unaffected food without letting the knife touch the mold. "Soft" foods such as tomatoes, melons, cream cheese, and peanut butter should be thrown away. If you mess around with these and many other soft foods, you may pay a high price. Moldy foods should be thrown safely away so they can't be gotten into by curious kids and hungry animals.

Bacteria need moisture to grow, and many strains found in foods can be very tough to kill. Some of the more nasty varieties toxic to humans can form *spores* that are very resistant to being eradicated. Moldy "wet foods" such as canned goods can become havens for the bacterium *Clostridium botulinum*, or botulism, one of the most deadly forms of bacterial food poisoning around. The toxin created from the growing bacteria is the culprit and is reportedly so potent that one teaspoon of the botulism toxin is capable of killing hundreds of thousands of people.

Because of this, don't screw around with bacterial spoilage in any type of wet food, whether fresh, home-canned, or commercially canned from the store. **Any canned goods that are bulging, leaking, smell bad, or that squirt liquid when you open them should be thrown away!** As with moldy foods, make sure you dispose of them safely away from kids and pets. (Note: Canned foods that have gone bad will have at least two of the above traits. Some cans that have been physically dented will squirt fluid when opened with a can opener, as the volume inside the can has been reduced, thereby putting the canned goods under pressure.) However, IF IN DOUBT, THROW IT OUT!

Using Salt to Reduce Moisture

It would be almost impossible for dry grains and legumes to grow harmful bacteria due to the lack of moisture. They can, however, grow mold. There is an easy method used to keep the moisture content in certain stored foods low that involves our friend salt. For food products such as rice, dry beans, dried peas, and pastas (other grains will require a different method), putting one inch of salt in the bottom of a container such as a food-grade five-gallon bucket before adding the food will hold the moisture content below 10 percent. This eliminates the environment required for molds to grow and prevents many insect eggs from hatching. Don't separate the salt from the food. Just pour the food right on top of the salt. As we know from our salt talk, the salt will store indefinitely and can be used as is. This method is a great way to have salt work for its storage space until it's used for its own sake.

The Dizzying World of Food-Storage Strategies

The technical information involved in storing foods is incredibly intense and has been the subject of dozens of books. I have only so much room in this book so you're on your own to research the other methods used to increase the storage times of

food. Other home storage strategies might include Mylar bags, flushing with carbon dioxide and nitrogen, special enamel-coated cans, moisture-absorbing desiccants and oxygen absorbers, dry ice, vacuum sealing, and food-grade diatomaceous earth. Your local LDS (Mormon) church might have a cannery near where you live and you may be able to use their food-packing facilities for a fee. If the option feels right to you, it doesn't hurt to ask.

Come on, Man, Tell Me . . . How Long Do Stored Foods REALLY Last?

I wish I knew for sure, other than the obvious good keepers such as salt and white sugar. In the months of research I did for this book, I came across many, many contradictions as to how long stored foods will last. Some sources say whole wheat lasts for six months, others, indefinitely. And I could go on and on with the discrepancies. This is the main reason that I don't include a one-size-fits-all, handy-dandy food storage chart stating exactly how long your stored food will last. I looked at several such charts and many of them have very different answers for the same food product.

I personally have experimented with dried pinto beans (among several other things) that have been stored for more than fifteen years, still in the paper sack in which they were bought! Other than requiring a lot of soaking time and extra fuel to cook, they're fine . . . or are they? I don't have the resources to take my beans to the neighborhood laboratory and have them analyzed for nutritional content and microbes, as I'm sure is true for many other food storage "experts" who've undoubtedly experimented likewise. So I have fifteen-year-old pinto beans in a paper sack that are still edible, so what? I live in Arizona, land of limited moisture. How would that sack of pinto beans do in a closet in Washington state?

As with human nature and Mother Nature in a survival scenario, food storage is fraught with variables as to how the story will end. There is no question that following the rules of food storage will increase the shelf life of your stored food. How long it will really last is anyone's guess. Take all prophetic advice about how long your vittles will be vital with a grain of salt. The sure way out of this dilemma is to *rotate your food by storing what you eat and eating what you store.*

Bugs, Mice, and Rats: It's What's for Dinner

When the times get tough, the tough look for alternative food sources. I don't like killing things for food, but I realize the importance of knowing how to do so if that's my only option. So do the students who take my classes on survival skills, some of whom have been vegetarians or vegans. Animal meat doesn't originate on a Styrofoam plate covered with plastic wrap. I'm convinced the world would have a lot more vegetarians if people who chose to eat meat had to kill it themselves. Doing so is an awesome responsibility and very humbling. That said, every urban, suburban, and rural area will have their share of smaller critters that hardy survivors can exploit to their advantage—bugs and rodents being the most common.

Eating What Bugs You

Eating bugs has gotten a bad rap, most recently from stupid television shows designed to shock people that seem to have nothing better to do. Most insects and bugs can be eaten and almost all contain a high amount of protein. Stay away from stinkbugs in the Southwest, caterpillars in general, and beware of insects that can hurt you such as bees, wasps, yellow jackets, and the like. Some insects should be cooked to kill potential parasites they carry, such as grasshoppers.

I realize your family will more than likely protest to worms being on the menu. Such an opinion is just that, an opinion based on cultural conditioning and being grossed out by the appearance of a foreign-looking creature. Bugs aren't gross; they just *look* gross to most people. If you knew the ingredients of a hot dog you would eat bugs. Most bugs and insects have a very mild flavor that can easily be disguised with spices or other food. Their shapes can be disguised by cooking and grinding them if necessary into a powder. This homemade protein powder can be added to soups and stews or something else to help your family achieve the nutrition they need—without the gross-out factor. If your survival food stash is getting low, cutting it with bugs will help extend the rations. For the most palatable results at the dinner table, think twice before telling other family members what you've done—and don't tell Vinny!

Remarkable Rodents

Mice and rats are extremely adaptable creatures. They are also easy to catch and kill with a little advanced preparation. My "Really Cool, Gotta Have It, Multiple Use Stuff" list presented later in the book includes traps for mice and rats. Rattraps are simply mousetraps on steroids. I have killed rats in mousetraps, and vice versa, but unless the mousetrap comes down on a vulnerable part of the rat's anatomy, you

Handy HOMEMADE RODENT DEADFALL

EXTREME CLOSE-UP

B

A

BAIT

A

B

YOU WILL NEED...

- Two sticks, pencils, or whatever works 7-8 inches long

- One piece of string a few inches longer

- Something heavy to act as the "deadfall," such as a large book or flat rock

- Bait & bait stick

- The will to kill

- A tasty victim!

LOOKIE HERE!

Block the sides to help prevent super quick escapes!

will more than likely lose your mousetrap to the rat. Unless the powerful critter gets stuck in a small space while trying to navigate with the trap attached to its body, it will disappear to a place only the rat knows about.

The most common mouse and rattraps are the Victor brand found at most hardware and grocery stores. There are two choices, the old-fashioned type with the metal bait area and the ones with the yellow plastic bait pad. The latter ones rely on a substance that's imprinted into the plastic itself to attract the rodent and don't require bait. These work okay when fresh, but they quickly lose their attractant, even when stored new within their original plastic. Even so, I like these the best, and use them successfully, even with no bait or commercial attractant left on the yellow pad. The answer to my success is easy if you think like a rodent. I place the loaded traps with the yellow pad nearest the wall, preferably right after or before a tunnel of some kind, such as a board propped up against the wall. Rodents are creatures of habit and love cruising along walls in the dead of night. If the wall also features some protective cover, such as our board example, all the better. The yellow bait pad has a large surface area and traps the rodent as it scurries across the trap, no bait needed.

Follow Robbie's instructions to make your own deadfall trap using everyday stuff around the house. Use caution with this trap as it can smash fingers and kill pets as well as rodents. To learn how to cook your critter, head to the Crucially Creative Cooking chapter.

SUPER SIMPLE SUMMARY

- ⮌ In the strictest sense, stored emergency food should be treated as rations, not regular meals. Its main focus is to provide the survivor with sugar in order to minimize catabolism and dehydration and increase survival time.

- ⮌ At minimum, have a two- to four-week supply of stored food on hand for possible emergencies. This food should be easy to access, portable, require no cooking, and meet all of your nutritional needs. Don't forget to store food at the office and in vehicles as well.

- ⮌ If the power goes out, eat the food in the refrigerator first, and then the freezer. In a well-stocked, well-insulated freezer, foods will usually still have ice crystals in their centers—meaning they are safe to eat—for at least two days.

- There are three macronutrients in foods: *carbohydrates, proteins, and fats*. All contain different amounts of calories, or stored energy, and "burn" or metabolize at varying rates within the body. Stored foods should contain all three macronutrients when possible for maximum nutrition and energy.
- Of the three macronutrients, proteins require the most water from the body to metabolize. Avoid proteins and salty foods when water supplies are scarce.
- Along with the nutritional content in quality food, salt and fats (cooking oils, etc.) are required for life. Fats are difficult to store for long periods of time but salt will store indefinitely.
- Your basal metabolic rate (BMR) is the amount of calories you burn at rest doing no physical activity. Physiological factors that increase BMR are being male, young, tall, and muscular. Doing any physical activity whatsoever will increase the amount of calories you burn, as will certain illnesses and being in cold weather without adequate clothing or shelter.
- Several factors will determine what your family chooses to store for food. These include the family's preference for what they like to eat, the supposed duration of the emergency, the age and health of family members, your home's unique storage environment, family finances, and pets.
- *Warning!* Don't take food storage for granted. Forced low-calorie diets of semistarvation will have far-reaching psychological and physiological effects. Leave living-off-the-land mythologies to Hollywood.
- Be discreet about your food storage program and its location. It's no one's business but your family's.
- There are several types of prepared foods that can be successfully stored. The more common options are canned goods, dried or dehydrated, freeze-dried, whole grains or legumes packed in buckets, and MREs (meals ready to eat). All have their pros and cons in preparation, cost, palatability, storage life, and nutrition.
- Basic rules of food storage: Store what you eat, rotate what you store, store your food in the best possible

conditions for maximum storage life using food-grade containers, and *keep things simple*.

- ➲ In general, canned foods are great for food storage plans as they are widely available, durable and portable, cheap, easy to open with no preparation or cooking required, and store well for up to two years.
- ➲ How much food to store is dependent upon the intention and needs of each family. Keeping track of consumed food is helpful for purchasing larger quantities. As an example, a family wishing to store six months of food can estimate the amount of food required to purchase by keeping track of all food eaten within a one month period and multiplying by six.
- ➲ For maximum storage life, foods should be stored in a *cool, dry, dark* location in food-grade, *oxygen-free* containers. The containers should also keep stored foods protected from rodents and insect infestations. All food should be dated and faithfully rotated.
- ➲ When purchasing bulk grains or legumes, buy only from reputable dealers who quickly sell large volumes of quality product. The more they sell, the fresher the product will be and the less likely it will have an insect problem.
- ➲ Insects, and their larva and eggs, can be destroyed with sufficient heat or cold. Keep food storage areas clean to avoid attracting pest problems in the first place.
- ➲ Some molds in foods produce dangerous mycotoxins that are toxic to humans. These toxins make their way deep into foods, last for long periods of time, and are *not* destroyed by heat.
- ➲ *Warning!* All "wet foods" such as canned goods, whether home-canned or commercially canned, that are *bulging, leaking, smell bad, or squirt fluid when you open them* should be safely discarded out of the reach of children and animals. Deadly bacterias such as botulism can quickly kill your loved ones. *If in doubt, throw it out!*
- ➲ The easiest way to prevent decreased nutritional content and spoiled food is to faithfully rotate your stored food using the "FIFO" method, *first in, first out*.

SAVVY yet SIMPLE
Significant Substitute
SANITATION

"And thou shalt have a paddle upon thy weapon; and it shall be, when thou wilt ease thyself abroad, thou shalt dig therewith, and shalt turn back and cover that which cometh from thee."

—Deuteronomy 23:13

Improper sanitation is directly or indirectly responsible for the deaths of hundreds of thousands of people worldwide every year. Some slum settlements today in Africa require up to 150 people to share a single toilet, forcing many to defecate in plastic bags, known as "flying toilets," which are thrown on the roadside. Disease from improper sanitation has at times proved just as deadly as the wars which provoked the situation. During the American Civil War, more than 70,000 soldiers died from dysentery. The same plight killed more soldiers than bullets during the Spanish-American War. Currently, more than 2.6 billion people live without proper toilets or drains, leaving ample opportunity for disease. Should an act of devastation take out your town or city's sanitation system, an alternative means for dealing with human waste should rank high on your list of survival priorities.

Early efforts at sanitation, at least for the wealthy, have been traced back as early as 3300 BC to the Mesopotamians, with the Greeks, Romans, and others following suit. For the "common man," going to the john usually meant something different. For early Romans, it was routine to throw the contents of the chamber pot out the window and onto the street the next morning. Countless supposedly advanced civilizations had for the most part no clue about proper sanitation. Many cultures simply pooped in unhygienic pits or threw the contents of their primitive privies over the walls of towns and cities. Medieval Paris had to extend its protective city walls as the pile of poop had grown so tall outside the original wall that invaders could climb the pile and attack the city. The thousands of pounds of excrement dumped into rivers even stopped some of them from flowing. Needless to say, the smell of many medieval towns and cities was totally obnoxious and dangerously unsanitary. It wasn't until the mid-1800s with the likes of potty pioneers Thomas Twyford, Thomas Crapper, and George Jennings that improvements in the toilet and sanitation started to create less of a stink.

A lack of sanitation facilities following a major disaster can quickly create disease epidemics unless basic guidelines are followed. Unfortunately, modern urbanites have an "out of sight, out of mind" mentality regarding the aftermath of going to the bathroom. We have grown accustomed to doing our duty, hitting a lever, and

letting someone else deal with our shit, literally and figuratively. Sooner or later, however, similar to one who blames other people or circumstances for his or her troubles, our waste products will catch up with us to be redeemed.

The average person produces two to three pints of urine and one pound of feces every day. Imagine your family's toilet after one day of use without the ability to get rid of its contents. Besides rating high on the gross-o-meter, it's a great way to get your entire family sick, especially during the warm season. As clean as your family might be, the truth is, flies, pests, and pets love poop and will stop at virtually nothing to partake in the feast. After dining on your turd, flies won't think twice about landing upon your sandwich or whatever survival cuisine you may be enjoying at the moment. The ensuing results from fecalborne pathogens can be disastrous to you and your loved ones' health.

P(ee)P(ee) and D(oo)D(oo): Decisively Dealing with Dangerous Dung

Over the years I have ushered hundreds of people into the wilderness for survival and primitive living skills courses. Within hours of our arrival at our backcountry home, we discuss the nature of doing one's business in nature. These helpful hints are just as applicable in your backyard as they are out in the woods. Use the "PPDD" formula as ground rules for the toilet options discussed later in this chapter.

PPDD Stands for Privacy, Proximity, Depth, and Drainage

Privacy

Unless your potty plan produces privacy on the part of the participant, you will quickly fall from grace within your family. The last thing that anyone needs during a survival scenario is to be stressed out about where to go to the toilet. Undo stress and concern about being seen while going to the bathroom can psychologically and physiologically cause a person to "bind up" inside, preventing a bowel movement through constipation. Unless this is remedied, your loved one may become impacted, forcing a kind of kinship better left to the imagination and the virtues of a rubber glove. Along with providing privacy, tell your loved ones to RELAX and consciously think about the process while doing the job. If they are tense or strain, the sphincter muscles contract and make evacuation more difficult. This, along with squatting to keep the sigmoid colon properly aligned (outlined later) and adequate roughage in the diet should do the trick. Once again, an ounce of prevention is worth a pound of . . . well, you get the picture. A simple tarp or other barrier might be all that is required to have your family pooping in peace.

Proximity

I have had people get lost in the woods while looking for the perfect private haven to go to the toilet. They walk so long and so far that, upon their return trip, they become disoriented from camp—an embarrassing predicament at the very least. While this point might not be applicable for your situation, make certain that your place of business is located within the realm of your loved ones finding their way back to the house. Stress, fear, darkness, weather, or other variables might make your backyard or back lot trip a bit more challenging than usual. Having a designated place to go to the bathroom that is private will prevent a person's instinct to wander until they find a spot in which they feel safe.

Depth

According to the U.S. Forest Service, one should dig a small hole at least twelve inches deep to poop in. Doing so in most of the state of Arizona will require a backhoe due to incredibly hard desert earth. Sometimes, in remote areas during intense desert heat, I leave scat uncovered; it gets baked by the desert sun and decomposes much more rapidly than if covered. In this case, I am on a cross-country hiking course and am permanently leaving the area and the fly connection. For our urban/suburban purposes, plan on covering your poop. There are a few different applications in regards to the depth and the size of the hole, which I'll cover later in the chapter.

Drainage

Poor sanitation habits are stereotyped to be the curse of developing countries and their largely "uncivilized" population. Recent history has proved otherwise. The Serbian/Croatian conflict mentioned earlier is case in point. Unfortunate families downstream from the upstream poopers bore the brunt of the effects. Entire families became ill due to fecal pathogens as rampant dysentery ruled day and night.

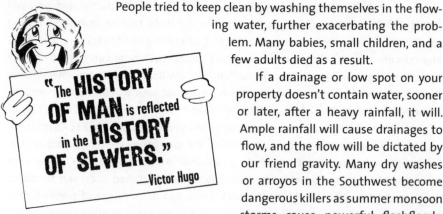

People tried to keep clean by washing themselves in the flowing water, further exacerbating the problem. Many babies, small children, and a few adults died as a result.

"The HISTORY OF MAN is reflected in the HISTORY OF SEWERS."
—Victor Hugo

If a drainage or low spot on your property doesn't contain water, sooner or later, after a heavy rainfall, it will. Ample rainfall will cause drainages to flow, and the flow will be dictated by our friend gravity. Many dry washes or arroyos in the Southwest become dangerous killers as summer monsoon storms cause powerful flashfloods, washing away cars, cows, and campers.

It's tempting for some to go potty in drainages, as excess vegetation caused by extra groundwater enables one to squat with some semblance of privacy. Pathogens in fecal matter can travel more than three hundred feet through the earth, thereby contaminating above- and below-groundwater sources with a bevy of nasty things.

If you go potty in that private little wash in the back of your property, when it does flow you risk infecting your neighborhood with the gift that keeps on giving. Think like a raindrop when you decide where to station the outhouse—your family and neighbors will thank you.

Using Your Existing Toilet

If the water mains are broken, it's still possible to use your indoor toilet with no water in the back tank. Before doing the following suggestion, *make sure there is no problem with the local sewer mains!* Flushing your toilet when the town's sewer infrastructure is in pieces will further complicate your locality's sanitation emergency. Eventually radio or some other media will broadcast bulletins concerning the status of your sewer lines and whether it is safe to flush.

After going to the bathroom, pour water into the toilet bowl itself (not the tank in the back) from a five-gallon bucket or other large container and your toilet will flush. Obviously, use this method only if water is an abundant resource.

If for some reason your toilet cannot be flushed you can still use it for the seat that it is. First, remove the water from the bowl. Next, tape or otherwise anchor a heavy-duty plastic bag (I would double the bags) under the toilet seat and let the bag fill the cavity of the bowl. After the bag is comfortably full (two-thirds at most), untape the bag, add a small amount of powdered disinfectant like wood ashes or quicklime, tie it very securely, and place it within a preprepared slit trench or durable container such as a plastic five-gallon bucket (lined with a trash bag) or a trash container (lined with a trash bag) with a tight-fitting lid. Don't be cheap and have too much poop in the bag or it will be a living nightmare to tie up and dispose of.

The Five-Gallon Bucket

I love five-gallon buckets as they have endless uses. They are *containers*, and hunting and gathering cultures around the world evolved around the container and how it could be used, from carrying food and water to babies and bedding. Have several buckets on hand and keep the plastic ones out of the sun so they don't prematurely deteriorate and crack and fall apart.

Five-gallon buckets lined with a couple of heavy-duty plastic bags can be used as portable toilets indoors or outside. When the bag is too full for comfort, tie it off securely and dispose of it in a preprepared slit trench or secure container for disposal when your emergency is over. Some camping stores sell buckets complete with a toilet-seat lid, custom-made for going to the bathroom. Sitting on the uncomfortable rim of the bucket can be dealt with by laying a couple of boards across the bucket's top and pooping in between the boards. At the onset of an emergency, any container will do that has a cover and will hold the contents until you can dispose of it. Many varieties of sanitizing chemical packets and disinfectants can be purchased from camping and RV stores and can be added to the contents of the bucket.

Basic Backyard Bathrooms: A Potty Primer

You would be amazed at how many people have never gone to the bathroom outdoors. If you are one of those amazing people, no problem, there's always a new day and another opportunity! The following outdoor recommendations are basic, yet tried and true.

Most families have a variety of options to deal with human waste after a grid meltdown, especially those with access to a little bare ground in the backyard or elsewhere. **Extreme caution** should be used in areas where the groundwater table is high; raw sewage can easily infect underground water supplies, wells, springs, creeks, rivers, and lakes. If possible, locate your trench WELL AWAY from all potential water sources, above and below ground. The United States Forest

I DIG IT!!

the SLIT TRENCH

The cat hole

Homemade empty can with wire handle scoop with optional pail of wood ashes or quicklime

Board for covering trench

Use existing fence or side of structure as part of privacy screen

Privacy screen made from blankets or tarps

Presence of coffee can toilet paper holder signals bathroom is "free"

Service recommends a minimum of two hundred feet between your poop site and any open water source. (Consider this a bare minimum, as waterborne pathogens have been known to travel more than three hundred feet to contaminate above- and below-groundwater sources.) Nevertheless, if your yard's topography directs rainfall runoff through the latrine, and then into the stream, rethink your location regardless of the two-hundred-foot rule. Fierce storms can dump amazing amounts of rain in a very short time. After the carnage, it's easy to study the ground and see where the next storm's runoff water will go by the tiny and sometimes not so tiny ravines created by the initial storm.

Use common sense, and wherever you go to the bathroom, *think like a raindrop* and visualize the area covered with water and notice where the flow would go. There may be times, due to the right topography, that you'll be fine having a cat hole fifty feet or so from water, especially if it's used for only a few days. If you're unable to safely dig cat holes or pit trenches, don't bury your human waste. Store it instead on the premises in containers with tight-fitting lids. I'll talk more about this type of containment later.

The Slit Trench

If you have the space and the time, a slit trench is a great way for the family to unload its troubles in a contained manner with minimal potential for sanitation problems. Slit trenches take more effort to create than cat holes but can be used for extended periods of time and by larger families.

The Cat Hole

The cat-hole method speaks for itself with a few human, sanitary considerations thrown in. The next time Whiskers or Fluffy takes a dump, notice what they do. First, they find a diggable area which meets their psychological profile regarding privacy. Next, they dig the hole, do their business, and bury the results. Cat holes are good for single uses or more. Posthole diggers are marvelous for efficiently excavating fairly deep pilot holes good for several poops. Manual or mechanical augers, if available, are even better.

You will be *squatting* to go to the bathroom for both slit trenches and cat holes. Get used to this thought now. If need be, you can always improvise something to sit on to suspend your derriere over the hole. If family members are older, have bad knees, or some other physical disability, you can creatively build things out of 2x4s or knock out the bottom of a chair to support a butt over slit trenches and cat holes.

A Word on "Squatting"

Unless you're lucky enough to be a catcher for a baseball team, most Americans are not accustomed to squatting while going to the bathroom. If you have traveled to many locales on our planet, from India to Asia, the chances are high that you have

SAVVY SQUATTING STRATEGIES

1 Have your heels higher than your toes. Put rocks or boards under your heels, squat on a slope, etc.

2 If helpful, stretch beforehand to help loosen tight muscles. Go ahead and laugh ... until the night you have dysentery over your trench.

3 If wearing shorts or pants, take off one leg, or better yet, take them off completely before squatting. This provides greater mobility, lessens the need for accuracy, and eliminates the stress of crapping on your clothes. Dresses are

wonderful for squatting and can provide some semblance of privacy when going to the bathroom in less than private scenarios. Take off your underwear and simply lift the dress up, bunching it around your waist. Men can do the same with kilts—how can a 250-pound, axe-wielding Scottish warrior be a sissy?

4 Anchor some type of grab bar such as posts, a suspended rope, or have your trench near a helpful bush or tree limb to hold onto to assist you in getting back into a standing position. Grab bars are critical for obese, elderly, or physically impaired family members.

already practiced squatting. Squatting properly positions the body more naturally, keeping the sigmoid colon in a more vertical position, and lets the abdominal cavity be supported by the tops of the thighs to help eliminate waste more efficiently.

Conditions and Materials Needed to Construct a Slit Trench or Cat Hole

1 *The bodily need.* If you have a large family or expect to be doing your business for an extended period of time, constructing a slit trench might be the best option. Cat holes work for short-time uses or smaller families, depending on how much land you have.

2 *Access to dry or moist (not wet) diggable ground that is safe from contaminating above- and below-groundwater sources and safe for access and use by all members of the family.* If you have the opportunity and are thinking ahead, locate your trenches and cat holes around areas where your family's fecal matter will nourish the earth. Multiple cat holes around the perimeter of your fruit trees will fertilize the tree, thereby providing a more healthy and abundant crop in the future. Don't dig too close to the tree or you'll run into roots.

3 *Something to dig with.* Shovels (and picks and digging bars in the case of most of the Southwest) and post-hole diggers work well for creating a comfortable ca-ca cavity in most earth. If you own a small backhoe or garden tractor with an auger attachment, you'll be your neighborhood's best bathroom barter buddy.

4 *Privacy barriers.* Unless your poo place has built-in privacy from fences, trees, shrubs, or whatever, plan on making Aunt Betty's potty practice pleasurable by erecting sheets, extra blankets, opaque tarps, or some other visibility barrier. Again, a word to the wise: If you fail to make your bathroom spot psychologically comfortable for the user, they won't use it. This can lead to uncomfortable results such as constipation and possible fecal compaction. Do you really want to know your family this well? Like everything else in this book, plan ahead and get to know your family's comfort zone now.

5 *Something to cover the poop and fill in the hole.* Remember, flies and other critters, including many family dogs, love poop, so it's important to cover it over to decrease the possibility of problems. Your family can simply use the dirt that came out of the hole but flies can be aggressive little diggers. If you're worried about kids or pets rooting through the debris, get aggressive about blocking off the opening of the trench or hole with boards or something else. Wood ashes from your fireplace or woodstove or a thin layer of quicklime can also be used as cover. Both have somewhat disinfectant properties that not only make it harder for flies to dig for the goodies but also provide a barrier that flies (and most pets) disagree with. Ashes and quicklime are also powderlike in their makeup, thus they cover poop thoroughly. Agricultural lime is *much, much* stronger than quicklime. Too much agricultural lime will disrupt the pH of the soil, affecting plant growth, depending on the ecosystem. If agricultural lime is all you have, cut it at a ratio of one tablespoon lime per five-gallon bucket of wood ashes.

When your slit trench or cat hole is full (about a foot from the top), spread a thin layer of quicklime on the contents and fill it in with dirt.

You'll have more dirt leftover because you've been adding poop to the hole. This is good as you want to mound up the dirt over the trench or cat hole as the earth will settle with time. When the trench is full, walk on the mound to pack the earth down.

After the Turd

Your colon is empty, the results have been safely buried, and life is looking up...now what? Before you make everyone a survival sandwich or hug the baby, it's time to take action about washing your hands. I always wipe my butt with the same hand, but I thoroughly wash both. Hand washing is critical, especially in group scenarios, as the majority of sanitary health problems and kitchen cases of food poisoning are a direct result of improper food handling by kitchen workers with unclean hands. Always stock waterless hand sanitizer (usually an alcohol base) in your bathroom whether or not you have a water-washing option available; water may be hard to come by at some point in your ordeal. At my water-miser homestead, I use waterless hand sanitizer full time in the bathroom. Put one or two squirts into the palm of your hand and briskly rub your hands together until the sanitizer dissipates. If thirty seconds of brisk hand rubbing have passed and your hands are still wet with sanitizer, use less next time.

Another option is to have a small basin of water with enough household bleach 5.25 or 6 percent in it to make the water smell strongly of chlorine, usually two and a half capfuls (one tablespoon) for every gallon of water. As the size of bleach caps

Break the **FECES + FLY + FOOD = YOU** Equation!

vary, some folks tie a measuring spoon to the handle of the bleach bottle. Chlorine bleach dissipates into the air over time so pay attention and add more bleach often to retain the chlorine smell. Change the water frequently, depending upon use. Be aware that heat inactivates bleach and in very cold water it takes longer to work. *The rule of thumb is, if your hand-washing water doesn't smell like chlorine, add more bleach!* While somewhat sketchy, in the outdoors when I have no water, bleach, or hand sanitizer, I use "clean" sand, gravel, or earth to wash my hands. Vigorously rub your fingers and hands with the above for thirty seconds or more and you should be good to go in a pinch.

Optimal Hand Washing

Hand washing, especially when preparing food for yourself and others, is the single most important procedure for preventing the spread of infections and is defined as a vigorous, brief rubbing together of all surfaces of lathered hands, followed by rinsing under a stream of water as described below: Consider it to be your sacred civic duty.

1 Wash hands in soapy water, including top, bottom, sides, in between the fingers, and under the nails. (CAUTION! Soaps containing ammonia should not be used with chlorine bleach as they are a toxic combination. Check for possible warning labels on the soap to see if it's unsafe to use with bleach. As a small boy, I made the mistake of peeing into a toilet into which my mother had put chlorine bleach to clean it. I still remember the toxic gas created and gasping for breath as my parents held my head out of an open window for fresh air.)

2 Rinse the soap off.

3 Then re-rinse hands in a bleach solution.

4 Allow your hands to air dry! (by shaking, NOT wiping)

Hand-washing stations can be easily made from a gallon jug with the bottom cut out and tied upside down to a post, fence, tree, or shrub. Punch holes in the cap (the new "bottom" of the jug), and add water to the "new top" as needed so it can sprinkle out the holes like a makeshift faucet. These jugs can be anchored above an existing sink or outside in an area where drainage is not a problem. You can also use the larger, two-and-a-half-gallon-size water jugs with the built-in spigot in the front. Cut a flap in the plastic toward the top, back part of the jug, and you can refill it with water whenever it runs low. I used this method while I was living in my yurt. I elevated my two-and-a-half-gallon jug using a couple of boards screwed together and put a cheap plastic basin underneath the spigot. I used this system not only to wash my hands, but my dishes as well for several years. If used as a regular hand-washing facility, clean the spigot regularly with bleach water. If you provide bar soap at your wash station, keep it in a container with drain holes in the bottom.

Just like the family camping trip, you will want to reemphasize the importance of hand washing and keep things and people as clean as possible. When the modern conveniences that we take for granted are gone, people tend to get lazy about proper sanitation. DO NOT let your family become complacent about their sanitation practices or you will all suffer the consequences.

Safely Storing Scat

There may be times when the little man in the truck doesn't show up to take away your waste products for some while. You will be left holding the bag, so to speak, of your family's (and neighborhood's) health and safety. If you have the space or the land to dig a hole, bury your waste. Read the other sections on where and how to do so safely. Be mindful that local authorities might discourage you from burying human waste. If you don't have the space, you'll have to store it aboveground. Many people talk about burning their waste. While most of your toilet paper will burn, have you ever tried to burn a fresh turd, or even one that's a few weeks old? OK then . . . this is where having a couple of extra-large garbage cans with tight-fitting lids will come in handy. These should be lined with paper and/or plastic trash bags. Even if the lid is already a tight fit, anchor it down with ropes or bungee cords and stake the entire garbage can to the ground or tie it off to a tree or shrub so it can't be knocked over. Arizona has white-collared peccaries—wild

Safely **STORING SCAT**

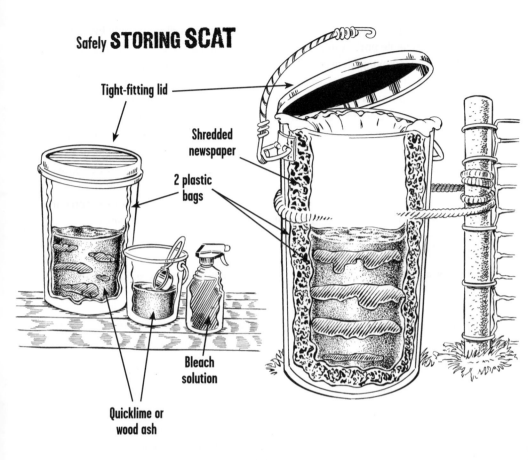

Tight-fitting lid

Shredded newspaper

2 plastic bags

Bleach solution

Quicklime or wood ash

piglike creatures—that love to push over people's trash cans and eat the contents. Roaming dogs can manage just as well, and you can imagine the result. Add a small amount of household disinfectant, a thin layer of quicklime, or wood ashes between each "deposit" from your emergency toilet until the garbage can is reasonably full. These cans can be stored if need be until the public sewage system is up and running or emptied into safe ground pits if they become available. Insecticides and deodorants can be used to control odors and bugs breeding in storage containers that can't be immediately emptied.

What about Apartment and Office Building Poopers?

Instead of using large garbage cans to store poop, apartment dwellers can use smaller covered pails or whatever sealable containers are available. As mentioned, sealable five-gallon buckets can be double-lined with garbage bags and used as an emergency potty as is. Sprinkle or spray your fresh deposit with a disinfectant before sealing up the bucket for the next user. You can also add shredded newspaper as described below between the garbage bags before putting them in the five-gallon bucket.

Waterproof paper containers, similar to barf bags on airlines, should be kept as portable, disposable potties in places where yards and conventional toilets are not an option. After spraying bleach disinfectant on the contents, seal the bags individually and store them in doubled- or tripled-up large-capacity garbage bags (if pails or other sealable containers are not available) until an opportunity to properly dispose of them arises. You're not living in ancient Rome, so don't throw these parcels out the window to help start a disease epidemic. What comes around goes around, so take responsibility for your poop and pee. You can make your own portable potty bags by putting a large grocery bag inside another with a layer of shredded newspaper or some other absorbent material between the bags. Keep a good supply of grocery bags, large-capacity trash bags, old newspapers, and a gallon of 5.25 or 6 percent household bleach around the apartment or office for just such emergencies.

No Toilet Paper? No Problem!

"I'VE LEARNED . . . THAT LIFE IS LIKE A ROLL OF TOILET PAPER. THE CLOSER IT GETS TO THE END, THE FASTER IT GOES."
—ANDY ROONEY

Toilet paper is a recent phenomenon. My own grandparents wiped their butts with corncobs and the good ol' Sears and Roebuck catalog. Some corncobs were softened in water before use and even dyed pretty colors to spiffy up the outhouse décor. Royalty of days past, believing their butts more sensitive than those of the working class, used strips of silk and goose feathers, still attached to the dead goose's skinned neck for maximum wipability.

I don't allow students to take toilet paper into the field on my survival classes. As I prepare them with this reality, I have seen many eyes go wide and faces turn white. God only knows what they're thinking. Some sit uncomfortably while others rage and protest as if their lives depended on the stuff. I have several reasons why I don't allow toilet paper during field courses, and the main one is simple. The last thing that should stress you out during a survival situation is what you're wiping your butt with. Once I instruct students how to go potty without using toilet paper, and they experiment with the information outdoors, the mystery is gone. It's no longer an "unknown variable" to place something other than Mr. Whipple's recommendation in contact with their backsides, and they are free from one more self-imposed limitation.

Cool Things to Wipe Your Butt with

Over the years my profession has led me to wipe with almost anything you can imagine that's not still moving, thorny, or has spines. In my more naïve years, I once wiped my butt with poison ivy on the third day of a month-long backpacking adventure, so I'm able to empathize with you about any non-toilet paper scenario your might find yourself facing. Below are a few of the safer items you have in your backyard, back lot, or in the garage. It's your job to identify any noxious plants particular to your area or personal sensitivities you may have.

- *Rocks*. Rocks are a favorite of mine as there seems to be a shape and size for every orifice, but watch out for the sharp parts. Note: If it's too hot to pick up, it's too hot to wipe with. Watch for critters such as scorpions or fire ants in the Southwest.
- *Sticks*. Be careful of sharp broken ends.
- Grass. I like long grass. Pull up enough grass to create, when folded over onto itself, a thickly padded spoon-shaped utensil.
- *Leaves*. Beware of poisonous plants. Use several at a time, overlapped, or your fingers will bust through.
- *Snow*. An invigorating "wake-up-and-smell-the-coffee" experience that wipes and cleans at the same time.
- *Tree branches and shrubs*. You will quickly learn that some are "directional." Identify whether a plant might irritate (before using on your buttocks!) by

rubbing some of the plant on your wrist or some
other area less sensitive and critical to your comfort.

➲ *Rags.* There are dozens of uses for rags and this is one
of them. Use them sparingly due to the other choices
you have.

➲ *Newspaper.* Crumple it up a few times beforehand
and the paper will become softer and more absorbent. It also works great for cleaning your windows;
something about the printer's ink.

➲ *Magazines.* While somewhat slippery and oily feeling,
crumpling up the pages can improve its wiping abilities. What better way to honor yet another enlight-
ening article about Paris Hilton?

Helpful **HARDCORE** *Hints*

No Toilet Paper? . . . or Anything Else? . . . No Problem

In the event that you run out of anything to
wipe your butt with after going to the bathroom, you still have an option, your hand and
water. In many parts of the world, toilet paper
will not be waiting for you in the outhouse.
Instead you will find a water-holding container
of varying design. There are a few techniques
in using the water/hand combination and I'm
sure you'll find which method works best for
you. Some folks have tried the water/hand method and never gone back. Most people recommend that you wipe with one hand and eat with the other, use water to
rinse with, and wash your hands thoroughly, but that's where the commonalities in
the advice end. Below are some options worth exploring.

Techniques for Wiping Your Butt with Your Hand

(*Caution!* Beware of cuts or abrasions on your hand(s) that could come in contact
with fecal matter.)

1 First, make sure you have some sort of container
filled with water that is reserved for this purpose
only. Have hand-washing supplies ready to go
at the site of your defecation.

2 Go poop in some think-like-a-raindrop-
approved location.

3 Using the hand that you don't eat with,
try one of the following methods:

> a. Slowly pour/splash water up from the water container as you use your fingers to wipe and dislodge fecal matter from your anus ...
> OR

> b. Pour water from the container slowly down your lower back and into your butt crack while doing the same as above with your fingers ...
> OR

> c. Have some water container that can create velocity, such as a bicyclist's squirt bottle or commercial drinking water container with the pop-up squirt top. Direct the stream of water at your anus while using the fingers as mentioned above ...
> OR

> d. Entertain the family by inventing a unique method of your own.

Note: Some people prefer to wet their fingers first as they feel the poop is less likely to stick to their fingers: your call.

Regardless of which water/hand method you employ, WASH YOUR HANDS WELL after you're finished. If using this method, it will be a great advantage in comfort and cleanliness to keep your fingernails trimmed as short as you are able. Plan on using water to wash, not just waterless hand sanitizer, and have a bleach solution rinse, and maybe a fingernail brush, somewhere in your hand-washing routine.

Pertinent Potty Paraphernalia

The following are emergency sanitation supplies that will help you out when dealing with human waste. Purchase them now before the next emergency. Unlike canned corned beef, they will never go rancid, and they will always be useful for something.

> Toilet paper (if the hardcore tips above didn't grab you, keep a month's supply on hand at all times)
> Waterless hand sanitizer
> Bleach-based spray disinfectant and/or a bottle of chlorine bleach—sodium hypochlorite 5.25 or 6 percent (Dry bleach is caustic and not safe for this type of use)
> Antibacterial soap (alcohol-based)
> LOTS of heavy-duty plastic trash bags with ties
> Large trash can(s) with tight-fitting lid

- ➲ Two or three five-gallon buckets with tight-fitting lids. Apartment owners might opt for these alone instead of the large trash can
- ➲ Shovel or other digging tool(s)
- ➲ Moistened towelettes or baby wipes
- ➲ Quicklime or woodstove/fireplace ashes
- ➲ A bunch of old newspapers (two or three weeks' worth). Use for making toilet paper or absorbent, homemade, portable potty bags, wrapping up garbage, lining large garbage cans for storing poop, and a variety of other sanitary uses
- ➲ Four- to six-mil plastic sheeting. This roll of plastic has multiple uses, well beyond the realm of sanitation. If one of your tribe gets dysentery, using plastic sheeting to cover and protect his or her sleeping area will be a godsend

Making the Most of Your Meals: Composting Your Family's Poop and Pee

One of the blasphemies of modern society is the primitive way in which we deal with our waste products by using one of the most sacred elements of survival, water. The fact that your survival scenario can leave you high and dry, with no way to replenish your family's potable water supply, is not only possible, it's probable. If given a choice, using one of your most critical survival resources to stem the effects of one of your most critical sanitary needs begs the question whether you should remain in the gene pool. In the drought-stricken southwestern United States, towns and cities continue to flush millions of gallons of precious water down the toilet to whisk a turd to a place of residence where it can begin its redemption process, using yet more water, energy resources, and dangerous chemicals. There has to be a better way, and there is.

There are several no-water or, at least, low-water ways in which we as a society can deal with our waste and, frankly, they are not being promoted with any fervor or regularity. Sadly, America's aversion to simple and common-sense sanitation strategies dates back more than a century. Back in the late 1800s, New York City was having a problem getting rid of all the poo from its residents. After chucking it into the surrounding water proved to be a stinky situation, New York City for a time hauled its dung to New Jersey. After the Garden State proved unable to accommodate the needs of the Big Apple, New York looked to France for a solution. The French had been successfully composting human manure for a long time in a process called *poudrette*. Unfortunately, the composting process was voted down by an unimaginative city council, due to its inability to view composted human poop as plant fertilizer, and the ignorance largely continues. On the hopeful side, in many areas major home-building and hardware stores now carry very low- or no-water use commercial toilet systems that have all of the comforting

HOW to COMPOST your POOP

Add composted compost to vegetation and enjoy the fruits of your labor!

First, make a potty.

Get some organic matter (grass clippings, leaves, and other stuff works too).

1-quart saucepan

Let compost pile compost.

Add two scoops of sawdust to cover the bottom of the poo-bucket.

Do the doo (and pee is okay, too).

Use a quart or two of grey water and wash empty poo-bucket.

Empty full bucket into compost pile and cover with layer of straw or other organic matter.

(Made with free pallets!)

Cover each poop with sawdust.

statistics needed to convince and reassure skeptical city planners as to their efficiency and safety.

The art of composting has been around for as long as people have. Back in the days of common sense, people actively used composted waste products from themselves, animals, food scraps, and other items to enrich the earth with nutrients. The thermophylic composting process brought the various items in the compost pile up to a certain temperature for a sustained period of time in which all of the harmful pathogens were killed. The end result was a safe, rich humus material that was then added to the garden, orchard, or field. The enriched earth would in turn give back to the people in the form of greater and more nutritious yields of fruits and vegetables—a closed-loop system in which everyone benefited. While composting might seem unrelated to an urban emergency situation, if more people would consider composting, we could deal with the cause of some of our problems instead of paying later to clean up their effect.

Just in case you're inspired to reap the harvest from your family, so to speak, see the previous illustration for how to compost your waste. For further reading and entertainment, I highly recommend *The Humanure Handbook* by J. C. Jenkins. J. C. lays out the facts regarding composting human waste in a scientific yet humorous way that won't bore you silly. He also addresses how to deal with the legalities of composting human waste in an urban environment full of fear and closed minds.

SUPER SIMPLE SUMMARY

- ⮑ After a major disaster, due to destroyed infrastructure and swamped emergency response personnel, improvising proper sanitation methods will rank high on the list of your survival priorities.
- ⮑ Improper sanitation directly or indirectly kills hundreds of thousands of people each year.
- ⮑ Flies, other pests, and the family dog love poop and will transfer dangerous fecalborne pathogens to family members if given a chance. *All fecal matter should be thoroughly covered!*
- ⮑ Use the PPDD method (privacy, proximity, drainage, and depth) when planning the location for your outdoor potty place. *All outdoor pit toilets should be located at least 200 feet from all water sources!*
- ⮑ Slit trenches and cat holes, two basic styles of alternative pit toilets, can be created with a pick or shovel

in suitable ground. These styles of toilets will require you to squat to go to the bathroom unless a seat is improvised. Privacy barriers can be created from an extra blanket or tarp. Discontinue using slit trenches and cat holes when they fill up to within ten to twelve inches from the top of the ground. Fill them in with earth and pack it down.

- Existing toilets in the home can be used by pouring water into the bowl itself to flush. *Warning!* If using this method, make certain that your area's sewer lines are intact! The existing toilet can also be used as a "seat" by suspending and anchoring doubled-up plastic bags into the empty bowl itself. Partially filled bags with added disinfectant are then tied up securely and disposed of in a safe location.

- *Important! Adequate hand washing is the single most important procedure for preventing the spread of infections.* Thoroughly wash hands after going to the bathroom. Chlorine bleach-dip solutions, antibacterial soaps, and alcohol-based waterless hand sanitizers can be used in conjunction with the mechanics of proper hand washing.

- If burying waste products is not an option, use containers with tight-fitting lids such as five-gallon buckets or garbage cans to safely store waste products temporarily. Garbage cans should be thoroughly staked down to prevent them from being knocked over.

- Toilet paper can be improvised from newspaper, magazines, and rags, as well as an assortment of outdoor options such as grass, leaves, sticks, and rocks.

- Have sanitation supplies on hand to improvise emergency sanitation needs such as digging tools, five-gallon buckets, chlorine bleach, toilet paper, hand sanitizers, plastic trash bags with ties, old newspapers, plastic sheeting, and antibacterial soap.

"I GREW UP with SIX BROTHERS. That's how I learned to DANCE—WAITING for the BATHROOM."

—Bob Hope

16

HELPFUL
Highlights
of HYGIENE

"Keep your own house and its surroundings pure and clean. This hygiene will keep you healthy and benefit your worldly life."

—Sri Sathya Sai Baba

The following are tips to help keep your family reasonably clean when conventional means for doing so have disappeared. Attempting to continue regular hygiene habits will help prevent the spread of disease, increase morale, and offer a predictable routine, thereby reducing stress.

The Amazing Towel Bath:
Four Simple Steps to a Cleaner You and a Better Attitude

Let's face it, life sucks with a smelly crotch and armpits. Eating the can of survival beans next to Uncle Ted's wafting pelt can be a trying experience for the wee ones as well as the older members of the family. I remember my grandmother (one of seven kids) cringing as she told me the story about her bathing experiences on the old South Dakota homestead. Once a week her mother would fill a washtub with water heated on the woodstove. Then, one by one, the entire family would take turns bathing in the same water. The littlest kids went first, often peeing in the water. On the bright side, maybe it kept the water warmer longer.

It's amazing how a somewhat clean body can have a positive effect on your attitude. If survival situations become long term and really grubby, "cooties" can get out of control and offer up a number of skin infections that are no fun to deal with. Crowded shelters, especially during hot, humid weather, can cause skin diseases to flourish. It's very important to wash off sweat and dead skin cells from your body. In sticky, humid weather, these skin cells will stay on your body and start to decay. At the same time, bathing with soap too often washes off normal skin oils and can cause the skin to prematurely dry out and crack, especially in dry, cold environments.

While emergency scenarios can put a damper on supplies, especially hot water, with a little ingenuity, your family can feel like half a million bucks with minimal effort. In the past, my solar shower experiences have been more of an experiment than a shower during the winter months. Thus I have become well-versed in perfecting the towel or sponge bath, as some prefer to call it.

The following recipe for cleanliness is good for one adult.

Ingredients:

- ➲ **Heat source to boil water**
- ➲ **Medium-sized pot or container**
- ➲ **One-half quart, give or take, of potable or nonpotable water**
- ➲ **One medium-sized hand towel, large kitchen towel, large clean shirt, or whatever**
- ➲ **Your naked, smelly body**

Directions:

1 Put water in pot, cover with lid, and begin to bring to boil on heat source. Using a lid will save fuel, time, and water.

2 Check frequently. As water starts to steam and form small bubbles at bottom of pot, remove pot from heat source. (*see Tried and True Towel Tips below.)

3 Slowly and carefully immerse towel into pot. Move towel around slightly to let capillary action of cloth wick up hot water. If towel is completely saturated, use less water next time as a fully wet towel will be too hot to pick up, let alone wring out, and it will drip all over the place.

4 When towel is very hot but not too hot to handle (**see Tried and True Towel Tips), pick up towel and vigorously wash body.

I like to start with my face (washing long hair is a separate event, folks), and then my arms and torso, back, legs, armpits, and the crotch last. I use every part of the towel, front and back, being careful not to rework the crotch part of the towel over some other part of my body. Believe it or not, I then take the towel, crotch part folded in the middle, and spot mop the floor of my house. While this may seem extreme to many water-rich parts of the country, I can sense my fellow desert rats and rain harvesters nodding in approval. Regardless of your mopping the floor with your towel or not, the towel is now dirty and should be laundered or at least sun-washed before future use (*** see Tried and True Towel Tips).

Tried and True Towel Tips:

*Fully boiling the water will make it too hot for immediate use, but if you're bathing with funky, nonpotable water, you may choose to boil the water for one minute or at least bring it to a boil to ensure the destruction of weird, waterborne pathogens.

**The towel will transform from being too hot to handle to cool within a phenomenally short amount of time so move with speed!

***The more you encourage your loved ones, especially the kiddies, to wipe and clean their butt cracks with something disposable **before** wiping it with the towel, the easier it will be to clean the towel for future use and make certain that it's properly disinfected. Washcloths, underwear, socks, and other high-use items can be disinfected by putting them into boiling water for a minute or two. Disinfecting these items, not just washing them, is the most important health objective under difficult shelter conditions. Unless plenty of water is available for rinsing, don't disinfect clothing by putting it in a chlorine bleach solution. Also, see the sun-washing section later in this chapter.

Spiffy Spray Bottle Showers

Spray bottles can be made into improvised showers allowing you to use very small amounts of water for bathing. Many household goods come in a spray bottle or they can be purchased new at most hardware stores. If you choose to recycle a spray bottle for use as a shower, don't choose one that held bug poison or some other toxic goo. Clean and rinse out the bottle thoroughly. Most spray bottles have an adjustable spout that will let you choose from a fine mist to a squirt-gunlike stream depending upon your needs. Fill up your bottle with warm water or set it in the sun. Bottles can be painted a dark color to speed up the absorption of shortwave radiation from the sun to heat up the water, but the smaller size of most bottles usually makes this unnecessary. Next, get naked, and in an appropriate place, use a combination of spraying and wiping with a rag or small towel to get clean.

The Super-Sized Spray Bottle Shower

Multigallon capacity, manually pressurized spray bottles with an attached hand-held wand that are normally used for spraying weed killer or fertilizers can be purchased at hardware stores. As the majority of my house is concrete, I used one of these sprayers (and the smaller handheld spray bottles) to paint my house using concrete dye. Just like their little brothers, these big brother spray bottles can be painted black or some other dark color, filled with water, and set in the sun to get hot, or at least warm, depending on where you live and the season. The container holding the water has a pump that allows you to pressurize the water inside, eliminating the need to continually pump the handle for you to have a pressurized shower. Simply fill the clean container with warm/hot water or set it in the sun, pressurize the holding tank, and enjoy a serious spray of water. The handheld wand can be modified and mounted in a number of ways to offer hands-free operation. **Chemical Caution:** Don't use a sprayer that has held toxic weed killer or chemical fertilizers for extended periods of time. Plastic absorbs the contents of whatever is stored within it so even intense scrubbing may not be enough to clean a sprayer that has been used for these purposes. Use common sense and test such a sprayer on something other than your crotch.

Greasy Hair

To temporarily clean greasy hair, try rubbing small amounts of baby powder into the scalp and hair. Any extra should be brushed or combed out. Visually, this method works best for blondes, as dark-haired people might look like they have a wicked case of dandruff—but who cares if you're more comfortable. Baby powder is a cover-up and doesn't deal with the cause of greasy hair, but it helps to stretch out the time between rare showers, if need be.

Temporary Toothbrushes

New toothbrushes are dirt cheap, so having a few spares around the house is easy. When they wear out for humans, they're still great for cleaning stuff. The following are options for keeping teeth clean in a crisis. Toothpaste is overrated. I haven't used it for nearly twenty years and four out of five dentists surveyed say I have great teeth. Here are some toothbrush and toothpaste substitutes:

➲ **Fabric, rags, or washcloths and baking soda. Pioneer folks, including my grandparents, used wet pieces of fabric (hand towels work great) with salt or baking soda (toothpaste substitute) and simply rubbed their teeth and gums clean.**

➲ **Willow (*Salix* species) or cottonwood (*Populous* species). Willows and cottonwoods contain *salicin* and *populin*, ingredients in aspirin that also double as a great plaque fighter. Simply cut a fresh twig of either about as big around as a pencil and chew the end until it's fuzzy. Use this as your toothbrush and scrub away. At first, both have a slightly bitter taste but it's not all that disagreeable; some people even like it.**

Dental floss is very hard to duplicate in nature. I have used fibers of yucca and agave plants here in the Southwest but if your teeth are "tight," forget it. I think we have all experienced the agony of having something wedged in between the teeth. You may also be eating who knows what as part of your survival diet in which floss rates higher than dessert. In my first book, I pay homage to the multiuse virtues of dental floss and always carry some in my survival kit. Follow the advice and have some extra floss around the house.

"Hygiene is **TWO-THIRDS** of HEALTH."
—Lebanese proverb

Worthwhile Waterless Washing

If water is hard to come by, *externally* smelly areas of the body such as crotches, armpits, and feet can be dealt with using a variety of alcohol-based products and a paper towel or rag. While not truly getting you clean from dirt, the alcohol kills the critters that cause the stink instead of just masking the smell with a fragrance. In my dubious water situation, I commonly use waterless hand sanitizer to knock down the funk factor and it works wonderfully. Funky smells are not only a real romance killer,

SELF-CLEANING CLOTHING?

"During Desert Storm most casualties were from bacterial infections rather than from accidents or friendly fire. We have treated T-shirts and underwear for soldiers who tested them for several weeks and found that they remained hygienic, as the clothing was actively killing the bacteria. They also helped clear up some skin complaints in those testing them."

—Jeff Owens, scientist, U.S. Air Force

Scientists have created a coating that repels water, resists stains, and even kills many of the bacteria in human sweat that cause odors. While the clothing would still need to be laundered, it would need to be washed much less often and would wash much easier. The technology involves using microwaves to fix microscopic nanoparticles, which have "attached" chemical properties such as water repellency or the destruction of bacteria, to clothing fibers. Although the coating wears off over time, makers claim it can be restored by soaking the material in a fresh solution of the same chemicals.

U.S. Air Force scientists initially became involved in the research in hopes that soldiers' clothing could offer protection during biological warfare. Initial tests discovered that the process could kill anthrax and other weaponized bacteria.

The coating, especially its antibacterial properties, could revolutionize sports and backpacking clothing as well as offer hundreds of other possibilities, from hospital bedding, doctor and nurses' uniforms, and chefs' aprons to air conditioning filters on planes and cruise ships.

they are also harbingers of skin diseases ready to manifest themselves and should be dealt with seriously. Obese friends and family members may have the same bacterial buildup between the folds and rolls of their fat, caused by no light and high-moisture conditions. Help them keep as clean as possible through regular methods or wiping with one of the following alcohol products. Like mom does for baby, high-moisture areas can be treated and kept dry by using baby powder or cornstarch to absorb excess moisture.

- ➲ Rubbing alcohol. This is very drying to the skin so use sparingly and stop if problems arise
- ➲ Lotions containing alcohol
- ➲ Shaving lotions and face creams

➲ **Baby towelettes**
➲ **Waterless hand sanitizer**

Super Sun-washing

While doing the laundry is not a disaster priority, I'll share the following tip nevertheless. Between extended field courses in outdoor survival and unique living situations for the majority of my life, I have found myself at times unable to do the
laundry. Professional slobs will tell you that there are various levels of "dirty" that
clothing can become before it should be burned. Most urban folks don't have dirty
clothes at all as there is no dirt to dirty them within their environment. The majority of metropolitan dirty clothes are unclean due to perspiration and sloughed dead
skin cells from the owner. Add cigarette smoke, pungent food odors, stains from Al's
Garlic Deli, and animal hair from the family pet, and that usually rounds out the
equation. Unclean, yes, but dirty? I don't think so.

As the fabric of your clothing continues to take on your dead epidermis and glandular fluids, the fibers become clogged and the dead air space, or insulation value of
the clothing, starts to decrease. For nearly two decades, I have experimented with
wearing the same shirt for several days unless it becomes dirty, i.e. caked with earth,
weeds, or something else picked up in the backcountry. I'm so sensitive to this routine
that I can literally feel the increased insulation value of a clean T-shirt as opposed
to a dirty one. In other words, if it's cold outside, I feel warmer with a fresh shirt.
Remember, clean clothing is a plus if your survival situation happens when it's cold.

If you have to wear your shirt for two or three days, take it off and shake it occasionally. If you shake it vigorously in a beam of sunlight, you will witness a small
cloud of skin particles waft off the fabric. Clothing that is worn for days on end with
no cleaning can cause various skin rashes and problems, and that is in addition to
its losing its insulation value and you looking like hell. There is a direct relationship
between these skin problems and the "skin dirt" from your body lingering in the
dark, humid environment of your clothing.

As we now know, sunlight contains ultraviolet radiation, which, if given enough
time and in the right concentration, is used to kill entire legions of waterborne
pathogens in order to make nonpotable water potable. These same disinfecting
benefits of ultraviolet radiation can also work wonders on the "yuck" within the
fabric of your clothing. The more potent the sunlight, the better and faster the following method will work.

1 Gather up dirty articles of clothing (or your sleeping
     bag, blankets, etc.), turn them inside out, take them
     outdoors, and vigorously shake out each one.
2 Spread out clothing in full sun, off the ground if
     possible, on a bush, a fence, a porch, or something
     else. The more the entire surface area of the fabric is
     exposed to direct sunlight, the better.

3 If you're tight for time or sunlight or both, flip the article of clothing in the middle of the day. If time is not an issue and you have a few days of good sun, you might leave one side of the clothing exposed for an entire day and flip it in the morning.

4 How much sunlight your wardrobe requires depends on the intensity of the sun in your area, how much time you have, and how fussy you are. A hot summer day here in the Southwest will "clean" a shirt in a few hours. A sun-washed garment will both smell and feel cleaner, as the ultraviolet radiation has cooked many of the critters that revel in your sweat and dead skin cells.

Decisively Dealing with Dead Bodies

Even the best survival plans can fail. One of the most difficult circumstances you may be forced to deal with is the death of a loved one or someone else. Although it takes much courage to do so, especially if the dead person is a family member, you may be required to cowboy up and dispose of the body yourself for a number of reasons during or after a major crisis.

The methodology that goes into dealing with human remains after a mass disaster is staggeringly complex and run by an army of experts from more than a dozen fields. Every effort should be made to contact and wait for the proper authorities to dispose of the body of a loved one or an unknown person. Doing anything with a dead body in this day and age will open you up to unbelievable scrutiny. *Document everything in writing* such as the name of the individual, their age, sex, what they were wearing, and the location and position in which they were found. Estimate the time of death, the cause of death, and any and all circumstances that you feel will help the authorities piece together what happened. If you have access to a camera, take pictures of everything you do. Although no crime was committed, the disturbing of a body will destroy many clues from the "crime scene" as far as investigating authorities are concerned. Be aware that there is an actual series of regulations for removing a body, including inspection of the site, examination of the body, collection of possible evidence, photographing the scene, questioning those who found the body, and much more. When authorities look and ask for this sort of evidence, don't take it personally; it's a boilerplate procedure when dealing with a corpse. The more you document the circumstances surrounding your situation, the greater help you'll be to authorities (and yourself) when the officials show up. If the identity of the body is unknown, think twice before getting involved and be extremely meticulous with your documentation.

The Importance of Having a "Funeral Ceremony"

Regardless of your faith or lack thereof, it's wise to have some sort of funeral ceremony or rite-of-passage ritual upon dealing with a dead body. It will initiate healing and closure, especially if it's a loved one. If time and opportunity allow, basic respect and dignity surrounding the preparation of the body will resonate with the living and have a lasting positive effect upon the morale of your family. Book after book has been written about the delayed emotional trauma experienced by survivors who were forced to deal with distressing events without proper closure and healing. I have attended more than one conscious-dying process of friends who have chosen to die at home surrounded by loved ones. The experience of everyone who was involved in the process was profoundly life-changing. Although this drawn-out ritual is much different than dealing with the sudden death of a family member, the hands-on, heart-open approach of being fully present with the end result of a dead family member is the same.

Throughout the world's history, hundreds of thousands of people have lost loved ones, some killed purposefully right in front of their eyes. These people have had to move on, literally and figuratively, and sometimes very quickly in order to live another day. You are not alone in the experience of having to manage the death of a family member. Your loved one is no longer that body. Prioritize what needs to happen to protect the living from further danger first, deal decisively with the dead body next, and then allow yourself and your family to consciously move through the healing process in whatever way works best for the good of the whole.

Dead Bodies and Disease . . . Fact or Fiction?

In 2002, the World Health Organization (WHO) issued a statement saying, "Dead or decayed human bodies do not generally create a serious health hazard, unless they are polluting sources of drinking water with fecal matter, or are infected with plague or typhus, in which case they may be infested with the fleas or lice that spread these diseases." Medical opinions offer that dead bodies are not as dangerous as people think in regard to the spread of disease. The reason given is that after death the body temperature drops rapidly, killing the most resistant viruses and bacteria, thus preventing them from spreading. The dead bodies of both humans and animals that might pose a health risk need certain specific environments for that risk to become manifest. The factors that cause a health risk include the following: the microorganisms that caused the disease need to be able to keep living in the dead host or in the environment after the host dies; the bodies are host to a disease that is common for the area; or the environment supports the spread of the disease, such as the chaos of severed sanitation systems or overcrowded shelters.

There are documented exceptions such as outbreaks of typhus and bubonic plague that can be at least partially contributed to bodies being accessed and the diseases transmitted by flies, mice, rats, etc. Isolated events of cholera, hepatitis B, and hepatitis C have also been reported. Although most of these outbreaks happen in developing countries with less than savory sanitary practices and resources, any modern urban area can quickly be reduced to the same set of variables in a long-term, major disaster. Other diseases can cause a problem as well. The HIV virus has been found still active within a body sixteen days after its death, and tuberculosis is highly contagious. Bodies suspected of having tuberculosis should have a piece of material put over their mouths and be handled in open areas with plenty of ventilation.

Regardless of scant exceptions, evidence supports that death caused by blunt-force trauma, drowning, or other nonepidemic scenarios, whether human-, animal-, or nature-caused, will not result in bodies that spread disease. After all, diseases and putrefaction are caused by different microorganisms. Someone who died without having cholera isn't suddenly going to create the disease when already dead. *The common misconception that all dead bodies spread disease takes the focus and precious resources away from the survivors.* Mass cremations have occurred in other countries after major catastrophes, such as with Hurricane Mitch in 1998, in which extremely limited fuel supplies were used to burn bodies thought to have been spreading disease, at the expense of that fuel being used to disinfect water and provide warmth, light, and transportation. Sometimes, such as happened in Sri Lanka following the December 2004 tsunami, entire "life-giving" hospital wards have been converted into morgues for fear of stopping an impending infection of the living.

The common practice in some countries of mass cremation or burying the dead in mass graves can cause great emotional trauma. Families receive closure when they have a chance to identify the body. Not being able to do so adds to the financial burden as well. In India, bodies must be identified in order for the families to receive monetary compensation. In the United States and other countries, the lack of official notification of a death can delay insurance payments for years.

The risk factors for disease after a disaster that is nonepidemic in nature come primarily from the scope of the disaster and the characteristics of the population regarding the following: the availability of adequate sanitation and potable water, the degree of crowding in shelters, the general health of the population, and the availability of healthcare, among other variables—*NOT dead bodies.* Immediately after a disaster, the priorities of the survivors should be in caring for other survivors by providing effective emergency sanitation, disinfecting drinking water, providing food, modifying shelters and so forth, not urgently disposing of the dead. Only after the immediate needs for the living are dealt with should the disposal of bodies commence.

What Happens to a Dead Body When It Decomposes

In days past, most cultures buried their dead near the home. Cemeteries didn't appear in cities until the seventeenth century. In a disaster situation, temporary burials may be necessary until outer conditions normalize to allow the transfer of the body to its final place. Dead bodies left exposed to the elements will putrefy and be the cause of much unpleasantness, especially in hot weather. Aside from heat, the main factor that influences the rate of decomposition of a body is the amount of bacteria already present within the intestines. This unknown variable will cause one body to noticeably start the decomposition process within a couple of hours, while a body a few feet away may not show the same signs for twelve hours or more. The stench and visible sight of the dead are a real buzz kill and will cause the morale of your tribe to suffer. While in some seasons a body will freeze solid, it will eventually "un-freeze" and must be dealt with just the same. In addition, roving packs of hungry animals from dogs and cats to coons and coyotes will dine on the dead and spread the body all around the neighborhood. When the danger of the initial emergency has passed, do whatever you need to do to fill yourself with courage and get into action to deal with the body as quickly as possible. The fact is that the body you see is no longer your loved one; it's just a shell. *The sooner you deal with a dead body, the less unpleasant your experience will be from its impending decomposition and its effects.*

While I have no direct exposure with bloated human corpses, I have a scientific collection permit from the Arizona Game and Fish Department that lets me legally harvest most species of animal roadkill for teaching purposes. This unique opportunity has allowed me to witness a wide variety of bodies in various stages of "yuckiness."

All decomposing flesh reacts the same way. Critters, both seen and unseen, just love dead stuff. Depending on the season and climate in which the death occurred, flies will be the first to join the party and will enter any available orifice to lay their eggs. Many hours later, the resulting hatched young (maggots) will make the body's skin literally crawl as they feed upon the corpse. Soon after, packs of flesh-eating beetles will arrive, usually black and orangish-red in color. Some are big, the size of a cockroach, and some are the size of a ladybug. Shortly after death, tiny microorganisms start to have their say within the body, and the resulting decomposition creates gas that causes the abdominal cavity of the body to swell up. The pressure from this gas will eventually get so intense that it will release itself out one of the body's orifices. Since decomposing flesh is greatly weakened, this gas might also burst through and release itself from the skin over the torso, thus spraying you with an assortment of liquids that are better left unsaid. Herbivores, having multiple stomachs, such as cows, will bloat up to a massive size from the putrefaction of grasses within the stomachs. These natural stages of decomposition make the body a literal putrefaction factory that greatly disfigures a dead body.

As I have no direct experience with a decaying human, I asked a local mortician what to expect, visibly, when someone dies. He started by telling me that 90 percent of the population could not possibly imagine what a body begins to look like when undergoing decomposition. Depending on heat and bacteria already present within the intestines, a dead body will turn green and then black. The face will swell up, as well as the belly, sometimes to almost twice the person's original size, making the body's identification nearly impossible. The body will eventually blister and the skin will peel away. Fluids will leak from the entire body, not just from body orifices. The body will purge itself, especially if it is moved, and stomach contents will be forced out through the mouth and nose due to the pressure from bloating. These processes can manifest themselves in a day, or within several days, depending upon the variables stated earlier.

I'm not writing this to gross you out or make light of the fact that someone you loved died. I'm writing this to let you know that the body of whoever died, if allowed to decompose in the open for even a short period of time, will look very different. Know this now so you're not scared or freaked out if and when you see it in the future. Our modern society has made death, and the results thereafter, all but invisible to the majority of the population. Bodies that are viewed at a funeral have undergone serious modifications, and Aunt Betty is made to look as if she's only sleeping. Major disasters will stretch emergency response personnel to the limit, and all of the wonderful firemen, police, and medical personnel who would normally save you from having to witness death in its raw state may be unavailable to be a first responder in your situation.

How to Dispose of a Dead Body in a Pinch

Basic precautions should be followed when handling all bodies, regardless of their apparent state of decomposition. *Although most organisms in a dead body are not likely to infect a healthy person, some infectious agents may be transmitted to those who are in close contact with blood, body fluids, and tissues of a body that died with infectious diseases.* Handling dead bodies increases risks for bloodborne viruses caused from direct contact with leaking blood or body fluids. Since dead bodies commonly leak feces (one drop of feces contains millions of microorganisms), gastrointestinal infections can easily be contracted from direct contact with the body, soiled clothes, or contaminated vehicles and equipment. The following are basic precautions to take when needing to prepare for and dispose of a dead body.

➲ ***Ensure universal precautions against blood and body fluids at all times!***

➲ **When handling dead bodies, do not smoke, eat, or drink, and avoid touching your mouth, eyes, or nose.**

➲ **Wear disposable latex or vinyl gloves when handling the body or anything associated with the body. Cover all of your cuts and abrasions with waterproof bandages or dressings. If you don't have disposable gloves, improvise mittens from zipper-lock bags, anchoring them at the wrists with rubber bands or tape. If nothing else, sacrifice a pair of winter gloves or mittens. Dispose of them or wash and disinfect them afterward.**

➲ **To prevent exposure of blood or bodily fluids to the mucous membranes of your eyes, nose, and mouth, wear masks and protective eyewear or face shields when coming in contact with a corpse. These can be improvised from construction-related equipment, such as dust masks and goggles or masks used for operating power saws or welding equipment.**

➲ **Wear gowns, aprons, or other improvised coveralls when doing anything that will likely splash blood or other bodily fluids. Be sure to thoroughly disinfect and wash these garments. The disinfection method used before washing or disposal should be done** by soaking the items for thirty minutes in a freshly prepared 0.1 percent chlorine bleach solution (1:50 dilution.) If disposing of these items, wrap them up securely in a plastic bag and discard in a safe place or burn them in a fire-safe environment. Coveralls can be made with fifty-five-gallon barrel liners or plastic lawn and leaf bags, a cutting edge, and duct tape, or improvised from plastic "painter" coveralls or rain gear. The sooner you deal with a dead body, the less it will be affected by the decomposition process.

➲ Wash hands and other parts of your body thoroughly if they come in contact with bodily fluids. Even if no apparent contact was made with bodily fluids, wash up thoroughly anyway. Your hands should be washed immediately and dipped in a chlorine bleach solution (see page 254) upon removing your gloves and disposing of them properly.

➲ Disinfect all equipment, vehicles, and contaminated surfaces after disposal of the body with a freshly prepared 0.1 percent chlorine bleach solution (1:50 dilution). Any spilled blood or body fluids should be carefully wiped up with a 1 percent chlorine bleach solution (1:5 dilution).

➲ Use body bags whenever possible. If need be, these can be improvised from triple or quadruple (or more) layers of fifty-five-gallon barrel liners, or roll the body up inside several layers of plastic sheeting. If in doubt, use more layers of plastic, as the containment of blood and body fluids are the main concern and a decomposing body will leak fluids more and more as it breaks down. The plastic bags or sheeting should be secured tightly with duct tape or something similar. Don't use safety pins or anything that will puncture the plastic. If you need to transport the body or handle the "plastic package" more than usual, and the outside of the plastic bag gets blood or body fluids on it, wipe the bag down with a 0.1 percent chlorine bleach solution (1:50 dilution). Note: Wrapping the body up with impermeable materials will cause the body to decompose more rapidly and temporarily prevent the earth from neutralizing some of the mess. However, your duty is to prevent the living from being exposed to blood or body fluids

from the corpse. If the identity of the body disposed
of is unknown, and the body is exhumed in the future
for identification or transfer to a permanent resting
place, authorities should have no problem identifying the corpse through the use of DNA testing. Even
so, you may consider sealing any identifying objects,
such as items in the pockets or jewelry, in a plastic
bag and burying it with the corpse.

⊃ Graves should be dug at least one hundred feet away
from all surface water sources and the bottom of any
grave must be at least five feet above the water table
with a two-foot unsaturated zone. Use common sense
and reread the sanitation chapter if necessary. (Note:
While I personally support cremation over the burying
of bodies, cremation in a time of disaster will use up
precious fuel and pose a risk to the living through fire
danger. Think how much heat is required to cook a
burger on the grill, let alone to completely consume
a 150-pound body. Cremation will also make identifying the body in the future, if its identity is not already
known, next to impossible.) Dig a hole in accordance
to the size of the body. A standard cemetery hole is
eight feet long by three feet wide and seven and a
half feet deep. This depth is to compensate for a traditional casket, so your hole can be much shallower. If
need be, two people can be buried, one on top of the
other. The depth of your hole will be affected by what
tools you have to dig with, the hardness of the earth,
groundwater levels, and what kind of critters might
try to dig up the body. Some people, before covering the body with earth, have covered the body with
thorny bushes such as blackberries, raspberries, or
other painful vegetation that will physically stop dogs
and other animals from reaching the body. Attempt
to have the body under at least three feet of earth.
Mound up the earth several inches on top of the hole
and tamp it down by walking on it; newly deposited
earth will settle over time. Mark the grave for future
location in a way that identifies who is buried there, if
known, or at least that a body has been buried there,
if you don't know its identity.

⊃ If blood or body fluids from the dead body enter
your body through "splash exposure" into the eyes,

mouth, or any mucous membranes or through an exposed injury, wash the injured or exposed areas with copious amounts of disinfected running water. Encourage minor penetrating injuries to bleed. Use liberal amounts of topical disinfectant like povidone iodine 10 percent, lightly cover with a breathable sterile bandage, and seek medical help if possible for further treatment of the exposure.

○ Initiate a funeral ceremony or rite-of-passage ritual to begin closure and healing for the family and all concerned.

○ *Ensure universal precautions against blood and body fluids at all times!*

Handy Hygiene Stuff

Duplicates of the following supplies in your home, car, office, and bug-out pack, as per your family's needs, will make life less of a drag during emergencies.

○ **Cornstarch or baby powder**
○ **Fingernail clippers and emery board**
○ **Sanitary napkins and/or tampons**
○ **Toothbrush and dental floss**
○ **Insect repellent**
○ **Toilet paper**
○ **Two or three hand towels**
○ **All purpose soap**
○ **Petroleum jelly**
○ **Small mirror**
○ **Waterless alcohol-based hand sanitizer**
○ **Liquid chlorine bleach**
○ **Optional: Disposable baby diapers**

SUPER SIMPLE SUMMARY

➲ Staying as clean as possible after a disaster will help prevent the spread of disease, increase morale, and reduce stress by offering a predictable routine.

➲ Water-saving baths and showers can be improvised using hot-water-soaked towels and large and small spray bottles filled with warm water (sun-warmed or otherwise).

➲ Toothbrushes can be improvised with rags and certain plants. Toothpaste can be improvised from baking soda or salt.

➲ Alcohol-based, waterless hand sanitizers can be used externally to spot disinfect smelly body parts, as can other common bathroom products such as baby tow-elettes. Pure rubbing alcohol dries out the skin and should be used with caution.

➲ Ultraviolet radiation from strong sunlight can be used to clean dirty clothing, blankets, or sleeping bags.

➲ Although it will be emotionally and mentally chal-lenging, you may be forced to deal with the dead body of a loved one or a stranger after a disaster.

➲ If authorities are unable to recover the dead body in a timely manner, document in writing everything you can about the scene including the individual's name, age, sex, time and cause of death, position found, and any other details you feel will help the authorities piece together what happened.

➲ *Important!* Dead bodies in them-selves normally *do not* create a serious health hazard unless they died of a contagious disease such as plague or typhus. (In these cases, the disease is carried and spread by fleas, lice, rats, and mice in contact with the body.) Bodies suspected of having

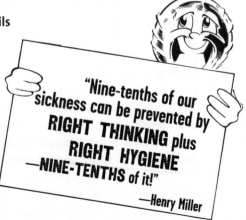

"Nine-tenths of our sickness can be prevented by RIGHT THINKING plus RIGHT HYGIENE —NINE-TENTHS of it!"

—Henry Miller

tuberculosis should have a piece of cloth put over
their mouths and be handled in open areas with good
ventilation. Dead bodies can pollute water sources
due to leaking feces.

- ⮑ The misconception that dead bodies spread disease
takes valuable resources away from survivors. Fulfill the
needs of survivors first and then deal with the bodies.

- ⮑ The two main factors that cause a dead body to
putrefy are heat and the amount of bacteria already
present within the intestines. The second factor is the
unknown variable for how quickly a body will begin
to decompose. All dead bodies will become greatly
disfigured when they decompose.

- ⮑ *Caution! When disposing of a dead body, ensure
universal precaution against blood and body fluids
at all times!* Wear protective clothing and wash and
disinfect hands, clothing, and all equipment after the
fact. Body bags can be improvised from barrel liners
or sheet plastic and duct tape.

- ⮑ Graves should be dug according to the size of the
body, at least one hundred feet away from all surface water sources and at least five feet above the
water table. Reread the sanitation chapter if necessary. Upon burying the body, make sure it's covered
with at least three feet of earth, mound it up, and
tamp it down.

- ⮑ If accidentally exposed to blood or body fluids in your
eyes, mouth, mucous membranes, or into a penetrating injury or cut, wash the area profusely with disinfected water, use liberal amounts of topical disinfectants, lightly cover the area with a sterile, breathable
bandage, and seek medical help for further treatment if available.

- ⮑ Create a ritual or "closing ceremony" to aid in the
healing process of the living.

- ⮑ Have hygiene supplies on hand such as baby powder,
fingernail clippers, sanitary napkins and/or tampons,
toothbrushes and dental floss, insect repellent, toilet
paper, towels, soap, disposable diapers, waterless
hand sanitizer, and liquid chlorine bleach.

17

LUMINOUS
and Liberating LIGHTING

"Anthra!" (Translation: "Fire!")
—*Quest for Fire*, the movie

Light is a form of energy, which can be emitted through a variety of processes including incandescence, fluorescence and phosphorescence, and laser generation. According to anthropologists, incandescence in the form of the element fire has been manipulated by someone or something for more than 2.5 million years. For indigenous peoples the world over, this flickering delight had limitless uses. It cooked food, disinfected water, made tools and weapons, regulated body temperature, and kept wild critters at bay. Nevertheless, one of the more profound and lasting attributes that fire could gift a growing world was the promise of light for the night. From coast to coast and culture to culture, humanity's aboriginal lighting was a simple by-product of one of nature's four sacred elements.

All flame-type lighting devices produce gases, which when burned feed the flame. Stuff that was burned for light over the centuries was incredibly varied and included pine pitch, birch bark, and the oils and fats from a number of animals, fish, and plants.

In Ice Age Europe nearly 40,000 years ago, the invention of stone, fat-burning lamps heralded the first effective, portable means of exploiting this aspect of fire. So profound was this shift in technology that it coincided with other remarkable changes in culture including the emergence of art, personal adornment, and complex weapons systems.

In the 1600s, early colonial settlers in America made candles just like the Indians taught them: from sections of conifer trees (pitch wood) that were cut into segments and burned. Later on, folks wanted to burn larger and larger things for brighter light. A container was devised, called a *cresset* or fire basket, that was nothing more than a noncombustible containment device made from clay, stone, or metal.

"We SEE LIGHT, not dark. But it is IN THE DARK that we FEEL GOBLINS and GHOSTS."
—Rex Brandt

Cressets, although not designed for burning liquid fuels, were amazing as now people could light streets, the decks of boats, and more. Using the fat-lamp concept, people started making all sorts of lamps and lanterns from clay, metal, stone, shells, and glass—anything that was liquid-worthy and could thus be filled with burnable oils such as olive oil, fish oil, whale oil, or sesame oil, among others. This light source had a wick made from dried moss, plant fibers, fabric—almost anything that would conduct the fuel to the flame. The wick could be adjusted as needed for more or less light, thereby conserving precious fuel.

Lighting technologies rapidly advanced and changed through the centuries from coal oil and camphene to kerosene and paraffin. From 1800 to 1850 alone, more than five hundred patents were granted for improvements in lighting devices.

In the 1850s, kerosene lighting was largely replaced by natural gas, which was in turn replaced by electricity in the 1880s. As the world rockets into the twenty-first century, who knows what lighting method will replace our current standard?

A Bump in the Night

Within every twenty-four-hour cycle on our planet, with few exceptions, we can all count on standing in the dark for several hours. For the past few decades, however, the vast majority of towns and cities have covered up this fact with a barrage of artificial lighting. Urbania's addiction to lighting, and the ease with which this addiction can be pacified, cause many people on the grid to think about lighting only when they don't have it. Lighting has become common enough to be completely taken for granted. Entire neighborhoods, towns, and cities sprout a blinding array of 24/7 indoor and outdoor lighting, literally blotting out the nighttime sky and any hope for seeing what grandma used to call stars. Many urban areas are so well-lit that darkness, and the psychological learning that comes along with it, never happens.

Few modern people have the psychological stamina to deal with life's burdens and fears when the lights go out. They have never trained or even considered what to do when it's pitch black. This complacency has worked its way into our psyches to a point that, when the darkness finally comes due to a power outage or other means, many of us feel helpless and lost. Don't believe me? Venture into the woods with me on one of my wilderness courses where I don't allow artificial lighting of any kind. Time after time, I have witnessed countless people become hopelessly confused and humbled when darkness descends upon the camp. And the majority of these people have a good degree of outdoor experience.

Adequate lighting not only comes in handy when trying to find the canned beans during a power outage, but it is also vital for long-term sanity. Several studies regarding the proper design and use of underground nuclear fallout shelters all came to the conclusion that people go nuts when subjected to continuous, long-term darkness. The good news is that very low levels of light, in which a simple

outline of a human form is all that can be distinguished, will prevent the crazies. Total pitch blackness, the kind where you are unable to see your hand in front of your face, is the kind of darkness that's the most difficult to deal with, especially if you have other people freaking out in your proximity. While holing up underneath the petunias in the backyard is off-focus for the intention of this book, becoming familiar with the ins and outs of emergency lighting, especially during low-light winter months, is not. Luckily for us savvy survivors there are several gadgets on the market that light up the night with little effort.

Let There Be Light! Banishing Fright from the Night

Fantastic Flashlights

The first flashlight was invented in the 1890s by Conrad Hubert, founder of the Eveready Battery Company. The lighting device got its name because at that time the batteries were not strong enough to power the light for a sustained amount of time, thus the user had to literally "flash light" for a moment in front of himself in order to conserve power. Early commercial flashlights started as a novelty and consisted of a small light, which was attached to a man's tie or a woman's barrette.

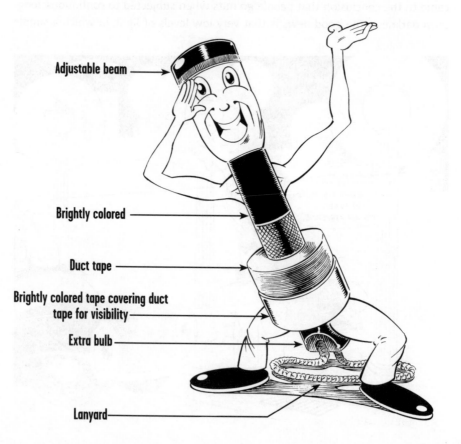

Adjustable beam

Brightly colored

Duct tape

Brightly colored tape covering duct tape for visibility

Extra bulb

Lanyard

It was necessary at the time to carry a large battery pack, which was sure to have been a buzz kill regardless of the cool gadget attraction.

Although all households in the modern world have a flashlight or two in their midst, odds are the batteries haven't been replaced since the 1990s. Being able to see in the dark is a gift. Flashlights have saved me more than once from having to spend an unplanned night out in the wilderness, and I use them regularly at home. In fact, there's a flashlight situated at virtually every entrance to my house.

There is little substitute for a high-quality flashlight. Even so, I have witnessed supposedly worthy lights take a dump on their owners at compromising times. There are many flashlight shapes and sizes available, although the AA-battery-size flash-lights are typically cheap, compact, widely available, and have enough candlepower to get the job done for the lion's share of household chores. In addition to the AA variety, I recommend that you consider the larger C- or D-cell-size flashlights as well. Having one or two of these around the house will really light up your life; some are extremely bright for larger nighttime jobs or backyard missions where extra light is advisable. As a side note, most airborne Search and Rescue teams use night-vision equipment during their missions. Night vision makes a small AA flashlight look like a truck with its high beams on. To give your rescuers the best visibility possible, sweep the flashlight beam from side to side of where you are; don't point it at the pilot.

Choose the most dependable, widely available, brightly colored flashlight pos-sible or make it that way with brightly colored tape. We are a visually oriented culture so making your preparedness gear strikingly obnoxious is a bonus. My AA flashlight has duct tape wrapped around the end as a bite piece. I often hold my flashlight in my mouth thereby freeing up my hands for various tasks, and teeth and aluminum don't mix. The hundreds of uses for the extra duct tape speak for itself. At the end of my light is a lanyard that allows me to secure it to my wrist. The lanyard is necessary in situations that might physically separate me from my light such as violent storms, flooding, deep snow, or heavy brush. The flashlight I carry is widely available, cheap, has reasonably priced, easy-to-obtain spare bulbs, stores a spare bulb in its end cap, and has an adjustable beam. Flashlights are reasonably kidproof and should be high on the list for families with children.

The Wild World of Specialty Flashlights

I shy away from specialty flashlights if for no other reason than the spare parts and bulbs are a pain to find on a good day, let alone during the end of the world. I want to be able to replenish my stock with a minimum of hassle and most of us don't need much of an excuse to procrastinate buying, repairing, or rotating emergency sup-plies. Some flashlights are so powerfully bright that they could almost cause sun-burn, to say nothing of what they could do to your eyesight. I do admire their bright-ness but that strong light comes at a price, literally and figuratively; these flashlights eat batteries like a politician hugs babies during an election year. I have no interest in paying for, storing, and feeding these types of lights for daily household use. Analyze your situation and see if one of the bright boys fits in with your survival plan.

Lately there are some very cool LED (light-emitting diode) lights on the market that spit out a surprising amount of light for their size and have a tremendous bulb and battery life. Some flashlights that use standard bulbs can be modified to use this technology. The mini-mag brand of flashlight, in the AA battery size, has an LED addition that can be purchased from many outdoor stores. This option replaces the standard bulb with three LED bulbs that are renowned for their long life. You can also purchase an end-cap piece that allows you to push a button to turn on the flashlight instead of twisting the bulb end of the light. Gone will be the option of a focused or wide beam from the standard mini-mag bulb, and if you purchase the push-button end cap, the neat little metal loop for easily attaching a lanyard will also disappear.

The Beautiful yet Baffling Battery: Choosing, Storing, and Rotating Your Batteries

There are many types of batteries on the market although not all of the batteries listed below are used in flashlights; some are for hearing aids, pacemakers, and the like. While most are categorized as "primary cells," meaning they are one-use wonders and can't be recharged, there are many options for "secondary cells" or batteries that can be recharged. Types of batteries under the primary-cell heading include alkaline/manganese (the most common household battery type), carbon-zinc, lithium, mercuric-oxide, silver-oxide, zinc-air, and other types of button batteries.

Secondary-cell choices include nickel-cadmium and small sealed lead-acid, along with a few alkaline varieties. Many of these batteries, when spent or having grown tired of several recharges, are extremely toxic. Nickel-cadmium, for example, a popular but outdated rechargeable battery (it's been replaced by nickel-metal hydride), is supposed to be disposed of at a household hazardous waste collection site. Rechargeable batteries are not on the top of our list, as much as I love them (as mentioned, my entire home runs on solar power so this book is being written with sunlight and, of course, the batteries that hold the solar power when I write at night!). Remember, the reason you are using a light is because the grid has gone down; where is the power going to come from to recharge those rechargeables? Also, nickel-cadmium and nickel-metal hydride batteries self-discharge quickly, which means they lose juice just sitting in the drawer. In fact, they lose about 25 percent of their power each month with a shelf life of two to three months: not the best choice for an emergency flashlight battery. There are batteries on the market that recharge using the sun and come with their own photovoltaic panel to harness energy from sunlight. Some flashlight bodies have a built-in photovoltaic panel and need to be simply set in direct sunlight to recharge. Depending on where you live, rechargeable batteries such as these might be a worthy investment.

Good Ol' Alkaline Batteries

Confused about the many choices of batteries yet? I go to the discount or grocery store and buy the brand name batteries they have on the shelf, usually the alkaline type, which were invented more than forty years ago by a scientist named Lew Urry. More than 2 billion alkaline batteries are sold each year, dwarfing all other battery sales combined. On average, alkaline batteries have a shelf life of five to seven years. Look at the date printed on the batteries at the store and buy the ones with the latest date. After seven years, the batteries might still retain 80 percent of their juice but they won't perform as long or as well, so, in other words, use at your own risk and get used to rotating your battery stock each year. Regular alkaline batteries are available in common sizes and are used in all sorts of battery-operated devices, so rotating your stock and buying fresh ones shouldn't be a big deal; another plug for simple flashlights that use simple batteries without the bells and whistles of the specialty lights.

Store your batteries like you should store your flashlight: at room temperature, out of direct sunlight, and in a dry area—NOT in the refrigerator. Moisture absorbed by batteries from the tuna surprise casserole can cause the battery to not work and/or drastically reduce their shelf life and performance. Keep extra batteries in their original package for storage. Contact with other metal items, including the batteries themselves, can short-circuit the battery so don't carry loose batteries in a pocket, purse, or pack. As to which brand of batteries to purchase, Consumer Reports found very little difference between brand name battery companies and their product despite the commercials. I have found that Duracell batteries seem to work and hold up better in the cold than Energizers, but to each his own. In years

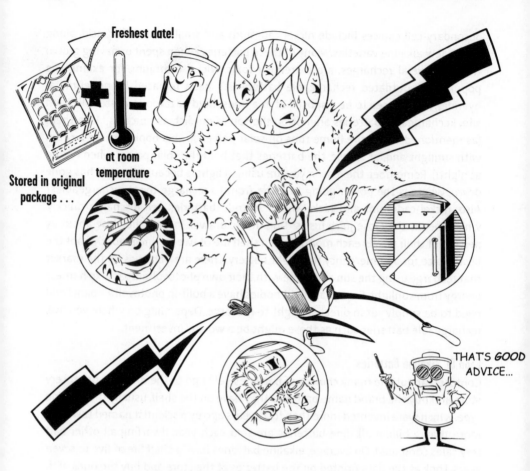

Freshest date!

Stored in original package . . .

at room temperature

THAT'S *GOOD* ADVICE...

past alkaline batteries contained mercury, which made them bummers to dispose of. In 1996, however, Congress banned mercury from all household batteries. Now they can be safely thrown away in typical household trash when they poop out, or you can recycle them at some electronic stores such as Radio Shack.

More expensive lithium batteries, now commonly available at most grocery stores, have up to a fifteen-year shelf life. That's where the advantage ends, however, for our emergency flashlight motives. Lithium batteries are typically reserved for devices that require a lot of power in a short amount of time such as MP3 players, digital cameras, and CD players. Just in case you're getting testy and want to argue the lithium battery point, call the Energizer battery company 1–800 number available on the Internet like I did. They will tell you that other than the longer shelf life, lithium batteries for flashlights are, and I quote, "a waste of money."

Spare alkaline batteries carried in my survival kit for one year give approximately four hours of light with the first three hours being the brightest. The last hour of light is marginal but still useful for close-up household tasks. You should rotate your batteries in the flashlight as well as your spares every year, whether you have put them to use or not. I bind my spares together with brightly colored tape and write the month and year they were purchased in permanent marker on the tape. This takes the guesswork out of when you should rotate the little gems.

The ends of batteries corrode quickly, even in the arid Southwest, so get in the habit of inspecting your spares a few times a year. If you live in a wet climate, plan on rotating them more frequently. Although in a pinch the corrosion can be scraped off the ends, it's a safer bet to replace them entirely. As a bonus, batteries—even AA batteries—can be placed end to end and used in conjunction with superfine steel wool to start a fire.

Light Sticks

Light sticks are just one application of an important natural phenomenon—luminescence. Generally speaking, luminescence is any emission of light that is not caused by heating. Among other things, luminescence is used in televisions, neon lights, and glow-in-the-dark stickers. It's also the principle that lights up a firefly and makes some rocks glow after dark.

Since their inception twenty-eight years ago, chemical light sticks have made their way well into urban culture and are available at many camping and big box stores. Nearly every little kid during Halloween becomes a glowing example of the power of two chemicals mixed together. Light sticks are used for a variety of applications from scuba diving to the rave dance scene. I use them to mark base camp shelters in the winter woods and desert caches of water at night for weary travelers on my field courses.

While not super cheap (two to four dollars apiece), light sticks are reasonably priced and put out enough light to get a range of close-quarters tasks accomplished with minimum hassle. These bulbless, batteryless wonders are light and portable and, dare I say it, more or less kidproof. The chemical reaction that takes place within the light stick generates absolutely no heat so parents don't have to worry about junior lighting the drapes on fire, scorching the pet cat, or otherwise burning down the house. This point should not be taken lightly as, aside from flashlights, finding a decent lighting alternative that is also kid-safe is a challenge.

How light sticks emit their glow is fairly simple. They consist of a small glass vial, or activator, filled with a hydrogen peroxide solution. This glass vial is housed inside the middle of a larger plastic vial, containing a phenyl oxalate ester and dye solution. The last two chemicals make up the majority of the light stick's guts. By bending the plastic stick, the glass vial breaks open, and the two solutions flow together. The chemicals immediately react to one another in a process called *chemiluminesence* and the atoms begin emitting light. The particular dye used in the chemical solution gives the light a distinctive color, of which there are several to choose from. The white ones put out the most light, next yellow, and then take what you can get.

Depending on which compounds are used, the chemical reaction may go on for a few minutes or many hours. By heating the solutions, the extra energy will accelerate the reaction, and the stick will glow brighter, but for a shorter amount

LIGHT MY FIRE! USING BATTERIES AND STEEL WOOL TO MAKE FIRE

Helpful **HARDCORE** *Hints*

For this method, avoid using batteries smaller than the AA size. Box-shaped batteries that feature both terminals on the same battery can also be used. Put two batteries together end to end, the nipple of one touching the base of the other. Hold one end of the steel wool to the base end, and touch the other end of the steel wool to the nipple end. Then put the glowing result into a suitable tinder bundle and gently blow it into a flame. If you wish to use a car battery, and it's still in the car, open the hood and let the engine compartment air out. Volatile gases from batteries can explode so use caution and common sense. Don't use a longer or thicker piece of steel wool than necessary to reach the opposing battery terminal as it will require more voltage from the battery. Also, keep the ends of the steel wool fairly loose yet neat, not tightly compressed. Take it away, Robbie!

of time. Put an activated light stick in boiling water for a few minutes and see for yourself. If you cool the light stick, the reaction will slow down, and the light will dim. If you want to preserve your light stick for the next day, put it in the freezer or outside in cold weather—it won't stop creating light but it will drag out the reaction considerably. However, the light emitted at this point is not something you'd choose to read a book by.

Candles

Candle manufacturer surveys report that 96 percent of all candles are purchased by women and are used in seven out of ten U.S. households. With more than 350 commercial, religious, and institutional manufacturers of candles in the United States alone, as well as countless small craft producers, it's no wonder that retail sales of candles in the United States is estimated at $2 billion per year, excluding the sales of candle accessories. Major candle manufacturers may offer up to 2,000 varieties

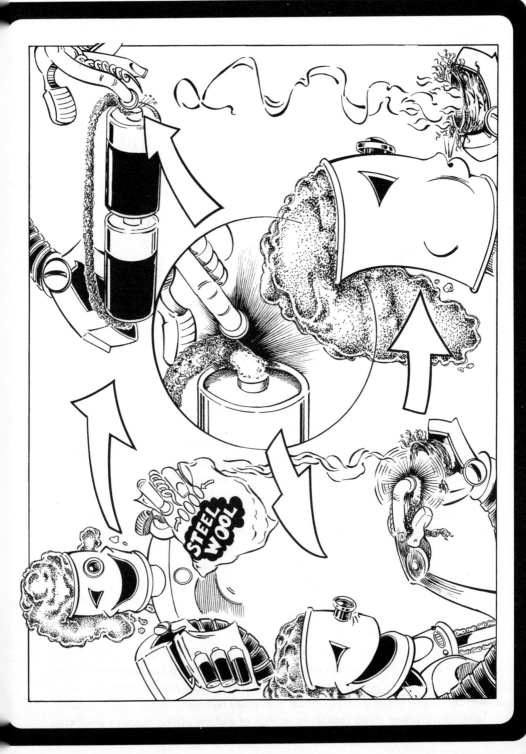

of candles in their product line, including tapers, straight-sided dinner candles, columns, pillars, votives, wax-filled containers, and an assortment of specialty candles in a variety of sizes, fragrances, and colors.

Not much is known about the origin of candles. Some scholars think they were first developed by the Egyptians, who used torches called "rush lights." They were made by soaking the pithy core of reeds in melted tallow or animal fat, although they had no true wick like a candle. The Romans win the prize for developing the wick candle, and they used it for everything from lighting homes and traveling at night to illuminating churches for worship. Similar to the Egyptians, they used tallow, the rendered fat from cattle or sheep, as the fuel element. Two-thirds of the tallow came from the solid fats palmitin and stearin with one-third from the liquid fat olein. Candles made from tallow smoked like crazy and emitted a certain odor that wouldn't go over well on a first date. In the Middle Ages someone finally discovered the wonders of beeswax and its delightful, clean-burning flame, although it was expensive at the time.

In the late eighteenth century, the whaling industry boomed partly due to the discovery of a wax called *spermaceti* that was obtained by crystallizing sperm whale oil. Fortunes were made and by 1792 the whaling port of Nantucket alone had ten candle factories. This wonder fuel could be produced not only in quantity (one sperm whale could contain hundreds of gallons of the precious goo), thus making the price cheaper, but it also burned just as clean as beeswax, had a higher degree of candlepower than anything else, and was harder and didn't bend in the summer sun.

In 1850, much to the relief of a diminished whale population, a substance called paraffin wax was made from oil and coal shales. The greatest advantage of paraffin was its cost; it was the cheapest to produce of anything that had been tried as a candle fuel. This, along with the discovery of an additive called stearic acid, solved the problem of paraffin's low melting point. With the introduction of the light bulb in 1879, candle making declined until the turn of the century when a renewed popularity for candles emerged.

Technically speaking, a candle is defined as one or more combustible wicks supported by a material that constitutes a fuel that is solid, semisolid, or quasi-rigid at room temperature, 68 to 80 degrees F (20 to 26 degrees C). It can also contain additives, which are used for color, stability, odor, or to alter the burning characteristics, the combined function of which is to sustain a light-producing flame. A candle flame burns its fuel in distinct regions within the flame itself. The differences are reflected by the various colors appearing within the flame. The hotter-burning blue areas burn hydrogen that has been separated from the fuel to form water vapor. The brighter, yellow part of the flame is carbon soot being oxidized to form carbon dioxide. Thus, a well-made, properly burning candle produces mostly harmless water vapor and carbon dioxide. The chances of carbon monoxide poisoning with candles is almost nonexistent as you would need many, many candles in a very confined space.

A fairly simple invention, a candle consists of a *wick* and *fuel*. The candlewick is responsible for moving the liquefied fuel upward via capillary action where it is vaporized within the candle's flame. Wicks can be composed of everything from dried moss or twisted cloth to finely braided glass fiber. Today, there are more than one hundred different wicks on the market from domestic and imported sources. For the most part, a high-quality wick is made from a braided fabric (the majority of which are 100 percent cotton or cotton-paper combinations), while a lower-quality wick is twisted, such as those used in birthday candles. The most common wicks are flat wicks, square wicks, cored wicks, and specialty and oil lamp wicks. Flat wicks are very consistent, flat-plaited wicks that curl in the flame for a self-trimming effect. Square wicks are braided wicks that also curl in the flame and are preferred in beeswax applications and can help inhibit clogging of the wick

"Don't CURSE the DARKNESS— LIGHT A CANDLE."
—Chinese proverb

CANDLE SAFETY TIPS —COURTESY OF THE NATIONAL CANDLE ASSOCIATION (NCA)

The nature of a candle is a direct flame burning within whatever environment it's used, thus their use is not without risk. According to the U.S. Fire Administration (USFA), irresponsible candle use is responsible for approximately 10,000 residential fires each year, along with 1,000 civilian injuries, 85 fatalities, and $120 million in property loss. National fire safety agencies in the United States report that the vast majority of mishaps with candles occur from stupid actions or negligence. To set the record straight and make sure that you're on the straight and narrow regarding your family's candle use, the National Candle Association recommends the following safety tips when burning candles. Many of these common-sense tips will apply to any radiant-flame lighting devices, such as lanterns and oil and fat lamps.

   (*Warning!* Any fuel-burning lighting source poses a risk for **fire danger.** Have a quality fire extinguisher on hand at all times and make sure that it's rotated and replaced or serviced on a regular basis.)

- Always keep a burning candle within sight. Extinguish all candles when leaving a room or before going to sleep.
- Never burn a candle on or near anything that can catch fire. Keep burning candles away from furniture, drapes, bedding, carpets, books, paper, flammable decorations, etc.
- Keep candles out of the reach of children and pets. Do not place lighted candles where they can be knocked over by children, pets, or anyone else.
- Read and carefully follow all manufacturer instructions.
- Trim candlewicks to one-fourth inch each time before burning. Long or crooked wicks cause uneven burning and dripping.

Always use a candleholder specifically designed for candle use. The holder should be heat resistant, sturdy, and large enough to contain any drips or melted wax. Be sure the candleholder is placed on a stable, heat-resistant surface.

Keep burning candles away from drafts, vents, and air currents. This will help prevent rapid, uneven burning, smoking, and excessive dripping. Drafts can also blow lightweight curtains or papers into the flame where they could catch fire. Ceiling fans can cause drafts.

Keep the wax pool free of wick trimmings, matches, and debris (aka dead moths and other unrecognizable flying insects) at all times.

Do not burn a candle for longer than the manufacturer recommends.

Always burn candles in a well-ventilated room.

Extinguish the flame if it comes too close to the holder or container. For a margin of safety, discontinue burning a candle when two inches of wax remain (one-half inch if in a container). This will also help prevent possible heat damage to the counter/surface and prevent glass containers from cracking or breaking.

Never touch or move a votive or container candle when the wax is liquid.

Extinguish pillar candles if the wax pool approaches the outer edge.

Candles should be placed at least three inches apart from one another. This is to be sure they don't melt one another or create their own drafts that will cause the candles to burn improperly.

One of the safest ways to extinguish a candle is to use a candlesnuffer, which helps prevent hot wax from spattering.

Do not extinguish candles with water. The water can cause the hot wax to spatter and can cause glass containers to break.

Flashlights and other battery-powered lights are much safer light sources than candles during a power failure.

Never use a candle as light when you go into a closet to look for things.

Never use a candle for light when fueling equipment such as a lantern or kerosene heater.

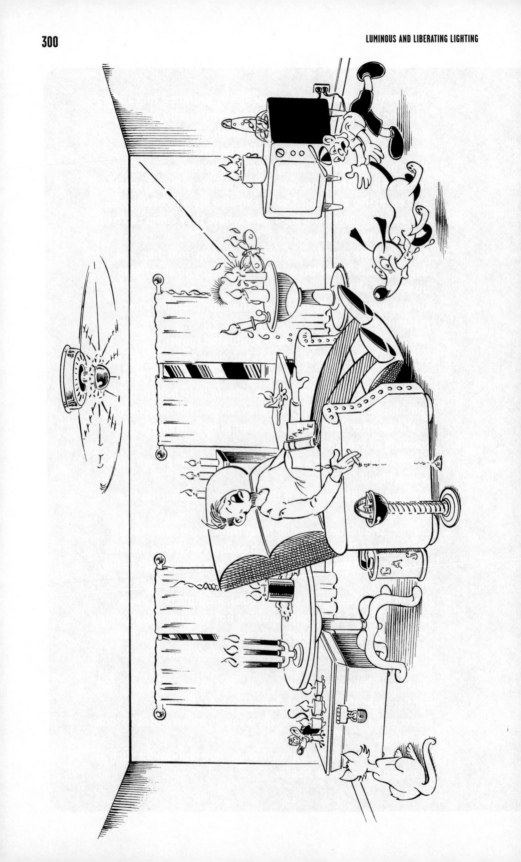

when high levels of noncombustible materials such as pigments and fragrance are used. Cored wicks are braided wicks with a round cross section and are designed to remain straight while burning. These wicks contain a separate core material of zinc, tin, cotton, paper, or dangerous lead, and are used in jars, columns, votives, and devotional lights. Specialty and oil lamp wicks are designed specifically for burning oil lamp fuels and insect-repellent flames.

The fuel element of a candle can consist of everything from mule deer fat and shortening to paraffin, beeswax, or, as colonial women figured out, boiling down the grayish green berries of bayberry bushes to produce a clean-burning, sweet-smelling wax.

An important note about lead wicks: More than twenty-five years ago, members of the National Candle Association, which makes 90 percent of the candles in the United States, agreed to ban lead wicks from their products; but how to tell if you're buying one of the other 10 percent is hard to figure out. Imported candles, most notably those from China and the religious candles made in Mexico, have been found to contain lead wicks, so do some research on what you are buying. To test candles for possible lead-core wicks, take a piece of white paper and rub the tip of an unburned candlewick onto the paper. If it leaves a light grey, pencillike mark, it has a lead-core wick. User-safe zinc or tin-core wicks should not leave any mark on the paper.

Storing and Using Candles

I burned candles and oil lamps for years as the primary source of light in my home before my investment in solar photovoltaics. Candles require thought regarding their storage, especially in areas of extreme environmental heat. I have trashed many a candle in unrelenting Arizona temperatures. Store your candles in a cool, dark, dry place. Longer dinner or taper-type candles should be stored flat to prevent warping. Think about candle placement in your home for safety and greater efficiency. Candles placed on a windowsill can deform or melt in the sun. High areas in homes such as lofts and attics, while shaded from direct sun, can reduce a candle to a puddle from the simple fact that hot air rises.

A well-made candle should not soot or smoke when burning properly. Smoking will occur, however, whenever a candle's flame is disturbed, which allows unburned carbon particles (soot) to escape. Any candle can be made to smoke by causing the flame to flicker from a draft. Although the soot produced by quality candles does not present a health concern, it can be a drag in close quarters with minimal opportunities for ventilation. Minimize candle flickering by trimming the wick to one-fourth inch before lighting, as well as keeping the candle free from blower vents, obnoxious drafts, and strong air currents.

Tips for Getting the Old Wax out of Your Candleholders

Poorly fitting candles caused by old wax stuck within candleholders can be dangerous as they are more prone to being knocked from their holder. To make cleaning your candleholders easier:

- ➲ run very hot water over them or leave them (metal holders) outside in hot summer sun
  OR

- ➲ place the holder in a freezing environment, allowing the wax to shrink and pop off
  OR

- ➲ for votive candles, think ahead and add a few drops of water to the glass before inserting the candle. A word of caution: Do not add more than a few drops and don't add water unless you intend to burn the candle immediately afterward. If not burned immediately, the candle's wick can, over time, absorb the water and no longer burn properly. Don't use a sharp object to remove old wax from glass holders as it could weaken the glass, causing it to break upon subsequent use.

Making Sense of Scented Candles

Our sense of smell is one of our most powerful senses, and fragrance experts say that some smells can have a deep affect on people's psyches. Candles are available in a seemingly endless variety of fragrances from blooming flowers to baked goods

BURNIN' DOWN THE HOUSE

According to data from the USFA's National Fire Incident Reporting System and the National Fire Protection Agency, most candle fires (44.5 percent) occur in the bedroom (wink, wink!); followed by the living room, family room, or den (18.6 percent); the bathroom (11.4 percent); and the kitchen (7.2 percent). The most common materials to go up in flames were mattresses or bedding (12.8 percent); cabinetry (10.1 percent); and curtains, blinds, or drapes (8.4 percent).

Forty percent of the fires occurred because candles were left unattended, abandoned, or inadequately controlled. Nearly 20 percent occurred because a combustible item was too close to the candle. The following figures represent the leading causes for residential candle fire incidents:

Candle left alone—19.3 percent
Candle too close to combustibles—19.1 percent
Candle misused—11.4 percent
Inadequate control of flame—10.2 percent
Out-of-control kids—8.7 percent
Abandoned material—7.4 percent
Falling asleep—4.5 percent

to apple cider to pine trees. Believe it or not, according to data from the National Candle Association, the most important factor that people look for when buying candles is their fragrance. While scented candles may help folks feel relaxed, refreshed, and calm, they can also antagonize allergies and tempers and be a real turn-off, especially in tight quarters or locations with minimal airflow. Some environmentally sensitive people that I know can't even be in the same building with scented candles as the smell makes them sick. While you may dig the aromatherapy effects of scented candles, Cousin Jack might not. Play it safe and reserve burning the scented candles for use in the outhouse or the next holiday dinner.

Homemade Primitive Candles

Fat or Oil Lamps

One of the most well-known indigenous candles is the Inuit fat lamp or *kudlick*. Fat lamps or oil lamps, in one form or other, have been around for thousands of years cross-culturally. All indigenous peoples needed to make a fat lamp was a container, fat or oil, and a wick. In ancient Greece and Rome, lamps were fueled by olive oil; in India, ghee was used; and in ancient Persia they used petroleum that was freely

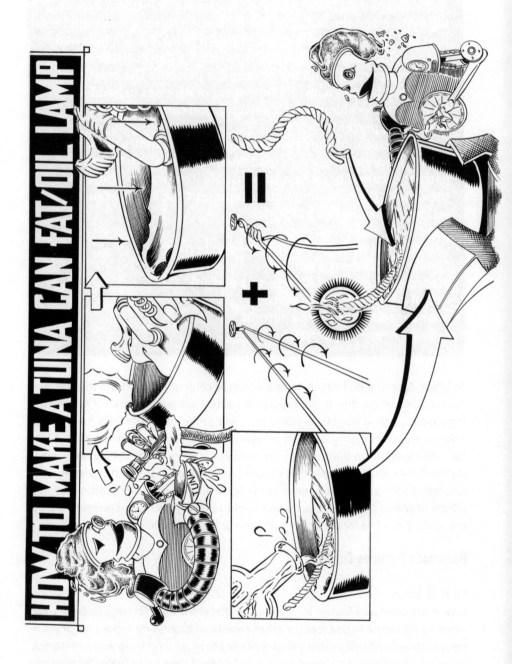

HOW TO MAKE A TUNA CAN FAT/OIL LAMP

oozing from the ground. Olive oil lamps continued to be used in countries around the Mediterranean Sea up until the nineteenth century. A recent experiment in the metrology laboratories of Kodak-Pathe, France, used modern replicas of Paleolithic fat-burning lamps to investigate how much light they put off. It was found that although the lamps lacked the light intensity of a candle, they were still good enough to illuminate the way for navigating through a cave or to light up fine work such as creating a cave painting when placed close to the work. Recent experiments of my own using primitive lamps in various teepees, wickiups, and wall tents have shown the same results.

You can make your own fat lamp using everyday household items following Robbie Rubbish's instructions. Any sort of noncombustible container can be used such as clean metal cans, bottles, or clay jars, along with an assortment of different fats and oils, such as olive oil, corn oil, vegetable oil, vegetable shortening, liquid paraffin, and others. Even bacon grease and lard will work but must be cleaned first of debris in order to burn reliably. Good wicks, through capillary action, "wick" heated liquid fuel up their length and convey it to the free-burning end without being consumed too quickly. Serviceable wicks can be made from an assortment of items from jute or cotton string to pieces of rag or clothing. Some mosses, lichen, grasses, and fibrous plants, such as juniper bark and dogbane, will work as they are or processed into cordage. Even twisted-up toilet paper or paper towels will work. The amount of light put out by the fat or oil lamp is determined by the quality of the fuel and the length of the wick. More wick usually means more light, at the expense of burning more fuel. The type of fuel, what the wick is made from, and how the wick is adjusted will determine the amount of blackish smoke and smell coming from your lamp, so go for the cleanest-burning fuels possible. In my oil lamps, I use commercially available braided "glass" wicks, as they smoke the least and last for an eternity. Even so, playing four hours of Monopoly around a couple of oil lamps will cause you to have black boogers the next time you blow your nose. All orange and yellow flames produce harmful carbon monoxide gas so use caution.

Pitch Wood Candles

Some earthy-yuppie catalog retailers sell resin-saturated wood by the name of "fat wood," or pitch wood. If you live in or around evergreen woods, you can gather it by the ton with no cost other than your time. Pitch wood refers to conifer trees in which, for whatever reason (usually it's because the tree has died), their highly combustible sap has been condensed into focused areas. It's easy to distinguish from regular wood as it's a lot heavier and denser. In an area where an evergreen has died and mostly rotted away, pitch wood might be the only pieces of wood left, as it's fairly rot resistant. Take a knife to a piece of pitch wood and carve off a bit of the outer layer and you'll see a honey color that will smell strongly of sap. Pitch wood burns like crazy. It can be split and made into emergency candles for lighting or used to help ignite and burn wet fuel.

To make a candle, find a piece of pitch wood in which the grain runs from end to end. It can be a piece as big around as a pencil or your finger or larger, and six to twelve inches long or longer. Make a split on one of the ends about an inch deep. Split it the other way as well so that the end has four distinct "prongs." I wedge a couple of tiny pieces of wood into the splits to keep the prongs away from each other. This allows oxygen to infiltrate your "candle." Unlike a blob of pine pitch, which will burn in a chaotic, bubbling mess, the grain in the pitch wood acts like the wick of a candle, helping to stabilize the flame for controlled burning. Pitch wood candles take some fussing around and put off an intense black smoke, but they may have applications for your family if you're down and out on the back forty.

Lovable Lanterns

In general, a lantern is a portable lighting device that's used to illuminate large areas. There are many types to choose from. Some lanterns are used for decoration, others for general outdoor camping, and others are safe enough to bring into the house. Most of these lanterns are fuel-based of one type or another, whether kerosene, white gas, propane, or wax. CAUTION! All fuel-burning lanterns can be hazardous, and the dangers include burns, the potential of fire, dealing with flammable and toxic fuels, and carbon monoxide poisoning. If you have kids or pets, think twice about using fuel-burning means of illumination.

Candle Lanterns

Candle lanterns have been around for a very long time and consist of some sort of glass container, which lets the light through but protects the candle flame from the wind. Centuries ago, the Chinese captured fireflies and added them to transparent containers for cool but short-lived lanterns. In the past two decades, candle lanterns have become vogue in the camping and backpacking scene by companies who have designed lightweight, telescoping lanterns for easy packing. You can easily make your own by putting a candle inside a glass jar and anchoring it in sand or dirt. Wire can be wrapped around the top of the jar or around the jar itself so the homemade lantern can be suspended where convenient. Caution should be used with ANY direct flame method of lighting your house, so reread the previous candle safety tips.

Kerosene Lanterns and Lamps

Flat-wicked kerosene lanterns, sometimes called hurricane lamps, were commonly used since the late 1800s for lighting homes, barns, and outhouses, as well as horse-drawn carriages, railroad cars, and early automobiles. They were also used as an early method of navigation and signaling on both land and sea and had interchangeable colored globes of glass to signify different needs and intentions. They are still available at discount and camping stores. While these lanterns are cheap and durable, they provide little light and are not suited for reading. They also require a periodic trimming of their wick and regular cleaning of soot build-up from the inside of the glass chimney.

These lanterns were originally designed as a more portable and durable version of the kerosene lamp. Cheaper kerosene lanterns should not be brought into an airtight house, as they stink (especially when using poor grades of kerosene), can be dangerous if tipped over, and are more likely to cause carbon monoxide poisoning than more expensive and better-burning kerosene lamps.

Just a few generations ago, *kerosene lamps* were the mainstay of lighting up almost everyone's life. My grandparents grew up with them and have passed a few on down to me. The king of kerosene lamp makers was The Mantle Lamp Company of America, which was founded in Chicago, Illinois, in 1908. The company changed its name in 1949 to Aladdin Industries. In 1999, a group of lamp collectors called the Aladdin Knights purchased part of the company and renamed it the Aladdin Mantle Lamp Company.

Aladdin created some absolutely gorgeous kerosene lamps for the home that have modern lamp collectors drooling. Aladdin also trashed the poorly perform-ing flat-type wick and developed a specialized cylindrical wick with a central air-flow tube that works awesomely with the high and uniform heating demands of mantle-type lighting. Mantle-type lanterns use a woven, ceramic-impregnated gas mantle to accept and reradiate heat as visible light from a flame. The mantle itself doesn't burn, although the cloth matrix carrying the ceramic must be "burned" with a match prior to first using a new mantle. When heated by the flame, the mantle glows incandescently, and some have a comparable light output of a standard 60-watt light bulb or more! To stabilize the airflow and to protect against the high temperatures that are created, a cylindrical glass shield called a "globe" or chimney is placed around the mantle.

Conforming to modern times, Aladdin later went on to manufacture electrical lamps as well. Even today, Aladdin lamps enjoy a cult following and it shouldn't be hard to buy obscure parts for your lamp with a little searching on the Internet.

"Why is it called **'AFTER DARK'** when it **REALLY IS 'AFTER LIGHT'?"**

—George Carlin

While kerosene lamps rate high on the nostalgic cool meter, and they do work well, they can be quite complex to operate (and expensive to buy) and must have an owner that doesn't mind fiddling with this and that to get the best results. Unless you already have experience with this type of lighting, leave it to the collectors for use during an emergency.

Grades of Kerosene

There are different grades of kerosene, and if you do decide to use a kerosene lamp in the home, you will want the best grade possible. The grade or quality of the kerosene, how clear and clean it is, will influence how often you'll need to replace the lamp wick, how clean a burn and how much light you'll get, and how much the lamp smells. The better the grade of kerosene, the longer your wicks and your health will last. Supposedly the best grade of kerosene that can be purchased for lamps with the least amount of odor is from the Aladdin Company and is called Genuine Aladdin Lamp Oil, which is available from any Aladdin dealer. Although it's called "oil," it's really kerosene in this instance.

The next-best grade of kerosene is called "K-1" and is usually available at most hardware stores in the paint section. However, due to a recent government law on motor fuel tax, quality K-1 kerosene is harder and harder to find. Rural gas stations may also have bulk, taxed kerosene at the pump. There are different grades of K-1 as well so check to see if the stuff you're about to buy is as clear as water and virtually odorless. If you can, avoid grades of kerosene that have been dyed red, stink badly, or are yellowish in color. These impurities will reduce the light output of the lamp, shorten the life of the wick (the dye clogs the wick), and potentially shorten your life if you use them in tight, enclosed areas. For the lamp collector in you, crummy grades of kerosene can also discolor the lamp bowl itself, and some older Aladdin lamps go for hundreds or thousands of dollars.

Some lamps look and operate much like a kerosene lamp, but burn lamp oil instead. Commercial lamp oil typically comes in two grades and is available by the pint or the gallon. For indoor use, get the best quality oil you can find such as 99 percent pure paraffin lamp oil. The other cheaper variety is usually reserved for tiki torches or other outside lighting options. Many stores that sell lamp oil only do so during the holidays. Be aware of that limitation and stock up when you can.

White-Gas Lanterns

A few decades ago, no camping trip was complete without the familiar, forest green, manually pressurized, Coleman brand white-gas lantern in the one- or two-mantle model. "White" gas is a purified form of gasoline—without additives or dyes—that's not suitable for use as a motor fuel. While still very popular (I must have three or four of them), white-gas lanterns are being phased out for the more convenient propane or electric lanterns. White gas can also be used in camp stoves. If you have and use the white-gas variety, use caution about storing and using the fuel, especially around kids and rambunctious pets.

Propane Lanterns

Propane (a fuel that becomes liquid when compressed) lanterns are more convenient, safer to use, and less messy than the older-style white-gas variety. I prefer storing propane containers over white gas any day, as they have a veritably indefinite shelf life if the containers are protected from moisture (which can cause corrosion of the container) and excess heat. Although pressurized propane canisters can be deadly, there is usually not much that can go wrong, as the fuel stays inside the canister until it's needed. How long the canister will last, like any fuel, depends on how high you turn up the lantern, and all mantle-type lanterns do kick out great light.

"All **SUNSHINE** makes a **DESERT**."
—Arabic proverb

Operating a newer camping-size propane lantern is easy. Preburn the new mantles (if the old ones are shot) and put back on the glass globe that surrounds them. Then screw the propane canister directly into the bottom of the lantern. Attach the included plastic base to the bottom of the propane canister and you're ready to turn on the fuel and "click" the automatic sparking lighter, no match required. The Coleman brand lantern also has a really cool break-apart design where everything except the propane canister fits neatly and securely into its own plastic carrying case. Buying the smaller propane canisters is the more expensive way to go (although they do go on sale at the discount stores), and it sucks to throw them all away, but . . . many hardware stores sell an attachment that allows you to refill the smaller canisters from a larger propane container. You know how things work today, so check local rules and regulations to see if your area allows for the refilling of small containers.

Propane lanterns are my choice for lighting up the night on some of my vehicle-based survival skills courses. Their extreme durability and packability, along with the convenience, simplicity, and relative safety of the fuel, make them great options around potentially "green" and clumsy students in the field. And of course, the same small propane canisters can be used with the forest green Coleman cook stove.

Battery-Powered Lanterns

Battery-powered lanterns are a super option for families who have small children. Short of junior throwing one at his little sister, or knocking it over, breaking the glass globe, and rolling in the aftermath, they are as safe as any battery-powered flashlight. Although models are available that use a standard bulb, the fluorescent-bulb models are more battery efficient. Battery-powered lanterns put out a good amount of light (although not as much as their propane and liquid-fuel-powered brothers) and have zero weird fumes or the potential fire danger of fuel-based models. Some feature an adjustment knob that allows the user to choose how much light is needed—from dim to full blast—which will, of course, determine how long your batteries will last. Depending on the make and model, these lanterns may use regular disposable batteries, rechargeable replaceable batteries, or permanently installed rechargeable batteries. Some of the rechargeable battery models must be brought to a full charge every few months whether they are used or not. Some rechargeable battery-powered lanterns can be literally plugged into an electrical outlet to charge, or can be charged using an automobile 12-volt system or by being attached to a small photovoltaic solar panel. Fancier rechargeable lanterns can be left plugged in full time and set up to turn on during a power failure. I know these conveniences are nice, but use caution when setting up your emergency system to rely on grid power when the grid itself is in question.

Whatever brand of lantern you choose, whether liquid fueled or battery powered, choose a high-quality model with easily available fuel and replacement parts. For parts that are destined to naturally wear out, buy spare parts now and safely store as much fuel as you think you'll need for your emergency.

Solar Photovoltaics

At my place, anything that requires electricity runs off my independent solar power system, from an electric cement mixer to a microwave, blender, stereo, washing machine, computer, refrigerator, power drills, saws, and all kinds of lighting. While *passive solar* involves taking advantage of the sun's free energy for heating through the proper orientation of a structure, *active solar* requires many more moving parts such as photovoltaic panels that collect sunlight, inverters that change DC current to AC, batteries for storing the harnessed energy for nighttime use, charge controllers, wiring, and a bunch of other doodads needed to produce and maintain electrical power.

That said, lighting is one of the easiest things to accomplish with a solar power system. Even many of the larger discount stores now carry compact fluorescent, energy-saving bulbs, and with the advent of LED lights, power draw on a solar system can be next to nothing. The compact fluorescent lightbulbs that I use have a light output of 900 lumens, the equivalent to a 60-watt lightbulb, while using only 13 watts of energy! As an added bonus, they have a supposed life span of 10,000 hours. I've been using my bulbs for nearly two years straight and haven't needed to replace one yet. Folks, crisis or not, get your butts down to the store and change out as many of your old incandescent bulbs, when they blow, as you can with these energy-efficient wonders. I've even bought them on sale at prices lower than conventional light bulbs.

Anyhow, my solar system was not cheap to purchase and install—and I received discounts from friends who sold me the stuff and installed it. It won't make sense for many homes to convert to solar power from the expense standpoint alone. Mini-systems that will run basic essentials in an emergency can be put together fairly cheaply—real cheaply if you buy some of the items used. My first solar system consisted of a used solar panel I found in the classified section of the newspaper, one battery with a dinky charge controller, scrap wiring, and a 175-watt cheapo inverter available in the auto section of most discount stores. That was five years ago and it's still running strong, capable of powering a couple of lights, a laptop computer, and a small stereo all at once.

Solar-powered electricity is a possibility for most parts of the nation depending on terrain and climate, but don't fixate on needing to run your electric lights or dishwasher in the face of a catastrophe—use balance in all things, never forgetting your survival priorities.

Portable Battery Packs

Several manufacturers make a portable suitcaselike power source built around a sealed lead acid battery. Most of these have a cigarette lighter adapter, a light, and jumper cables to jump-start your vehicle from the stored power. They also feature an AC power cord to let you charge up or keep the battery charged until it's needed. My model even has a built-in air compressor in case of a flat tire. These battery packs can run stingy power use LED lights for quite a while before losing their juice. While handy and reasonably priced at most discount or auto parts stores, they can be finicky about being charged and holding the charge when they get older. Pay attention to the directions if you get one and do what they recommend for the maximum life of your unit.

Generators

During the Y2K insanity, generators were sold out for weeks at all the hardware stores. I do love generators, as noisy and smelly as some of the larger ones can be. I still have the one that helped build my home by running an assortment of power tools and lighting. Many people are attracted to generators, as they offer the allure of being able to function normally, as far as appliances go, in the aftermath of a disaster. For some places, such as a hospital, it makes perfect sense to have backup power. Only you know how important it will be to use the washing machine and dishwasher when the sky is falling.

Larger generators made to power an entire household can be wired directly into the home by qualified personnel and can even turn on automatically if and when the grid goes down. Special care should be given to the toxic carbon monoxide fumes put off by the running generator. It should be adequately vented away from the house, which the installation professional you hire should be acutely aware of.

Smaller generators are very common and can be seen daily in the back of many building contractors' pickup trucks. These generators will not run your house, but will allow you to operate an assortment of appliances. Similar to solar photovoltaics, you can research the wattage of what you wish to operate and compare it to the wattage power put out by the various-sized generators. The more things you want to run at one time, the bigger the generator you'll need.

Generators are not cheap; the cheaper the model the more problems you are likely to have. If a generator is a major part of your survival backup plan, buy the best one you can afford. However, the more your family relies on a system that involves many moving parts for their safety and comfort, the more you're putting yourself between a rock and a hard place when, not if, those moving parts fail. Generators are like kids and require maintenance and upkeep. They will need to be fed on a regular basis and flammable fuels in any quantity are sketchy to store safely. They might be cranky on cold mornings and not want to start. They will be noisy, which can irritate neighbors and telegraph to the entire neighborhood that you have power. They can smell from leaky oil, carbon monoxide fumes, and the fuel they require to operate. And of course, if it's not already apparent, generators generate only electricity, so will do nothing for your natural gas or propane appliances such as heating systems, stoves, and ovens. Do you want to spend hundreds or thousands of dollars to have your lamps work and run the refrigerator?

I woke up one night to the sound of an engine near my rural homestead. As I had never heard the noise before from that direction, I went outside to investigate. It was my neighbors visiting their land from the big city. They were sitting around a peaceful campfire, yelling over the racket of their generator a few feet away that powered a single light bulb for who knows what purpose. Separate your family's wants from their needs now. Whether a generator is right for your family or not, don't forget the sacred aspect of simplicity in all things. The simpler your disaster plan, the easier it will be to initiate and follow in times of intense stress and fear.

SUPER SIMPLE SUMMARY

- ⊃ Light is a form of energy, which can be emitted through a variety of processes including incandescence, fluorescence and phosphorescence, and laser generation.
- ⊃ Most modern people lack the psychological stamina and practice to deal with nighttime tasks and fears without adequate lighting.
- ⊃ In the long term, such as in an underground survival shelter, adequate lighting to at least be able to see the dim outline of a form in front of you is vital for long-term sanity.
- ⊃ Flashlights, such as the AA battery size, are cheap, compact, widely available, and have enough candlepower to get the job done for most household chores. Having a larger C- or D-cell-size flashlight will work well for larger nighttime jobs or backyard missions where extra light is needed. Buy them brightly colored or make them that way with highly visible tape. Unlike many other fuel-burning lighting devices, flashlights are safe to have around children.
- ⊃ Buy and store regular brand name alkaline batteries commonly found at the grocery or discount store. Look at the date on the package and buy the newest ones. They will have an average shelf life of five to seven years but they should be rotated much sooner. Store them at room temperature, out of direct sunlight, in a dry area—NOT in the refrigerator. Keep extra batteries in their original package for storage and don't carry them loose in a pocket or purse.
- ⊃ Chemical light sticks are widely available at camping and discount stores and are child-safe alternatives for certain low-light needs.
- ⊃ Unscented candles of all types and sizes are available for emergency lighting. All should be used with

caution around kids and pets, and kept well away from combustible materials such as drapes and bedding. Avoid candles that have lead wicks, such as those commonly imported from China and Mexico. Store longer taper-type candles flat in a cool, dry location to prevent warping.

⊃ A few fuel-burning lighting options can be made with homemade fat, oil, or pitch sticks from dead conifer trees.

⊃ Lanterns come in many forms, from battery-powered to propane, kerosene, and white gas, although the first two listed may be the easiest to use for the majority of people.

⊃ *Caution!* All fuel-burning lanterns can be hazardous due to the dangers of dealing with flammable and toxic fuels, the potential of fire or burns due to the high temperatures involved, and deadly carbon monoxide poisoning. Be careful if you choose to bring this type of lantern into the house, especially around children and animals.

⊃ Solar photovoltaic systems consist of photovoltaic panels that collect sunlight, inverters that change DC current to AC, batteries for storing the harnessed energy for nighttime use, charge controllers, wiring, and more. While larger systems can be very expensive, smaller emergency systems can be purchased fairly cheaply, especially if some of the parts are preowned.

⊃ Fuel-burning generators can be purchased to generate electricity and run the entire household or a few appliances. All will require basic upkeep and fuel and will cost from a few hundred to a few thousand dollars. When using a generator, beware of toxic carbon monoxide fumes.

18

Crucially **CREATIVE COOKING**

"ed•i | ble (ed´ə_ b_l) *adj.* fit to be eaten"
—Merriam-Webster's Collegiate Dictionary

There are many ways to cook or heat up food when conventional methods are no longer an option. Whether you need to cook food at all depends on what's for dinner. Canned foods are precooked and can be eaten straight from the can. In summer months here in the Southwest, canned foods can be set in the sun for a few hours and then opened to enjoy a warm to hot meal depending on the sun's intensity and the length of the exposure.

Many foods, such as grains and legumes, require heat to make otherwise indigestible components digestible or at least palatable. Below are many suggestions and items to have on hand that will make your kitchen experience a little less challenging during rough times.

Handy Things to Have around the House for Preparing Food after a Crisis
Major disasters will spell an end to a normal kitchen for days or weeks. Have the following goodies on hand to ease your food preparation until things get back on track.

Cooking Utensils
If nothing else, a good quality metal two- to four-quart pot with lid will serve you well for many meals. Number 10 cans from stored food or coffee cans can be used as cook pots in a pinch. Many of these cans have plastic coatings inside which must first be burned away before they can be used. Build a fire in a safe location outdoors or in your woodstove or fireplace. Place the can, opening down, on top of the fuel and light your fire. It shouldn't take more than five or ten minutes of decent flame to burn out the plastic coating. After the fire subsides and the can cools, take it out and wash it thoroughly

with soap and water. In water-stingy desert locales, I've "washed" by aggressively scouring the can out with earth and sand before use. You can get fancy if you like and knock two small holes on opposite sides of the top rim with an ice pick, nail, and hammer, or a Swiss army knife attachment. Salvaged wire can be doubled up and anchored through each hole, providing a convenient bail or handle to suspend the pot over a heat source, to carry it when hot, or lash it down to a pack when hitting the road. Make sure your emergency cooking utensils are made from metal, as glass and ceramic cookware can easily be broken.

Eating Utensils

Many foods can be eaten with the hands. Doing so, however, increases the risks of gastrointestinal problems when forced to use emergency sanitation techniques. Why take the chance? Although Martha Stewart would disapprove, there is no need for a fork, spoon, and knife unless you think there is. Campers have used the famous "spork"—a combination of fork and spoon—for decades. A simple eating spatula can be carved in seconds from a piece of wood. Chopsticks from a couple of twigs can be improvised even quicker, and like the spatula, can be added to the fire or thrown away after the fact, saving time and wash water. With individual bowls, spoons are not required as you can "slurp-drink" your soup from the bowl itself. Although not a good sanitary habit, I have slurp-drunk stew from the cook pot along with everyone else who was present. We simply passed the pot around the circle of people, as no one had any containers or utensils.

Spoons are great for canned goods and most survival fare, which usually manifests itself at some point as soup or stew. Stew is a great excuse to throw into a pot anything that might be edible, along with a bouillon cube for flavoring. Knives might be necessary if your survival cuisine gets tough and stringy. Although plastic silverware is convenient at first, it's weak and constantly breaks. If you pack only one eating utensil, make it the mighty spoon. Larger camping stores sell extremely strong Lexan plastic spoons if you're fickle about weight.

Paper Plates, Cups, and Towels

Paper utensils and napkins are great when washing dishes is a drag due to knocked-out services. Paper plates come in several qualities and prices, as do paper cups and towels. The dirty dishes can be burned in a safe location or buried in the pit latrine, saving precious water and eliminating the chance of dirty or poorly washed dishes attracting flies and other disease-spreading critters. Paper cups can be purchased with built-in

"It is NOT NECESSARY TO ADVERTISE FOOD to hungry people, fuel to COLD people, or HOUSES to the homeless."
—J. K. Galbraith

handles that make holding hot beverages more pleasant. Paper cups are also more durable than Styrofoam cups, which can easily crack and break and produce noxious fumes when burned in the living room fireplace or woodstove. Paper towels provide both safety and convenience for wiping up nasty things without worrying about storing the towel for later washing. Although paper products are perhaps not eco-friendly, their short-term use saves immediate resources far more precious to the survivor.

Heavy-Duty Aluminum Foil

Heavy-duty aluminum foil can be used to protect food that can then be thrown directly onto a hot bed of coals to cook in the fireplace. You can also fold aluminum foil into improvised containers that can hold food for cooking or water for boiling and disinfecting. Foil can also be used to reflect the light from a candle flame when mirrors are absent to achieve brighter lighting. I have aluminum foil covering the ends of my energy-conserving fluorescent lightbulbs. The larger bulbs stick out from many conventional lighting fixtures and their exposed glare can be annoying. The foil bends nicely to whatever shape is required and is worry-free against the hot bulb. Several sheets of heavy-duty foil can be used to make an improvised fire pit outdoors for heating and cooking. The foil can be used repeatedly or rolled up and discarded when cold to the touch. Foil can be used to line homemade solar ovens or scrunched up and stuffed into holes or cracks to prevent mice and other rodents from chewing and entering the opening. Layers of foil can be made into an insulating mat to act as an improvised lid for cooking pots or formed into energy-efficient skirts to put around burners and cook pots to maximize heat and conserve fuel. And of course, aluminum foil can be used to wrap and protect food for use at another time.

Several Ways to Light a Fire

Fire is king, and the art of how it's made, used, and extinguished can be incredibly complex so I'll save it for another book. For our urban adventure, have several conventional ways to make fire on hand at all times. While you can make fire with certain chemicals, sticks, parabolas, fresnel lenses, optics, mish metals, batteries and steel wool, "flint and steel," and even sunlight and the two-liter plastic pop bottle used for disinfecting water with the SODIS method, having and using matches and lighters is a lot easier under survival stresses. Both produce the instantaneous flame much sought after by more unconventional methods. Have two or three ways to make fire and, if you need to evacuate, carry them with you in three different places. Don't put all of your survival eggs in one basket. All responsible family members should be equipped with the necessary means to create fire.

Regardless of the small amount of space I dedicate to fire in this book, your family's ability to create it and control it is of paramount importance to their comfort and survival. Practice *now* how to light a fire in all weather conditions and with all types of fuel. Seek hands-on training from a reputable instructor about how fire is made, used, and extinguished. Know well the three elements of the fire tri-angle—*fuel, ignition or heat,* and *oxygen*—as in these lie the keys to success for not just creating flame, but in controlling and putting it out completely for the safety of your home, neighborhood, and town. Ignorance can kill, especially when dealing with fire. Unfortunately, due to the majority of Americans being ignorant about how fire is created and used, you can count on many buildings (and towns) burn-ing after a prolonged crisis due to carelessness and a lack of emergency response personnel and equipment.

A Manual Can and Bottle Opener

Years ago, Gary Larson's *Far Side* cartoon featured a couple inside a bomb shelter after nukes had gone off in the distance. The husband and wife were surrounded by canned food, without a can opener, as the wife yelled her discontent at her hus-band's memory lapse in proper preparation. Many homes have electric can openers, which will, of course, be useless during a power outage. If the lion's share of your emergency food is canned, a quality can opener or two is a must. Swing-A-Way makes a good brand of manual can opener that's easy to use, lasts for a long time, is readily available, and relatively inexpensive. Cheap can openers are a bummer to use; they result in mangled cans, spilled contents, and children learning bad words uttered by the pissed-off user. Military P-38 can openers are great. I have one on my keychain and use it often. They are cheap, lightweight, compact, and very fast with practice. Not all are created equal; discount stores carry brands made from cheap metal that bend and break. Try military surplus stores for the real deal. I've seen bottles opened with plastic combs, the sides of tables, and teeth (not recom-mended). The Swing-A-Way can opener also has a handy hook for opening bottles, as do most Swiss army knives.

Camping or Backpacking Stove with Fuel

Portable two-burner camping stoves are great for cooking grub when standard options are on the fritz. They're convenient, relatively safe when used properly, readily available, and easy to service and buy parts for. Larger two-burner stoves fold down into their own briefcase-sized container and include everything you need except fuel and a pot. I've used various models for years as a regular part of my kitchen experience. Basic two-burner camping stoves are available at many discount stores and are perfect for most families. I especially like the "matchless" models that use a self-generated spark to light the burners, thereby eliminating the need for matches or lighters.

Due to its weight and bulk, it would be suicide to pack the above-mentioned two-burner stove in case of a hasty evacuation. Miniature backpacking stoves are cool when weight and space are at a premium, but their smallness and one-burner capacity make them a poor choice to use for a family of any size. Picture the size of the pot that it would take to feed your family, and then picture it sitting on the dainty, unstable single burner. Their scaled-down size makes them a pain in the ass

NO CAN OPENER, NO PROBLEM!

With practice, canned food can be easily opened with a little elbow grease and an abrasive surface. The raised lip on the top of a can is actually folded metal. By wearing through this "fold," the top will pop right off. To impress your family and friends (after practicing), start by firmly holding the bottom of the can, the raised lip pointed toward your abrasive surface. I like slabs of concrete, block walls, brick, sandstone common in the Southwest, or some other relatively flat, hard surface that has the grit required to wear through the metal lip. Firmly grip the can of food, put the lip in contact with the abrasive surface, and make a series of small, forceful circles like you're sanding a piece of wood with the top of the can. In a matter of a minute or less if you're really going at it, you'll see liquid from the inside of the can start to stain the "sanding surface." Fiddle with the lid to see if the metal is connected at any point; if it is, sand some more emphasizing the area that's not worn through. Other than a little grit in your grub, you should be good to go. Although more tedious, the can of food can also be held and a smaller abrasive surface worked around the lip of the can.

to use on a regular basis and the teetering pot perched atop the engineering marvel can easily be toppled by kids, pets, or inclement weather, increasing fire danger if used in your home. Rabid designers may be able to make a cell phone smaller, but who cares if your fingers are too fat to make a call. Backpacking stoves are also expensive in comparison to larger two-burner models and you may be forced to endure elitist snobbery from sales people at high-end outdoor stores when deciding which God's-gift-to-ultralight-stoves to choose.

The most common camping or backpacking stoves burn white gas or propane, although some burn alcohol (such as homemade stoves that can be created from an aluminum pop can) and even sticks and leaves. As described in the lighting chapter, white gas is more hazardous to store and not as neat as propane, as it can be easily spilled. Having a stove that runs on the same fuel as your alternative lighting options is a wise choice, be it white gas or propane canisters. Whatever fuel you choose, pack away extra for a rainy day in a safe location.

Even though newer camping and backpacking stoves have a warning on the package about using them indoors due to concerns about carbon monoxide poisoning, it's fine to have them in your kitchen to prepare food. If you live in a dollhouse covered with plastic wrap or your shelter or kitchen area is tight, crack a window when utilizing the stove to allow fresh air to enter the room and always use them on a stable, noncombustible surface. For God's sake, don't bring the stove into your home with the intention of using it to heat your house. Cooking, yes. Heating? Absolutely not!

> "As a child, my family's menu consisted of TWO choices: **TAKE IT OR LEAVE IT.**"
>
> —Buddy Hackett

Other Food Cooking Alternatives

Charcoal and Barbeque Grills

Kiss the cook! Dad will have a blast cooking up survival meals just like he does in the summertime with his famous hamburger cookouts. Most barbeque grills run on propane tanks and will last a surprising amount of time depending on what you cook. Many grills have a side burner perfect for heating up items in pots. I love my outdoor propane barbeque grill and use it mainly when I entertain company or for quickly cooking up rodents and rabbits without having to hassle with a fire pit.

Due to their shape and volume, spherical-shaped charcoal grills allow you to easily use almost anything that will burn as a fuel source long after the briquettes run out. They're basically a fire pit with wheels, ending the need for you to bend over your fire pit to cook your food or disinfect your water. *Caution!* Carbon monoxide fumes from charcoal briquettes have killed people who brought the grill inside for warmth during power outages, so use caution and common sense. *AT NO TIME should a charcoal briquette- fueled barbeque grill be brought into or near the house.* If necessary, reread about carbon monoxide poisoning on page 122.

Mini-stoves with Fuel Tablets

Some cooking stoves are nothing more than a collapsible metal grate in which hexamine tablets are placed underneath to heat whatever. They're neat and will simmer water in your Sierra cup, but they could cause vexed family members to bludgeon you to death as they painfully wait for their tepid dinner, one cup at a time. They would be useful if you are forced to hit the road due to an evacuation.

Candles

Although slow and tedious, with patience, a simple candle flame can heat up many foods. Canned foods can be opened, the paper label peeled off if necessary, and the can set directly upon an improvised fireproof grate over a candle flame.

Woodstoves

Many woodstoves feature a flat area on top of the stove that's perfect as a cooking surface. The main drawback with using a woodstove to cook or heat food is that it's in your house. If your emergency happens in the middle of July, it's doubtful you'll fancy firing up the stove to heat the survival beans when it's 95 degrees F (35 degrees C) outside.

Fireplaces

Any Hollywood movie depicting medieval times has a shot of the family fireplace in which all meals are prepared and cooked. With a metal pot and grate, matches, firewood, and ingenuity, you'll quickly learn what works best if you choose to incorporate your home's fireplace as part of your kitchen cookery. Fire safety from neglected chimneys is of prime importance so reread the alternative heating section on page 116.

Campfires

There are many, many variations of campfire lays in regard to how things are set up to cook food with fire. Radiant flame contains the most heat but the smoldering coals provide a more even heat without scorching. Until you get a cooking system down, your metal pot will drive you mad as it will either be too far from the heat source and will take forever to warm up or suffocate the fire of oxygen by being too close. Every year I watch my students from urban backgrounds attempt to cook their food over an open fire in the wilderness. It's comical and somewhat pathetic at first, but by dinner on the third night they're almost pros at getting the fire and pot to bend to their will for great results. If you're subjected to using an open campfire to cook your food, go slow, use common sense, and have patience with yourself and others. Things will only get better with practice. When building a fire outside, do it away from buildings and don't build it under a carport, as heat and sparks can easily start a house fire. Learn how to start a fire safely—don't use gasoline to get a wood or charcoal fire started.

Some camp cooking fires are built on the ground and others are raised up to eliminate bending over. Outdoor cooking options can be quite elaborate and include earth or rock ovens, pit baking, flat stone griddles, green stick grills, clay baking, and more. In each instance, their commonality is how to most effectively and efficiently

FOIL AS LID

get the heat to the food. The problem with an open fire, especially in the wind, is that only a small percentage of its heat reaches the container to cook the food. The rest is lost to the environment.

You can suspend a metal pot with a handle over fire or coals using sticks, dig a narrow trench that allows a fire underneath, or have the pot sit on rocks, among many other variations. Open fires have a way of trashing cook pots by turning them permanently black, so be warned. If you lack a noncombustible container or heavy-duty tinfoil, which is hard to imagine in an urban setting, food can be stone boiled in a variety of otherwise combustible containers. I routinely "stone boil" food such as clams, crayfish, beans, or corn in gourd pots using rocks that were heated in a fire. Indigenous peoples used tightly woven baskets, wooden containers, and animal parts to achieve the same means. Rocks gathered from low-lying areas, whether the stones were in water or not, should be heated up carefully, as the trapped water within the rock can rapidly expand and cause the rock to explode when heated.

Canned foods can be opened and put directly into a bed of coals or near the fire; occasionally stir the contents with a spoon or stick so it doesn't scorch. Food products such as ashcakes, described on page 229, can be put directly onto the hot coals or skewered and suspended on sticks like you did with marshmallows and weenies when you were a kid. Whatever method you choose, there is no escaping the fact that the more you know about how fire works, the easier (and safer) it will be to cook your food using its power.

Be Fire Safe!
Make sure any fire is well contained. Strong winds can blow embers into dry grass or other fuels and have your neighborhood go up in smoke quickly. Many idiot campers put massive fuel on a tiny heat base and then fight over the sitting area that's not smoking like crazy. You don't need a huge white-man fire to cook your lentils. It wastes fuel, attracts attention, creates a terrible fire danger, and burns food and people, as it's too damn hot to get near to stir the beans.

IN THE KITCHEN, SIZE DOES MATTER

Whole grains and legumes should be left whole until days or hours before cooking, as this ensures the least amount of oxidation to damage the food's nutritional value. To save time, water, and fuel, these food types should be broken up before cooking to allow the greater surface area to speed up the cooking process. The perfect tool for this is the manual food grinder or grain mill. There are many varieties to choose from in all different qualities. Buy the best, most simple hand-crank mill you can afford and it will give you a lifetime of service.

A low-tech alternative is to create a *mano* and *metate* from rocks in your backyard. A veritable prehistoric grain mill used for thousands of years, the mano is the grinding stone you hold in your hand(s) and the metate is the larger stone surface that you grind upon. Many authentic metates have deep depressions worn into them by years of faithful service. I have made quickie mano and metate sets on the fly during wilderness courses to pulverize or grind up corn or mesquite pods for easier cooking and digestion.

I usually dig a rectangular trench about six inches deep to put my fires in and use the earth to build up a small embankment around the fire. This trench is dug in mineral earth, free from roots and other combustibles underground. Fire pits encircled with rocks turn into trash cans in the woods, but if you have to use rocks to contain your fire, do so. In an urban setting, bricks or concrete blocks work great. Some people use metal drums or charcoal grills to build their fires.

Be sure to properly extinguish any fire when you are through with it. All parts of the fire, including the black carbon, should be *cool to the touch*. Remember the fire triangle: heat, fuel, and oxygen. Remove any one of them and the fire goes out. The easiest way to put out your fire in low- or no-water situations is to burn very small fuelwood and let it burn out. In other words, think ahead about when you want the fire out and STOP ADDING FUEL!

The Dutch Oven

In the hands of experienced people, Dutch ovens are capable of cooking nearly anything, from stews to chocolate cakes. All they require is food, fuel, and someone who knows what they're doing. Many Dutch oven artists like the model with three or four metal legs and a lid with a rim around its circumference. These design features allow for the easy distribution of hot coals under and on top of the oven for heat to evenly penetrate and cook the meal inside.

Pressure Cookers

Pressure cookers make short work of hard-to-cook survival fare foods such as rice or beans, saving fuel, time, and water. When foods are stored for long periods of time, they will become slightly tougher and harder to cook, hence the virtues of the pressure cooker. There are many cheap ones on the market (some of which have exploded under the pressure!), and some of the best to be found are lingering on a back shelf at the thrift store. My grandmother could work magic with her pressure cooker and I fondly remember its "rattle and hiss" that inevitably meant something tasty would be on the table soon. Purchase a quality pressure cooker as you'll have it for life.

Solar Ovens

According to one source, the first formal solar cooker was developed in 1767 by Horace de Saussure, a Swiss naturalist. Since the sun has been drying people's food for thousands of years, my guess is that the sun was being used to cook food much earlier than this; we have yet to find the proof.

I absolutely adore my solar oven. I can cook almost anything and during the summer months my oven can get to temperatures of 375 degrees F (191 degrees C) in less than half an hour—all with the free power of the sun. How hot a solar cooker gets is primarily determined by the number and size of the reflectors used and, of course, the sun's intensity and its duration. High temperatures are not required for cooking and food will cook just fine as long as the oven reaches about

200 degrees F (90 degrees C). Foods containing water can't go above 212 degrees F (100 degrees C) at sea level anyway, unless a pressure cooker is used. High temperatures in cookbooks are for the sake of convenience and to achieve effects on food such as browning. Lower temperatures allow foods to cook slower, like in a crockpot, so people can do other things and come back to a hot meal. Higher oven temperatures cook food faster, in larger quantities, and give your oven a boost during partly cloudy or hazy days.

There are three basic types of solar cookers: *box cookers, panel cookers*, and *parabolic cookers*. Box cookers are probably the most common variety and can evenly cook large amounts of food. Some communities use homemade box-cooker ovens that hold and roast an entire turkey. Reflectors can be added, like the petals of a flower, to further focus the sun's rays into and around the solar cooker "belly" where the food rests. Panel cookers consist of various flat panels that focus the sun's rays onto a container inside a glass bowl or clear plastic bag. These can be made very cheaply with few materials. Parabolic cookers are reflective concave discs that focus the sun's rays onto the bottom of a pot. They are more complicated to make but follow the same principle as my Radio Shack solar cigarette lighter that I use for fire demonstrations. Parabolas you may have around the house that can be used to make a fire are the inside reflective bowl of a good-sized flashlight or the reflective bowl from the inside of a car headlight. Parabolas focus the sun's rays into a concentrated area and can cause wicked eye damage to people who insist on using their lighter to see how much gas they have left in their fuel tank.

As a general rule, solar ovens take about twice the cooking time as a conventional oven. One of the beauties about box cooker ovens is you really have to work to burn something in them. Point it toward the sun, put the food in, adjust it once or twice as needed, and walk away—the perfect free crockpot. A friend of mine sets up his solar oven and points it south before he goes to work each day. Upon returning from work, his food is cooked and he sits down to a hot meal each evening.

They also work well to simmer or at least pasteurize nonpotable water. Commercial solar ovens and many homemade ones are so efficient that even hazy days or the reduced insolation of the winter sun simply adds a bit more cooking time to yet another amazing meal. The taste of food cooked with the sun is "pure," and hard to describe as there is no taste hint of any fuel that you get with other methods.

"An **EMPTY BELLY** is the **BEST COOK.**"

—Estonian proverb

The Perfect Pot

There are many opinions about what type of pot to use in a solar cooker. Here in the desert, it doesn't seem to matter much. Dark-colored metal pots won't reflect

HERE COMES THE SUN

In many countries, poor residents (mostly women and girls) are forced to walk for hours each day to find firewood (a scarce commodity for two billion people in developing countries). When wood is scarce, people have to burn dung and crop residues which would otherwise have been composted to enrich poor soils for growing food. The time involved gathering fuel to cook food takes away from their educational opportunities, such as school or from learning various trades for greater independence, and sets them up for violent assaults common in locales such as Darfur in Africa.

Sitting around a poorly burning camp fire each day is not healthy, as the chemicals in smoke cause long-term health effects. If solar ovens, which don't produce toxic smoke and can also pasteurize unsanitary water, were used in these countries, countless children would not be killed by waterborne and smoke-related diseases, which are the primary killers of children in developing countries. Poor urban families spend a good part of their meager paycheck on cooking fuels. The European Commission as well as solar cooker experts estimate that 165 to 200 million households could benefit from solar cookers.

Today hundreds of thousands of solar cookers are being used on a regular basis, mostly in parts of India, China, and Africa. Slowly but surely, thanks to organizations such as Solar Cookers International (SCI) and many others, solar cooking can and will liberate hundreds of thousands from dependence on dwindling wood supplies, saving countries from continued environmental degradation and pollution caused from processing and burning human-made fuels, as well as saving families money and increasing their health. Far more than just a cool survival option, solar cookers can literally revolutionize the world and empower people with the free and limitless energy of the sun.

as much long-wave radiation as shiny pots, but I've used both and they both work. Clear or colored glass works, too, as well as Corningware. If all you have are shiny pots, and you feel strongly about using a black pot, using it to cook over an open fire a few times will solve the problem, maybe forever. As a general rule, use dark-colored, shallow, lightweight metal pots.

Making Your Own Solar Box Oven

There are several designs in books, magazines, and on the Internet for making your own solar oven. For our purposes, we'll make one out of cardboard although you can use much more expensive materials if you wish. Paper burns at 451 degrees F (233 degrees C) and your oven won't get that hot. Cardboard works great unless it gets rained on, but hey, this is a solar oven so what's it doing in the rain? If you expect frequent moisture or want greater durability from your cardboard oven, paint the outside with house paint.

The Robbie Rubbish Radically Right-on Radiant Range

Robbie dug deep into the landfill of opportunity to come up with this solar oven design. He knew from looking at other designs that the cover or top of the solar oven was the biggest challenge to create. To avoid this pitfall, he used a box with a lid. Robbie said he found a bunch of heavyweight cardboard boxes with lids at printing shops and copy centers, as that's what their paper comes delivered in.

The inner walls of Robbie's oven are covered with an old reflective space blanket, although heavy-duty aluminum foil works great too. (Robbie knows that the smoother and shinier the surface, the better it will reflect radiation, so he chose the salvaged space blanket.) The space blanket or aluminum foil reflects the impending long-wave radiation after the shortwave radiation from the sun enters the box. As the heat from long-wave radiation has a hard time getting back out through a barrier such as glass or plastic, it continues to bounce around the interior of the box. He feels this works better than painting the inside walls black. Although the color black may get "hotter" on the oven walls, he's not interested in eating the oven and the subsequent reflected long-wave radiation is a better use of heat.

For the window, instead of using glass, Robbie uses a clear plastic oven bag that can withstand temperatures of 400 degrees F (204 degrees C). He likes to cut the oven bag in half, thus using only one layer of plastic for slightly greater solar gain. You can also leave the bag in one piece so the two sides form an insulating air pocket, but be sure to tape or glue the bag shut or it may collect water vapor between the layers of plastic and block sunlight. Oven bags don't have ultraviolet protection so they will eventually become fragile and need to be replaced, but they are common and cheap enough to do so with a minimum of hassle. Plastic is also lighter and safer than glass, especially around kids.

Robbie's not going to insulate the oven walls, as he knows cardboard is already a decent insulator due to its corrugations. He also knows that heat rises, and will mostly be lost through the oven's top plastic panel which is necessary to let in the sun. He won't insulate the bottom either, although he'll pay attention to where he sets the oven to be mindful of potential colder conduction from the ground. After all, he's dealing with a solar oven, meaning the sun will be striking all around the ground where he sets the oven, warming the surface.

With all the materials at hand, I watched Robbie make an oven in less than forty-five minutes. Follow Robbie's solar-oven instructions or create your own!

Materials

- ➲ Cardboard box with lid. (The one Robbie found was eighteen inches long by ten inches high by fourteen inches wide)
- ➲ Space blanket or roll of heavy-duty aluminum foil
- ➲ Sharp knife and scissors
- ➲ Glue
- ➲ Duct tape
- ➲ Clear plastic, turkey-size oven bag
- ➲ Scrap piece of wire

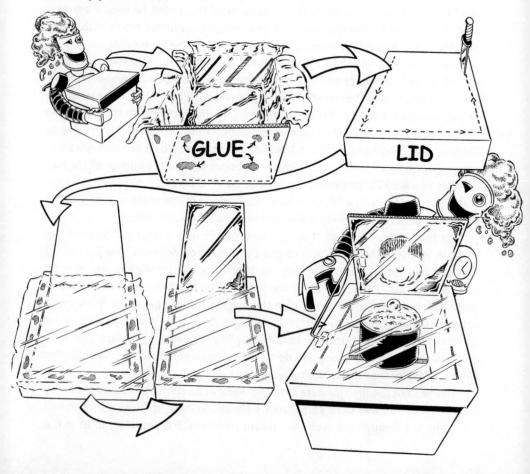

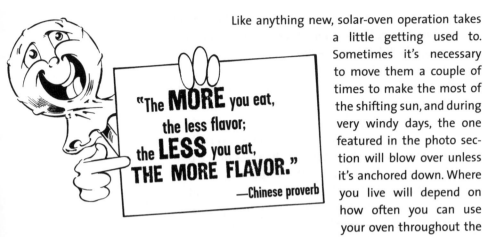

"The **MORE** you eat,
the less flavor;
the **LESS** you eat,
THE MORE FLAVOR."
—Chinese proverb

Like anything new, solar-oven operation takes a little getting used to. Sometimes it's necessary to move them a couple of times to make the most of the shifting sun, and during very windy days, the one featured in the photo section will blow over unless it's anchored down. Where you live will depend on how often you can use your oven throughout the year.

Cooking Tips and Techniques for Getting the Most Fuel Bang for Your Buck

All fuel sources after an emergency will be like gold. Whether it's gasoline or firewood, its presence is like money in the bank for the savvy survivor. Knowing how to make these precious resources stretch is all-important.

The efficiency of a heat source used for cooking can be thought of as having three parts. The first part is the *efficiency of combustion of the fuel* and the second is *the efficiency of heat transfer to the cooking container.* The third variable is the *competence and skill of the person doing the cooking.* Over all, maximizing the second variable will result in the greatest fuel savings. Use the techniques listed below *now* to save energy and get yourself accustomed to doing more with less.

Many of the following tips can be incorporated into cooking over a campfire as well. Outdoor campfires will be under the influence of weather variations and require much greater attention to variable number one when compared to a premixed propane-fueled stove that's used indoors.

- ➲ *Choose a good pot!* Broad-bottomed pots are better than narrow ones. Thick metal takes more time to heat up but also holds and radiates more heat when the heat source is removed. Pots with short handles on either side, as opposed to one long handle, will be easier to incorporate into a hay box (featured next). Your pot must have a lid.
- ➲ *Keep a lid on it!* Hot air rises. Food cooks much slower in a pot without a lid, thus it uses the same amount of fuel but for a much longer duration. The same amount of heat enters the pot but less of it is used for the cooking process, hence an uncovered pot is a less successful heat exchanger. Lids should be tight

fitting to keep the steam inside the pot. Lids can be insulated by putting several layers of aluminum foil in or on the lid. When the lid becomes hot, turn down the burner but keep the lid on.

➲ *Wear a skirt!* Use a noncombustible, reflective skirt of double or tripled layers of heavy-duty aluminum foil or unpainted, ungalvanized aluminum roof flashing to encircle the cooking flame and pot, reradiating otherwise lost heat toward the sides of the pot. This increases the heat transfer value for the same amount of fuel. The skirt can be as tall as the pot on the stove with about half an inch to a quarter of an inch of clearance away from the sides of the pot. Double up the material encircling the pot a few inches and anchor it with a large metal paper clip. Some folks simply put a large metal mixing bowl upside down over the entire cooking pot.

➲ *Shorten the distance!* Keep the cooking container as close as possible to the heat source without suffocating the flame from receiving oxygen.

➲ *Keep the heat focused!* Flame blasting up around the edges of a pot is wasted. Turn the burner down until the flame is focused upon the middle of the pot, yet covering as much surface area as possible. Smaller flames may take longer to cook but will yield greater cooking results for the fuel consumed. Doing so will also eliminate much burnt food stuck to the bottom of the pot, thereby saving food and washing time.

➲ *Center the pot directly over the cooking flame!* This sounds like common sense but check out where the pot is located tonight at dinner. Ninety percent of the time it's off to one side of the flame.

The Hay Box: The Power of Heat-Retained Cooking

Precious fuel creates the heat that is then used to cook your food. But what if you could harness the heat from the food in your pot to do some of its own cooking? Doing so would allow you to turn off the stove that much sooner, thereby maximizing limited fuel resources. This heat-retention cooking concept is exploited to its fullest by using something which is commonly referred to as a *hay box*. A hay box is nothing more than a superinsulated box in which food that has been heated to cooking temperature is placed to continue cooking. Its fuel savings, depending on the type of food and how much cook time it requires, can be from

20 to 80 percent! The longer a food item takes to cook on the stove, the greater the savings when using an insulated cooker. Insulated cookers can be used anytime, not just after emergencies, to save a tremendous amount of cooking fuel and energy.

The concept behind insulated cookers is simple. When food in a container is put near a heat source, the food climbs to the boiling temperature and then stabilizes. The food within the stabilized temperature then "cooks" for a given period of time. Any heat beyond the boiling temperature is merely replacing heat lost to the surrounding environment by the pot. When the container reaches its top temperature and then is removed from the heat source and placed in a super-insulated box, the food inside continues to cook. In heat-retained cooking, food is brought to a boil, simmered for a few minutes depending on the particle size of the food, and then put into the hay box to continue cooking. (Simmer smaller grains such as rice for five or six minutes. Simmer larger food such as dried beans or whole potatoes for fifteen to eighteen minutes. Presoaking and draining beans always makes them easier to cook, as well as to digest. Red meats such as a roast can be simmered for twenty to thirty minutes. Note: As a safety precaution, meats should be recooked before serving.) The insulation prevents most of the heat in the food from escaping, thereby eliminating the need for a continued heat source for cooking.

As a general rule, hay-box cooking times are usually one or two times the regular cooking time on a stove. It's like having a free crockpot, cooking the food and keeping it warm, without burning the contents, until you're ready to eat. Like many techniques in this book, experimentation will prove what works best.

Making a Hay Box

Quickie hay boxes can be made by wrapping up a cook pot with extra blankets, pillows, or sleeping bags. However, as the pot will be very hot, there are a few rules to follow when making or improving your heat-retaining cooker. Essentially, a hay box is any heat-safe insulating material that can be safely wrapped around a pot. Four to six inches of insulation is best, although it depends on the type of insulation, as not all are created equal. Several kinds of insulation have been used such as straw, hay, wool, feathers, cotton, rice hulls, cardboard, Styrofoam peanuts, newspaper, fiberglass, fur, papercrete, rigid foam, and others. Whatever insulation is used should fit as closely as possible to the pot for maximum efficiency. Using aluminum foil or a reflective space blanket against the pot will not only protect the insulation from some of the pot's heat but will reflect the long-wave radiation (heat) back to the pot. Heat-safe insulation can be placed directly around the pot after putting the pot in a cardboard box or it can be stuffed between two boxes and the pot placed inside the smaller box, among numerous other variations. Some people create an insulated kitchen drawer as a hay-box cooker. After simmering on the stove, they simply pop the pot into the drawer, fold the insulation down around the top, and shut the drawer while dinner cooks.

Rules for Optimal Insulation

You can get away with a lot and still have a heat-retaining cooker work well but, by adhering to the following points, your hay-box cooker will be superefficient at maximizing trapped heat. The insulation for your hay-box cooker should have the following characteristics:

- ⮑ It must be heat resistant and withstand cooking temperatures of up to 212 degrees F (100 degrees C), the boiling temperature for water at sea level.
- ⮑ It should maintain an adequate loft. Even the best insulation can be compromised by squishing it up tightly or spreading it out too thin.
- ⮑ It must be pliable or custom-fit to the cooking pot itself in order for it to fit around the pot as closely as possible to minimize heat loss.
- ⮑ It should not release any toxic fumes when heated. Some foams will need to be protected and should not be used directly against the pot.
- ⮑ It must be kept dry. Rising steam from the pot will dampen insulation, thus causing it to lose some of its insulating properties. Mylar space blankets or aluminum foil can pull double duty as a reflective and moisture-proof barrier.
- ⮑ All cooking containers should have tight-fitting lids to prevent the escape of heat and moisture. The larger the cook pot, the more thermal mass it will have, thus it will store a greater amount of heat to cook food after being removed from the heat source.

Other Hay-Box Advantages

Conserving fuel is not the only gift a hay box can give. Preparing multiple meals can be a hassle with a single or even a two-burner camping stove. Hay boxes allow you to simmer items for a few minutes and then stash them away to cook further, thus freeing up the burner to heat other dishes for the meal. Since water won't be simmering away, you'll require less stored water to cook grains and legumes. Because of this, reduce added water to foods by one quarter. If dried beans require two cups of water for cooking, try

"HUNGRY MEN think the cook is **LAZY."**
—Anonymous

using one and a half cups instead. Hay boxes cook food using reduced temperatures, thereby preserving more of the food's original nutrition and flavor.

The Survival Kitchen

Survival kitchen: anyplace you happen to be that is used to prepare food after a catastrophe.

The following tidbits can make life a lot easier when needing to feed the herd. No doubt trial and error will go a long way in your learning curve toward doing more with less under very great stress.

Kitchen Control

In the outdoors, there is nothing worse than a student haphazardly walking over prepared food, especially in sandy conditions. The "sand sandwich" leaves much to be desired. After emergencies, when kitchens must be created in unconventional areas, it may be necessary to set up boundaries to keep things sanitary and prevent kids and pets from knocking things over or creating major first-aid episodes.

Kitchen boundaries can be objects on the ground, such as coolers and tables, or consist of string or surveyor's tape stretched out around the kitchen perimeter, similar to a crime scene. String or rope can also be used for hanging towels or other implements to dry and sanitize in the sun.

The Deluxe Dishwashing Station

After the paper plates run out, washing the dishes for a large family without modern conveniences can be interesting. You will want to stay on top of dishes or they will attract unwanted critters. Dirty dishes lying around are a morale killer in general. I have seen the following method used to service hundreds of people at a time in the outdoors. The more people, the more the water, soap, and chlorine will need to be changed.

Get four containers that hold enough water to fit your dishes into. If nothing else, five-gallon buckets work great. Some folks add one more container at the beginning of the line that serves as a receptacle for uneaten food and table scraps. (If you're not eating what's on your plate during a survival situation, close this book immediately and go watch TV.)

The buckets or containers function as follows:
1. *The prerinse.* This one is filled with water and takes the major goop off the plate to extend the life of the next container.
2. *The washer.* This one is filled with hot potable water, soap, and a pot scrubber if you have one.
3. *The rinser.* Yep, filled with plain potable water.
4. *The disinfector.* This container is filled with potable water to which a couple of capfuls of chlorine bleach

are added. Depending on how much water you have,
use about one part chlorine bleach to ten parts water.
The disinfectant rinse should smell like chlorine and
be prepared fresh before each use after mealtime.
If it doesn't smell like chlorine, add more. A bleach
water rinse followed by air drying is the simplest way
to effectively sanitize pots, pans, and utensils. Boiling
water is another option but much more fuel con-
sumptive and liable to cause accidental burns.

Change the water as needed depending on the number of people using the dishwashing station. Get the buckets off the ground to keep animals and small kids out
of them. If the rinse water starts to get sudsy early, knock back on the soap in the
washing container so the rinse water will last longer. Too much soap residue left on
washed dishes can also cause diarrhea. You may want to prepare your wash station
before preparing the food. This allows you to wash kitchen utensils as you go and
the containers can be refreshed quickly when needed.

While this might seem like a lot of water to use to wash dishes (and it is if all of
the containers are full), fill the containers with only as much water as your family
needs. You'll figure it out after the first time or two.

The Desert Deluxe Dishwashing System

In my arid region, the above method would be unacceptable unless attending a
Rainbow Gathering or a heavy-metal concert. Deep in the wilderness, when hauling potable water is a pain, and even at my house, we wash dishes in a far different way. Personal bowls are half-filled with potable water. Using the spoon you ate
with, swish and scrape the bowl until it is clean, thus cleaning the bowl and spoon.
The "dishwater" is then drunk on the spot. The dishes are then laid out in the sun
to disinfect.

The quicker you wash your dishes, the easier they will be to clean. At my house
I use cold tap water (and rarely any soap) to wash dishes, which I do immediately
after eating. I then lay them out to dry, and the collected dishwater is periodically
poured onto plants in my xeriscape garden. The food particles never sit long enough
to turn into a bacterial nightmare, and the drying dishes likewise don't become a
habitat for anything funky that might want to propagate. The better you clean your
plate when eating, the less food you'll have to wash off. While not recommended,
there was a gentleman I knew of that had his dog do the dishes, after which he
would stack them back in the cupboard—no doubt a single guy.

Chilling Out

Conventional refrigerators are a fairly recent invention. Both of my grandparents utilized basements and root cellars to keep food cooler during the year, and
I remember standing in both with flashlights and radios due to tornadoes. Almost

"The belly RULES the mind."

—Spanish proverb

every household should have a cooler that can be used to store food in a pinch. Keep it outside in the cool of the night and bring it back inside during hotter day-time temperatures and store it in the cooler part of the house. In the winter-time, keeping food cool is sometimes not the problem, it's how to keep it from freezing—better frozen than not cold enough, however. Many times a cooler will prevent foods from freezing unless the temperatures are extreme, as insulation works for both hot and cold.

The easiest way to not rely upon a refrigerator is to not need one. Canned goods of the proper size ensure there will be no leftovers. Store dried or freeze-dried foods and *prepare only what your family will eat at each meal*, unless it's something that doesn't require refrigeration such as bread. While the eat-as-you-go method takes more time and uses more fuel, it's better than dancing with diarrhea from *staphylococcal enteritis* or some other busy bug.

I created built-in cooling tubes in my house in the hope that they would suffice as refrigeration. Due to a design flaw, I was wrong, but they're still great places to store food at a cooler temperature than the rest of the house. Try what my grand-mother did for cooling with water and burlap (page 129). Or consider the following method: An African potter devised a homemade cooler by using two unglazed clay pots, one larger than the other. He put the smaller pot into the larger pot and filled the void between the two with wet sand. Both of these devices are built upon the principles you already know about: conduction, convection, and evaporation.

Compost

Unless things get over-the-top hardcore, there will be items on the dinner plate that you will want to get rid of. Vegetable and fruit scraps, eggshells, and many other food wastes can be composted. And while gardeners will cringe, for our pur-poses compost the meat scraps as well. Men in garbage trucks might not appear for a while so plan ahead about dealing with your waste products. If you don't already have a compost pit in the backyard, make one. Mine consists of free wooden pal-lets screwed together into a square. You can also cut the bottom out of an existing garbage can with a lid, throw a screen in the bottom, set it on the bare ground, and pitch food directly into it. Quickie compost areas can be nothing more than a hand-dug pit, identical to a latrine for going to the bathroom, or you can simply throw food scraps into the poop pit.

After food scraps are added to your compost pile, cover it with earth to shield it from critters. If your compost area is protected with a fence or some other means, you won't have to use as much earth (thus you'll have to dig new holes less often) to cover the table scraps to keep Fido from digging up the goods. When the contents come to within a foot of the surface, fill in the hole completely. Like the sanitation latrine, a mound of dirt is left on top to level out by itself as the garbage underneath decomposes and settles. It will be a great place to plant a garden when the emergency is over. If used only for kitchen scraps, compost pits can be located fairly close to the kitchen.

The art of composting is fairly involved and can take many forms. Compost piles can generate heat that inactivates all bad pathogens, or they can be propagated with red worms to eat the contents, thereby producing pathogen-free yet yummy worm castings that plants adore. I have heard of some compost piles getting so hot that they burst into flames. Although this is rare, don't have the pile next to the house.

If you're an apartment dweller, treat your food scraps the same way you do your poop and pee (according to the sanitation chapter) until something better comes along. Believe me, food scraps will smell and look almost as nasty as poop after a few days in hot weather so don't casually throw them into the corner of your room. Human waste and food waste are both major pest magnets.

Grey Water

Every household produces *grey water* and *black water*. Grey water is produced from the kitchen sink or the washing machine, black water from the toilet. Pathetically, Arizona just recently legalized grey-water systems for watering plants and trees around homes. As usual, human nature waits until things get bad instead of looking ahead at preventing the cause of a pending shortage. Better late then never, guys; we were all using grey water to water our plants anyway.

Large plants and trees will aggressively gobble up the nutrients available in grey water. If you water your vegetation, you'll need to consider things such as not adding toxic stuff to your wash water. Use biodegradable soaps and rotate grey water onto different plants to let them rest between soakings.

If you don't plan on adding grey water to plants (and why not?), it should *not* be thrown into the compost or pit latrines in quantity, as it will water down the organisms that break down the contents. Grey water can start to smell if no plants are present to utilize the water so plan on digging a separate hole just for grey water. The size of the hole will depend upon how much water gets tossed in and how well the ground "perks" or soaks up the liquid. Start with a two- by two-foot hole and make it bigger if necessary. This grey water "sump," as it's called, can be located next to the kitchen compost pile.

Food Preparation, Serving, and Handling

Be mindful that preparing food is a serious responsibility. The preparer has the power and opportunity to get the entire family sick. The food-prep person should be meticulous about personal sanitation and should have thoroughly washed his or her hands before commencing to prepare or serve any and all food items. An adequate wash station for hands, which both cook and patron should use, should accompany all kitchens. Tables or other objects should be used to keep food

"Red meat is **NOT BAD FOR YOU.** Now BLUE-GREEN meat, **THAT'S BAD** for you."

—Tommy Smothers

preparation off the ground and should be covered when not in use. After each meal, wash the surfaces with soapy water, rinse, rinse them again with bleach water, and then allow them to air dry in the sun. Keep the food preparation table(s) free of personal items at all times.

In large families or group settings, for better management of potential sanitation breaches, one person should serve the entire family or group. The server should have the person hold their personal bowl near the edge but not touching or directly over the serving container. This avoids food running down the potentially contaminated sides of the dish and back into the serving container. Some outdoor kitchens use a plastic funnel with the bottom cut out to facilitate getting food into narrow containers. Foods should be served in a manner that the serving equipment NEVER touches the individuals' eating bowl or plate.

Keep serving containers covered when not in use and keep the serving utensil in a separate container other than the food pot, as organisms can travel down the handle into the pot to multiply. When taste-testing food for seasoning, drop a sample into a personal bowl to avoid contaminating the serving utensil. Prepared foods, raw or cooked, should be served and eaten promptly.

Helpful **HARDCORE** *Hints*

Preppin' and Cookin' the Critter: How to Eat Your Trapped Rats and Mice

If you've followed the advice on trapping rodents given in the Familiar yet Fantastic Food chapter (see page 240), or if you're a natural hunter, I'm assuming you have fresh meat for the grill. Congratulations!

As a general rule, check your traps in the morning and evening, or whenever you feel the need to do so. Rodents that have lain dead in a trap all night long will still be OK to eat, even in hot climates, so don't weeny out and think it's been sitting too long to be edible. If you heed the advice given in the first sentence of this paragraph, rotting rodents won't be a problem.

I rarely see fleas on the rats and mice I trap. In truth, at closer glance they are very clean and beautiful creatures. Part of this is because the body has cooled off and the fleas have split. Still, I have watched rodents be caught and, upon inspection of the still warm body, didn't find any fleas. Other small critters such as ground squirrels, tree squirrels, and cottontail rabbits might be literally crawling with fleas and ticks. You can put the body in a zipper-lock bag until it's butchering time if you wish, or let the body cool naturally, away from your living area.

CAUTION! Small rodents can be carriers of *hantavirus* or *bubonic plague*, especially in the Southwest. Use caution and common sense when processing rodents by wearing rubber gloves if you have them, or at least avoiding contact with the cuts or abrasions on your body with the body fluids from the animal. If these two diseases are prominent in your area, process the animal in an area with plenty of ventilation and sunlight and do your best to cut out, contain, and safely dispose of all feces and urine (bladder). Plague is transmitted by infected fleas. In known plague areas, I sometimes throw the body of the dead animal—fur and all—into a waiting fire to kill all suspected fleas. Plague will sicken the animal itself and it will eventually die. The problem is that you're not going to witness its sickly behavior before it dies in your trap. Look any animal over carefully before processing it. Does it look like hell, or does it look normal and healthy, even though it's dead? Mice and rats should look pretty good, plump with shiny, clean coats. All animals that look to the contrary should be discarded in a safe place away from curious pets and children. You should also inspect the internal organs to look for discolored spots, worms, or other oddities that just don't seem right. East Coasters should watch out for ticks and Lyme disease. In a healthy rodent, proper cooking will destroy anything that's unsafe for consumption.

If the rodent body checks out healthy upon your inspection, it's time to clean it. I have kept unprocessed rodents in the refrigerator for up to three days before finally cleaning and eating them. Regardless of this, eat them as soon as you can. If you're eating rodents and still have the use of a grid-powered refrigerator, it makes me wonder about you.

Mice Are Nice

Mice can be put directly onto the coals of a fire whole. You can use other heat sources as well but the coals of a fireplace, woodstove, or campfire work great. You can skin them first, but it's a hassle. The heat from the coals will singe off the fur, but it will take some rubbing with a stick and a few attempts turning as necessary to get off all the hair. Singed hair would make a T-bone taste awful so do a good job. If after the singeing process you think skinning is easier, be my guest. The skin will peel right off after precooking in the coals.

As the hair is being singed, the mouse will start to bloat up from the heat. Take this opportunity to scrape lightly at its abdominal cavity with something or gently tear it open with your fingers. At this time, most of the guts should begin to pop out of the opening you created. Near the end of the intestines, you will clearly see mouse turds heading toward the anus. Get rid of all this stuff, but the heart, lungs, and almost everything else up near the head and middle of the body is good eating. Once the mouse has been gutted and the hair singed, it's time to cook it on the coals. I like to cook them until they're between crispy and chewy, turning as necessary. Don't undercook them, but don't turn them into a piece of charcoal either from overcooking.

By the time you're ready to eat the mouse, it won't look like one. The tail and legs will have burned away and the body will resemble a blackened hotdog-like object. There are three bites to a mouse, the middle and rear being the best (in my opinion), so the next task is to jockey for position regarding who gets what bite. The head isn't bad, but eat it hot, as mouse brains suck when they're cold.

Rat . . . the Other, Other White Meat

I love the taste of packrat. It has a delightful, slightly nutty flavor that's neither too subtle nor too overpowering. The Yavapai Indians from my area called pack-rat *mahlgah* and considered it a delicacy; in the past, young Yavapais cooked and crushed it up so older, toothless relatives could savor the flavor.

I've never had Norway rats, most common in big cities, but I would treat them much the same way as far as preparing and cooking. You'll want to skin rats and do cool things with their hides. Once skinned, the rat should be gutted, although you can gut the rat before you skin it if you wish. Process this animal in much the same way as you would a larger, big game animal. Open up the abdominal cavity with a knife or sharp object and pull out the guts. The internal organs can be eaten like you did with the mouse. Keep in mind the meat is raw in this case so use caution and keep things as sanitary as possible when cleaning. The rat can also be thrown onto the coals whole like the mouse but it doesn't work as well, as it's a much bigger animal. If you land a Norway rat the size of a house cat, definitely skin and gut it first before cooking.

Once the animal is gutted, wash it off with clean water. If water is scarce, this step can be skipped. The skinned, gutted, and cleaned rat can then be spread out flat and put on coals or grilled on the barbeque. Turn as necessary and cook it like chicken. Yummy … then eat the meat right off the bones and don't forget about the internal organs. In cases of extreme need, the entire cooked animal can be pounded up Yavapai-style, bones and all, to extract the most amount of nutrition possible.

Recipes: From My Kitchen to Yours with Love

No survival book is complete without at least a few recipes. The following dishes allow you the flexibility to entertain like a star whether the disaster just happened or has been dragging on for weeks. Enjoy!

"The Week After" Rat-A-Touille

Yield: 4 servings (serving size 1 1/2 cup)

- ⮩ 1 tablespoon olive oil
- ⮩ 1 to 4 rats, skinned and boned
- ⮩ 2 medium-size zucchini, unpeeled and thinly sliced
- ⮩ 1 small eggplant, peeled and cut into 1-inch cubes
- ⮩ 1 medium green pepper, cut into 1-inch pieces
- ⮩ 1 medium onion, thinly sliced
- ⮩ 1/2 pound fresh mushrooms, sliced
- ⮩ 1 can (16 ounces) whole tomatoes, cut up
- ⮩ 1 1/2 teaspoon crushed dried basil
- ⮩ 1 clove garlic, minced
- ⮩ 1 tablespoon minced fresh parsley
- ⮩ Black pepper to taste

Heat oil in large nonstick skillet. Add rat meat and sauté about 3 minutes, or until lightly browned. Add eggplant, zucchini, onion, green pepper, and mushrooms. Cook about 15 minutes, stirring occasionally. Add tomatoes, basil, garlic, parsley, and pepper; stir and continue cooking about 5 to 10 minutes, or until rat is cooked and tender. Serve over rice.

Survival Rat-A-Touille

Yield: 4 servings (serving size depends upon amount of initial ingredients)

- ⮩ 1 tablespoon olive oil (or whatever oil isn't rancid)
- ⮩ 1 to 4 rats, skinned (gut, but save organs, dry out
  bones to pound and add for nutrition)
- ⮩ 2 cans mixed vegetables
- ⮩ 1 can corn
- ⮩ 1 cup dandelions or other edible greens you have in

your yard (beware of those previously doused with
weed killer)
- ➲ 1 can (8 or 16 ounces) mushroom pieces (optional)
- ➲ 1 can (16 ounce) whole tomatoes, cut up (optional)
- ➲ 1 1/2 teaspoon dried basil, crushed (or whatever herbs
you have left that you think will work)
- ➲ Black pepper and onion and garlic powder to taste

Heat oil in large nonstick pot with lid suitable for later putting in hay box. Add rat
meat and organs and sauté about 3 minutes, or until lightly browned. Add canned
vegetables and mushroom pieces if available. Use juice in can to save water. Cook
about 15 minutes, stirring occasionally. Add canned tomatoes, dandelions, garlic
and onion powder, basil, and pepper; stir and continue cooking about 5 minutes.
Put in hay box for 1 to 2 hours, or until rat is cooked and tender. Reheat for a few
minutes and serve over rice if you have any left.

SUPER ✦ SIMPLE ✦ SUMMARY

- ➲ Many foods, such as grains and dried legumes, require
heat to make otherwise indigestible components digestible. There are many options to cook food when conventional methods are no longer available.
- ➲ A two- to four-quart cooking pot with lid, eating utensils, paper plates, cups, and towels, heavy-duty aluminum foil, ways to light a fire, a manual can opener, and a
camping cook stove with fuel are nice items to have for
the preparation and cooking of food after a disaster.
- ➲ A can of food can be opened by sanding the top of the lid
on an abrasive object such as a cinder block wall.
- ➲ Other options for cooking or heating food are charcoal
or barbeque grills, candles, woodstoves or fireplaces,
campfires, Dutch ovens, pressure cookers, and solar
ovens.
- ➲ Solar ovens can easily be made with cardboard and an
oven cooking bag. Cooking pots that work the best in
most solar ovens are dark-colored, shallow, lightweight
metal pots.
- ➲ Reducing the size of some foods before cooking such as
dried beans will allow them to cook quicker, using less

water and fuel. Hand-crank grain mills work wonderfully for this purpose.

- ⊃ Maximizing the efficiency of cooking fuels is important. Choose a good pot with a lid and keep the lid on when cooking. Make a noncombustible skirt out of aluminum foil and place it around the pot to reflect radiation to the sides of the pot. Keep the pot close to and centered over the flame.

- ⊃ Make sure all fires are well contained. Strong winds can blow embers into dry grass or other fuels and cause wild fires. Six-inch-deep trenches in mineral earth can be dug to contain the fire. Use rocks if you must, bricks or concrete blocks, or metal drums and charcoal grills.

- ⊃ Extinguish all fires when done. All parts of the fire should be *cool to the touch*. Think ahead about when you want the fire out and burn small fuel or stop adding it altogether to make the fire easier to put out.

- ⊃ Hay boxes allow you to save cooking fuel by using the heat of the food within the container after being cooked for a short time. The pot is then put into a superinsulated box to maximize the radiated heat. Insulated cookers can be used anytime, not just after emergencies, to save a tremendous amount of cooking fuel and energy.

- ⊃ Survival kitchens should be set up with attention to keeping people, pets, and kids out for maximum safety, germ control, and efficiency. They should have areas to dispose of compost and grey water as well.

- ⊃ Most group dishwashing systems should have multiple containers in which to scrap, wash, rinse, and bleach-dip dishes.

- ⊃ The easiest way to not rely upon a refrigerator is to not need one. Canned foods of the proper size ensure there will be no leftovers. *Prepare only what your family will eat at each meal,* unless it's something that doesn't require refrigeration such as bread.

- ⊃ For better management of potential sanitation breaches when serving food to large families or groups, one person should serve the entire family or group.

- ⊃ Rats and mice can be easily caught in homemade or commercial traps, checked for health, cleaned, cooked, and eaten.

19

FUNDAMENTAL First-AID

first'— aid' *adj.* emergency treatment for injury, etc.,
before regular medical care is available
—Merriam Webster's Collegiate Dictionary

There's not a hospital in America that is fully prepared to deal with the effects of a wide-scale disaster in which hundreds if not thousands of people would need urgent care. To staff and equip a medical facility to do so full time would quickly cause bankruptcy under normal operating conditions. In order to combat the guaranteed shortage of health care personnel after a major emergency, there is an effort by some authorities to train civilian volunteers in a quick course on medical needs to ease the burden on regular health professionals. While this is a smart move and would greatly release physicians and nurses from some of the more mundane tasks of patient care, a weekend crash course in disaster medicine can only accomplish so much. Have you ever spent time twiddling your thumbs in a hospital emergency waiting room under normal, calm conditions?

Do yourself, your family, and your community a favor by enrolling in a basic first-aid and CPR course. Call your local community college, fire station, hospital, CERT (Community Emergency Response Team) program, or the Red Cross extension in your area today to learn the basic skills necessary to support life when accidents happen or health-related emergencies fall into your lap. Many basic first-aid and CPR courses last a day or two at most and give you a condensed version on what to expect and how to deal with rudimentary injuries and health issues.

For those who wish to know more, Wilderness First Responder (WFR) courses are taught that go well beyond a standard first-aid course and are extremely handy when you're beyond traditional medical care, such as in the wilderness or after a disaster when emergency services may be slow to respond. Many community colleges also offer Emergency Medical Technician (EMT) training for a more advanced look at the human body and how it can be repaired. EMT courses, while worth their weight in gold, rely heavily on transportation to a regular medical facility and technical goodies beyond the scope of ordinary folks. Many ambulance and fire-fighting crews also have a paramedic onboard for even more advanced life-support options. The human body is what you're trying to keep alive, yet it's amazing how little survival students and even survival instructors know about human physiology. The more you know about the human body and how to patch it back together, the better off you may be after a crisis.

Home Sweet Home?

According to a dated, 1985 version of the book *Family Safety and First Aid,* put out by Readers Digest, about 9 million Americans each year called a physician to deal with an injury sustained in their home. Within a twenty-four hour period, 63,000 people cut, bruised, scalded, poisoned, or burned themselves while in the comfort of their own homes. More than twenty years later, this number has probably doubled or tripled if not more. Most of these accidents could have been prevented by simply paying attention, or by correcting the potential causes of accidents in the first place.

What do you think would happen to these statistical numbers after an emergency? How would they be affected if people were forced to rely on unfamiliar disaster supplies for a number of days or weeks? There can be little doubt that even a well-stocked family has not taken the time to learn how to use their supplies on a sunny pleasant day in the backyard let alone when all hell is breaking loose environmentally and otherwise.

If your home is an accident waiting to happen, it ain't gonna get any better under extreme stress. Get your ducks in a row by making needed repairs and upgrades as soon as possible for the safety and convenience of your family.

The Creepin' Crud and You

"WE DON'T KNOW THE TIMING OF THE NEXT PANDEMIC, HOW SEVERE IT WILL BE. WE DON'T KNOW WHAT DRUGS WILL WORK. WE DON'T HAVE A VACCINE, YET WE ARE TELLING EVERYONE TO PREPARE FOR A PANDEMIC. IT'S TRICKY . . . THIS IS SCARY AND WE DON'T KNOW . . . THAT'S THE MESSAGE."
—DICK THOMPSON, WORLD HEALTH ORGANIZATION (WHO)

Despite annual vaccinations, run-of-the-mill influenza in the United States kills more than 36,000 people and lands 200,000 more in hospitals each year. In addition to the body count, influenza is annually responsible for a total cost of over $10 billion in the United States alone.

There are very nasty things floating around the planet such as SARS and the avian flu (bird flu). Apparently forgetting about the sinking of the continents Lemuria and Atlantis, Secretary Michael Chertoff of the Department of Homeland

Security said, "The avian flu bears the potential for societal disruption of unprecedented proportion." According to the Centers for Disease Control (CDC), a pandemic, or worldwide outbreak of a new influenza virus, could make the above paragraph look like a fart in the wind. A flu pandemic in this day and age would utterly overwhelm this country's health and medical capabilities, with effects, to quote the CDC, "potentially resulting in hundreds of thousands of deaths, millions of hospitalizations, and hundreds of billions of dollars in direct and indirect costs." Pandemics

have occurred throughout history. The last three occurred in 1918 (40 million dead), 1957 (2 million dead), and 1968 (1 million dead) worldwide. The Spanish influenza epidemic of 1918 has been studied by health professionals over and over again for clues on how to better mitigate a modern-day pandemic, and unfortunately, it has left more questions than answers.

According to the CDC, the next pandemic "is likely to come in waves, each lasting months, and pass through communities of all sizes across the nation and world. While a pandemic will not damage power lines, banks or computer networks, it will ultimately threaten all critical infrastructure by removing essential personnel from the workplace for weeks or months." A worst-case scenario pandemic plan from the CDC involves the general public staying in their homes; no school, no shopping, no nothing, for up to three months. Do you have the supplies, skills, and psychological fortitude to stay in your home for three months? You sure would have time to put a dent in that favorite book you've been wanting to read (or write!).

REDUCING THE SPREAD OF THE FLU FROM YOU

According to the CDC and common sense, an infection carried by one person can be transmitted to dozens, even hundreds of other people. Because of this fact, your action or lack of in mitigating the spread of disease is perhaps the most important part of preparing for a pandemic outbreak. If you or one of your family members gets the flu, take the necessary steps to prevent it from spreading to others. Be prepared to follow public health recommendations that may include limiting attendance at public gatherings and travel for several days, weeks, or months. The obvious end result of this is to have the necessary emergency supplies in your home to deal with isolation for a long time. Fear mongering? Paranoia? Months at home you say? Yep. And it's not my opinion. All of the information in the above paragraph was pulled from the Centers for Disease Control Web site about a potential influenza (flu) pandemic.

STUFF YOU CAN DO TO AVOID THE FLU

- Stay healthy. Eat right, exercise, and limit bad habits, such as smoking, drinking alcohol, and having too much stress.
- Wash your hands frequently with soap and water.
- Liberally use waterless hand sanitizers.
- Cover your nose and mouth with a tissue if you cough or sneeze.
- Safely dispose of your tissues in a wastebasket.
- Cough or sneeze into your upper sleeve if you don't have a tissue.
- Wash your hands after coughing or sneezing or use a waterless hand sanitizer.
- Avoid touching your eyes, nose, and mouth.
- Avoid close contact with others who are ill. Take precautions and wear a medical mask or quality dust mask purchased from a hardware store if necessary.
- Stay home if you're sick.
- Purchase several copies of this book to give to friends and family.
- Pay attention, use common sense around others, and maintain a positive attitude. After all, the true nature of all disease is "dis-ease."

Our little hamlet has already done a body count, so to speak, on how many corpses the county could handle at once due to a flu pandemic by compiling information on available space from local hospitals and morgues. No doubt your town or city has done likewise although you haven't heard anything about it—which is not necessarily a bad thing.

There are researchers who study not just diseases, but how human minds and emotions will react to diseases when they threaten to manifest themselves as full-blown epidemics, and the results are not pretty. The first thing researchers learned is that the mob is indeed fickle, and people either act irrationally by rushing to hospitals before they have symptoms or stay home even when they are extremely ill and need treatment. And, of course, chaos breeds more chaos, so the more "freaked" people become after an outbreak, the more difficult the disease is to contain. This irrational behavior spawned by a lack of prevention training could hit America's pocketbook hard. Estimates from the Congressional Budget Office put the potential costs of a flu pandemic at $675 billion. And, as proof of our nation's half-assed preparedness training for the public, half of this cost will be because of fear and confusion! How much preparedness training could the American people get for a little over $337 billion? We have some of the best-trained disaster response personnel in the world, but the general populace—forget about it!

> **WE HAVE BECOME FAMOUS FOR EXPERTLY PICKING UP THE PIECES OF THE SMASHED LAMP INSTEAD OF REALIZING IT WAS TOO CLOSE TO THE EDGE OF THE TABLE TO BEGIN WITH.**

Now, the chances are very high that if you're reading this book, you are not a dyed-in-the-wool "sheeple" (people + sheep = sheeple). You have the intelligence and foresight to recognize what the government apparently has not, that strength and independence come from the ground up, and that the best disaster plan is to have everyone empowered, prepared, and on the same page—not just the wonderful agencies who are expected to mop up the mess after the fact. We have become famous for expertly picking up the pieces of the smashed lamp instead of realizing it was too close to the edge of the table to begin with. Fortunately, you have the choice to prepare as you want for the unexpected, and it's you who should ultimately prepare for the safety and welfare of your family, not the government. If you need a refresher on the concept of self-reliance, flip back to the first part of the book.

Although I'm a wilderness EMT, I'm not about to cut and paste together a chapter on emergency first aid. It's not my forte, although I know a lot about human physiology and its repair, and the psychological nuances that influence it. What I do want to cover in this chapter are basic remedies and preventions for some of the more common problems that may be experienced during and after a compromising situation. Trials such as nausea, diarrhea, blisters, or burns will be common for a population that is suddenly forced to whip out and use their survival supplies under stress. I repeat, take a qualified class on first aid with a known health care provider in your area. Do it soon—don't put it off and have to learn the hard way when all hell breaks loose.

Open Wounds

Flesh wounds will be a very common injury during a disaster. There are many types of wounds, from incisions and scrapes to puncture wounds and full-on amputations. Some require specialized treatment, yet there are more similarities than differences when the protection of the skin is breached.

Control the Bleeding

Wounds that bleed freely must be controlled. The following guidelines should be used when you need to prevent excessive bleeding. *Protect yourself from blood and body fluids at all times!*

1 If you have the time, wash your hands with soap and water before caring for a wound.

2 Put on latex gloves to protect yourself from bloodborne infections and body fluids. These can be improvised from plastic bags or other nonpermeable membranes.

3 Have the patients sit or lie down. If large amounts of blood have been lost, they will experience shock, so keep them warm and have them lie on their back and elevate their legs nine to twelve inches. Even small wounds can cause people to become nauseous, dizzy, or faint, so play it safe and get them on the ground.

4 Expose the wound and apply direct, even pressure over the entire wound area with a clean dressing or cloth for five to ten minutes or longer until the bleeding has stopped. Bleeding from an extremity such as an arm or leg can be slowed by elevating the limb above the heart while applying the pressure. If the bleeding continues after ten or twelve minutes, apply greater pressure over a greater area of the wound or use a pressure dressing, which is nothing more than tightly tying thick dressing materials over the wound site using bandaging material such as a strip of fabric or clothing. If using a pressure bandage, don't tie it so tightly that you reduce the circulation in the rest of the limb. If the limb feels colder or turns a blueish color, loosen the bandage. If the dressing material that was used on top of the wound is removed too quickly in order to clean the wound, it may pull away the blood clots that have stopped the bleeding. Use discretion and seek medical care for large wounds.

Cleaning and Caring for the Wound

The next step in proper wound care is to properly clean and bandage the wound to prevent infection and promote proper healing. While wounds should be cleaned and kept as clean as possible, I have pushed the envelope many times over the years on back-country field courses. As I go barefoot most of the time, I've lost count of how many superficial wounds I've had on my feet with which I've marched through miles of filthy water and dirt for several days with no other initial care than washing off the blood in the river. I don't bandage or cover the wounds as it would fall off anyway due to environmental circumstances. In each incident the wound healed fine. I'm not recommending that you blow off treating your wounds, yet some wounds, especially the superficial kind, can go through hard times with a minimum of care and be OK. Don't psych yourself out that you'll lose your arm or a leg because you can't keep a wound spic-and-span clean.

The following guidelines for the treatment and care of generalized wounds are standard practice and can prevent many simple mishaps from growing into a major infection problem.

Basic Wound Care

Shallow Wounds

1 Clean the wound and the surrounding area thoroughly with soap and water. This may restart bleeding but it needs to be done. Smaller wounds should be encouraged to bleed at first to flush out potential debris that may be in the wound itself.

2 Cover the wound with a sterile or clean dressing and bandage in place. Although I rarely do so myself, you can use a thin layer of antibiotic ointment on the cleaned wound before covering with the dressing.

3 Inspect your wound(s) for infection morning and evening for the first few days and clean and change bandages as needed.

Deeper Wounds

Deeper wounds will need to be "irrigated" as part of their cleaning ritual. Irrigation involves forcefully squirting potable water into the wound itself to wash out pieces of dirt, sand, metal flakes, blood clots, tissue or anything else that will start an infection. (Note: See the water disinfection methods starting on page 161 for treating nonpotable water. Don't use full-strength topical disinfectants such as iodine or povidone-iodine in the wound itself as they may damage the tissue and delay healing. Instead, use them to disinfect the skin around the wound. A diluted povidone-iodine solution using ten to twenty parts clean water can be used directly on the wound if desired.)

You'll need to spread some wounds open to reach their depths for proper irrigation. Protect your eyes and mouth when irrigating wounds as things can get messy. Many first-aid kits have a large-diameter syringe that can be filled with fluid for this purpose. You can easily improvise an irrigation option from a clean zipper-lock freezer bag or other baggie although it will not be as effective as a syringe. Fill the baggie with the disinfected solution and use a needle sterilized with a flame to pop a small hole into one of the corners of the baggie. Squeeze the baggie as necessary to obtain as much of a forceful spray as possible. Any chunks of foreign matter that remain will need to be wiped out or picked out with sterilized tweezers.

Small, clean wounds can be closed with tape or butterfly bandages if the edges can be pulled together. Deeper, larger wounds can be treated in the same manner but may need advanced medical care. Large gaping wounds should be cleaned the best that you can, packed with sterile dressings, and carefully bandaged until the person can receive proper medical care.

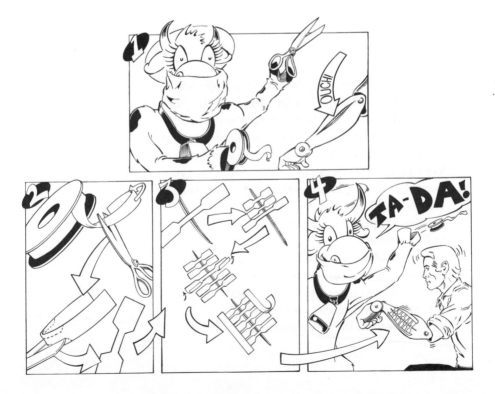

Inspect the wound(s) for infection morning and evening for the first few days and clean and change bandages as needed.

Infection

Any breach in the skin provides an area for possible infection. Deep or large wounds that are difficult to clean and keep clean are the most susceptible to infection but even superficial surface abrasions can become infected. Some of the following signs will be experienced in a wound without an infection but will be much more pronounced when infected. The pain from most soft tissue injuries begins to subside after two or three days. If the pain continues or increases, the wound is infected.

Signs of Infection

⊃ Redness surrounding or spreading from the wound. In more advanced cases of infection, a "red line(s)" or streak(s) may travel from the wound to the heart. (I've had more than one friend involved in the art of brain-tanning deer hides whose small cuts on their hands became open doors to infection from nasty funk from the hides. In each case, they required large doses of intravenous antibiotics at the local hospital to kill the infection.)
⊃ Increased pain and tenderness
⊃ Swelling
⊃ Pus. Pus can be off-white to light green, pinkish, or even straw-colored or clear and drain directly from the infected wound or collect in an abscess or boil under the skin. The discharged pus may or may not smell. Abscesses will eventually form a whitehead like a pimple (which can be accelerated by hot compresses or soaking in hot water) and should then be drained and kept clean
⊃ Swollen lymph nodes, usually whichever is closest to the wound
⊃ Limitation of motion due to swelling and pain
⊃ Persistent, above-normal oral body temperature
⊃ Chills and fever (strong indications that the infection has spread into the blood and can become life threatening)

Dealing with a Wound Infection

1 Wash hands with soap and water and clean the surrounding skin area with a topical disinfectant.

2 If not already opened, open the wound gently using a sterile object to allow the buildup of pus to drain. Soaking the wound in warm water beforehand will help the wound drain more easily by dissolving the crusty serum and pus that sometimes keeps a wound closed. Pus can form in multiple pockets deep within a wound so inspect it to see if there are others that need to be drained other than the obvious. It's very important that infected wounds be allowed to properly drain. As long as an infection is present, don't allow the wound to close on its own. This can be accomplished by inserting a piece of dry, sterile gauze into the wound, which should be changed whenever the dressing is changed.

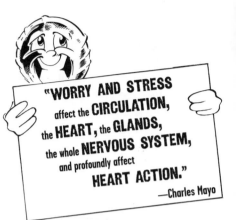

> "WORRY AND STRESS affect the CIRCULATION, the HEART, the GLANDS, the whole NERVOUS SYSTEM, and profoundly affect HEART ACTION."
> —Charles Mayo

3 Soak the wound in warm, disinfected water four times per day for twenty to thirty minutes, with or without a small amount of added povidone-iodine. The warm water also helps in the healing process as the heat dilates the blood vessels, bringing more blood to the infected area.

4 After soaking, carefully dry the affected area and change the dressings as often as required to keep them clean and dry.

5 Give over-the-counter pain medications if needed such as ibuprofen, aspirin, or acetaminophen. Aspirin is a blood thinner so use with caution.

6 For advanced infections, the use of antibiotics will most likely be required. Important Note: Most antibiotics are available by prescription only and, like any other drug, have a shelf life. Consult with your family physician about having a ready supply of topical antibiotics for a disaster scenario in which medical response may be severely limited or delayed. People traveling to remote countries often take with them a doctor-prescribed supply of oral antibiotics due to meager resources or to deal with just-in-case scenarios.

Burns

Burns will also be a very common injury due to the flourishing use of alternative lighting devices and the general population's renewed reliance on fire for heating and cooking. Thanks to gestapo-like federal forest regulations regarding fire use and the neutered, unrealistic views of banning campfires in the back country by gear-addicted, politically correct outdoor companies, even well-seasoned outdoorsmen and women are hopelessly clueless about the creation, use, and extinguishing of fire. Can you imagine the burn injury rate if every household needed to use fire to get their needs met as was done for thousands of years?

Burn Classifications

There are three types or classifications of burns, *first degree, second degree,* and *third degree.* In a first-degree burn, the outer layer or epidermis is affected and the skin appears mildly red, swollen, and painful, but no blisters are formed. Almost everyone has experienced this in the form of a common sunburn. Second-degree burns pass through the epidermis and extend into the dermis or secondary layer of skin. The pain and swelling is moderate and blisters are present. Both of these burns are classified as partial-thickness burns. Third-degree burns reach into the underlying fat and muscle tissue of the body and are termed full-thickness burns. The skin appears charred and leathery, is numb to the touch from the burn victim's standpoint, and for all intents and purposes is "dead." Much like a piece of wood in a fire, a single burn upon the body can exhibit characteristics of all three burn classifications.

    How much of the body was burned, where the burn(s) occurred, and whether the burns are partial or full thickness will determine how the patient is treated and what their odds for survival are. Burns to the face, neck, hands, feet, genitalia, and buttocks are serious. Facial burns can cause serious damage to the respiratory tract and compromise breathing. Burns completely encircling the body (circumferential burn) can have a tourniquet effect on the body. I won't go into the details for major burns or burns that involve much of the body, as people with these burns will need hospitalization if they are to survive. With no hospitalization they will most likely die from "burn shock" caused by damaged capillaries allowing blood serum to leak into the burned tissue. This fluid loss reduces the blood volume of the body and rapidly causes shock just like a major bleeding incident. People with severe burns require massive amounts of fluids to survive, which must usually be given intravenously. *Important! All serious burns will need advanced medical care as soon as possible!*

Dealing with a Burn

Immediately STOP the burning! Pour cold water over the burned area as quickly as possible and remove burned clothing. Clothing and jewelry around the burn should be removed before swelling takes place. To lesson the pain, smaller, partial-thickness burns will benefit from "cold" such as a towel soaked in ice water or the immersion of the burn into clean, cold water. Like any other open wound, clean the burn of all debris, keep it clean, and prevent blisters from rupturing.

After cleaning and drying the burn, most medical manuals recommend covering all second-degree burns and some third-degree burns with a thin layer of antibiotic ointment. Cover the wound with a clean or sterile nonstick dressing and bandage. If the burn is wet or oozes, wash the area daily with clean warm water, dry, and reapply a new dressing and bandage. For most third-degree burns, it's recommended that you cover the area with a dry, sterile, or at least clean, dressing. Ibuprofen is probably the best over-the-counter remedy for the pain associated with the burn. Burn victims will be dehydrated and should be encouraged to drink extra water although, as indicated above, advanced injuries will require intravenous fluids. Serious burn victims should be transported to the nearest medical facility for advanced care.

Although rarely mentioned in medical manuals, pure honey is amazing when applied topically to burns. Use only quality honey, not the cheap stuff cut with corn syrup. In this case the honey is used similar to the antibiotic ointment mentioned above. After cleaning the burn, apply honey and then a clean dressing, bandaged in place.

Dreadful Diarrhea

Diarrhea is caused by a number of variables that will be all too common in survival land. Intestinal infections from poorly disinfected water, food poisoning from eating spoiled stored food or from sampling weird food options, food sensitivities and allergies of family members that you never knew had an allergy to powdered milk, and plain old stress can all cause the screaming turkey trots.

There are two main types of diarrhea. One is the less serious and more common *"traveler's diarrhea."* The other is the more invasive *bacterial diarrhea*. The difference in their effects is that bacterial diarrhea will have the added gifts of chills and fever, along with blood, obvious pus, or mucous in the stool. This type of diarrhea is very serious and will need to be treated with antimicrobial medication. Antidiarrheal medications such as Pepto-Bismol or Imodium AD should NOT be used with bacterial diarrhea as they could prolong the illness. Affected people under three years old, over sixty-five, who are pregnant, or who have had severe diarrhea for more than forty-eight to seventy-two hours with abdominal tenderness along with the above added symptoms should seek medical care as soon as possible.

Traveler's diarrhea caused by critters, usually *E.coli* bacteria, has an incubation period of twelve to forty eight hours and lasts from two to five days. Besides copious, horrid-smelling watery squirts, the symptoms of abdominal stress, obnoxious bowel sounds, and cramps are unmistakable to most everyone. Besides being a major bummer, severe diarrhea (categorized as ten bowel movements per day or more) and the severe dehydration it causes can kill very young, very old, or weaker family members, especially when visiting the hospital might be dubious at best after a calamity.

"DOCTORS prescribe MEDI-CINE of which they KNOW LIT-TLE, to cure DISEASES of which they KNOW LESS, in human beings of which they KNOW NOTHING."
—Voltaire

Treatment for Traveler's Diarrhea

The replacement of fluids and electrolytes (sodium and potassium) is of prime impor-tance to all victims of diarrhea. Remember to check your pee for adequate hydration levels (urine should be clear, frequent, and copious) and use the homemade elec-trolyte replacement solution as needed as mentioned on page 143. Broths, soups, and fruit juices can also be consumed. To keep up with the dehydrating effects of diarrhea, you may need to drink several quarts of fluid each day. It may also help to avoid milk products and meats for forty-eight hours afterward as well as diuretics such as coffee.

Antidiarrheal medications (Pepto-Bismol, Imodium AD, or Lomotil) vary in their potency and effectiveness person by person. Some medical professionals feel that their use prolongs diarrhea, even traveler's diarrhea. They should be used at your discretion for controlling painful cramps or during circumstances that are far more dangerous or uncomfortable than diarrhea itself, such as needing to stay in a bath-roomless basement during a tornado or having to pile into an evacuation bus with dozens of other victims. Prolonged, moderate diarrhea caused by stress and fear (irritable colon syndrome) is best treated by hydration and electrolyte replacement, reassuring and comforting the person, and, of course, dealing with and eliminating the cause of the stress if possible.

Constipation

On the other end of the spectrum, survival stresses such as the consumption of monotonous, "different," stored survival foods, dehydration, erratic schedules, and

STAPHYLOCOCCAL ENTERITIS: IT'S WHAT'S (WAS) FOR DINNER

Staphylococcal Enteritis bacteria are present on nearly half of the population's hands on a good day, let alone during a survival situation, thus the bacteria commonly contaminate foods during hands-on preparation. Any food can become contaminated with the bacteria but they are more commonly a problem in milk products and other food such as mayonnaise and meats. Staphylococcal toxin is produced when contaminated food goes without refrigeration for several hours (such as during a power outage), causing the toxin to multiply. Once it's present, even boiling the food doesn't kill the toxin. Only refrigeration or consumption of food immediately after it's prepared can prevent this bug and others like it from doing their thing. Cramps, diarrhea, and sometimes vomiting begin within one to six hours after eating the suspect food and last until the food is emptied from the body, usually six hours. I mention it here, as it could be a common dinner guest at the onset of any power-failure-related emergency.

stress in general can cause constipation, which is more the passing of hard, dry stools rather than the frequency of a person's bowel movement. Different people have different bowel movement schedules. Some people poop three times a day and others poop once every three days. Only you know when your schedule is off.

I have had more than one student become constipated on a stressful field course and not have a bowel movement for three days or more. A change in diet, dehydration, and the low-level stress of being at the mercy of a freaky guy in the woods takes its toll on their colon and they "lock up," so to speak. If the problem doesn't take care of itself in the field when they eventually get used to the routine and settle down, once back in the comfort of their own homes, they gleefully give birth to the mother lode.

Constipation Cure

Most constipation can be remedied with an adequate fluid intake coupled with consuming high-moisture (fruits) and high-fiber foods such as bran cereals. Simply calming down and relaxing can do wonders for your colon as well as your psyche. Although in most circumstances laxatives will be unnecessary, the most effective and safest is Milk of Magnesia.

Mr. Jelly Finger: Fun with Fecal Compaction

Ignore the signs and symptoms of constipation and you'll be forced to get to know one of your family members better than should be humanly allowed. When one

STEEEERETCH!

ignores the need to defecate for whatever reason—having to poop in a weird potty, in a weird place, with a bunch of other weirdos, such as in a public shelter after a disaster— normal bowel reflexes might cease to function and allow fecal matter to pile up and get hard in the rectum. Add the previous pitfalls of dehydration, strange food, and stress to the problem, and fecal compaction can quickly become a reality.

According to medical books, the best way to determine if someone has fecal compaction is to insert a gloved, lubricated finger into the rectum. If the finger runs into a brick wall, so to speak, the hardened fecal matter must be removed. This is best done by breaking up the fecal matter and removing the pieces as carefully as possible to avoid damaging the rectal and anal tissues. If the tissue is torn during the extraction, and subsequent bowel movements are painful, the person should eat a lower-fiber diet of soups and such, temporarily, while consuming one tablespoon of mineral oil two times per day to lubricate the stool and reduce pain. (Note: Prolonged diets of low-fiber foods will create constipation and you'll start the fun all over again. Mineral oil is a lubricant, not a laxative.) See how much easier and pleasant it is to drink your water and go to the bathroom when you have to?

Upset Stomach, Nausea, and Vomiting

"DUDE, IF YOU'RE GONNA HURL, HURL IN THIS."
—GARTH OFFERING NAUSEOUS FRIEND A SMALL PAPER CUP IN *WAYNE'S WORLD*, THE MOVIE

Vomiting can be a sign of many issues ranging from motion sickness and head injuries to pregnancy, hyperthermia, or stumbling across a decomposing corpse. When you puke, you lose water, not to mention breakfast. If you keep puking, you'll continue to lose water (until the alcoholic dry heaves) long after breakfast has hit the pavement. Nausea and vomiting will be one of the side effects of drinking water that wasn't completely disinfected. Many waterborne pathogens that enter your system require treatment with drugs; others, although the effects are hell, will seem to go away on their own, albeit with part of your intestines, or so it would seem.

An unconscious person vomiting is at risk of asphyxiation; just ask John Bonham and many other rockers. Even at the expense of a possible spinal injury, the patient must be carefully rolled on their side with their head lowered to allow the vomit to clear the airway.

Prolonged vomiting is serious and the person should immediately be taken to a hospital. Similar to diarrhea, the replacement of lost water and electrolytes are all-important to the healing process. When the patient is finally able to keep stuff down, feed them bland foods, preferably liquids such as soups for the next day.

Most people are able to keep down about a teaspoon of water every twenty minutes, so keep a medicine cup and timer or watch handy.

Bogus Blisters

Blisters, although seemingly innocent, can stop the foot-bound traveler in his or her bloody tracks. After a major disaster, many forms of transportation will be unable to operate due to clogged roads, debris, or a lack of fuel. You will be "hoofing it" to get from place to place, and you may very well be doing so in fashionable shoes created by people who wouldn't walk more than fifty feet wearing their own creation.

Advanced blisters are painfully crippling and can take days to properly heal. Ruptured blisters are an invitation for infection, especially during the gnarly conditions present after a catastrophe. Imagine being a Hurricane Katrina survivor with open blisters walking knee-deep in the toxic goo that was once called water. Bad idea and a set-up for an infection that left unattended could easily mature into a life-threatening condition.

Before the Blister

Blisters are caused by excessive friction and result in a buildup of fluid beneath the skin. They most commonly manifest themselves on the heels or toes, but I've seen them happen all over the feet, even on top. New boots or shoes are notorious for causing blisters. All survival footwear should be thoroughly broken in, yet still be in great shape, not worn out. The infant blister will first appear as a hot spot on the foot, and this is the easiest time to deal with it. Stop, take off your shoes, dry out your socks if possible, and apply a piece of first-aid tape, duct tape, "second skin," or adhesive felt (moleskin) over the hot spot. Make sure to cover a larger area than necessary so the dressing doesn't peel off. Don't use a regular bandage over a hot spot as the nonadherent pad will continue to rub.

I often use duct tape for this purpose but it should be used with caution as it doesn't breathe. If left on for several hours and hurriedly pulled off, the weakened, moist skin underneath can easily tear. The need is to dry the foot out (and change your socks if you have a clean dry pair) and stop the rubbing of the affected area. In the outdoors, I've even applied pieces of bark or leaves over hot spots with positive results.

Since I go barefoot most of the time, when I do wear sandals, I pretape my heels with duct tape *before* donning my sandals. I know that the sides and tops of my feet are particularly sensitive to friction as they rarely have anything in contact with them.

Many people use two pairs of socks within their boots to avoid blisters. The thinner liner sock next to the foot will take much of the friction when walking. As in all things, an ounce of prevention will save you a lot of future pain and misery.

After the Blister

Once a blister manifests, you can create a pad from moleskin or some other material that is built-up with a cutout for the blister in the middle, like a donut. This keeps the pressure away from the blister itself.

Unbroken Blisters

If you're certain you can eliminate all pressure from the affected area, such as being able to lounge around your home barefoot for several days, don't pop the blister; let it heal naturally. If this isn't an option, and the blisters are painful, wash the area with soap and water, sterilize a needle with a lighter or match flame, and pop the blister around its edge in several places and gently push out the fluid. Leave the top flap of skin over the blister intact and place a nonstick bandage over the area.

Broken Blisters

Wash the area with soap and water. Broken blisters can have debris such as dirt or sand under the affected area that needs to be cleaned out. If necessary, gently cut off the flap of skin over the top of the blister to clean it out. Cover the blister with a sterile nonstick pad and then cover this with tape or moleskin. Watch for signs of infection (redness and tenderness extending beyond the blister, discolored blister fluid, or pus) each day.

The Basic First-Aid Kit

There is no one portable first-aid kit that will cover all of your needs, and there is perhaps no better way to start an argument between otherwise good-natured and intelligent people than trading opinions about what to carry in a first-aid kit. Yet compiling a good first-aid kit is basic and relevant for every household on earth. Your kit should reflect the amount of first-aid training your family has. A family comprised of a physician and nurse might have a very elaborate first-aid kit, as they have the training and the know-how to use it. We greenhorns will have far fewer bells and whistles, yet there's no reason we have to sit on the bench and watch the action happen. Like the contents of a survival kit, the contents of your family's first-aid kit will reflect many variables and should be custom-made to conform to your family's situation. Variables such as bulk, weight, cost, the number of people, and the proposed duration of your emergency will all factor in. Some items are staples, such as bandages and triple antibiotic ointment. If you live with a diabetic or someone on treatment for another medical condition, tailor your kit to reflect such a reality. One-size-fits-all first-aid kits are just as mythological as one-size-fits-all survival kits. Even if you live down the street from a hospital, don't assume it will be your saving grace after a catastrophe.

The following list, while solid for many first-aid needs, simply reflects a foundation upon which to build your custom kit. Be self-reliant and dare to think for yourself. The below supplies may be all you need, maybe even less. Although it seems like a lot of stuff to carry, most of it is very small in volume and weight. Be sure to pack the items separately in a well-marked pouch stating "First Aid." Don't throw the items into a huge jumble along with shampoo, deodorant, and breath mints. I have the majority of my first-aid items double-sealed in two zipper-lock freezer bags to keep the contents dry. The clear plastic makes it easy to locate certain items before opening the seal. Your first-aid container should be waterproof, highly visible, simple to open and use, and yet be rugged enough to protect its precious contents.

Foundational, Portable First-aid Kit Contents

(Important Note: The amount of medications and bandages will need to be increased for families. Stay-at-home kits can be larger but make sure to have a portable version for hitting the road.)

- Latex gloves—5 pair
- Bandages— small, medium, and large—10 or more of each
- Sterile gauze pads, 4-inch squares—6 or more
- Nonadherent gauze pads—6 or more
- Butterfly strips—10 or more
- First-aid tape, 2-inch width—one roll
- Kling wrap (self-adhering roller bandage)—one roll
- Elastic bandage, 3-inch width—one roll
- Moleskin (for blisters), 4-inch squares—4 or more
- Safety pins—5 to 10
- Irrigation syringe, 20 cc—one
- Triple antibiotic ointment—one tube

- ➲ Topical antiseptic towelettes—10 or more
- ➲ Topical anesthetic cream—one tube or pads
- ➲ One- to four-ounce bottle of povidone-iodine 10%
- ➲ Pain and anti-inflammatory medications, 50 tablets or more of each: acetaminophen tablets (Tylenol) 325 mg; ibuprofen tablets and aspirin, 200 mg. (*Special note about pain relievers:* In the case of serious body trauma, you will want the biggest, baddest pain relievers on the block. Many outdoor expeditions don't mess around with the realties of devastating mechanical injuries and remote locations. They typically carry Tylenol III, codeine, meperidine, and/or morphine. Check into the legalities of obtaining these and having them in your possession. Talk to your family physician, tell them your intention, and see what they recommend.)
- ➲ Small bar of antibacterial soap or waterless hand-sanitizer packets
- ➲ Decongestant—10 or more tablets
- ➲ Antihistamine—20 or more tablets
- ➲ Antacids—10 or more tablets
- ➲ Hydrocortisone cream—one small tube
- ➲ Antidiarrheal tablets—10 or more
- ➲ Laxative tablets—10 or more
- ➲ Cough drops—10 or more
- ➲ Sunscreen—one small tube
- ➲ Lip balm with sunscreen—one tube
- ➲ Insect repellent—one small tube or towelettes
- ➲ Powdered electrolyte replacement solution—4 to 6 single-use packets
- ➲ Small notebook and pencil (wrap duct tape around pencil)
- ➲ Tweezers—one pair
- ➲ Small scissors—one pair
- ➲ One small flashlight
- ➲ Scalpel with blades, a few single-edged razor blades, and/or a small, very sharp knife
- ➲ Matches or lighter
- ➲ One large needle
- ➲ One bandana
- ➲ Motion sickness tablets, optional
- ➲ Antibiotics (Note: As with the big guns of pain relief, antibiotics such as penicillin will need to be pre-

scribed by a physician. Some family members may have serious allergies to several types of antibiotics. Talk with your family physician about your intention.)
- ⊃ Good first-aid book
- ⊃ A positive attitude and a little luck

SUPER SIMPLE SUMMARY

- ⊃ After a major disaster, assume that all hospitals in the area will be overwhelmed.
- ⊃ Every family member of age should enroll in a basic first-aid and CPR class from a nearby provider as soon as possible. Wilderness First Responder (WFR) and Emergency Medical Technician (EMT) courses are also available for those who want to learn more.
- ⊃ The average American home is the site of millions of medical emergencies every year, many of which can be avoided by paying attention and initiating home repairs or upgrades.
- ⊃ Despite annual vaccinations, influenza in the U.S. kills more than 36,000 people and causes another 200,000 to enter hospitals each year.
- ⊃ According to the Centers for Disease Control, having another flu pandemic is simply a matter of time.
- ⊃ One person can transmit the flu to dozens and even hundreds of other people. Use basic safe-hygiene skills, such as containing sneezes and coughs, washing hands, avoiding touching your nose, eyes, and mouth, and staying home if you are ill. Stay healthy by eating right, exercising, and keeping a positive outlook about life.
- ⊃ The possibilities of mass chaos during a pandemic are very real, as well as the realities of limited travel opportunities for buying needed supplies. Keep your family prepared with what they need to survive without outside assistance.
- ⊃ Wounds will be very common after a disaster. Ensure precautions against body fluids and bloodborne pathogens and stop the bleeding, clean the wound,

and dress with a clean or sterile dressing and bandage to minimize infection.

➲ Any wound can become infected. Common signs of infection are redness, swelling, increased pain and tenderness, pus, swollen lymph nodes, elevated temperature, and chills and fever for advanced infections.

➲ Infected, pus-filled wounds must be allowed to drain and should not be allowed to reseal when the infection is still present. Soak the wound in warm, disinfected water four times per day for twenty to thirty minutes, as the warm water helps in the healing process. After soaking, carefully dry the affected area and change the dressings as often as required to keep them clean and dry. Over-the-counter pain medications can be given if needed.

➲ Burns will be very common as people use their disaster supplies. STOP the burning, clean the burn of all debris, keep it clean, and prevent blisters from rupturing. Cover the burn with a thin layer of antibiotic ointment and then a clean or sterile nonstick dressing and bandage. Give over-the-counter ibuprofen for the pain. Burn victims will be dehydrated and should be encouraged to drink extra water.

➲ People with severe burns require large amounts of fluids to survive, which must usually be given intravenously. *All serious burns will need advanced medical care as soon as possible!*

➲ Diarrhea may be common after an emergency. There are two types of diarrhea, the less serious and more common "traveler's diarrhea" and the other, more invasive bacterial diarrhea. The latter is very serious and will require advanced medical care.

➲ *The replacement of fluids and electrolytes (sodium and potassium) is of prime importance to all victims of diarrhea.*

➲ Antidiarrheal medications such as Pepto-Bismol, Imodium AD, or Lomotil should be used with discretion for controlling painful cramps or during circumstances that are far more dangerous or uncomfortable than the diarrhea itself.

➲ Due to stress and an irregular diet, constipation is possible. Most constipation can be remedied with an adequate fluid intake coupled with consuming high-moisture (fruits) and high-fiber (bran cereal) foods. Calming down and relaxing can help as well. Although mostly unnecessary if the above is followed, the most effective and safest laxative is Milk of Magnesia.

➲ Go to the bathroom when you need to, stay hydrated, and eat healthy to avoid fecal compaction.

➲ Nausea and vomiting are common side effects from drinking nondisinfected water. The replacement of lost water and electrolytes are all-important to the healing process. When possible, feed the victim bland foods, preferably liquids such as soups, for the next day.

➲ Serious blisters caused from repetitive rubbing can be very painful and impede foot travel. Stop the rubbing, keep feet dry, change socks, and deal with hot spots before they mature into blisters. Keep blisters clean and watch open blisters for possible infection.

➲ All families should compile and have ready a portable first-aid kit. What you choose to carry in a first-aid kit is dependent upon your family, the duration of your emergency, cost, weight, volume, and other variables.

➲ First-aid containers should be waterproof, highly visible, simple to open and use, and yet be rugged enough to protect their contents.

20

Sensibly SERIOUS SELF-DEFENSE

"Though defensive violence will always be 'a sad necessity' in the eyes of men of principle, it would be still more unfortunate if wrongdoers should dominate just men."

—St. Augustine

This book is based upon the virtues of taking responsibility for your actions and whether or not you choose to actively prepare for an emergency. Much like opinions about knives in a wilderness survival context (how big, how many, what type of steel for the blade, etc. ad nauseam), the very nature of "self-defense" has strong supporters on both sides of the fence. These beliefs are spawned by many circumstances and ideologies, from the teachings of various religious doctrines, or personal experiences, to political slants or views on life in general.

I have included this chapter for reasons that should be obvious at this time in our planet's consciousness. My responsibility is to give you the best possibility in surviving your family's crisis. What you do or don't do with the information presented in this book is your business. The more tasks that you are able to perform yourself, the better off you'll be, and the less drag you will be on emergency response personnel in times of chaos. Self-reliance in any particular skill or commodity, and the mind-set and actions that go with it, give you *options*. These options provide you with alternatives to mitigate or deal with problems when outside help and resources are not available.

My Interview with Professor Mark Bryans of the American Combato System

As my expertise in "self-defense" is minimizing and combating risks to your life from nonphysical threats of violence, I wanted to talk with someone who specializes in personal and family self-defense. I have always had an interest in self-defense training, but I was not interested in walking on rice paper and catching a fly midair with my toes in order to be able and willing to defend myself in a hairy situation. Survival and self-defense scenarios are identical twins in that, at their core, both deal with potentially life-threatening emergencies under extreme stress. In the same vein, both arts have a few ego-saturated jerks who either willfully or out of ignorance distort the truth about what is and what is not important in dealing with these life-threatening emergencies. The myth is coddled and fed by producers and editors in film, television, magazines, newspapers, and online who have zero experience in the realities of either genre. At the viewer or reader's expense, they shamelessly tout information that often is more geared toward supporting ratings than delivering sound advice.

Mark Bryans is blunt, unflattering with the truth, uncompromising in his ideals of self-defense, has zero tolerance for the bullshit in his field, and is completely driven to be and teach the best practical, real-life self-defense possible to his students. In short, he walks his talk. Some of his answers will shock you, make you uncomfortable, and cause you to think. Be shocked now, and then prepare, long before some whacko charges at you with a butcher knife.

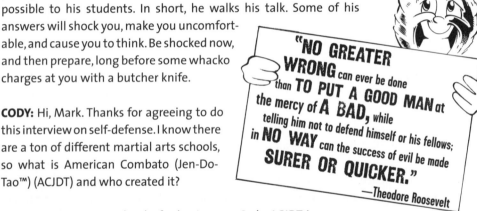

"NO GREATER WRONG can ever be done than TO PUT A GOOD MAN at the mercy of A BAD, while telling him not to defend himself or his fellows; in NO WAY can the success of evil be made SURER OR QUICKER."
—Theodore Roosevelt

CODY: Hi, Mark. Thanks for agreeing to do this interview on self-defense. I know there are a ton of different martial arts schools, so what is American Combato (Jen-Do-Tao™) (ACJDT) and who created it?

PROFESSOR BRYANS: Thanks for having me, Cody. ACJDT is a complete, comprehensive martial arts system focusing entirely on close-quarters combat and self-defense. Our students are trained mentally, physically, and tactically to defend themselves against deadly, unavoidable, and unprovoked attacks. The system was created by Bradley J. Steiner in 1975 and has absolutely no sporting or competitive application whatsoever. Professor Steiner combined his background and training in Eastern martial arts, western boxing, and wrestling with the immense knowledge and training programs taught to various operatives and soldiers during World War II. He also used his training in Taekwon-do, Ju-Jutsu, Indian varmannie, and Chinese-Hawaiian Kempo Karate, along with western boxing from the practical wartime methods of the Applegate system, Helson system, O'Neill system, Fairbairn system, Brown-Begala system, Sigward system, and the Biddle-Styers system.

CODY: Wow, it sounds pretty comprehensive.

PROFESSOR BRYANS: It is. Steiner also added miscellaneous modern Special Forces approaches, commando techniques, and the brutal tactics of rough-and-tumble "street," "prison," and "alley" fighting. He drew also upon his deep involvement in physical training and the art of progressive-resistance exercise and studies into the crafts of hypnosis, mind-control techniques, and other unusual philosophies as these things relate to combat arts, as well as his exposure to the world of secret intelligence. Cody, all methods of combat can be divided into offensive and defensive methods. ACJDT is the first martial-arts system in history to offer a comprehensive and in-depth syllabus of attack combinations and methods of planned aggression as well as "self-defense" techniques which we call counterattacks. The AC student is trained to be aware of an attacker before he attacks and to focus upon "attacking the attacker" once he perceives the beginning of the attacker's violent action or intention. We don't teach a student to react to the attacker's specific attack, whether it's a punch, grab, or weapon acquisition. We teach students to simply and destructively launch their own attack with nonstop destructive action to knock the attacker unconscious. The counterattack portion of the system prepares the student to "attack the attacker" if taken by surprise.

CODY: Now that you've filled us in on the system itself, what's your background?

PROFESSOR BRYANS: I've been studying American Combato with Professor Steiner since 1979. I was the first individual to achieve black belt ranking in ACJDT, and am currently the highest-ranking instructor in the system outside of Professor Steiner himself. My current ranking is sixth-degree black belt whereupon I was awarded the title of professor in the system. I've been operating my own school since 1992 where I teach all types of people from private citizens to the military and the police. The majority of my students are, and will continue to be, private citizens. I also work with individuals and groups in all aspects of mental and physical conditioning, including drilling of offensive and defensive combat methods, progressive-resistance training (i.e. weights), and mind-set development.

CODY: Exactly what does it take to defend yourself and what are the qualities an individual will need?

PROFESSOR BRYANS: By far, the most important attribute is the combative mindset. This is not the attitude of the "tough guy" or of the paranoid. It is simply the deeply held conviction of self-respect and understanding that no one has the right to initiate force against another, that force is to be used *only* in retaliation against unavoidable, unprovoked attack and only against those who initiate its use. As I've heard Professor Steiner say, "Any rational person prefers peace over violence and that all such individuals are pacifists until they are attacked." If you should find yourself under criminal attack and escape is not possible, then you should proceed without hesitation to viciously destroy your attacker by launching your own attack. All students learn during their first lesson to "attack the attacker." The individual seeking defensive, protective capability must know, subconsciously, that the attacker is wrong and that what the attacker is doing is evil and that any action and damage that the defender MUST inflict upon the attacker is right and necessary. Realize that the defender's motive is always defense, but the means is *offense*: The defender must master a few, simple, direct offensive attack combinations, and commit to relentless, brutal follow-up to their initial attack until the attacker is rendered harmless. Now, the attacker is harmless when he is unconscious, if he flees—don't pursue him—or if the defender can safely escape. Realize also that the defender must absolutely expect to be hurt, perhaps seriously injured, during any self-defense encounter and this is true even for an expert.

These attributes must be coupled with a *relaxed alertness* that does not allow a surprise attack. When one realizes attack is imminent, one will instantly "attack the attacker" with total surprise. Never should anyone show any aggression prior to being attacked. Don't agree to fight, don't argue, leave the area if possible, or apologize, even if you don't actually feel that way if it will make the peace. But, if you are about to be injured, or an innocent loved one is about to be injured, explode into the assailant or assailants with all the destructive fury you can muster.

CODY: You mentioned the importance of fostering a combative mind-set, and the need to "attack the attacker," but how does one develop those abilities in today's world?

PROFESSOR BRYANS: Good question. First, cultivate righteous indignation by questioning the nonsense that is being programmed into all of us through the mainstream channels. When you read a story or hear in the news about an innocent person or family being attacked by the all-too-common scum that are allowed to roam free, anger and rage should be your reaction. If you think that such a response

"Among the natural rights of the colonists are these: first, **A RIGHT TO LIFE,** secondly **TO LIBERTY,** thirdly **TO PROPERTY,** together with the right to defend them **IN THE BEST MANNER** they can."

—Samuel Adams

is inappropriate, you just proved that such programming has been successful. Why isn't rage appropriate when horrors occur daily such as abduction, sexual assault, the murder of children, home invasions, and attacks on the elderly? . . . and on and on the list goes. These serious crimes are almost invariably committed by repeat offenders who are let loose on the good and innocent people of our nation. Cultivate the combative mind-set, which is prerequisite to any effective self-defense action to be done.

Second, hook up with a good self-defense school that teaches and drills students in simple, adaptive, retainable skills that blind, disrupt the breathing, break bones, rupture internal organs, and create trauma to the monster who attacks the innocent. These simple procedures must be *overlearned* by repetitive training against an imagined adversary and training dummies and targets until they become second nature if one should ever need them. Developing a few things really well breeds confidence. The need to overlearn the techniques is essential to gaining competence and having an automatic retaliatory attack response if or when the need arises.

CODY: Are these techniques difficult to learn and develop?

PROFESSOR BRYANS: No. Techniques in self-defense have to be simple and direct. If the techniques cannot be understood and learned in a short amount of time they won't be available in an emergency. Once the techniques are learned they must be *practiced repeatedly* until they become automatic and reflexive.

Let's go through some of the things Combato students learn in their first private lesson. First, the students must learn how to stand and position themselves when dealing with unknown individuals. Your position should be balanced with one foot back and to the front of the rear shoulder, lead foot slightly turned in with the body at an angle to the potential threat. The *relaxed ready* position should be learned from both the right and left position to enable you to attack from either side. Next, the hands should be up, mid-chest level or higher, in any configuration that doesn't look aggressive or tie up your hands. Keep your eyes on the individual who has approached, letting your gaze rest easily on the head and shoulder triangle area; and always be aware of the individual's hands. Don't allow the person to crowd you and keep him just out of arm's reach. This way, if the individual were to attack, he would have to step in, therefore telegraphing his movement, and you can attack the attacker where he has left himself open. From this relaxed ready position, you, the defender, will be able to avoid many circumstances in the first place by being aware, and go to all lengths to avoid physical confrontation. If the attacker should attack, you will have the element of surprise by unexpectedly launching your own preemptive strike. If two or more individuals approach, always step to the outside. Learn to interact in all circumstances without diverting eye placement, and whatever your hands are doing, let them remain unencumbered at mid-chest level or higher (in any configuration that doesn't look aggressive).

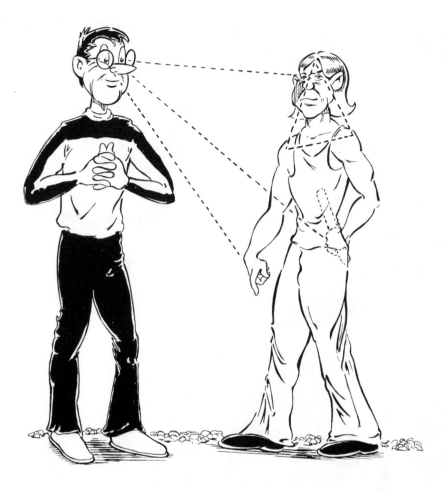

For example, someone asks you for the time, show him your watch, but don't look down at your watch. Never put your hands in your pockets. If a person asks directions, keep your eyes on him and point him in the right direction without turning your back to him.

CODY: Mark, you mentioned the students attacking with a preemptive strike if necessary when they realize they are under attack. How could this be done, I mean, what are some of the techniques the Combato system teaches?

PROFESSOR BRYANS: Yes, let's cover four basic strikes often taught to all beginning students—the *chop*, the *chin jab*, the *side kick*, and the *fingertip thrust*. First the chop. This weapon is formed by flattening the hand with the palm down, striking with the edge of the hand out. The impact of the blow should come from the edge of the hand near the wrist where the metacarpal bones meet the carpal bones. This will give more penetration and focus to the strike. Also, the entire outside edge of

the arm, the ulna bone, can be used for the impact point. The throat and the bridge of the nose are great targets for this strike.

The *chin jab* smash is done by pressing the hand back as far as possible, so the impact point is at the heel of the hand. In this way the head of the attacker, when struck under the chin, is driven up and back, smashing and breaking the neck. This blow, like the chop, is done close in, half-an-arm's reach or closer. It's an upward strike with the primary target being under the chin. Secondary targets are the eye sockets, the nose, the temple, and the jaw hinge. The chin jab blow is done primarily off the rear side. The chop, with the lead hand, followed by a chin jab with the rear hand, is a practical application of these two basic strikes.

The third technique is the *side kick*, sometimes called the king of all self-defense moves. The side kick targets the knee joint or lower but the knee joint is ideal. It doesn't matter if it's the front of the knee, the outside of the knee, or the inside of the knee; the knee breaks relatively easy. Now, the kick is done in a side-facing position. The lead foot is lifted up about knee height, perhaps a little higher and close to the standing leg. It's thrusted out in a piston-type action stomping in a downward action through the knee joint. The impact is with the bottom of the heel or with the entire foot, although the heel is best.

The *fingertip thrust* is done palm down, while flattening out the hand and extending the fingers. Drive the extended fingers in a straight line into the attacker's eyes. This technique embodies simplicity, ruthlessness, and brutality and anyone can do it.

CODY: OK, Mark, you talked about some simple, basic techniques that Combato offers but how do I practice? I mean, do I need a partner to practice with, can I do this alone in my garage; how would you recommend that someone learn these skills?

PROFESSOR BRYANS: Well that's a great question, Cody. What you need is to *overlearn* some very simple skills and to practice them against an imagined attacker. The techniques can be done in the air, imagining the attacker in front of you, but at some point it will become important to have some sort of object to hit into such as a striking board, a heavy bag, or a striking dummy. You don't need a training partner but a partner can be helpful at times where you're working on certain types of counterattacks such as a front choke escape or a bear hug hold. In these cases, working with a partner should be done at reduced speed and there should be *no contact* with any of the blows involved, as they're very destructive. If it's effective for self-defense it needs to be destructive. You can't spar with combat techniques.

CODY: So the entire family can partner up if desired and train together using these simple techniques?

PROFESSOR BRYANS: Yes, but you can never make actual contact with a live person. Blows must be at a very reduced speed in the beginning, and all striking should be done on dummies.

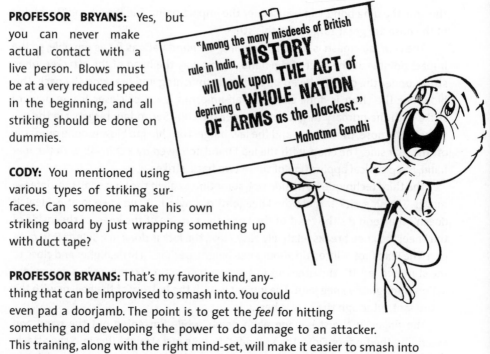

"Among the many misdeeds of British rule in India, HISTORY will look upon THE ACT of depriving a WHOLE NATION OF ARMS as the blackest."
—Mahatma Gandhi

CODY: You mentioned using various types of striking surfaces. Can someone make his own striking board by just wrapping something up with duct tape?

PROFESSOR BRYANS: That's my favorite kind, anything that can be improvised to smash into. You could even pad a doorjamb. The point is to get the *feel* for hitting something and developing the power to do damage to an attacker. This training, along with the right mind-set, will make it easier to smash into a real human when necessary. Three 2x4s can be glued together (make sure not to use any nails) and buried three feet into the ground. The boards are then padded with carpet, closed-cell foam sleeping mats such as backpackers use, or anything that will get the job done. The height above the ground is about six feet and the striking surface should flex dependent upon each individual's needs.

CODY: What I've stated in this book is the need to practice motor memory skills, not just physical skills, so when someone is subjected to a real-time survival situation, they've gone through that scenario in their mind again and again and again and are more mentally and emotionally prepared to act. It sounds like this is true for Combato as well, is that accurate?

PROFESSOR BRYANS: That's absolutely true, Cody. People want to be entertained by new things and complicated techniques but it's not the way to train for real-world self-defense. In self-defense, the motive is always defense, but the means to achieve this are by offense. Trendy training methods that are popular are not necessarily the best choice, as you know in your field. The things that you see in movies or the cage fights are not conducive to effective self-defense for a number of reasons. Techniques need to be simple, direct, destructive, and highly adaptable, allowing them to be used under a variety of conditions. Using complicated techniques—I don't care if the person is an expert tenth-degree black belt—is going to get the you-know-what kicked out of you if you attempt it against a street predator. You want to *keep things simple* and develop a few basic techniques. The four techniques we outlined—the chop, the side kick, the chin jab, and the fingertip thrust—need to be *overlearned*. The process is this; you begin by first learning the technique at a slow rate, perhaps watch it being done, and as you get the technique down you build up speed. But then you do hundreds and hundreds and hundreds of repetitions coupled with the right mind-set. The person's mind-set should be on the complete destruction of the attacker with an offensive spirit coupled with instant action. Techniques for effective, practical, real-world self-defense should be overlearned so they are literally more available as a motor skill to someone who's scared and pumped up with adrenaline. You need to attack and keep on attacking until the attacker is unconscious.

CODY: No secret walk-on-rice-paper thing there, right? Just good old-fashioned work and common sense.

PROFESSOR BRYANS: Absolutely.

CODY: OK. Well, since this is an urban survival book based upon preparing the home, what should readers have at their house to protect themselves should the need arise?

PROFESSOR BRYANS: One of the worst things happening in our society today is home invasions where attackers are coming into homes with the family present to do their dirty work. There are a number of ways that home invaders enter a home. One obvious way is that they kick the door down or perhaps pick the lock or break a window. Oftentimes, however, they manipulate their way into the home in some way. Children especially should

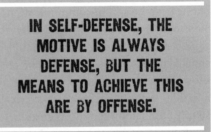

IN SELF-DEFENSE, THE MOTIVE IS ALWAYS DEFENSE, BUT THE MEANS TO ACHIEVE THIS ARE BY OFFENSE.

be taught never to open the door to any stranger. Of course, the first thing to do in any encounter is to try to avoid it altogether by advanced preparation. First, families should develop specific signals to be used among each other that have various meanings depending on the circumstances. How, when, and what type of signals will be used is up to the needs and creativity of the family—and it could be at any level of the attack.

Let's say somebody is at the door and no one knows for sure what the person's intent is. The father or whoever answers the door could have a specific question that could be asked to the visitor that would alert family members that something wasn't right. The signal could also be a light left on or turned off that would signal there was a problem. It could be to the point where a gun is pointed at a family member's head and everything's at critical mass and somebody is going to make a move, deciding it's time to defend and a statement was made such as, "Geez, guys, can't we talk this over!" And the family knows when that statement comes out ending with the word "over" that they're going to make their move all at once. My family has a specific statement that we use in public. If my wife or daughter notices something that doesn't seem right, and says the signal words, I know to pay more attention to something that I'm not seeing.

CODY: That's perfect! So you have many sets of eyes out there, not just one, if everyone's paying attention to what's going on.

PROFESSOR BRYANS: You bet, and what a feeling to be on top of things to simply avoid an altercation altogether. In addition, the concept of a *safe room* is a great idea—where there's one room in the house where it would be very difficult for the attackers to break into. This doesn't have to be as extreme as the movie where the woman had a bank vault in her house, but if you have the money, all the more power to you. Having a good carpenter come in to beef up doors and windows in a specific room would be wise. If you're in the middle of building a home, you have all kinds of opportunities to make one small area that is defensible that could be used to retreat into if the need arises.

As mentioned before, the family could have a specific signal for retreating into the safe room. Safe rooms should include provisions that the family thinks are important for their scenario, especially after reading this book, and of course a cell phone or some sort of communications to allow for the alerting of the authorities. Safe-room provisions—in fact, everything regarding a family's preparedness—should not be advertised but should be kept private within the family. No one should know that you have this kind of thing going, which of course is just common sense. When I was a boy, my mother always had plenty of canned food on hand, and there was no emergency or survival situation going on; it was simply based upon common sense.

Now of course the ownership of firearms depends on where you live. Here in Arizona, it's perfectly legal to own and use firearms, but the person thinking about purchasing a home-defense weapon should check local laws before doing so. Certainly, having a weapon to defend yourself makes complete sense, as long as it's purchased and used in a legal way. For home defense, I would recommend a 12-

"Gun control? It's the **BEST THING YOU CAN DO** for crooks and gangsters. I want you to have nothing. If I'm a bad guy, I'm always **GONNA HAVE A GUN.** Safety locks? You will pull the trigger with the lock on, and **I'LL PULL THE TRIGGER.** We'll see who **WINS.**"
—Sammy "The Bull" Gravano, Mafia informant

gauge shotgun or a .45 automatic pistol. A woman can manage a 12 gauge if she is properly trained, but a 20 gauge, although not as effective as a 12 gauge, will be sufficient and easier for her to manage. For the shotgun, double-ought (oo) buckshot is most commonly recommended and it's a great round. In some cases, there might be some danger to people in other rooms if this round is used—going through walls and such—and a number four round might be better, but I don't think you can go wrong with either one. It would also be a good idea to have a couple of boxes of slugs on hand as well. The most important thing about firearms is to have one that you're comfortable using and that meets your needs.

As far as precautions around the home, avoiding the confrontation altogether is superior in every way. Take a look at homes around the neighborhood sometime; windows are left open and they just look so easy to break into. Although any home can be broken into, you don't want to make it easier for intruders to do so. It should be difficult and the attacker should have to make a lot of noise. They should have to break windows and give you plenty of warning that they're coming. Various security measures can be done, from roll-down shutters and stronger locks to thorny shrubs at the base of windows to make it more difficult to get into that window. Predators most often are looking for an easy target. Have the best alarm system you can afford, along with adequate lighting around the house, including motion detector lights. If the power goes out, remember that darkness can be helpful; you know your house layout and the assailant doesn't.

Dogs can also be very effective. Now, if you want to get an attack-trained dog, you need to go to a qualified trainer, as that dog needs to be treated very differently. It can't be socialized with just anybody. Personally, I prefer having an ordinary dog around. A dog is a good alarm; he usually doesn't allow someone to sneak in undetected. Predator types are very frightened of dogs because they know they can't intimidate a dog. Even a little dog is going to yap away. All this is conducive to keeping potential attackers away, as they like to do their evil deeds in the dark and in secret.

CODY: Mark, I know there are a lot of inner and outer "politics," for lack of a better term, in which the concept of self-defense has taken a beating. What would you say to concepts and opinions expressed that look down on the right to self-defense?

PROFESSOR BRYANS: Frankly, Cody, anybody with that type of attitude, I don't care what they think, they're idiots. I think the term that comes to mind is paranoia, and paranoia is when someone is not interpreting reality correctly. They're out of touch with reality; they literally cannot function. Now you tell me, is it paranoia to recognize the fact that there are some dangerous people out there in this world and people are being hurt all the time? To take a reasonable, rational approach and realize that violence could one day come to me and I might need to defend myself so I better be ready to go, I think is quite reasonable.

I also find that people who are very frightened of the world out there, when they start to learn some self-defense skills—and this really applies to kids—their

"The most foolish **MISTAKE** we could possibly make would be to allow the subjected people **TO CARRY ARMS;** history shows that **ALL CONQUERORS** who have allowed subjected people to carry arms have prepared **THEIR OWN FALL.**"
—Adolf Hitler

confidence goes way up. They're finally seeing that, hey, I have some options of what to do; instead of intensifying that fear, it starts to allay the fear. Now they can go about their business with greater awareness, paying attention to what's around them, and, for the most part, there's usually nothing to bring about that fear in the first place. Learning quality self-defense skills reduces fear; it doesn't intensify it. I've trained hundreds and hundreds of people over the last ten years and I find that their confidence increases tremendously and it starts to relieve some of the fear and anxiety that they initially felt. I'm sure it's much the same with your clients and what you do with survival training.

CODY: Yeah, it's true. I think fear is frequently a reflexive response to the unknown. So the more people learn about unknown variables and how to deal with them, the more apt they are to survive a crisis or, better yet, use their training to avoid one in the first place. I know that the Combato system mentions *command presence* in its training. What is command presence and how can it be developed?

PROFESSOR BRYANS: Command presence is not something you can teach per se, although perhaps you can develop it in someone. Have you ever been in a situation, and I know you have, where there's an emergency and there's a certain person present who takes control and inspires confidence? Take a simple thing such as going into a convenience store to buy a carton of milk. Most people are walking around, staring at their feet, almost apologizing for breathing the air around them, versus someone who has their head up and knows what they're doing and has a no-nonsense demeanor about them. It's not an arrogant thing; it's just simply and confidently going about the things you need to do. As confidence increases through training, command presence comes automatically. You can't affect command presence; you can't fake that kind of thing. Faking confidence is instantly seen as weakness, especially by predator types.

CODY: You mentioned some of the Combato techniques earlier. In the average home there are lots of things lying around. Can people improvise self-defense weapons from common household items, such as a stapler or a pencil, that can be used in an emergency?

PROFESSOR BRYANS: Yes, absolutely. The natural weapons of the body do a number of things. One, they prepare us for situations where we don't have a weapon at hand. But why would you defend yourself against a deadly attack and not use a weapon? A gun is great but might not be available or legal, so learn how to use everyday objects to deliver the knockout you need to stop the attacker. Pens, cell phones, remote controls, bottles, lighters, chairs, books and magazines, dirt, forks and spoons, rulers and more can all be utilized to the defender's advantage.

CODY: How about a pen? I have a pen sitting right here for this interview. How would you use that?

PROFESSOR BRYANS: Well, perfect. So if we're going to chop an attacker in the throat, let's think about what we're trying to do—we are trying to damage the airway. Now if I simply, with my palm down, grasp the pen and let it protrude out, maybe an inch or two, and now chop with the impact point being the pen, doing destruction to the airway or to the eye socket, clearly the effectiveness of that strike has increased. The chin jab smash uses the heel of the hand up under the chin. The key point here is brutally smashing up under the chin. This book could be held in two hands and the binding driven up under the chin to great effect. Clearly, this would only be justified in a life-threatening situation where no other alternatives exist.

CODY: I mention canned goods in the food section. Could someone hold a can of food and strike with that?

USING A MAGAZINE OR NEWSPAPER AS A WEAPON

Helpful **HARDCORE** *Hints*

1. Take a magazine or newspaper and roll it up tightly into a tube.
2. Grasp the magazine or newspaper in your striking hand.
3. Let an inch or two of it stick out from your clenched fist.
4. Use the hardened tube to attack the attacker's target areas such as the temple, jaw hinge, eye sockets, etc.

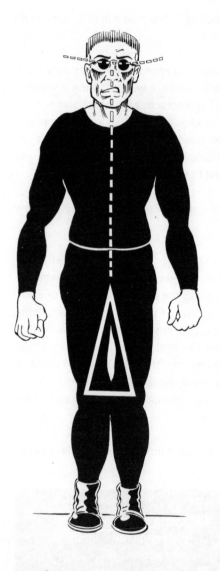

PROFESSOR BRYANS: That would be an excellent weapon. The chin jab held with a can upright in the hand could be driven up and under the chin as a weapon. The can could be thrown in the face of the attacker, a side kick delivered to his knee, followed by a chin jab, followed by another can grabbed to smash the head. The choices are endless. A cell phone in the hand could be used to chop with and so forth.

There are different types of improvised weapons. Some are going to bludgeon, some are going to be impact weapons, and some are going to be cutting weapons. But the point is they all do more trauma to the human body. There are three areas of the body that are generally attacked: *the band, temple to temple; the centerline of the body;* and *the kicking triangle* composed of the knees and testicles.

Any type of impact weapon or cutting weapon could be used in the band area, to the eyes for example. Something as simple as a car key can be held and driven into the eye. You need to do the most damage as quickly and ruthlessly as possible to knock the attacker or attackers unconscious or allow you to safely flee the area. As you can imagine, improvised weapons could be the subject of a book in itself. If an item can't be used to directly strike an assailant it can be thrown into the attacker's face, such as throwing dirt into the eyes, to distract them in order to set up the next defensive attack combination.

CODY: I've heard of several scenarios in the news where someone robs a restaurant for instance, and then starts hassling the people, who choose to do nothing, as opposed to people who started doing things such as throwing salt shakers, glasses, or ketchup bottles at the assailant. Is this a good thing to do?

PROFESSOR BRYANS: That would be an excellent thing to do. We don't want to just let the attacker go unchecked in what he's doing. There was an incident a few years ago where people were lain out prone upon the floor to be executed. One of the survivors was interviewed and said there was nothing he could do but lay on the floor and wait to be killed. This is not the combat mind-set. *Move*, get into action, throw something at the attacker, flee, do SOMETHING, and get into action to get the attacker under stress!

CODY: So it sounds like, as with a lot of my training, that mind-set is everything and with the proper mind-set, you can take almost anything from your environment and use it to your advantage to help stay alive in a self-defense scenario.

PROFESSOR BRYANS: Well put, Cody. Technique is always subservient to mind-set.

CODY: As it's so critical, let's talk a bit more about mind-set. What exactly is a combat mind-set?

PROFESSOR BRYANS: The *combat mind-set*, simply put, means that a person under attack is going to feel intense rage at the person coming after them and feel very natural in the process of going about destroying them. Really, a mind-set is simply a collection of beliefs pertaining to a certain area. So when you cultivate mind-set in your students, you're perhaps changing beliefs in certain areas about certain things, as I am with my students. There are several areas of belief that often need to be altered in a situation of self-defense. For example, sometimes a person firmly believes it's never right to injure another person under any circumstance. Or another belief that is often firmly embedded and gets in the way of a person defending himself is that he is not going to succeed and will only make matters worse if he fights back. Of course, in a self-defense situation these are totally irrational. Again, the combat mind-set is simply a belief structure that revolves around a combative situation. The proper response to someone trying to hurt you should be rage, anger, and action.

CODY: So I think it's probably safe to say that every mother, if any harm were to be directed at her children, would have a natural combat mind-set.

PROFESSOR BRYANS: You bet. I'll train women and often they'll say, "Oh, gosh, Mark, I don't know if I can do that attack technique or not." I then ask them

"I declare to you that WOMAN MUST NOT depend upon the protection of man, but must be TAUGHT TO PROTECT HERSELF, and there I take my stand."
—Susan B. Anthony

what they would do if someone was going to hurt their son or daughter. Instantly their facial expression changes, they start to grit their teeth, and they'll often say something like, "I'd kill that son of a bitch!" I then remind them that they are just as important as their kid. Sometimes the combat mind-set is easier to apply to protect a loved one than to protect the individual herself. Again, we're back to altering belief structures—maybe their self-esteem just needs a little boost.

CODY: In my field, a lot of survival training is bogus as it assumes the survivor will be a physically fit, twenty-four-year-old Special Forces soldier with a gung-ho mind-set. Is it the same for self-defense training? I mean, what about a typical home where there are going to be women, children, and maybe even grandparents living at the house? Can these people defend themselves?

PROFESSOR BRYANS: Of course they can defend themselves, and, unfortunately, they're going to be the ones who are targeted, as predators will go after the weakest individuals that they feel they can easily victimize. Nothing really changes with these individuals other than it behooves them all to understand that they are in a deadly circumstance every time. They need to realize that they are fighting for their lives and that they must do the most decisive, destructive thing quickly. Weapons, or at the very least having something in the hand to strike with, will become more important. One of the things to keep in mind with these individuals is that they have a tremendous advantage with the element of surprise if they learn how to use it. No one would ever expect an elderly person to even fight back, let alone fight back effectively. So in a situation where the attacker is threatening, or the attack is mounting, a woman, elderly person, or child can fain compliance, go along with them, convince them that they aren't going to fight back, and thereby create an opening that might not exist for someone like you or me. In other words, the attacker might be less wary and open himself to being attacked with a quick chop to the throat, which would pave the way for more follow-up strikes.

CODY: So family members don't need to feel out of place, they could even set up a counter-decoy for the more able-bodied family members to fight back. So there's a place in self-defense for each family member, is that what you're saying?

PROFESSOR BRYANS: That's correct. When you look at actual incidences of self-defense, you'll note that the people who do successfully defend themselves usually are not martial artists or athletes. They are everyday women, children, and elderly people. The common denominator that I see, other than luck, over which we have no control, is that they all *take action*. Oftentimes women who fight back will defend themselves against rapists. Their mind-set is right and they are not about to be taken into that car or whatever. With this combative mind-set, their chances for success go way up, whether they fight back well or not, they should *just fight!*

CODY: As far as improvised weapons go, I guess Grandma could use her cane or whatever, right? Nothing changes concerning using improvised weapons with the elderly, kids, or women?

PROFESSOR BRYANS: Correct, other than they are more justified in their use and won't have to fear any kind of legal repercussion if the situation is handled properly when the authorities show up.

CODY: What about a smaller person needing to defend herself against a larger, more powerful attacker?

PROFESSOR BRYANS: First off, keep in mind that people do it all the time. Smaller individuals defeat larger, stronger, more skilled individuals regularly. This isn't a sport; you're not in the ring; you're not squaring off with this individual. Remember that the attacker will have no idea that you are prepared and ready to launch a preemptive attack against him. When looking at a larger person, the smaller person needs to realize that you don't look at the strength of the individual. Look at his eye sockets. Are they any stronger than anyone else's? The throat, not much stronger than anyone else's; the testicles, same thing, and so forth. You have to look at the weak parts of the body, use the element of surprise, and destroy these targets. *Perhaps the single greatest advantage that the defender has is the element of surprise.*

CODY: Are there any basic assumptions that one can make regarding an attacker?

PROFESSOR BRYANS: Absolutely. You should always assume, regardless of your size or strength or ability, that your attacker will be stronger, bigger, more skilled, and faster and that he will be determined to fight to the death. Also, if you're doing everything that this chapter has outlined to avoid conflicts in the first place, there is a very good possibility that you're dealing with a psychopathic personality, a very dangerous individual who would be willing to do anything to you. It's not uncommon that somebody might kill a clerk when they steal a six-pack of beer from a store. Assume that you're dealing with a very, very dangerous adversary every time.

CODY: What should people look for in an effective self-defense school and what kind of questions should they ask the instructor?

PROFESSOR BRYANS: Look for a school that focuses entirely on self-defense, that there is no sporting aspect to what they're doing. It should also be self-defense in the extreme, in other words, worst-case-scenario situations. What if the attacker is highly motivated or high on drugs? If so, it's going to take a lot to stop that attacker. The school's curriculum should focus on offense, attacking the attacker, not on defensive responses of how to deal with an attack once it's already underway. In my school we teach counterattacks such as how to escape choke holds and bear hugs, and many other scenarios, but this is secondary to preemptive striking when attack is imminent. Ask the instructor if they spar, in other words, how the techniques are practiced, if they compete in sporting systems, and how long their classes last. You don't want anything to do with sparring, sports-type systems for self-defense. The school should teach ruthless, brutal, violent techniques—it's the only way to stop a violent attacker.

"I don't even call it **VIOLENCE** when it's **SELF-DEFENSE;** I call it **INTELLIGENCE.**"

—Malcolm X

CODY: So what if I drop an attacker? Will I be prosecuted for defending myself?

PROFESSOR BRYANS: Well, first understand that this question can only be fully answered by an attorney. People should consult an attorney in their area about the laws of self-defense. Having said that, laws regarding self-defense differ from state to state. The place you would find the answer to these questions would be on the jury instructions for justifiable homicide. In the state of Arizona, for example, I can tell you that there are a number of things that are looked at—one of the biggest being what was the perception of the defenders at the time they defended themselves. Did they fear for their lives? Also, another thing that is commonly looked at is whether the defender had an escape option but did not take it. If you're ever in a situation where you have the time or the means to escape and you don't do so, you will never have a right to self-defense. It has to be unavoidable, unprovoked self-defense. Another factor in the state of Arizona is whether the defender provoked the self-defense situation in any way. If you get into an argument with somebody, and he pulls a knife and tries to stab you, you have a legitimate self-defense situation. But the legal courts may see it differently: if they decide that you provoked the situation, you will lose your right to self-defense. This all gets pretty complicated. Basically, go out of your way to stay out of trouble and not get into arguments—saying whatever needs to be said to appease the other person and only fighting when there is no other choice.

It's important that you are frightened for your life, and that you feel that you're going to be seriously harmed or killed if you don't take action. This needs to be made clear to the authorities. So if you are asked if you were afraid of this person, of course you were afraid of the person—drop the macho nonsense.

CODY: Will the elderly or women have any easier time, so to speak, in the courtroom compared to some 300-pound body builder?

PROFESSOR BRYANS: I would have to say no. An elderly person could successfully defend himself and when questioned by the authorities say, "I wasn't afraid of these punks for a moment, they got what they deserved!" The police will have no choice at this point but to arrest the elderly person because there was no perception of fear.

CODY: So what you say when the authorities show up is vitally important.

PROFESSOR BRYANS: Yes, and if someone ends up seriously hurt, you have every right to ask for legal counsel and not talk until you have someone who will advise you about what to say. Unfortunately, that's the system we live in.

CODY: So that gives credence to the Combato system of relaxed ready, too, doesn't it, because it's totally nonthreatening. If someone looked up from a crowd at a defender with their hands up, angled off, and they were saying, "Hey, I don't want any problem with you," that would be good from a legal aspect and yet that person is totally wired and ready to defend himself if necessary. Would you agree with that?

PROFESSOR BRYANS: Yes, I would completely agree with that.

CODY: This is primarily a home-based book on self-reliance, but the chances are high that at some point a member of the family will need to travel to another location, whether to get supplies or to evacuate because of a disaster. That said, what about dealing with a carjacking?

PROFESSOR BRYANS: First, understand that approaching your vehicle, being in your vehicle, and leaving your vehicle are all vulnerable times and should be minimized during times of unrest. Also, recognizing this fact should make you more aware during times of travel involving an automobile.

There are some rules for traveling. Whenever you are approaching your parked car, spot-check your vehicle before opening the door. Look behind the driver's seat to make sure no one is in the vehicle. If there is, escape immediately—do not confront the person—and call the police. The second you get into the vehicle, lock the door and then start the engine. Always maintain your vehicle, which is just common sense, and make sure you have at least a half tank of gas. Gas up at convenient times when it's safe to do so, such as in the daytime.

Should you ever discover that you're being followed, do not stop your vehicle. Keep driving. If you know the location of a police station, go there. Once you arrive, place your hand on the horn and keep blasting it until you get results from the police. Blasting the horn if you're being followed while you continue to drive is an excellent strategy in general, as it will attract attention. Never drive to your home if you're being tailed, leading whoever is following you to your home.

A carjacker is a potentially lethal assailant, and alertness is the key to avoiding the situation in the first place. Whenever you are stopped at a red light or a stop sign, stay alert to anyone who is approaching your vehicle. If someone approaches, drive away immediately. If an attacker, or a group of attackers, is in front of the vehicle, run him, or them, over.

CODY: What if someone wants to know more? Does the Combato system have any books or training information?

PROFESSOR BRYANS: Yes. There's an excellent magazine that Professor Steiner puts out each month called *Close Quarters*. The carjacking information we just talked about came from *Close Quarters* Volume 2, Issue 12, as an example. Our Web site has all the contact information regarding the magazine as well as courses at www.americancombato.com.

- ➲ The most important attribute necessary to defend yourself is *attitude*, more specifically, the combative mind-set. The individual possessing this will "attack the attacker."
- ➲ Techniques for self-defense must be simple, easy to learn and use, and able to knock out the attacker.
- ➲ Be alert to what is going on around you. If something seems "off," leave the area. If this is not possible and you are approached, go to the relaxed-ready position, keep the individual(s) out of arm's reach, and be ready to attack and destroy the attacker if he (they) attack.
- ➲ Striking the attacker is highly effective. Four good natural weapons are the hand-axe (chop), the chin-jab smash, the side kick to the knee, and the fingertip thrust.
- ➲ The general attack zones for striking the attacker are the band, the line, and the kicking triangle.
- ➲ Once you attack, *always follow up*. Keep on hitting, tearing, ripping, smashing, and cutting as you attack, attack, *attack!*
- ➲ Use any item at hand (improvised weapons) to bolster the attack.
- ➲ No sparring. When practicing, attack into strike pads or dummies.

21

CRITICAL COMMUNICATIONS

"The 911 system was overloaded within ten minutes of the outage. Call rates jumped to 500 calls per hour for five hours (2500 calls) when normally 200 calls would come in—which is a ten-time increase."

—Anonymous witnessed account of the infamous
1996 power outage that caused a massive cascading
failure of the power grid in the western United States

Emergencies rarely occur with any prior warning, and their effects can quickly cripple normal information sources. Even if you have all of your survival bases covered, you'll still want to know what's going on in the outside world. Emergency bulletins will give you extremely valuable information that may directly affect your survival, or at least let you know how long you'll need to eat rice. On the other hand, the broadcast may be full of sensationalism, half truths, or outright lies, perpetrated by networks to gain higher ratings ($) or by outright news-slut reporters desperate for the first and most likely inaccurate story. Cross-reference emergency

"Examine **WHAT IS SAID,** not **WHO SPEAKS.**"
—Arabian proverb

broadcasts whenever possible to try and get the straight story. Whatever type or types of communications you decide to use, don't put all of your eggs in one basket, and expect the unexpected.

Comprehensive emergency communications in and of itself is extremely technical, and more than one book has been devoted to the subject. If you feel your family needs more detailed information than what this chapter provides, then practice self-reliance and get off your butt to find the information you need. Remember, there is no one-size-fits-all emergency plan for every home.

Knowing Your Neighbors

"WON'T YOU BE, WON'T YOU BE, PLEASE WON'T YOU BE MY NEIGHBOR?"
— MR. ROGERS

At first glance, most assume communications refer to mechanical means of sending or receiving a message. While this is true, it shouldn't negate more basic, human forms of communication during an emergency. I have already written about the power of the tribe, of having many people who are all on the same page regarding a certain intention. A well-oiled and disciplined team can accomplish much more than the stoic loner. Any neighborhood that can be cultivated to prepare together for emergencies will be a force to be reckoned with when the chips fly. Although done so after the fact, tight-knit communities in New Orleans did what they had to do to take care of their own after Hurricane Katrina. Taking the bull by the horns, neighborhood "tribes" quickly sprung up to do what governmental agencies had failed to do.

These tribes had the courage and wisdom to effectively communicate their needs to others. This initial communication was fostered months and years before the hurricane struck by people who talked with each other on a daily basis. Even if they weren't friends, they damn sure knew who was in their neighborhood and their basic patterns and habits of movement. When the elderly lady who lived alone with her cat didn't put the cat out as she did each morning, her neighbors noticed and came running to check up on her. Everyone took the responsibility for being the eyes and ears of the neighborhood, before and after the disaster. The flip side of this is the elderly gentleman in New York state who spent an entire year in front of his TV, even though he was dead. Plumbers responding to damaged water lines due to frozen pipes found his literally mummified corpse sitting in front of the television, which was still on. When questioned by news crews, neighbors had assumed that he had been taken to a care home, regardless of the mail that piled up and spilled into the street from his mailbox.

I know it's difficult to know your neighbors in our fast-paced, individualized society, where cyber-friends are more common than human friends. Being an instructor and leader of people under great psychological and physiological stress in remote wilderness areas, I understand fully that getting people on the same page in a stressful time is similar to herding senile cats with three legs. You must try. You must try as hard as you can to put your personal agendas behind you and bend for

the common good of the whole. Once the situation goes the way of *Lord of the Flies*, you will be hard-pressed to restore any useful communication or cooperation with others. The "other people" variable, in other words, human nature under pressure, is perhaps the biggest wild card in your urban emergency. It may be one of the biggest challenges you will face as a leader as you try to piece your neighborhood back together one home at a time. (Whether you are conscious of the fact or not, the material in this book is priming you for your leadership role during emergencies.)

Neighborhood block watches are helpful, as at the very least you'll meet your neighbors. Wanting to know who lives near you and communicate basic plans and precautions does not mean you need to spill the beans about everything your family has stored to prepare for a crisis. Use caution, common sense, and let your intuition be your guarding guide as you sift through how you'll interact with neighbors. Although I want you to try to bridge the gap and put yourself out there to others, I'm well aware of the unfortunate fact that in this current day and age, loose lips can sink ships.

"All in the Family" Signals (The Emergency Game Plan)

The knowledge of knowing where your family members are after a catastrophe is pure gold. If applicable to your situation, agree upon a prior plan or plans of action

> **"I HAVE SEEN** that in **ANY GREAT UNDERTAKING** it is **NOT ENOUGH** for a man to depend **SIMPLY UPON HIMSELF."**
>
> —Lone Man (Isna-la-wica), Teton Sioux

about what to do when a crisis hits and you have no other means to communicate with each other. A form of this advanced game plan is common in the realm of the modern survival scenario where the outdoor enthusiast, *before* they leave for the outdoors, leaves a detailed game plan about where they are going and when they will be back with at least two loved ones. This 5-W game plan is composed of the following parts:

Where you will be going
When you will return
What vehicle you're driving (or whatever means of transportation you're using)
Who is in your party
Why you're taking the trip

If this seems extraneous for an urban situation, a minute's pause will confirm that most family members automatically do this anyway before they leave for work or school. Brother Jim (who) goes to his job (why) at the gas station (where), after which he'll return home a bit after 5 p.m. (when), and he's driving his blue and gray Toyota pickup truck with California license plate 0U812 (what). If something happens to Jim, or Jim needs to be contacted for whatever reason, the rest of the family is not totally in the dark about how to get a hold of him.

I strongly recommend that your family have a game plan about *what to do* and *where to meet* should a major disaster occur. All forms of communication, even smoke signals and signal mirrors, are composed of moving parts, and moving parts can fail under the real-time stresses of a survival scenario. If everything else goes to pot, your family game plan will give you a tangible goal upon which to focus your attention.

Using Your Home as a Signal to Emergency Response Personnel

There are times when using a simple signal from your home, whether you are in your home or not, can dramatically reduce the bureaucracy inherent within disaster mitigation. Each summer in the dense ponderosa pine forests surrounding Prescott, Arizona, the talk always turns to fire danger due to the prolonged drought in the Southwest. Many mountain communities are shoved deep into the hills, and the access and communications required to evacuate certain neighborhoods is sketchy at best.

Cooperating with local fire agencies *before* a potential deadly wildfire, many neighborhoods worked out a simple communications plan to alert the authorities as to whether they were still in their home or had evacuated to safer ground. This common-sense, no-frills system revolved around hanging a white towel from the front door as a signal that the home was empty. This simple yet effective idea saves precious time and resources, as emergency response personnel are relieved of having to knock on every door to alert homeowners of the need to evacuate. Firefighters know from the street whether homeowners have safely left their homes or not.

It would be very wise to get together within your family or community and do something similar; coordinate with local disaster response personnel to have a commonly understood and acknowledged system of communications before the next crisis.

Reverse 911

Some law enforcement agencies are using the "reverse 911" method to relay emergency information to households. The concept is to notify homes within the path of a pending disaster by using a prerecorded phone message. If your home lies within the corridor of an approaching tornado, for example, you would get a heads-up phone call providing information to help you mitigate its effect, whether you seek shelter or evacuate the area. Although some privacy advocates are bitching about this, I would much rather get a phone call about an approaching killer hurricane than not be pestered about buying car insurance or vitamins. If used responsibly, this is a great asset to get the word out about a potential disaster, but it's only effective if the phone lines are intact and you're home to take the call.

The (Disaster) AM/FM Radio

(*Important Note:* All of the following means of communication require a power source. For obvious reasons, always opt for battery-operated models or other forms of alternative power that are not subject to the whims of the conventional power grid. For this reason and portability issues, television is not recommended as a sole means for retrieving emergency information after a disaster.)

The more you can control the receiving end of a broadcast, the better off you may be. In other words, although satellite radio has more news channels than you have fingers, if the company that broadcasts them into your living room is down, you're left in the dark. Every home should have a basic AM/FM radio on hand that does not require conventional electricity to operate. AA battery-operated radios are the most obvious choice and there are a plethora of them to choose from. If you live in a more remote suburban or rural area, you might need a stronger radio that can aggressively pick up weaker signals. People living in heavily wooded or mountainous terrain may also suffer from broken, static-filled radio signals. The chances are high that you already know if your radio cuts out or not; but maybe not. With the advent of music technology from satellite radio to iPods, conventional AM/FM radios are becoming a thing of the past. Test whether your AM/FM radio works for your location. Don't worry so much about crystal clear reception as you're not concerned with listening to Mozart. Many AM broadcasts will trump FM broadcasts for disaster news, and some can be picked up from a very long distance, especially at night. *If a widespread emergency occurs, civil defense-affiliated stations are set up to broadcast survival information on the AM broadcast band.*

There are several battery-operated radios that also feature a built-in hand crank to generate power. These models are wonderful as you'll always have power, and the crank enables you to save stored batteries for other uses such as flashlights.

Beware of cheaper hand-crank models that flood the market, especially in dark and dingy military surplus stores. I've also seen radios with a built-in solar panel for self-charging during sunny daylight hours. I can't overemphasize how important this piece of gear can be to your family's survival, so spend the money to purchase a brand-name, reliable radio. Free-playing radios such as the "crystal radios" composed of a coil of wire, a tuning capacitor, a crystal diode, and an earphone are also a possibility. World War II soldiers improvised crystal radios from their trenches by using coat hangers, the lead from a pencil, and a razor blade, among other parts, to keep up with the daily news.

"**COMMUNICATIONS** is the number **ONE** [college] **MAJOR** in America today. **CNN** had **25,000 APPLICANTS** for **FIVE INTERN JOBS** this **SUMMER.**"

—Larry King

Cell Phones

While cell phone coverage and quality has improved over the years, it still has much to be desired. The motto of one well-known provider, "Can you hear me now?" is all too appropriate at times. I know people who have cell phones on steroids complete with directional antennae, the thickest antennae wire available, and an amplifier, and yet during times of rain still have a problem getting reception, even when dropping from digital to analog.

Cell towers rely on regular AC power for their operation. During times of mass hysteria even those towers with backup power will be compromised, as everyone and their pet will be attempting to use their phone. Cell phones can also, like anything else involving complexities with many moving parts and people, simply fail to work when you need them most. Satellite phones are available if you have the money to pay for the minutes, yet even these phones could be taxed beyond their limits if everyone decides at the same time to pull an E.T. and phone home.

Cell phone batteries at the current time are hopelessly short-lived and sensitive to fluctuations in temperature, especially the cold, which sucks the power from the battery even when the phone is turned off. It's now common knowledge that the cell phone battery itself is a "bug." It can be used as a listening device by certain agencies, whether it's in the phone or not, to listen and record conversations unbeknownst to the owner of the phone. At least we can be assured that this power won't be abused ...

While cell phones are cool, and they have saved many lives, they have also inadvertently killed stupid owners who put all of their welfare and self-reliance into

a fickle, battery-powered machine with finicky reception in geographically chal-
lenged locations. Many places out West still don't have any hope of getting a signal.
Ever try to make a cell phone call on the flats of the Painted Desert on the Navajo
Indian reservation ... can you hear me now?

Internet

Internet access to news, weather, and e-mail, like everything based upon electricity
and phone lines, is vulnerable to chaos. Even satellite Internet powered by independent solar power can have problems. You may fail to get online due to a storm near
your provider, hundreds of miles away, while the weather around your computer is
sunny with blue skies.

SUPER-SIZED SOLAR FLARES AND YOU

**"Our increasingly technologically dependent society is becoming
increasingly vulnerable to space weather."**
—David Johnson, director, National Weather Service

**Technology junkies take heart. According to scientists, many
forms of electronic communication and navigation, such as Global
Positioning Systems (GPS), are vulnerable to solar flares. So what,
you say? GPS is far from a glorified compass used only by people
navigating the great outdoors. It is integral in newer cell phones
to allow emergency personnel to find an owner after an accident
and is responsible for navigating airplanes, automobiles, and
ships, transferring currency to and from banks, and many other
government and commercial activities.**

**According to a recent news report, a jumbo solar flare last
December influenced every GPS device on Earth that was experiencing daylight at the time. Some GPS systems only burped
and were reduced in their accuracy while others were completely
knocked out of commission. Even more troubling and baffling
to the experts is that the flare also affected some satellites and
fiddled with the electrical grid. The ramifications of a more powerful solar flare are sobering; one could affect the entire way most
countries conduct business, from the sale of fuel to food.**

**According to experts, there is no quick fix and the options that
are available are very expensive. Put this pearl of wisdom in the
back of your noggin and know there is something to be said for
low-tech common-sense solutions to daily living.**

Citizens' Band (CB) Radios

Breaker, breaker, Teddy Bear! Remember the movie *Smokey and the Bandit* with Burt Reynolds? What a classic. It seemed that no one in those happily bygone days was without a CB radio, a dorky handle (CB name), and a souped-up black Trans-Am with a golden eagle on the hood. My grandparents had a blast with their base station CB, and all of us pain-in-the-butt grandkids abused it often to report from our vehicle CBs that we were stuck in the mud (again) at the old bass fishing hole. I learned early that excellent communications meant that you could ramp up the stupid meter in your cousin's pickup truck with virtually no consequences.

The Federal Communications Commission established Citizens' Band radio in 1958, and there are now over 51 million CB users throughout the United States. In fact, CB radios are the most accessible means of communication for the general public. Their range is typically ten to twenty-five miles but ranges of well over a hundred miles have been commonly reported. Since many users share only a few channels, interference from others can be common, especially during an emergency. CBs are useful as a neighborhood communications system or when on the road to get real-time information from other drivers about blocked roadways or other hazards.

Channel 9 is the nationwide official channel for emergency use and traveler's information. Volunteer members of the Radio Emergency Associated Communications Team (REACT) monitor channel 9 almost continuously all across the United States. These selfless guardian angels typically handle over 100,000 calls for help each year. Some highways and neighborhoods have REACT logo signs readily visible to alert others to their assistance with emergency communications.

Shortwave Radios

"[AFTER A DISASTER] . . . EVEN WITH TECHNOLOGY THE WAY IT IS, IT'S ALWAYS AMATEUR RADIO
THEY FALL BACK ON."
—LLOYD HALGUNSETH, DISTRICT EMERGENCY COORDINATOR, YAVAPAI AMATEUR RADIO CLUB

With a spectrum of 1.7 to 30 megahertz, shortwave radio puts you in touch with
the unfiltered world of international radio whether you live in town or country.
With the right equipment, it can also be used for two-way communications instead of just listening. Almost
every town of any size has an amateur radio club. These radio "hams"
can tell you whatever you want
to know regarding FCC licensing
rules and its use for ham radio
transmission, and members
often have new and used radio
equipment for sale. While some
shortwave radios require regular 120-volt power for operation,
there are many battery-operated
(and even a hand-crank or two!)
models available. The world of the
ham radio operator is almost limitless and a golden asset during and
after any emergency. Thank you,
ham operators, for your dedicated volunteer service to others in their time of great need!

"The **PROBLEM**
with communication . . .
is the **ILLUSION**
that it has **BEEN**
ACCOMPLISHED."
—George Bernard Shaw

Two-Way Radios (Walkie-Talkies)

Like everything else in the communications world, walkie-talkies come in a wide
variety of styles, channels, power outputs, and prices. They can be priceless when
needing to communicate with a minimum amount of interference when a loved
one is a short distance away. Several models feature built-in NOAA weather-band
reception that would prove a valuable asset to the survivor. I remember getting a
cheap pair of walkie-talkies for Christmas when I was a kid and they ranked high on
the "cool meter." They still do, especially when the cell towers aren't working. I have
used them on road trips between multiple vehicles when needing to keep in contact with the other car. Some businesses use certain models for their communication needs of up to three to five miles. Other models are commonly sold in outdoor
and camping stores and are frequently used in the backcountry for everything from
a couple of day hikers keeping in touch to hard-core search-and-rescue missions
involving the coordination of dozens of people. If you feel this type of communication is relevant for your family, research which model(s) would be most applicable
for your needs.

Field Telephones

Available from some military surplus stores, hand-crank field phones that run off D-cell batteries will allow communications for many miles. Although interconnected by a wire, they have their unique applications.

Scanners

Scanners allow you to receive broadcasted information from a variety of sources such as police, ambulance, firefighters, ATF and Border Patrol agents, U.S. Customs, the Federal Emergency Management Agency (FEMA), the National Oceanic and Atmospheric Administration (NOAA), and an unending number of ham radio operators. These people often have cutting-edge information regarding a wide variety of disasters or local emergencies. Volunteer Search and Rescue personnel (SAR) commonly use some type of scanner or scanner/radio combination to listen in on sheriffs' calls that would signal a search-and-rescue mission. You're advised to know the laws regarding intercepting another party's conversation, which mostly revolve around the no-nos of using the intercepted communications for personal gain or discussing it with others. For our intentions of keeping track of events before or after a disaster to keep our families safe, we should be in like Flynn. Regardless, check your state's laws regarding the legal use of scanners.

SUPER SIMPLE SUMMARY

- ⮑ Survival communications are vital to let you know what's going on in the outside world after a disaster. Emergency bulletins will give you extremely valuable information that may directly affect your survival. Because of sloppy reporting and sensationalism, cross-reference emergency broadcasts for bogus information whenever possible.
- ⮑ Don't rely exclusively on one type of emergency communications. Diversify your communication "eggs" and purchase only quality communications gear.
- ⮑ Know your neighbors before a disaster strikes. Cooperative neighborhood planning, and the power that comes from working together toward a common goal, can make the difference between you living or dying during a crisis.
- ⮑ Creating an advanced "signaling system" for whatever is needed within your community can save precious time and emergency response resources.

⊃ How other people react to an emergency, whether you feel you know them well or not, will be one of your biggest leadership (communication) challenges during a crisis.

⊃ Use caution and common sense, and let your intuition be your guarding guide as to what information you'll share with neighbors.

⊃ Your family should have a well-known game plan about *what to do* and *where to meet* should a major disaster occur.

⊃ Most emergency communications require a power source. Always opt for battery-operated models or other forms of alternative power that are not dependent upon the conventional power grid.

⊃ Battery-operated or hand-crank AM/FM radios are great for receiving emergency broadcasts. If a widespread emergency occurred, civil defense-affiliated stations are set up to broadcast survival information on the AM broadcast band.

⊃ Cell phones, the Internet, CB radios, shortwave radios, walkie-talkies, field telephones, and scanners all have their pros and cons for use during emergencies. See which combination works best for your family.

⊃ For CB radios, channel 9 is the nationwide official channel for emergency use and traveler's information. Volunteer members of the Radio Emergency Associated Communications Team (REACT) monitor channel 9 almost continuously all across the United States.

⊃ Amateur radio clubs around the nation are great resources for learning the tricks of the trade and for buying used or new equipment from knowledgeable people.

⊃ Scanners allow you to monitor the conversations of many emergency response authorities such as the police, the sheriff's office, or the fire department. Check your state rules and regulations for the legality of doing so.

Tangible
TRANSPORTATION

"There can be no doubt that the transportation sector is the most critical sector of our economy."
—Congressman Robert A. Brady

Although this book is based upon making your home more self-reliant, it assumes that you'll be home when the crisis hits. Whether you're at home, across the county, or at the office, your transportation options may be severely limited during the chaos. Perhaps no other country on earth is more enslaved to conventional, fuel-burning transportation than the United States. Transportation is the lifeblood of the economy, which would quickly collapse if the means for transporting needed supplies were disrupted in any way. Grocery stores commonly carry only a three-day supply of food. This statistical three-day surplus would disappear within a few hours during an emergency situation; a panicked populace would make sure of that.

Civilization is like a great web upon which all things are connected. Bop one strand and the whole thing jiggles. Consider for a moment the 1996 northeast power outage and some of the aftereffects that rippled across the nation. Gas stations closed due to a lack of power. Only a few stations had backup power to run gas pumps and were providing what little gas they had to lined-up customers for cash only. ATM machines wouldn't work so people were unable to get cash. Grocery stores closed due to their inability to scan the barcodes on food or to take credit cards. I won't go into the drama about power-dependent medical needs and water and sewage pumps.

Complacency as to the ease at which modern transportation systems operate can do wonders in dumbing you down as to what options you might have when the Pontiac is forced to collect dust. Below are some common-sense and exotic tidbits to ponder if you get caught out in the open away from your casa, or you need to relocate.

Preparing Your Motorized Vehicle(s)

Most of us in this country rely upon the automobile for getting around. As we have discussed in earlier chapters, anything that you have a strong reliance upon should be in the best possible working order, with backup options if possible. Keep in good repair the best vehicle you can afford. If you suck at car repairs, and aren't married to Mr. or Mrs. Goodwrench, it's all the more reason to keep on top of servicing your vehicle. Whether something is wrong or not, it pays to take your vehicle to a reputable shop at least once a year to have them do a top-to-bottom inspection. Like survival training, it's easier to prevent a problem than to suffer from its effects because you were too cheap or preoccupied to take your ride in for some TLC. Your car, truck, or SUV should carry basic supplies that will allow you to get back home (on foot if necessary) and accomplish minor repairs to the vehicle itself if needed. The "Should I Stay or Should I Go" chapter contains some general ideas for portable survival kits and bug-out packs.

You know your daily living schedule better than anyone. If your work takes you many miles from home, get into the habit of keeping your gas tank topped off. One of the main disadvantages of our current means of transportation is its slap-in-the-face dependency on petroleum fuel. The last place you want to be when chaos strikes is stuck in the two-mile line at the gas station because you failed to keep your fuel level on the high side. That's what your gas tank is for, to store fuel in times of need, so do it.

What about Public Transportation?

Even the most hardcore New York City cab driver is powerless when streets are stuffed with traffic. You will go nowhere fast, if at all. Mass exoduses like those preceding and following disasters such as Hurricane Katrina are case in point that it will be hell to negotiate traffic in a private vehicle, let alone rely upon public transit systems. If Lady Luck smiles on you in your quest to catch a bus or cab, congratulations, but don't count on it. Local, state, or federal governmental agencies that do manage to implement some type of public emergency transportation will more than likely limit their passengers to one carry-on bag, if that. Have an emergency bug-out kit ready to go at all times.

Bodacious Biodiesel and Veggie Oil

"THE USE OF VEGETABLE OILS FOR ENGINE FUELS MAY SEEM INSIGNIFICANT TODAY, BUT SUCH OILS MAY BECOME, IN THE COURSE OF TIME, AS IMPORTANT AS PETROLEUM AND THE COAL-TAR OF THE PRESENT TIME."
—RUDOLF DIESEL, 1912

For those with the opportunity, the interest, and a form of transportation or backup power that involves a diesel engine, there are pockets of people around the nation and world who are reclaiming their independence with the technology of biodiesel and waste cooking oils. *Biodiesel* is derived from biological sources, from rapeseed and soybean oils to animal fats and many others, yet it goes through a refinery process called *transesterification*. As a refined fuel, biodiesel is ready to use to power diesel engines and is not the same as burning straight *filtered vegetable oil*. Biodiesel has also been used as a heating fuel in domestic and commercial boilers. This alternative fuel is gaining more and more popularity as time passes and people feel the pinch of precarious petroleum. According to the National Biodiesel Board (NBB), the United States went from consuming 500,000 gallons in 1999 to 75 million gallons of biodiesel in 2005. Even country crooner Willie Nelson has been bitten by the bio bug and actively promotes the stuff.

"ALL PROGRESS has resulted from people who took UNPOPULAR POSITIONS."
—Adlai Stevenson

If you think biodiesel is made for hippies by hippies, you haven't explored its technical side, which involves aspects of extreme mathematics, chemistry, physics, and linguistics when trying to read through some of the technical papers. Some biodiesel advocates tout the recycling aspects of biodiesel by the fact that it can be manufactured from used vegetable oil. Others argue that to compete with the sheer volume of fuel needed to keep just America running at its current level, even biodiesel would have its problems in trying to meet the demand. Since the U.S. Environmental Protection Agency (EPA) states that restaurants in the United States produce 300 million gallons of waste cooking oil each year, and the estimated transportation fuel and home heating oil use for America is a staggering 230 billion gallons annually, they may be correct.

The art of making and using biodiesel or using filtered oils or fats in a modified diesel engine is a book in itself. Researching on the Web will pull up loads of information for those who want to pursue the matter further. You may already have a neighbor who has been commuting to work for years thanks to the dregs from greasy spoon restaurants. I know several people who make and use both biodiesel and filtered-waste cooking oils in their backyard processing plants. One of my clients owns a converted school bus he uses for cross-country trips that runs on filtered veggie oil. He simply stops at restaurants instead of gas stations and they are all too willing to give him the goop, which otherwise the restaurant must pay to have removed. They've driven thousands of miles with their veggie bus and, yes, the tailpipe smells like French fries.

Regardless of saving the world or not, after a calamity, alternative fuel options such as biodiesel and filtered cooking oils may be the cat's meow. If you have a diesel-burning engine in your car, truck, or generator, you might want to pursue this further. For a current list of who sells biodiesel around the nation, or for questions, and access to the largest library of biodiesel information in the United States, visit the National Biodiesel Board Web site at www.biodiesel.org.

Motorcycles, Mopeds, and ATVs

While the above-mentioned goodies are still slaves to OPEC, they excel at making the most out of a gallon of gas. Some hybrid electric mopeds claim to get an astounding 150 miles per gallon! Scooters and ATVs also have the advantage of being small and maneuverable, thus they are able to fit in and around places that would stop a car dead in its tracks. Remember seeing those motorcycle maniacs on the highway snake between vehicles like they were standing still? You acted disgusted but were probably jealous, right? "Quads" or All-Terrain Vehicles (ATVs) are very popular in my part of the country. Some can haul a ridiculous amount of gear due to generous cargo space.

One of my favorite alternative vehicles is the street-legal dirt bike. A good quality dirt bike that's well maintained will run almost forever with minimal fuss. In town or country, there is almost no terrain these bikes will not cross with a proficient rider. They possess a stupid amount of power that will peel your skin off, can cover rugged ground in a fraction of the time it takes a hearty four-wheel drive, and still get up to 120 miles on a gallon and a half of gas. A rider can purchase or make racks for hauling gear, or simply wear a backpack when needing to transport goods. Dirt bikes are truly modern horses that require minimal feed and no water, don't spook or become moody or go lame, and will take you like a rocket as far as your butt can stand to go.

Beautiful Bicycles

I love bicycles. After all, can zillions of Chinese folks be wrong? I spent a few years riding a mountain bike to work, school, and back up into the woods where I was living at the time. My stashed bike was easy to conceal in the bushes as I hiked toward my home, thus it left no trace that I was camped nearby. Bikes are simple, affordable, easy to ride or learn to ride, fairly easy to repair, commonly available, quick, quiet, and save tremendous amounts of your personal calories (food) and water, which is their only required fuel. Being able to coast and still cover ground is a gift in any scenario where food supplies may be compromised. Generic, cheap mountain-bike-style bicycles have the balls to cruise over everything from beer cans to bloated bodies with minimal effort. Many bikes on the market have options for saddlebags or other pouches that can carry all sorts of supplies to boot. You don't have to break the bank to purchase a battle-worthy bicycle, and for many urban dwellers, bicycles will be worth their weight in gold as a super-transportation option if the petrol gets pinched.

Animal Magnetism

Animals have been used for thousands of years to carry people and goods. My family owns horses and pack mules, and I have friends who own pack llamas. While these animals are not likely to be accessible in downtown San Francisco, you can mimic the intention with a decent-size dog. My family has owned several big dogs and all of them had doggie packs in which they carried their stuff and some of ours too on cross-country treks. Long before the horse, native peoples on this continent routinely used camp dogs and *travois* (two wooden poles laden with gear and anchored to the dog's back) to move their camp from place to place. The dogs also served as hunters, heaters, guard dogs, and emergency food—although I promised you I wouldn't talk about cooking the family pet in this book.

Walk This Way: Fabulously Functional Footwear

During prehistoric times people were very mobile yet had limited means of getting around other than by foot. Indigenous peoples across the world commonly embarked upon great journeys of hundreds of miles on foot through extreme wilderness with the barest of survival necessities made from Nature Herself. Reflecting upon the forced marches that were perpetrated upon our own native peoples in the late 1800s should foster within you a "can-do" attitude regarding walking across town if the grid goes flop. Even during good times, your hunter-gatherer ancestors migrated hundreds of miles each season in order to find what was needed to put soup on the table.

A crucial item for transportation is a comfortable pair of footwear suitable for walking long distances. Although it may sound obvious, look down at your feet. Could you walk a few miles across your town or city with what you're wearing now? Would the Snoopy slippers hold up? If you're living in a rural area, would your trashy tennies cut it for the journey across the woods or desert? Many urban dwellers don footwear, especially for the office or nightclub, that would cripple them in a mile or two. If you blister your feet during the first ten blocks while trying to make it back home, the remainder of your journey will be extremely painful if not impossible. I'm not trying to cramp your style scene, just have a pair of spare *broken-in* shoes or boots, along with an extra pair of socks, at the office or

"A man travels the world over in search of **WHAT HE NEEDS,** and returns home **TO FIND IT."**
—George Moore

in the car as a backup. *Take heed, there is nothing that will ruin your day, and your feet, quicker than ill-fitting, new, or inappropriate footwear when you need to walk even a short distance.* Your ability to walk or run may be your only option for evading surrounding dangers to your survival.

It's worth having at least one pair of quality footwear that will hold up to the stresses and strains of serious walking in all types of terrain. Cheap shoes and boots are just that, cheap, and should not be trusted if your compromising situation becomes long term. I have witnessed several pairs of discount-store sandals, boots, and shoes blow up on my field courses. Hot ground temperatures in the desert can completely delaminate a new pair of sandals in less than an hour. I'm not an authority on helping you choose quality boots or shoes, but shoe stores specializing in high-end footwear will be able to assist you. Make sure to break in your new purchase by wearing them several times for greater comfort and to help prevent blisters.

I'm a big fan of going barefoot for a variety of reasons, one of which is to keep my feet tough and conditioned for cross-country walking. There is a reason opposing militaries took the boots of POWs; tender feet have little hope of escaping and evading through challenging terrain. I'm not advocating going barefoot in cities. At least in the wilderness one has a chance to pay attention to variables that influence the growth of certain painfully pointy plants. In the town or city, you'll never know what terrain dangers lay around the next corner, from broken glass, to nails, needles, and much more. Because restaurant owners fear I've walked in dirtier places than other customers, and grocery store clerks lie to me about violating state health codes or worry I'll dance on the Cheetos, I carry a two-dollar pair of flip-flops in my vehicle. While I'm in no way recommending flip-flops as competent walking gear, my guess is they would beat the hell out of a pair of pumps or tight wing-tips. At

Helpful **HARDCORE** *Hints*

that price, there's no excuse for not having a comfortable pair of footwear within reach regardless of your budget.

Improvised Fabric Backpack

I've preached several times about hunting and gathering cultures whose lifestyles mandated moving from one resource to another. One of their most valued possessions—containers—were made from the resources at hand, whether from animal skins or hair, woven plant fibers, fired clay, wood, shells, or other natural niceties. These containers transported all that was needed for a portable household.

When needing to become suddenly portable, you'll want some means of carrying gear that doesn't tie up your hands. If you don't have access to a conventional backpack, you still have options. Several years ago, fellow "abo" Matt Graham turned me onto an improvised backpack that can easily be made from a four-by-four-foot piece of fabric, although smaller and larger pieces of fabric will work fine. The fabric can be a blanket, tablecloth, thin rug, or something else, but steer away from materials that are too thick as they will be difficult to tie and bulky to carry.

You'll quickly learn how to pack your stuff so that softer items are against your back as padding, and sharp objects aren't poking you. To pack your gear, lay the fabric on the ground and start placing what you want to carry in the middle of the fabric. Smaller individual "stuff sacks" can be bought at discount and outdoor stores or improvised from plastic bags, canvas book bags, Tupperware containers, etc. These smaller containers, similar to zippered compartments on and in commercial backpacks, will allow you to separate gear without it all blending together in one confusing mass. The four corners of the fabric will be tied together in pairs; the upper left and lower right corners will come together to form their own knot,

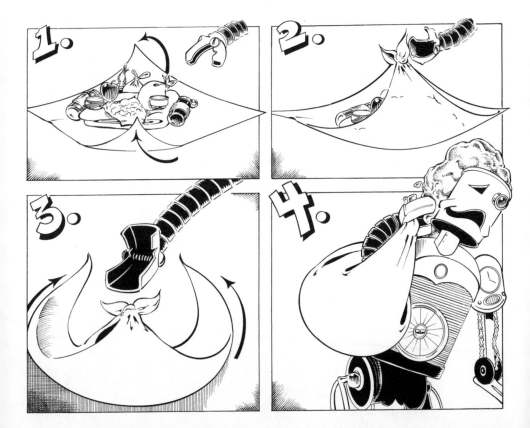

and the upper right and lower left corners will be tied together to form their own knot. (Check out the photo section for more details.) I like to position my gear inside the fabric knowing that I'll tie the upper left and lower right corners together first. These corners should be tied snugly around the bundle as they keep your gear inside the fabric from falling out. The upper right and lower left corners are tied together a bit looser as they will function as the "strap." Newer fabric will stretch and loosen, and things will jumble around causing you to retie the pack a few times. The fabric backpack can be carried in various ways, some of which are illustrated in the photo section. Similar to the hobos, smaller pieces of fabric can wrap up gear in much the same way and be carried suspended from a stick or broom handle.

I use two-dollar fabric backpacks on my outdoor courses side by side with my clients' two- to five-hundred-dollar commercial backpacks. The fabric itself is multi-use and can double as a ground cloth, sun shade, poncho, first-aid bandage, a sling to carry firewood, or bug protection to name a few.

Mobility-Impaired Loved Ones

If your loved ones are mobility impaired due to age, sickness, disease, being out of shape, or a physical handicap, think NOW about options they might use to move about under their own power when needed. Even though it may be inevitable, having to assist them in getting around will be very exhausting for all concerned, even with the luxury of a wheelchair. With aid and extraordinary adaptability, physically impaired people around the world have used anything and everything to get around, from sticks, shopping carts, and car dollies to wheelbarrows and skateboards. If you lack the proper means to transport your loved ones, use your powers of improvisation and adapt your surroundings to meet your needs. If you are unable to freely move about because you're out of shape, do your best to get back in shape or realize your self-imposed limitations. After all, what you're trying to keep alive is your body. The stresses you will experience during an emergency scenario will tax even the healthiest of bodies, so become familiar with what you can and cannot do. Once you know your limits, you'll know what extra goodies you'll need for your mobility issues.

- ➲ Before, during, or after a disaster, you may be forced to travel to another location.
- ➲ Disasters can strike at anytime when you might not be at home, thus making it necessary to make your way back to the house using some form of transportation. Due to the crisis, your transportation options may be severely limited.
- ➲ Keep your motorized vehicle(s) in good repair with the fuel tank full. Carry basic car repair tools in each vehicle.
- ➲ Have needed survival supplies in the vehicle that will allow you to get back home, on foot if necessary, if the situation allows you to do so.
- ➲ Don't count on public transportation after a disaster.
- ➲ While still a slave to gasoline, mopeds, motorcycles, and ATVs go much further on a gallon of gas and are highly maneuverable in tight situations such as clogged freeways and roads.
- ➲ Bicycles are simple, affordable, easy to ride and repair, commonly available, quick, quiet, and save tremendous amounts of your personal calories (food) and water, which is their only required fuel.
- ➲ Have a rugged yet comfortable quality pair of shoes or boots that will allow you to walk great distances if required. Wearing inappropriate footwear can cause painful blisters to manifest in a few short city blocks. If you go to work in high heels or wing-tips, have a back-up pair of walking shoes in the office or your vehicle.
- ➲ An improvised backpack can be made with a four-by-four-foot piece of fabric.
- ➲ Plan ahead for how you will transport mobility-impaired loved ones. If a wheelchair is not an option, use whatever is at hand to transport them under their own power, if possible.
- ➲ The stresses experienced during an emergency scenario will tax even the healthiest of bodies so become familiar with what your body physically can and cannot do.

Should I STAY or Should I GO NOW?

> "The ladies have to go first . . . Get in the lifeboat, to please me . . . Good-bye, dearie. I'll see you later."
>
> — John Jacob Astor, after putting his pregnant wife on one of the last lifeboats available from the *Titanic*

The World Health Organization (WHO) estimates that from 1900–1988, hurricanes left more than 1.2 million people without homes and directly affected the lives of nearly 4 million people. Floods affected another 339 million people and left 36 million homeless. Earthquakes, cyclones, and typhoons each affected 26 million people, leaving 10 million more without a home.

Although this is a home-centered book on self-reliance, statistics such as these prove that an emergency can quickly leave you homeless. I realize leaving your home, by choice or by force, will be an excruciating decision to have to make but remember, *you are trying to save your body and those whom you love, not material possessions.* If you're dumb enough to get killed because you refused to leave your stuff, you win the Darwin award and the planet's gene pool inches up a notch. I don't mean to discount the emotional and mental pain of having to leave your home—I know it's scary—but you need to remind yourself of your survival priorities, that it's YOU that you're trying to keep alive. Material wealth and comfort don't mean squat to a corpse.

Whether your family stays put or evacuates will depend on many factors.

> "NOTHING LASTS forever—NOT even your TROUBLES."
>
> —Arnold H. Glasgow

Such factors might be forced upon you by governmental agencies, approaching floods, hurricanes, and a bevy of scenarios worthy of a Hollywood movie. In any event, you should take the concepts presented in this book regarding shelter, food, water, lighting, etc., and adapt them to what is commonly referred to as a "bug-out" pack. A bug-out pack, not unlike a wilderness survival kit, contains within it a distillation of the most important gear your family will need during its emergency, all in one portable container. This pack should be fully loaded and ready to go *before* it's needed so you can grab it at a moment's notice in case of an evacuation. The concept of the bug-out pack can be used in your car or office as well. You might have two or three bug-out packs. Paranoid? No, just smart. Having all of your eggs in one basket has been a bad idea from the beginning. As much as I love my self-reliant house, there is no guarantee that I'll be home watching cheap pawnshop videos when the fan blades turn brown.

Consider building a family bug-out kit *first, before* outfitting your home. As this pack is portable, its volume will severely limit your ability to fill it with frivolous junk. You will be forced to pare things down to the bare minimum, packing only what your loved ones truly need to deal with their emergency. This forced, minimalist mind-set will train your psyche to define more clearly your needs from your wants, something that has to be continuously guarded against in our consumer society. After reading this book, and reflecting upon the basic intentions recommended, design your kit using the recommendations, dovetailed with your family's situation. When you begin to outfit your home with self-reliant goodies, simply purchase more of the same stuff that you packed within your portable disaster kit.

Basic Bug-Out Kits

The core intention of the contents of a bug-out pack is not unlike the motive of a wilderness backpacker. The modern backpacker carries whatever gear they think will meet their needs within a remote, backcountry setting. Some of this gear is necessary for survival, like proper clothing in cold weather, and some of it is fluff, like the portable espresso coffee-maker. As most outdoor enthusiasts are unfamiliar with using the natural landscape to meet their needs, the backpack becomes a scuba tank, so to speak. The backpacker can live in the ocean of the wilderness for only as long as the supplies in his or her backpack will let them. When supplies run low, they are forced to resurface back at the nearest trailhead or vehicle for resupply. Whether you find yourself in an urban or wilderness environment, the more you know about adapting

> **WHETHER YOU FIND YOURSELF IN AN URBAN OR WILDERNESS ENVIRONMENT, THE MORE YOU KNOW ABOUT ADAPTING YOUR SURROUNDINGS TO MEET YOUR NEEDS FOR SURVIVAL, THE BETTER OFF YOU WILL BE.**

your surroundings to meet your needs for survival, the better off you will be. Like the wilderness survival kit, all items within your bug-out kit should follow strict guidelines as to their usefulness in the environment you'll find yourself. Some items will be of equal value regardless of where you are on the planet, such as potable water. Gear that supports your family's basic physiological survival should be given the first consideration. That said, you may have family members who will function much better when allowed to have along some psychological comfort item. The teddy bear does not replace the coat in cold weather, but we have already discussed how a person's psychology can and does readily influence their physiology. As with all things, use common sense.

Preparing Your Bug-Out Kit

Below is a list of concepts you should consider when deciding what to pack in your bug-out kit. Some of the information was borrowed from my first book, *98.6 Degrees: The Art of Keeping Your Ass Alive!* In it, for those who want more detailed information on survival kits, I devote the second half of the book to describing in detail what I carry for desert and mountain regions. If the list of recommendations below seems anal retentive, remember that it's often a combination of little mistakes that kill people.

Your bug-out kit should be:

➲ **Relevant to the environment encountered**
➲ **Lightweight and portable**

- ⮑ Waterproof
- ⮑ Durable and dependable
- ⮑ Complementary to the physical fitness and expertise levels of the user(s)
- ⮑ Able to meet a wide variety of conditions
- ⮑ Comprised of multiple-use components
- ⮑ Comprised of calorie-conserving components
- ⮑ Panic-proof—containing components that can be utilized if you are injured
- ⮑ Comprised of components that can be easily purchased or made
- ⮑ Obtainable, *yet invisible*
- ⮑ Affordable, yet effective
- ⮑ Field-tested
- ⮑ *Simple!*

Relevant to the Environment Encountered

The world is full of many differences in geography and climate. If your on-the-grid house suddenly becomes off-grid, you will *feel* the landscape and weather variables in which your home sits. You and your family will be subjected to its variables in temperature, weather, and terrain. If your family lives in a hot, arid part of the world, your bug-out kit(s) should reflect this by packing hot-weather items for survival and vice versa for cold conditions.

Lightweight and Portable

Be prepared to leave the proverbial kitchen sink behind. If your kit is not lightweight and portable, it will be impractical to lug around, and it will prevent you from moving quickly. During an evacuation, governmental agencies might limit the amount of gear your fleeing family will be allowed to take, especially if you are forced to utilize public transportation. Attempt to have your hands free from carrying gear. In other words, limit the items you pack to what can be carried upon your back or body with the assistance of backpacks, daypacks, fanny packs, and straps in general. It will be easier to move quickly and you'll have better physical balance with everything packed up tight. Your hands are thus free for collecting, defense, and performing countless tasks for your survival. I have had more than one student ignore this recommendation and carry their camping gear in two duffel bags, one in each hand. This is NOT an efficient way to carry gear. They quickly became exhausted, dehydrated, and much more prone to injuries on the trail.

Waterproof

Many disasters involve large amounts of moisture, whether snow or rain. Even for dry disasters, you can't afford to let some items get wet, such as extra clothing, medications, or matches. In this age of plastic, there is little excuse for not keeping your lifeline dry. Put critical items in zipper-lock freezer bags and double line your entire pack with two garbage bags before packing the items inside. Depending upon the weight of the items packed, the double-lined garbage bags will trap a certain amount of air and possibly keep your bag afloat or allow you to use it as a float if needed. I routinely pack my outdoor gear in garbage bags within my homemade fabric backpack. When needing to swim across a pool within a canyon or whatever, I fold up the material pack, put it inside the garbage bag, retie the bag securely, and utilize the buoyant bag as a float as I kick myself across the water.

Durable and Dependable
To be blunt, the contents of your bug-out kit may be your last defense against death; so don't pack cheap gear.

Complementary to the Physical Fitness and Expertise Levels of the User(s)
Not all body types are the same, nor are levels of individual experience when using gear in scary situations. Unless your family is a group of special warfare soldiers, assess who will use your kit and evaluate limitations in physical fitness and usage competence before your kit is needed.

Able to Meet a Wide Variety of Conditions
Living conditions on the ground can radically change before, during, and after a disaster. The gear you choose to carry should be adaptable over a wide range of weird possibilities. The easiest way to allow your gear maximal adaptability is to stick to the basic concepts needed to support life.

Comprised of Multiple-use Components
Multiple-use components give you the option of doing more with less. The gear you carry should perform two, three, four, or more functions. Two prime examples of multiuse items are fire and a cutting edge. Both helped build every civilization upon this planet and can be used for literally hundreds of tasks. A tarp can shed rain, snow, and wind; block excess sun; catch rain for drinking; or be used as a privacy barrier or a ground cloth, among other uses. When you can no longer go to the store to fulfill your needs, you will be forced to foster an adaptive mind-set about your current resources. Think about this now, as it will dictate what type of gear you choose to pack to meet your desired intentions. The task doesn't have to be scary or a drag. Make a game out of it by posing realistic scenarios to your family with a "what would MacGyver do" analysis.

Comprised of Calorie-Conserving Components
Every time you move your body you burn through calories and water, both of which may be hard to come by in the chaos. Your body is like a battery and contains only so much stored energy reserves, and you don't know what shape your battery will be

in when thrust into a disaster. Keep your gear simple in nature and practice using it to develop a natural rhythm that will allow you to receive its benefits with minimal effort. Ultimately, you want to remain as lazy as possible while meeting your needs. For those with families, wisely distributing physical tasks will help even out the calorie-load demands upon the tribe.

Panic-proof—Containing Components That Can Be Utilized if You Are Injured
Unfortunately, the possibility of you or your loved ones sustaining an injury during an emergency is high. The combination of deteriorating fine and complex motor skills along with being hurt can leave your emergency gear extremely difficult to use. Don't assume that you'll have the use of both hands and feet during your crisis.

Comprised of Components That Can Be Easily Purchased or Made
Although I emphasized the importance of quality gear in your bug-out pack, it doesn't have to come from a one-of-a-kind specialty shop in Highmore, South Dakota. Specialty gear can not only be expensive, but it can also be a drag to find spare parts for, repair, or replace. While there are those who will travel to the middle of the earth for the perfect survival gear, most will not. Basic emergency supplies for your family should be obtainable in a few commonly available discount and hardware stores or rigged from something you already have in the closet or the garage.

Obtainable, yet Invisible
Your bug-out pack should be available for you to grab in a moment's notice, not for someone else to grab at a moment's notice. Be discreet about the look and placement of your emergency supplies, especially at the office or in the car. Blabbing about your kit to others will raise eyebrows for a variety of reasons, so keep your mouth shut.

Affordable, yet Effective
You shouldn't need to break the bank when purchasing your supplies. Firmly determining your tribe's intention about what is required and sticking to the basics will allow you to bypass the opinions of survival specialists and their inflated egos and prices.

Field-tested
Having gear in your bug-out pack doesn't mean squat unless you know how to use it. Decide what you're going to carry, change things around based upon common sense and the current situation, and get your butt out into the backyard and PRACTICE setting up your disaster supplies. Remember, things will not be happy, sunny, and calm when you use this stuff. If the efficiency in the use of your gear rates 100 percent when things are good, expect your performance to fall off by 50 percent or more when under disaster stress.

Simple!

All of the above concepts should harmoniously revolve around the innocence and power of simplicity. According to Murphy's Law, if the contents of your pack are not simple to obtain or make, pack and carry, use under stress, and repair or replace, you may pay for your self-imposed complexities with your life.

Bug-Out Kit Recommendations

If you were limited to a small backpack to carry gear relevant to your family's survival during an urban disaster, what would you choose? Pretty heavy decision to have to make, isn't it? Unlike a wilderness survival scenario where the statistics show that the vast majority of deaths are caused by lack of core body temperature via hypothermia and hyperthermia, there are no statistics that I'm aware of for how people most commonly die in an urban emergency. Some studies have shown that deaths associated with rapid-onset disasters are overwhelmingly due to blunt trauma, crush-related injuries, or drowning. We can make a few educated guesses as to the faces of death; surely hypothermia and hyperthermia are big contenders when people are forced from their homes during hot or cold weather, along with dehydration or drowning, crushing injuries, fires, falling, auto accidents, violent crime, and malnutrition, starvation, and disease for prolonged emergencies.

As the variables are so huge as to what could happen during a crisis, it's all the more reason to keep things simple and stick to basic core concepts for supporting life. If you live in an earthquake-prone spot, you should research earthquakes and modify your bug-out pack and everything else in your house to reflect this danger. *There is no one-size-fits-all bug-out pack any more than there is a one-size-fits-all home preparedness plan for every household.* Anyone who tells you differently is a fool or a liar and usually stands to profit from their opinion—at your expense. Take what you want from my recommendations below and modify them to fit your needs, which at this point should be fairly clear.

"**IF** you are **GOING THROUGH HELL,** keep **GOING.**"

—Winston Churchill

Bug-Out Kit Ideas

Remember, think like a backpacker and modify your "bug-out backpack" to take into account the variables of your urban wilderness. The art of *how* you pack your gear is important as well. Don't bury frequently used items under the sleeping bag. Think ahead about what high-use items you'll need from your pack and keep them easily accessible. Human beings are highly visual creatures so mark gear when appropriate with brightly colored tape. Individual stuff sacks help to separate and compartmentalize gear to make it easier to locate and identify when floating around in the bowels of a large-capacity pack.

Modify this list as you see fit based upon the needs of your family. In essence, much like the wilderness backpacker, your bug-out pack should hold the key to your independent and portable self-reliance when renewing your survival supplies is not an option.

Large-Capacity Backpack or Duffel Bag

How much pack room you'll need is dependent upon what you choose to put into it. You'll find that the following items, whether you carry all of them or not, will quickly fill even the largest pack. If you have several family members, items can be divvied up between your tribe using multiple packs. Even so, each individual should carry items critical to their survival such as adequate clothing and water should they be separated from the main group.

Tarp or Tent

I've already written about the virtues of tarps in the shelter chapter. Pick a style and size that's portable but still protects your family from the environment. Tents are easy-to-set-up, bugproof, portable shelters that keep you dry and out of the wind. Backpacking tents are extremely durable, compact, and lightweight.

Clothing Appropriate for the Season and Weather

Clothing is your first line of defense against the killers hypothermia and hyperthermia. Clothing is supremely important and should keep the survivor warm, cool, protected from the sun and from bugs, and be quick drying, durable, and nonrestrictive. I realize clothing is bulky and takes up a lot of space in your pack but you cannot afford to skimp on this item, especially during cold weather. Having a fresh, clean change of clothing will ensure optimal insulative properties from the clothing itself and give a lift to your morale. If applicable, it will also help to mask your initial appearance and help you better blend into the environment when people are "looking for the guy in the blue sweater."

Comfortable Walking Footwear

This is arguably one of the most important items on this list. If you trash your feet due to ill-fitting or inadequate footwear, your portable bug-out pack will no longer be portable as you won't be able to walk. The added weight from the pack and weird conditions or long lines you may be subjected to will take their toll on your tootsies so have comfortable footwear that also has the needed ankle support. Footwear is so important that I recommend you have an extra pair of durable sandals that can be easily clipped onto the outside of your pack. If appropriate for the season, sandals allow you to air out and dry your feet and socks; wetness is one of the main culprits behind the creation of blisters.

Wool or Synthetic Blankets or Sleeping Bag and Pad
Have the portable insulation required to sleep comfortably during outside temperature extremes. The ability to achieve adequate sleep is paramount to your attitude and overall survival for a number of reasons. Backpacking sleeping bags and foam sleeping pads are super-lightweight and portable and lash directly onto most conventional backpacks.

Space Blanket(s) (Large and Small Sizes)
Multiple-use space blankets come in handy in hot and cold weather and are explained in the shelter chapter.

Water Disinfection Method(s)
Water is your life's blood. The majority of found water sources will need to be disinfected after a disaster.

Water Bottles with Lanyard and Duct Tape
Durable storage containers will be needed to disinfect and transport potable water. Duct tape wrapped around the bottles can be peeled off and used for many tasks.

Sanitation and Hygiene Supplies
If you become sick during an emergency due to improper sanitation, your game might be over. Tampons or sanitary napkins can also be used on wounds or as fire tinder. Toothbrushes and dental floss take up very little space and make being on the road much more comfortable.

Garbage Bags/Barrel Liners
Lightweight, cheap, compact nonpermeable barriers can adapt to dozens of survival needs. A barrel liner can be put over yourself and your pack to keep both dry in the nastiest downpour.

Nonperishable, No-cook, High-energy Food
Lightweight, compact, long-lasting freeze-dried or dehydrated backpacking food fits the bill nicely. In a pinch, water can be added directly to the foil packets, heated or otherwise, and the contents consumed with a stick or by squeezing the foil pouch itself. Unless you have no other option, the weight and bulk of canned goods are oppressive and should be avoided when carrying your life on your back.

Heavy-Duty Zipper-lock Freezer Bags
These tough, collapsible, multiuse, food-grade plastic, waterproof containers are sent straight from heaven.

Methods to Light Fire
Along with the cutting edge, this item has helped build every civilization on the planet. Fire can be used to cook food, disinfect water, make tools, regulate core body temperature, signal for rescue, psychologically calm scared survivors, keep away bugs, consume trash, create light for the night, sterilize first-aid kit supplies, and more. Have three gross-motor methods to light fire in three different locations on and around your person.

Knife
Sharp metal knives have endless uses. As with fire, practice using them beforehand in order to be able to achieve the greatest number of uses with the safest results under stress.

Flashlight with Extra Batteries
A kid-safe light source makes life easier in hundreds of ways.

Rope or String
This is useful for countless tasks and to lash other gear or found items to your backpack without having to carry them in your hands. Dental floss is incredibly tough and compact.

First-aid Kit
A basic first-aid kit should be a part of everyone's pack. Don't pack medical gear that you don't know how to use.

Cook Pot with Lid
Use the pot for storing survival gear, cooking food, disinfecting water, digging a sanitation trench in soft earth, and much, much more.

Portable Radio
Super small radios are handy for keeping up with the disaster and the following emergency response.

Lightweight Leather Gloves
Survival tasks can be very rough on smooth city hands. Painfully blistered hands can seriously affect your ability to get even the most basic tasks accomplished. Open blisters are open invitations for infection due to decreased sanitary opportunities.

Game(s)

Boredom might be your biggest enemy. A simple deck of cards or some other small game to occupy the attention of survivors can be invaluable for morale.

Pet Supplies

Don't forget a leash, pet food, and whatever else is required if you plan on hitting the road with your pet.

Mirror

A small mirror comes in handy for removing foreign objects from the eye and checking on your sense of self. Although any mirror can be used to signal for rescue, the sightable military models excel at being able to hit the target under stress.

Whistle

The piercing blast from a brightly colored, "pea-less" whistle can be used to signal or warn the family or attract the attention of rescuers while saving vocal cords, water, and calories lost to shouting.

Bandana

Cotton or synthetic bandanas have hundreds of uses. It's a potholder, a headband, a scarf, a hat, a filter worn over the mouth for dusty or cold air, a wash cloth, a signal flag, a bandage, a sling, a container, cordage, pack-strap padding, a sediment filter for straining water, or anything else your imagination can come up with.

Sunscreen and Insect Repellent

Depending on the climate and season, these two items can make or break your experience. Remember that proper clothing should be able to deal with both.

Medications and/or Extra Glasses

Nothing else matters if you're dead before nightfall because you forgot your medications or couldn't see the approaching gang of thugs.

Money in Small Bills

Paper money talks as long as the system still supports its use. Throughout the centuries, people have bought off other people to save their own lives. Don't discount the unfortunate fact that greed will override altruism for many people when pushed to the wall by survival stress.

Identification and Pertinent Important Papers

You now require a passport to get back into the country when visiting other lands controlled by the United States. Don't give authorities the excuse to hold up your access to lifesaving transportation or supplies due to questions about your identity. Take the hint and carry the identification required to allow you to flow through roadblocks and other emergency response obstacles like greased lightning.

Cell Phone
Don't count on this working after a disaster but they are too compact, lightweight, and valuable to emergency communications to leave behind. Use sparingly to save the battery.

Watch or Clock
Knowing the time may be necessary to coordinate with other family members or to cooperate with emergency response personnel.

Car Kits
Whether you have a car kit or not and how comprehensive it is depends upon how important your vehicle is to your overall survival plan and how much space you have to store supplies. It's not uncommon in America to commute several miles to work. I know people who commute nearly a hundred miles per day, one way! If your vehicle serves you in this fashion, as a sort of home away from home, plan accordingly and make sure you pack the needed emergency gear whether you stay put at your current location or try to make it back to the house.

My vehicle is equipped with the bare necessities from the above bug-out kit list along with modifications. Many parts of the western United States are vastly different from the East in regard to distances between towns and cities. When I have hitchhiked back East, as soon as I was leaving one town I was entering another. In the West, there can be well over a hundred miles between the tiniest of trailer-park trash settlements, let alone a town of any size. Some of my vehicle survival kit components allow me to obtain supplies, if necessary, from the outdoors while making my way back to civilization. As I've said time and time again, there is no one-size-fits-all survival kit destined to meet every need, so modify your kit as you see fit.

Whether you pack the basics or the kitchen sink, make sure the components are in a portable container such as a spare daypack or duffle bag in case you need to hit the road while on the road.

Office Kits
If you feel you need basic emergency supplies at your place of work, by all means pack a daypack with gear and leave it stashed at the office. Although your car kit may be waiting for you in the parking lot, getting there during a power outage might be a challenge if you work in a huge multistory high-rise. Something as simple as a flashlight might save the day for you and the coworkers who gave you a hard time about your survival gear, allowing you to safely and quickly exit a pitch-black building. I remember when, three different times in two weeks, incompetent backhoe drivers unintentionally dug up the water main to the college campus I was working at. Since I had a water bottle with me and three gallons of water in my

PRIMARY PAPERWORK: IMPORTANT DOCUMENTS IN THE MODERN WORLD

Sometimes in our society, the one with the most important documents wins. If given half a chance (and not at the expense of your life!), keep the following items safe, some way, some how.

- ➲ Driver's license
- ➲ Passport
- ➲ Credit cards
- ➲ Medical and immunization records
- ➲ Birth and marriage certificates
- ➲ Social Security card and papers
- ➲ Bank records
- ➲ Titles and deeds
- ➲ Insurance policies
- ➲ Military discharge papers
- ➲ Religious records
- ➲ Wills
- ➲ Miscellaneous family treasures: photos, etc.

vehicle, each time I continued to get stuff done while others scurried off in search of something to drink throughout the day.

Lions and Tigers and Bears, Oh My! Persistent Paranoia or Prudent Preparation?

Survival kits in the house, the car, and the office—man, I can hear your friends and family giving you a hell of a time. You can never be overprepared, unless the act of preparation takes over your life and transforms you into a hyperparanoid, dooms-day freak. Once you have your bases covered, and you take a few minutes every six months to a year to rotate certain items in your kit(s), it's time to relax and enjoy life. This doesn't mean that you should drop your guard. Simply pay attention to your life and just enough of the news to keep in the loop regarding current affairs. I know people who have consumed themselves with survival preparedness. They live it, breathe it, and force others to listen to it. They are so busy preparing for the horrific variables of the future that they never truly live in the now. They rob themselves of life in the present moment due to their fears of an unknown future. Folks, this is not

> *"Do what YOU FEEL in YOUR HEART to be RIGHT—for you'll be CRITICIZED ANYWAY."*
>
> —Franklin D. Roosevelt

what preparing for an emergency is supposed to accomplish. If your survival plan doesn't increase your ease and confidence in life, then it's the wrong plan. I support you fully in being prepared, but not at the expense of your not living your life to the fullest and doing what you are here to do as part of your sacred pact with life.

On the other hand, you will need to tolerate and ignore, if possible, people that have been completely seduced by the modern conveniences of life to such an extent that they have become sheeple. Oblivious to most forms of common sense, independence, and reality, obnoxious sheeple will take great pleasure in criticizing all of your attempts at becoming self-reliant in your life. They will harass you about storing this or that and laugh at your "paranoid" behavior. Some of these sheeple might live in your house and you will be beholden to feed them if the brown stuff hits the fan. There have always been those throughout time that have mocked another's sense of intuition about preparing for the unseen. Don't let them disrupt your harmony. Do what feels best to you, like the ant, and pay no attention to the grasshoppers that cross your path. After listening however briefly to people on both sides of the fence, only you know if you're balanced in your family's emergency preparedness plan or not.

What About Running To the Hills?

"Run to the hills . . . Run for your lives!"
—Chorus from an Iron Maiden song, 1982

Due to my profession, I've been subjected to countless monologues about "getting out of town when the %@*# hits the fan to live off the land." Ninety-nine percent of these well-meaning people have no idea what living off the land entails, let alone the skills, the supplies, the landscape, or the guts to do anything about it. Yet somehow, the-grass-is-greener-on-the-other-side concept waxes strong within their psyches.

For those who are entertaining this concept, and torturing your family with it, have you ever tried to live off the land? Have you tried to do so in the wintertime?

Have you tried it with a dozen other armed crazies in the woods that had the same bad idea that you had? Have you tried to hunt and gather with your nagging kids and pissed-off spouse by your side? Have you been camping for more than a weekend or a week without the usual modern-day camping comforts that are guaranteed to distance you from how unforgiving the natural world can be? Have you been camping at all? Are the calluses thicker on your butt and fingertips from surfing online survival forums than from being outside practicing what you're blabbing about? Do you need to drive several hours in your SUV to find the land to live off? Are you (and every one of your family members) physically able to hike even one mile across a potentially rugged, backcountry landscape that will eventually be very hot or cold, and covered with biting and stinging bugs and plants that poke, prick, and tear at your flesh? Have you ever been hungry, *really hungry*, where your only option is to gather weird-tasting plants or attempt to kill something? If you have tried living off the land, how long did you last (be honest!) before raiding the energy bar stash in your camouflaged bug-out pack? Do you remember how you felt afterward, physically, mentally, and emotionally? If you thought your experimental living-off-the-land trip was successful, do you assume that Mother Nature will deal you the same playing hand the next time?

I have come across a few less-than-hidden survival stashes in the wilds of Arizona. I like to look at the contents and see what their creator(s) thought was important enough to haul out into the bush. One stash had not one, two, three, four, or five, but six different cooking pans; from a huge frying pan to various skillets and cook pots. I applaud his or her choice of at least one cook pot, but six? Maybe they thought they would be exceptional hunters and gatherers, thus requiring the extra cooking capacity. Along with this were dozens of paper plates complete with many pieces of plastic silverware. This gear alone took up more than half of the would-be survivalist's rickety wooden military ammo box, the one which animals had forced open and pillaged to eat the packets of instant coffee.

If I burst your bubble about living off the fat of the land . . . good. Be realistic about you and your family's physical, mental, and emotional abilities during times of extreme stress and leave the wild boar hunting from a tree up to Rambo.

Really Cool, Gotta Have It, Multiple-Use Stuff
The following items, listed in no particular order, contain many multiple-use options for the savvy survivor. Their practical uses in mitigating the cause or effects of emergencies are limited only by your needs and imagination. While this list is by no means all inclusive, it will give you a head start in your ability to adapt to changing environments. These are not all necessarily for your bug-out pack, although some of the same things are listed.

Methods to Make Fire

All hail the power of fire! It has the power to create, sustain, transmute, or destroy if the owner of the fire is ignorant about how it works. Lighting and safely maintaining a fire is a massive responsibility and one that demands that you receive the proper training. I've often wondered why local and federal fire officials are quick to ban fires on public lands during dry seasons yet offer no training whatsoever on how to responsibly make and build a campfire. The tools most commonly used to light the fire itself were covered on page 317.

Cutting Edges

Metal knives are the most obvious choice and are far from a tool used only in the wilderness. Try not to use a knife for a few days in the kitchen and you tell me how useful they are around the house. All cutting edges—knives, saws, axes, etc.— should be kept sharp and in good condition.

String and Rope

Indigenous peoples literally tied their worlds together. String and rope show up on every survival kit list in existence, both primitive and modern. This supremely multiuse gear is second only to my beloved cutting edges and fire.

Five-Gallon Buckets

Entire cultures revolved around the making and use of containers. Five-gallon plastic or metal buckets, especially those with tight-fitting lids, have unending uses for the survivor. Plastic buckets should be stored out of the sun as ultraviolet rays will eventually degrade and weaken the plastic.

Plastic Sheeting, Both Clear and Black

Native peoples the world over would have given their eyeteeth for a lightweight barrier that sheds rain, snow, and wind. It can make your house warmer or cooler, create an improvised window to keep out the elements, and wrap up a dead body. Along with crumpled up newspaper, duct tape and a cutting edge, plastic sheeting makes a pretty slick improvised diaper. Purchase plastic sheeting that's 4 mil or thicker to meet the widest variety of tasks.

Two- to Four-Quart Capacity Stainless Steel Pot with a Tight-fitting Lid and Bail (Handle)

A multiuse, fire- and waterproof container that will prove itself over and over again in its usefulness.

Duct Tape

I can't say enough about this wonder material. I've made handles, containers, cordage, sandals, and repaired many, many things, including packaging up broken body parts for transport to the hospital. There are many grades of duct tape available at the hardware store. Buy the thicker, more expensive stuff as you get what you pay for, yet I've seen some of the cheaper brand names perform well too. I have two or three different types of duct tape wrapped around my water bottles so I can choose the one that best fits my needs of the moment.

Rebar Tie Wire

I love this stuff. My entire home was lashed together with tie wire before being sprayed with concrete. Available at any hardware store or building supply center, its multiuse noncombustibility excels where duct tape cannot go.

Zip (or Cable) Ties

Zip ties offer strong, multiuse, static bindings without the complication of fine and complex motor skill knots.

Old Newspapers (At Least Two or Three Weeks' Worth)

Newspapers can be used as insulation against hot or cold temperatures in the home or in clothing. They have numerous packing, cleaning, and sanitary uses, can help with fire building, and can be read to keep your mind from being taken over by boredom or fear, among many other uses.

Fifty-five-Gallon Drum or Barrel Liners and Plastic Lawn and Leaf Bags

I've already mentioned the awesomeness of plastic sheeting and containers. So imagine the power of a collapsible plastic container! Both can be purchased at most hardware and building-supply stores in clear and opaque plastics. Their rugged, contained, nonpermeable disposability makes them excel at dealing with sanitary and storage issues from excrement to improvised body bags for the dead. They also make great raincoats.

Zipper-lock Freezer Bags, Quart and Gallon Size

The staggeringly multiuse "mini-me" version of the drum liner, except in this case it's food-grade plastic! They also double as disposable mittens that have any number of uses such as skinning rodents and moving the dead.

Plastic, Canvas, or Nylon Tarps

The ability to quickly create shade, cut the wind, or keep things dry might mean the difference between living and dying in extreme conditions as they all deal directly with the regulation of core body temperature. At the very least, tarps will help make your family more comfortable. Tarps work well for creating privacy around the improvised potty as well. While opaque plastic sheeting can double as a tarp in many ways, it lacks the durability and factory grommets that make the tarp such a great addition to any family's preparedness gear.

Mouse and Rattraps

A simple and effective way to put fresh, nutritious meat on the barbie during the most austere conditions. They also work great for eliminating critters that are raiding your food stash.

Backpacks, Daypacks, and Fanny Packs

Being able to move lifesaving gear from place to place might come in handy. Packs allow you to resupply your stock and gather useful improvised items or products on the move without tying up your hands.

Household Chlorine Bleach

How many times have I mentioned this stuff? According to the "find" feature on this computer, more than thirty times, and I'm not done writing. Chlorine bleach will disinfect everything from your dishes and drinking water to your doo-doo and your dead. Buy a gallon today and rotate it every year whether you use it or not.

Helpful **HARDCORE** *Hints*

How to Assess Remaining Daylight and "Tell Time" with Your Fingers

There are circumstances when knowing how much natural light you have left in the day can go from a welcome convenience to a matter of life or death. Although this method is accurate in telling human-created time down to within five minutes if you know the exact time of the sunset for the day, its primary purpose is telling you how many hours of sunlight you have remaining to find shelter, travel without the aid of artificial lighting, or accomplish the dozens of tasks so critical to your family's comfort and survival when no other lighting options exist. I have students use this method on almost every outdoor trekking course to accurately assess when they should stop walking and focus their attention on finding and creating a safe base camp for the evening without the use of artificial lighting.

This method is used for an average adult with an outstretched hand(s). Each finger equals fifteen minutes worth of daylight or time, so four fingers equals one hour.

1 Stretch your arm out in front of you toward the sun. Bend your wrist so that your palm is facing you and your hand is horizontal with your thumb on top. The bottom of the sun should rest on top of your index (pointer) finger.

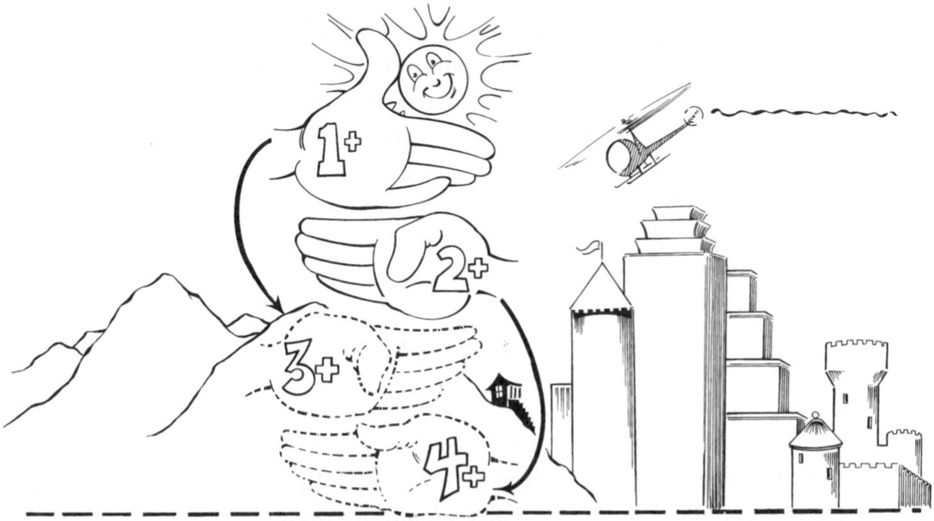

4 HOURS OF
REMAINING
DAYLIGHT

2 Put your other outstretched hand below the first.
3 Now move your upper hand under the second and continue "walking" your hands down toward an imaginary horizon line, counting the hands as you go. (If you're doing this on the ocean or in a Kansas cornfield, there won't be much to imagine about the horizon line.)

The accompanying illustration shows four hours (sixteen fingers) worth of daylight left. Be sure to keep your arms straight as you slowly walk both hands down toward the horizon. It's easy to get sloppy with this method by using only one hand or by putting your hand too close to your face because your elbows are bent. This method can also be used with the moon or to see how much sunlight has already passed in the late morning or early afternoon.

SUPER SIMPLE SUMMARY

- ⮑ Before, during, or after any disaster, you are trying to save your body and those whom you love, not material possessions. Although a potential agonizing mental and emotional decision, you may be forced to leave your home to stay alive or your home may be destroyed in a catastrophe.
- ⮑ A portable "bug-out pack" or disaster kit contains within it a distillation of the most important gear your family will need during its emergency. This pack should be fully loaded and ready to go before it's needed so you can grab it at a moment's notice in case of an evacuation. Some gear can be divvied up among family members so that all of the eggs are not in one basket. However, each family member should always carry basic needs within their individual pack, such as potable water and adequate clothing for the weather.
- ⮑ There is no one-size-fits-all bug-out pack so modify the contents according to your family's needs.
- ⮑ Compiling a bug-out kit first, before outfitting your home, will force you to pare survival necessities down to a manageable level. The motives and gear within your kit can then be simply expanded upon for your home.
- ⮑ The contents of your bug-out pack should be highly adaptable and meet a wide variety of conditions regarding the user and the environment in which the kit will operate.
- ⮑ As the variables are almost limitless as to what could happen during a crisis, keep gear and survival plans simple by adhering to basic core concepts for supporting life.

- *How* you pack your gear is important. Think ahead about what high-use items you'll need from your pack and keep them easily accessible. Mark gear with brightly colored tape for greater visibility and use smaller stuff sacks to make gear easier to identify and locate.
- At minimum, have on hand important identifying documents such as a driver's license and passport.
- Duplicate bug-out packs can also be kept in your vehicle(s) and at the office.
- Don't let overpreparation for an emergency consume your life. Once you have your bases covered, rotate certain items every six months to a year, pay attention, and relax and enjoy life.
- Running to the hills to live off the land is usually a bad idea and could hasten your death.
- There are several multiuse items that will allow you to create more with less, such as methods to light a fire, cutting edges, rope, five-gallon buckets, and plastic sheeting to name a few. Make sure your household has basic items that allow you to improvise and adapt from your environment what you'll need to stay alive.
- It's possible to tell how much daylight is left in the day, and the time, with the use of your outstretched hands and fingers. For an adult, each finger equals fifteen minutes worth of daylight.

24 EPILOGUE

"Nothing real can be threatened. Nothing unreal exists."
—*A Course in Miracles*

Perhaps the greatest survival skill of all is the ability to maintain harmony in the feelings in the face of seeming chaos. This is accomplished by having discrimination about where you put your attention, thought, and feeling, and how you choose to speak and act. You are on the planet for a purpose, for a mission only you can fulfill. You are given greater latitude for service in certain ways, by certain Laws because you have a physical body, because you are composed of the earth element. Keeping your body alive and in the best health that you can is your sacred duty in order to more effectively serve life using whatever gift it is that you radiate. Regardless of sometimes negative appearances, we must all sooner or later awaken to this destiny for the benefit of all.

This is not to say that attachment to the body is the point. If you are exclusively attached to your body, you will find a never-ending list of things and events to fear. You are not truly your physical body anyway, although it seems so in the short term. The close-up, "one-pointed" view of the mouse can be helpful when needing to focus in upon a single aspect of a need, yet to live in this myopic world full time invites self-generated patterns of a limiting and binding nature. Fluctuate between the balance and common sense of having the view of the hawk, as well as the mouse, soaring high above the big picture of whatever it is you wish to understand.

REALITY IS MERELY AN ILLUSION, ALBEIT A VERY PERSISTENT ONE.
—Albert Einstein

It is obvious that the Earth is going through a cycle of intense change at this time, and has been for several decades. If you choose to set the beer down, turn off the TV, shut your mouth and listen, *really listen*, this truth will become apparent. This *deep listening* is also what will prompt you to make correct choices and decisions that will keep your family safe during a crisis. Like any other time of flux, there will be leaders and there will be followers. If you have made it through the book to this point and paid attention along the way, you may be called upon by life to be a leader during very trying times in the future. You now know much more than the average person about what it takes to be prepared for a crisis and how to mitigate its effects after the fact. Who knows why you picked up or were given this book, much less read the contents. How it happened is not important—the fact is it happened.

CONFUSION IS A WORD WE HAVE INVENTED FOR AN ORDER WHICH IS NOT UNDERSTOOD.
—Henry Miller

As I've said before, one of the most challenging aspects of a survival situation will be dealing with the human nature of others. Even if you think you know someone very well, the stress of an emergency may show you a different aspect of that person that even they didn't realize was possible. This aspect can be positive or negative; it can be heroically altruistic or incredibly selfish. In times of great chaos and confusion, if you're open to the possibilities of receiving help—that for the most part is initially invisible to our physical sight—-the help will come. This is not blind hope or simple wishing, it is Law. When one part of the web of life genuinely tugs and asks for assistance, tremendous assistance will come, it *has* to come, as the web is all *one body*. If you inadvertently touch your hand to a hot stove, your entire body will assist you in removing it from the heat as quickly as possible. If you are open to greater-than-normal assistance being given to you during an emergency, you might be amazed at what is instantly downloaded into your life. Where there was initially borderline panic, you might suddenly possess the calm, peaceful, and determined command presence to instantly and effectively deal with a disaster scenario.

This concept is not a bunch of wishful thinking or hippy hooey. It is very real and has been "proven" by many, many people during crisis situations, from seasoned military combat soldiers and professionally trained disaster response personnel to the elderly and little kids. What was needed the most came regardless of scary appearances. You can intensify this action of assistance by *actively and purposefully asking for help* and then *expecting* it to come. *You must ask for the assistance you require and do so with great determination!* Do not be passive or wishy-washy, and don't second-guess as to what form the assistance may come. It will appear however it appears and the form is irrelevant, but pay attention so you don't miss it as sometimes the assistance can be subtle. The physical skills of survival are incredibly important and necessary to life, yet it's your "presence" as a person under stress, who you have become and what positive force you radiate out that will save more lives in times of catastrophic chaos. It's the "walk" not the "talk," the doing, not just the wishing that will accomplish the most good for your family and the planet as a whole. Like Gandhi said, "You must be the change you wish to see in the world."

I HEAR AND I FORGET. I SEE AND I REMEMBER. I DO AND I UNDERSTAND.
—Confucius

Don't be afraid to do what you're here to do. If you receive promptings from the heart to do certain things in life that after much quiet introspection and honest self-evaluation are deemed to be more than just the ego wanting to glorify itself, DO THEM. *In the grand scheme of things, it's not what you have stored that will save your life; it's who you have become as a person.* These past few paragraphs don't need to make sense intellectually. In fact, they will not make sense to the human intellect and ego with its desperate and infantile desire to justify itself by picking things apart, analyzing, ridiculing, and doubting them in order to create separateness from the One. Throughout history, there have always been individuals who have willfully missed the boat due to their own self-created falsehoods and limitations. Through openness and innocence, if this stuff seems to "click" on some level, if it feels good, even though it can't be explained, then don't be concerned.

Follow your intuitions and prepare as you see fit, physically, mentally, emotionally, and spiritually. Pay no attention to those who would choose to rip you down for doing so, but remain guarded. At all times, cultivate the wisdom of discrimination with others that allows you to know when to share information and when to remain silent. There is no need to defend an idea that remains invisible. As you work toward greater self-reliance in your physical world and otherwise, never give up. Never give in. Have courage, and don't compromise what's important to you. After all, when you finally lay your body down, you'll take absolutely nothing from this planet other than your honor.

THE GREATEST WAY TO LIVE WITH HONOR IN THIS WORLD IS TO BE WHAT WE PRETEND TO BE.
—Socrates

No one plans to find himself or herself in a survival situation. That's part of what makes those situations so terrifying when they happen. While there are no guarantees during a disaster, advance preparation, physically, mentally, emotionally, and spiritually can pay off handsomely for you and your loved ones. Even though this book is packed with technical information on surviving an emergency, don't forget about the art of simplicity and common sense in all things. If you find yourself facing a life-threatening emergency, calm yourself the best that you can, consider your options, and TRY. If you seem to fail and are knocked down from the effort, then get off your ass and try again! Your life and those of your family are precious. As long as there's breath in your lungs and a heartbeat within your chest, never, *never give up* and always remember to Party On!

TIMES OF GENERAL CALAMITY AND CONFUSION HAVE EVER BEEN PRODUCTIVE OF THE GREATEST MINDS. THE PUREST ORE IS PRODUCED FROM THE HOTTEST FURNACE, AND THE BRIGHTEST THUNDERBOLT IS ELICITED FROM THE DARKEST STORM.
—Charles Caleb Colton

For more information about Cody Lundin's Aboriginal Living Skills School, check out our web site at

www.alssadventures.com

or E-mail us at:

abodude@alssadventures.com

or Snail mail at:

ALSS, LLC
P.O. Box 3064
Prescott, Arizona 86302 U.S.A.

ALSS specializes in ancient and modern self-reliance training:

- ⮑ Urban, suburban and rural
  preparedness training and disaster mitigation
- ⮑ Real estate analysis and consultation for self-reliant living
- ⮑ Wilderness survival and indigenous living skills field courses
- ⮑ Sustainable design, building and living systems
- ⮑ Water harvesting methods for arid landscapes
- ⮑ Consulting, lectures, corporate training

The more you know, the less you need.

INDEX

Talk is cheap! Purposefully, peacefully, and patiently practice your preparation plan!